READINGS IN SOCIAL PSYCHOLOGY

The Art and Science of Research

Third Edition

Steven Fein
Williams College

Saul Kassin
Williams College

HOUGHTON MIFFLIN COMPANY

BOSTON NEW YORK

Publisher: Charles Hartford
Development Editor: Laura Hildebrand
Manufacturing Manager: Karen Banks
Marketing Manager: Jane Potter

Printed in the U.S.A.

ISBN: 0-618-40341-8

456789-CRS-06 05

CONTENTS

INTRODUCTION

The Purpose of This Book

One of the most rewarding aspects of teaching social psychology is that most students are interested in social psychological issues. Most of us—students as well as instructors—are interested in explaining the causes of others' behaviors, in predicting how people will react in various situations, and in understanding the attraction or hostility between people. But this interest can also present an important challenge to instructors. When people learn social psychological theories or findings that are at odds with their own intuition or personal observations, they may be too quick to dismiss these theories or findings as wrong or unrepresentative. Then when they learn other theories or findings that are consistent with their own intuition or personal observations, they may disparage the first theories and findings as mere common sense.

The difference between the discipline of social psychology and people's intuitions and observations is empirical research. Intuition and common sense can be frustratingly accommodating. One can, for example, cite, "Absence makes the heart grow fonder," to explain the continued success of a romantic relationship after the couple has been forced to spend some time apart from each other, and yet also cite, "Out of sight, out of mind," to explain the failure of a different couple to endure a similar amount of time apart. Social psychology, in contrast, cannot have it so easy. Social psychological theories must be more rigorous, and they must be supported by the results of systematic, methodically sound research. To fully understand and appreciate social psychology, therefore, one must understand and appreciate the research on which the field of social psychology has been, and will continue to be, based. Your textbook, the *Sixth Edition of Social Psychology* by Sharon Brehm, Saul Kassin, and Steven Fein explains much of this research clearly, concretely, and compellingly. The authors have made it a point to make this research come alive to students, to give students enough information so that they can imagine what it would be like to be a subject in many of these studies.

This book of readings was designed to take this emphasis a step further by presenting a diverse sample of important, unabridged, original research articles. Whereas a textbook and class lectures can offer summaries of a number of studies, only a sample of representative studies can give valuable insight into the process as well as the content of social psychology. The goal is to encourage students not only to learn the important theories and principles of the field, but also to think critically about them—to see where they came from, how they have been supported, why they have been supported, and what their potential flaws are. This kind of critical thinking not only makes the material more interesting and compelling but also leads to a deeper understanding of the material.

Another goal of this book of readings is to illustrate the creativity involved in designing studies to test one's hypotheses. In this process, social psychologists often are challenged to combine elements of theater and science. Their experiments must be controlled and precise; procedures should be identical across conditions, with the exception of the manipulated independent variable(s); and potential alternative explanations should be anticipated and ruled out. Within these constraints, however, researchers often need to create an artificial but very real world for their subjects. They need to anticipate the thoughts, feelings, and reactions of the people who participate in their studies, and they must create situations that are realistic and meaningful. "Doing" social psychology, therefore, often involves acting like a playwright; in conducting research, the social psychologist often must create characters, dialogue, and interactions among characters, must place these characters into various situations, and must create a setting, all with the intention of drawing the participants into this fabricated reality so that their reactions and responses are real and spontaneous.

Not all social psychological experiments require this level of creativity. Some studies are, by necessity, simple, whereas others are quite elaborate. Some involve a great deal of deception; others involve no deception. Some elicit strong emotional reaction; others are quite mundane. Some are conducted in a laboratory; others are conducted in the field. But whatever the level of complexity, the process that begins with a set of hypotheses and proceeds through the execution of a study to test these hypotheses is creative and enjoyable. We hope that the enjoyment of this process will become evident to the reader in this set of articles.

The Selection of Articles

In keeping with the goals outlined above, we have selected readings that we feel will help (1) inspire critical thinking about several of the most important issues raised in the textbook, (2) produce a better understanding of various important social psychological principles and findings, and (3) illustrate the creativity of the science of conducting social psychological research. Thus these readings not only present important findings, but they also describe interesting designs, procedures, or settings. We chose psychology journal articles that were written well and concisely and that can be understood and appreciated by people not familiar with all of the literature cited or details given. This is particularly significant because we wanted to present these readings in their entirety, unabridged, as the original authors wrote them. We emphasize this for a number of reasons. We feel there is no substitute for reading these important works firsthand, without the articles being diluted or filtered by anyone else. These are, after all, papers that have helped change the field of social psychology. In addition, an entire article can meet a variety of needs. Readers who want only the gist of the article and readers who want to study and learn the details of the research—such as exactly how some construct was measured or exactly why the researchers believed their results supported their hypothesis—can get what they want from the articles presented in this book. Perhaps most importantly, all students who read these articles must organize and synthesize the information for themselves—whether this means abstracting out the gist or outlining all of the important points and procedures—and this is an excellent way to improve understanding and retention of the information.

These articles include both classic articles that have withstood the test of time and contributed to the development of social psychology, and contemporary articles concerning research that has already made important contributions to the field and that is likely to inspire the research that will help reshape social psychology for years to come. The selection of both classic and contemporary articles can give students a sense of how the field has changed, and continues to change. For example, contemporary articles tend to feature more sophisticated methods and statistical analyses. Another difference is the language used in these articles. Some of the classic articles contain language that would be considered sexist by today's standards, whereas contemporary articles must conform to the American Psychological Association's guidelines for nonsexist language. Yet another example concerns the ethics of the research. Research today must be approved by a review board, and social psychologists today are more sensitive to the needs of those who participate in their research than they were in the past.

This is by no means an exhaustive set of the most important articles in social psychology. Rather, it is a sample of important classic and contemporary articles that report original, empirical research and that are readable and interesting. Moreover, these articles concern the variety of topics covered in Brehm, Kassin, and Fein's *Social Psychology*. Like the text, they are divided into four parts: Social Perception, Social Influence, Social Relations, and Applying Social Psychology. These readings concern issues raised in every chapter of the textbook.

We have briefly introduced each article to set the article in its proper context, including the sections in the textbook to which the article is most relevant.

NOTE TO STUDENTS: HOW TO READ THE READINGS

Several of the readings in this book were written in a style with which you are likely to be unfamiliar. They were written for psychology journals that have a particular format and set of norms. When approaching these readings, therefore, DO NOT BE INTIMIDATED. We selected articles that even those unfamiliar with the literature cited, jargon used, and statistical analyses reported should be able to understand without much trouble. The key is to know how to read these articles, such as what to read carefully and what to skim. Unless your instructor indicates otherwise, you don't need to understand all of the details.

The Four Major Sections of Many Articles

Many, but not all, of these articles share a particular structure. They begin with an Introduction, followed by a Method section, followed by a Results section, followed by a Discussion section. Articles that describe more than one study begin with a general Introduction and conclude with a General Discussion section; in between, each study reported is introduced with its own brief Introduction, has its own Method and Results sections, and may have its own Discussion section. The complete references of the literature cited in each article are listed at the very end of the article. Many of these articles also have a brief abstract, or summary of the entire article, before the Introduction.

In the Introduction, the purpose of the research is explained and placed into a general context, and hypotheses are developed. By the end of the Introduction, the research that was conducted to test these hypotheses is explained in rather broad detail. The Method section presents the specific details of how the research was conducted. The purpose of this section is to allow the readers to see exactly how the research was done so that they can evaluate the validity of the research and, if they so desire, try to replicate the study themselves. The Results section usually is the most detailed section. It reports the results of the statistical analyses that were used to determine to what extent the data collected were consistent or inconsistent with the hypotheses. The Discussion section summarizes these results and discusses such things as *why* the research found what it did, what the implications of the research may be, and what questions remain unanswered.

These articles can be described as having an hourglass shape: they start out relatively broad, usually by making general statements about a particular problem, then become more and more focused as they introduce the specific research conducted and results found, and then become more and more broad again as the Discussion section first summarizes the results and then discusses the broader implications of these results.

A Suggested Order in Which to Read the More Difficult Articles

To the extent, then, that some of these articles include details that are difficult to understand, how should you read them? First of all, you should be sure to have read Chapter 2 in your textbook carefully, particularly the sections concerning hypothesis, theory, basic research, and applied research; correlations; the essential features of experiments; the language of research, including independent variables, dependent variables, statistical significance, main effect, and interaction; and evaluating research.

Although you should check with your instructor, the way we suggest reading the more difficult (or less "user friendly") articles is to first read the sections that set the context and summarize the research most clearly, and then read the sections that provide more details. Thus, if the article begins with a brief abstract, or summary, begin by reading this carefully. Because of the jargon used, it is sometimes necessary to reread the abstract a few times until you understand the general purpose and findings of the research. Then read the Introduction. If the Introduction ends with a description of the research design and hypotheses, read this description carefully. Next, you may want to skip to the first few paragraphs of the Discussion section toward the end of the paper (this might be called the General Discussion section if there are multiple studies reported). The first paragraphs usually summarize the main points of the research findings. Once you understand these principal findings, you have the context needed to go back and read the rest of the article.

Next, read the Method section. As you read this section, it's often a good idea to jot down notes so you can keep track of the conditions of the study. Try to imagine yourself as a participant in this study. What would you be experiencing? What would you be thinking? Also, imagine yourself as the experimenter. What would you be saying to participants? How would you be observing or measuring their responses? If you come across jargon or references that you don't understand, don't worry about it. You may want to make a note of it and ask your instructor about it, but if you read ahead you should be able to understand the central idea. After you read the Method section, think about the predictions or hypotheses stated in the Introduction. Anticipate how participants will react differently in the different conditions of the study. You may want to go back to the end of the Introduction section where the hypotheses or predictions were stated and explained.

Reading the Results Section

Skim the Results section as best you can. Remember to familiarize yourself with each of the following from Chapter 2 of your textbook: correlations, independent variables, dependent variables, statistical significance, main effects, and interactions. In some of these articles, a number of statistical analyses will be reported that will be difficult, if not impossible, to understand. We'll give you a few guidelines in the following paragraphs to help you with these, but if you can't understand the Results section, you shouldn't be too concerned because you should be able to understand the most important results by reading the Discussion section and, if available, the Abstract.

As you read the results, go slowly and keep in mind the different conditions of the study and the hypotheses for these different conditions. Researchers are often interested in measuring the "average" response of participants in each condition. Suppose 20 participants in one condition were asked to rate how attractive some other person was, and 20 participants in another condition were asked the same thing. The researchers are interested in determining if the *average* rating given by the 20 participants in one condition was different than the *average* rating given by the 20 participants in the other condition. Whenever differences between conditions are reported, try to get a sense of the averages for each condition. The averages for each condition may be depicted in a table or figure, or they may be reported in parentheses, as in ($M = 3.47$), which should be read as "the mean, or average, of this condition is 3.47."

The next thing to look for is whether the differences between the averages of the various conditions are significant. As Chapter 2 indicates, the convention in psychology is to say that a difference between two conditions is statistically significant if the analyses suggest that the probability that this difference could have occurred by chance alone is less than 5 out of 100. For example, if you toss a coin 100 times, you may find that the coin landed on heads 53 times and tails 47 times. Is this difference significant? It is not significant because there is a very high likelihood that the difference reflects nothing more than a random outcome. What if you divide people into different conditions and have each of them rate something on a 100-point scale, and you find that the average response is 53 for the participants in one condition and 47 for the participants in the other condition? Is this significant? There is no way to determine whether this difference is significant without performing some statistical analyses.

The probability that a difference occurred by chance alone is usually reported as a number that comes after the phrase $p<$, where p means the probability. Thus, if $p< .05$, the probability that this difference occurred by chance is less than .05, or 5 out of 100, and so the difference is considered significant. Whenever differences between conditions are reported, you should try to get a sense of the averages for each group, and then see if the p level is less than .05.

When there is more than one independent variable in a study, researchers are interested not only in whether the average of one condition differs from that of another, but also in whether the independent variables interact with each other to create different patterns of results. Be sure to reread the section on interactions in Chapter 2.

In addition to differences between conditions, correlations also can be statistically significant or not. A correlation is an association between two variables that vary in quantity. It is positive when both variables increase or decrease together; it is negative when one variable increases as the other variable decreases. Chapter 2 explains and gives various examples of correlations. A correlation can occur by chance alone, such as if you flip a coin and roll some dice at the same time and find that rolling higher numbers with the dice was correlated with the coin landing on tails. This most likely was just a fluke. What if there is an association between watching a lot of television and being very aggressive? Is this a significant correlation? To the extent that the association between these two variables is a reliable one, it is more likely to be considered statistically significant. But if the probability that this association occurred by chance is less than .05, or 5 out of 100, it is considered statistically significant.

Again, it is important to keep in mind that if you begin to get lost in the details of the results, step back and gain perspective by rereading the Abstract and the beginning of the Discussion section.

PART I

Social Perception

READING 1

In his provocative self-perception theory, Daryl Bem (1972) proposed that people can learn about themselves the same way outside observers do—by watching their own behavior. To the extent that our internal states are weak or difficult to interpret, says Bem, we infer what we think or how we feel by observing our own behavior and the situation in which that behavior takes place. In an early test of this theory, Lepper and others (1973) reasoned that when people are rewarded for engaging in a fun activity, that behavior becomes *over*justified, or *over*rewarded, and can be attributed to extrinsic as well as intrinsic motives. The result is that they may begin to wonder if the activity was ever worth pursuing in its own right. As you read this study, think about the possible implications of this research in schools, businesses, and other settings. As you read more of the textbook, consider also how this research relates to theory and research presented in Chapters 3 (The Social Self), 4 (Perceiving Persons), and 6 (Attitudes).

Undermining Children's Intrinsic Interest with Extrinsic Reward: A Test of the "Overjustification" Hypothesis

Mark R. Lepper and David Greene
Stanford University

Richard E. Nisbett
University of Michigan

A field experiment was conducted with children to test the "overjustification" hypothesis suggested by self-perception theory—the proposition that a person's intrinsic interest in an activity may be decreased by inducing him to engage in that activity as an explicit means to some extrinsic goal. Children showing intrinsic interest in a target activity during base-line observations were exposed to one of three conditions: In the expected-award condition, subjects agreed to engage in the target activity in order to obtain an extrinsic reward; in the unexpected-award, condition, subjects had no knowledge of the reward until after they had finished with the activity; and in the no-award condition, subjects neither expected nor received the reward. The results support the prediction that subjects in the expected-award condition would show less subsequent intrinsic interest in the target activity than subjects in either of the other two conditions.

The process by which man seeks to understand his environment—to discern the causes of events which surround him and explain the behavior of others toward him—has been of central concern to social psychology for many years (e.g., Brunswik, 1934; Heider, 1958; Michotte, 1946); but only in the past few years have psychologists concerned themselves with the process by which man explains and understands his own actions and their causes (Bem, 1965, 1967, 1972; Jones & Davis, 1965; Jones, Kanouse, Kelley, Nisbett, Valins, & Weiner, 1972; Kelley, 1967). Recently, theoretical analyses of the process of self-perception or self-attribution by Bem (1965, 1967) and by Kelley (1967) have suggested that processes of self-perception have a common ground with those of other-perception.

When an individual observes another person engaging in some activity, he infers that the other is intrinsically motivated to engage in that activity to the extent that he does not perceive salient, unambiguous, and sufficient extrinsic contingencies to which to attribute the other's behavior. Self-perception theory proposes that a person engages in similar processes of inference about his own behavior and its meaning. To the extent that the external reinforcement contingencies controlling his behavior are salient, unambiguous, and sufficient to explain it, the person attributes his behavior to these controlling circumstances. But if external

SOURCE: Mark R. Lepper, David Greene, and Richard E. Nisbett. 1973. "Undermining Children's Intrinsic Interest with Extrinsic Reward: A Test of the 'Overjustification' Hypothesis," *JOURNAL OF PERSONALITY AND SOCIAL PSYCHOLOGY*, Vol. *28*, No 1, 129–137.

contingencies are not perceived, or if they are unclear, invisible, and psychologically insufficient to account for his actions, the person attributes his behavior to his own dispositions, interests, and desires.

Originally, self-perception theory was proposed as an alternative explanation of the large dissonance literature on "insufficient justification" (cf. Aronson, 1966), where subjects are induced to engage in unpleasant or attitudinally inconsistent behavior under conditions of either clearly sufficient or psychologically inadequate external justification. Typically, these studies have demonstrated that subjects given little extrinsic justification for the behavior they have been induced to perform come to believe that their actions were intrinsically motivated. In a self-perception analysis, this outcome is simply the result of a self-directed inference process. In the low-justification conditions, the subject infers from his behavior and the lack of apparent external pressure that he must have wished to act as he did; while in the high-justification conditions, the subject infers that his behavior was determined by the external pressures in the situation.

Besides its application to many classic dissonance paradigms, self-perception theory has a number of heuristic implications, one of the most intriguing of which could be termed the "overjustification" hypothesis—the proposition that a person's intrinsic interest in an activity may be undermined by inducing him to engage in that activity as an explicit means to some extrinsic goal. If the external justification provided to induce a person to engage in an activity is unnecessarily high and psychologically "oversufficient," the person might come to infer that his actions were basically motivated by the external contingencies of the situation, rather than by any intrinsic interest in the activity itself. In short, a person induced to undertake an inherently desirable activity as a means to some ulterior end should cease to see the activity as an end in itself.

While the existence of such an overjustification effect has been postulated by a number of authors (DeCharms, 1968; Deci, 1971; Kruglanski, Friedman, & Zeevi, 1971; Lepper, 1973; Nisbett & Valins, 1971), this proposition has received virtually no experimental examination. Nisbett and Valins (1971) reviewed several studies which, on reinterpretation, provided evidence consistent with this proposition, but the first study to intentionally pursue a directly related hypothesis was that of Deci (1971).

Specifically, Deci hypothesized that rewarding subjects with money and "closely related tangible rewards" for engaging in an intrinsically interesting task would decrease their subsequent interest in that task in the absence of such external rewards. To test this proposition, Deci asked college subjects to solve a number of inherently interesting puzzles during three experimental sessions. Following an initial base-line session for all subjects, one group of subjects was paid for solving a second series of puzzles, while a second group was not paid. In a third session neither group was paid. During a break in each session, subjects were left alone for a few minutes to do whatever they wished, including continuing work on the puzzles. During this time, the subjects' behavior was observed and recorded from behind a one-way mirror. Subjects who had been paid during the second session tended to show a greater decrease in intrinsic interest from the first to the third session than subjects who had not been paid. This result was consistent with the overjustification hypothesis, but unfortunately this finding was of only marginal statistical significance and depended as much on differences between the groups during the base-line session as during the final sessions.

Deci (1971) couched his hypothesis in terms of monetary or other material rewards. As an implication of self-perception theory, however, the overjustification hypothesis is formulated in terms of the perception of oneself as having undertaken an activity *in order to obtain some extrinsic goal*. The nature of the extrinsic goal should be of little consequence. Thus, an overjustification effect is predicted for any situation which results in an extrinsic attribution where previously intrinsic interest was the only salient attribution. Contracting explicitly to engage in an activity for a reward should undermine interest in the activity even when the reward is insubstantial or merely symbolic. Conversely, receipt of an unforeseen, unexpected reward *after* engaging in an activity should have little or no detrimental effect, even when the reward is a highly prized material one.

This analysis suggests two features necessary for an unequivocal test of the overjustification hypothesis: (*a*) a subject population intrinsically motivated to engage in a target activity and {*b*) a comparison of two experimental treatments—one in which subjects are asked to engage in this activity as a means to some extrinsic goal and one in which subjects are asked to engage in the activity for its own sake but subsequently receive the same extrinsic reward. Subjects who expect a reward should show less subsequent intrinsic interest in the target activity than subjects who do not. An appropriate test of this hypothesis requires a dependent measure taken some time after the experimental sessions and in a situation as different as possible from that in which the rewards were administered. Thus, in this study the rewards were delivered in an experimental room, while the dependent measure of intrinsic interest was obtained in a naturalistic field setting.

The present experiment was conducted with children in an educational setting in order to test the overjustification hypothesis in a context where its practical implications may be greatest. The notion of overjustification immediately raises issues relevant to two widespread "contractual" techniques—one old and one new—of controlling the behavior of school children. The long-established practice of giving grades, gold stars, and similar awards to children is, in the present terms, a contractual one likely to induce the cognition, "I am doing this [arithmetic, drawing, reading] *in order to. . . .*" The newly developed "token economies," in which children are offered redeemable tokens for desirable behavior, seem quite likely to produce the same cognition. The overjustification hypothesis implies that such contractual techniques may backfire for at least those children initially interested in the activities presented in such a context. Demonstrating an overjustification effect in an educational setting, therefore, would suggest the need for greater attention to the possible side effects and long-term consequences of powerful systems of extrinsic rewards.

METHOD

Overview

Preschool children showing initial intrinsic interest in a drawing activity during base-line observations in their classrooms were selected as subjects for the experiment, These subjects were blocked by degree of initial interest in the activity and assigned randomly to one of three treatment conditions: In the expected-award condition, subjects agreed to engage in the drawing activity in order to obtain an extrinsic reward—a certificate with a gold seal and ribbon. In the unexpected-award condition, subjects engaged in the same activity and received the same reward, but had no knowledge of the reward until after they had finished the activity. In the no-award control condition, subjects neither expected nor received the reward, but otherwise duplicated the experience of the subjects in the other two conditions. These experimental sessions were conducted individually in a room apart from the subjects' classrooms. The target-drawing activity was again introduced into the children's classrooms 1–2 weeks after the experimental sessions. Measures of subsequent intrinsic interest were obtained unobtrusively by covert observation of the classrooms from behind a one-way mirror.

Subject Population

Subjects were selected from the student population at the Bing Nursery School, located on the Stanford University Campus, These children, ranging in age from 40 to 64 months, were of predominantly white, middle-class backgrounds and of average or above-average intelligence. Three black children who would otherwise have been included in the experiment were arbitrarily excluded from the subject pool in order to increase the precision with which the population could be defined.

Observational Setting

The nursery school's facilities included three classrooms in which independent programs were run simultaneously. In each classroom, three different classes, each consisting of about 35 children and four to five teachers, met for either 2 or 3 half-days per week. The present study was conducted with four of these classes in the two classrooms equipped with one-way mirrors and sound equipment for observational purposes.

The program in these classrooms was such that with the exception of a single 15-minute "juice" break, children were free throughout the day to choose among a variety of activities. Some activities (such as building blocks, easels, housekeeping equipment, and outdoor activities) were available to them continuously; others (such as collage materials, "play dough," and drawing materials) were made available periodically by their teachers. Typically, at the beginning of each class session, children took note of the "periodic" activities, which had been set out for the day on each of three tables located near the center of the classroom.

For the purposes of the present study, the arrangement provided an opportunity to introduce a novel "target" activity into the ongoing nursery school program on a periodic basis. Moreover, the activity could easily be integrated into the normal classroom routine without the experimenters having to be present. It was thus possible to obtain an unobtrusive measure of the children's intrinsic interest in the target activity in a situation in which the activity was not associated with the experimenters or any extrinsic reward.

Experimental Activity

The experimental activity was chosen to meet three criteria: (a) sufficient similarity to other typical periodic activities so as not to appear out of place, (b) sufficient attractiveness to ensure that most children would express at least some initial interest, and (c) amenability of the activity to some objective definition of interest. These criteria were met handily by the opportunity to draw freely with multicolored felt-tipped drawing pens ("magic markers") not normally available in the children's classrooms.

Measurement of Intrinsic Interest

Base-line data on initial interest were collected during the first hour of 3 consecutive class days. On days when data were to be collected, a few minutes before the class began, the teachers placed a set of magic markers and a sheaf of fine white artist's drawing paper on a hexagonal table located directly in front of the observational mirror. After the first hour of class, these materials were replaced with some other table activity. Thus the target activity was available to a child from the time he arrived until the end of the first hour of class and was presented by the teachers as simply another activity with which the children might choose to play.

During this hour, two observers were stationed behind the one-way mirror, each equipped with a Rustrak eight-track continuous event recorder. The first six channels on both recorders were numbered to correspond to the six positions around the hexagonal target table. One observer was responsible for recording children's actions at Positions 1 through 4; the other was responsible for Positions 4 through 6 and Position 1. The data recorded on Channels 1 and 4 were used to test agreement between observers. For each observer, two additional channels (Channels 7 and 8 of each recorder) were available for recording behavior not clearly tied to one of the six positions at the table. Hence, the two observers were equipped to record data on up to 10 children at a time.

A child was defined as "interested" in the target activity whenever he either sat down in one of the six chairs at the target table or put his hand on a marker; he was considered no longer interested when he was neither sitting at the table nor in possession of a marker. In practice, typically, the first discrimination which had to be made by the observer was when the child should be considered "sitting." It was decided to regard the target table as a system with six regular inputs, such that whenever a child was effectively occupying one of these inputs to the practical exclusion of another child, he or she was considered to be sitting. This criterion was felt to be a more valid indication of interest than a "fanny-touching-seat" criterion and was only slightly more difficult to discriminate reliably. When a child reached for a marker before sitting down or got up from his seat to draw on the floor or somewhere else, his behavior was recorded by one of the observers on Channel 7 or 8.

The measurement procedure was highly reliable. A product-moment correlation of the records of the two observers for the 47 children who appeared on either Channel 1 or 4 proved close to unity ($r = .99$). To further ensure that this method of measurement would be as sensitive and accurate as possible, three slight modifications of standard classroom procedure were introduced. First, since the mere presence of an adult at any of the activity tables was highly correlated with the presence of several children, teachers and other adults were asked to defer all requests from children to sit at the table until the experimental activity had been removed. Second, highly similar materials (e.g., crayons, scissors, other paper, etc.) were made inaccessible to the children while the target materials were available in order to avoid forcing observers to make unnecessarily difficult judgments. Third, teachers recorded not only absences but also time of arrival for any children who arrived late on days of data collection. These data allowed the calculation for each child of a more precise index of interest, namely, the percentage of time that he chose to play with the experimental activity out of the total time that he was present while the materials were available.

At least some play was recorded during base-line periods for 102 of the 139 children who appeared in their respective rooms at any time during the 3 hours of measurement. All children whose total playing time exceeded 4 minutes of play with the target activity were blocked by class and sex within class and ranked in order of total playing time. Each of the eight class-sex blocks was divided into as many groups of 3 as possible, with extra children discarded from the bottom of the rankings. This procedure yielded a potential subject population of 24 boys and 45 girls. Within groups of 3, a table of random permutations was used to assign subjects to treatment conditions.

Experimental Procedure

Following the third hour of base-line observations in each class, the experimental materials were removed from the classroom until they were needed again for postexperimental observations. Experimental sessions began within 2 weeks after the baseline period and were completed for each class on 3 consecutive school days.

Two persons conducted each experimental session: The first experimenter brought the child to and from his classroom and administered the experimental manipulation; the second experimenter stayed with the child while he was in the experimental room and administered the reward. Two (male) experimenters each played the role of the first experimenter for subjects from two of the four classes, and four (two males and two females) assistants each played the role of the second experimenter for subjects from one of the classes.

Potential subjects were approached by the first experimenter in their classrooms, engaged in play and/or conversation, and then asked if they would like to come to the "surprise room" with him. Twelve of 45 girls and 2 of 24 boys refused to come to the experimental room on three separate occasions and hence were lost from the experiment. Thus, 55 subjects actually participated in the experiment (19 each in the expected- and unexpected-award conditions, 17 in the no-award control group).

Each subject was brought individually to the experimental room by the first experimenter. The subject was seated at a child-sized table containing a set of magic markers and a sheaf of paper. At this point, the first experimenter had in his possession a sample "Good Player Award," the extrinsic reward employed in this study. These Good Player Awards—colored 3 × 5 inch cards with the words "Good Player Award" and spaces for the child's name and school engraved on the front next to a large gold star and a red ribbon—have proved effective rewards in previous studies (e.g., Harter & Zigler, 1972).

Presenting the drawing materials to the subject, the first experimenter said,

> Do you remember these magic markers that you played with back in your room? Well, there's a man [lady] who's come to the nursery school for a few days to see what kinds of pictures boys and girls like to draw with magic markers.

For subjects in the unexpected-award and the no-award groups, the first experimenter continued,

> Would you like to draw some pictures for him?

For subjects in the expected-award condition, the first experimenter produced the sample Good Player Award and continued instead,

> And he's brought along a few of these Good Player Awards to give to boys and girls who will help him out by drawing some pictures for him. See? It's got a big gold star and a bright red ribbon, and there's a place here for your name and your school. Would you like to win one of these Good Player Awards?

Each subject indicated assent to the first experimenter's final question, typically with considerable enthusiasm. For all subjects the first experimenter concluded,

> Good. He should be right outside. I'll go get him.

The first experimenter introduced the second experimenter to the subject and then excused himself, leaving the second experimenter alone with the subject. The second experimenter sat down across the table from the subject, started a stopwatch, and asked the subject, "What would you like to draw first?" Most of the time the subject began to draw a picture immediately; when he did not, a little coaxing was always sufficient to get him started. During the session, the second experimenter was friendly but not overly responsive to the subject. Generally, he attempted to show interest in, rather than explicit approval of, the subject's performance.

Each subject was allowed 6 minutes to draw pictures. If the second experimenter felt that an interruption after precisely 6 minutes was inopportune, up to 30 seconds more was provided. This procedure was designed to control against confounding of the classroom measure by satiation effects. The drawings made by each child were kept to allow an examination of the child's performance, during experimental sessions, along both quantitative and qualitative dimensions. Ratings of these drawings on a number of descriptive indexes were made by judges blind to the subject's condition.

The second experimenter was completely blind to the subject's condition for the first 5 minutes of the session. At the end of 5 minutes, the second experimenter casually looked inside a manila folder which had been left on the table by the first experimenter to determine whether the subject was to receive an award or not. After this point, the second experimenter knew only whether the subject was in one of the two award conditions as opposed to the no-award control condition.

One minute later, the second experimenter looked conspicuously at his stopwatch and said,

> Well, it looks like our time is up. Thank you very much for helping me out by drawing these pictures for me. You really did a good job.

For subjects who were to receive an award, the second experimenter continued as follows:

> In fact, you have been such a big help to me that I have something very special to give you. [The second experimenter rose, got a Good Player Award and a black pen, and returned to the table.] I'm going to give you one of my Good Player Awards, with your name and school on it. [The second experimenter showed the award to the subject and wrote the subject's name and school on the award with a flourish.] Now turn around and let me show you our special Honor Roll board where you can put your award so that everyone will know what a good player you are! [The second experimenter stood as he spoke, walked to the corner of the room, and pulled back a standing slat screen to expose a bulletin board. This board was decorated with the title "Honor Roll" and contained a standard display of several Good Player Awards. The second experimenter escorted the subject to the bulletin board and placed a push pin through the top of his award.] You can put your Good Player Award anywhere you want on the Honor Roll Board. That looks very nice.

Then, for all subjects, the second experimenter said,

> Now, let's see if we can find [the first experimenter] to take you back to your room.

As the second experimenter opened the door, the first experimenter entered and returned the subject to his classroom.

Postexperimental Observations

The observational setting and data collection procedure were the same as during the base-line periods. Observers were blind to the conditions of the subjects. Data collection began 7 to 14 days after the last subject had been run in a given class and was completed over no more than 4 consecutive school days for each class. In three of the classes, one of the first three class meetings had to be skipped for reasons ranging from the unanticipated arrival of a goat in the classroom to equipment failure. Four subjects were lost during these sessions: Three were never in class during the three observational sessions; a fourth was present for only 10 out of a possible 180 minutes and was discarded, although inclusion of his data would not have affected the significance or pattern of the data reported. The final sample, then, consisted of 51 children—19 males and 32 females. There were 18 subjects in both the expected-award and the unexpected-award conditions and 15 subjects in the no-award condition.

RESULTS

The overjustification hypothesis led to the anticipation that subjects in the expected-award condition would show less subsequent intrinsic interest in the target activity than subjects in the unexpected-award and no-award conditions. The data relevant to this proposition—the mean proportion of time that children chose to play with the target activity in the postexperimental sessions—are presented in Table 1.

It may be seen that as predicted, children in the expected-award condition spent less time playing with the drawing materials than children in the other conditions. Preliminary analysis of the data by sex of child revealed no significant sex difference and no interaction of sex of child with experimental condition. The data were therefore collapsed across this dimension for purposes of analysis. Since the variances of the treatment groups were significantly different ($F_{max} = 5.39$, $df = 3/17$, $p < .01$) and the standard deviations of the groups were proportional to the means, a log transformation [$Y' = \ln(Y + 1)$] was performed on the data to produce homogenous treatment variances (Winer, 1962, p. 221). These transformed data were submitted to a one-way unweighted-means analysis of variance, which is presented in Table

2. This analysis yielded a significant effect of experimental treatments on subsequent intrinsic interest in the experimental materials ($F = 3.25$, $df = 2/48$, $p < .05$). To clarify the precise nature of this effect, a contrast was performed to test the specific prediction of the study. This contrast proved highly significant ($F = 6.19$, $df = 1/48$, $p < .025$), accounting for most of the systematic variance and indicating that subjects in the expected-award condition chose to spend a smaller proportion of their time playing with the target materials than subjects in either the unexpected-award ($t = 2.32$, $p < .025$) or the no-award ($t = 2.05$, $p < .025$) conditions.[1]

In addition, although blocking subjects on initial interest in the target activity of course eliminated any between-groups differences in this variable, it is of some interest to compare postexperimental interest with original interest within each treatment condition.

Subjects in both the unexpected-award and no-award conditions showed very slight and nonsignificant (both *ts* < 1) increases in interest from preexperimental to postexperimental measurement sessions. Subjects in the expected-award condition, however, manifested a significant decrease in interest in the target materials from base-line to postexperimental sessions ($t = 2.61$, $p < .02$).

TABLE 1
Mean Percentage of Free-Choice Time That Subjects Chose to Play with the Target Activity, by Treatments

Experimental condition	*n*	%
Expected award	18	8.59
No award	15	16.73
Unexpected award	18	18.09

TABLE 2
Analysis of Variance on Transformed Proportions of Time Spent with Target Activity

Source	*df*	*MS*	*F*
Between	2	3.96	3.25*
Contrast	1	7.55	6.19**
Residual	1	.37	< 1
Within	48	1.22	

*$p < .05$.
**$p < .025$.

Some readers may find it surprising that receipt of the award did not increase the interest of children in the unexpected-award group. It should be recalled, however, that subjects were selected on the basis of their relatively great initial interest in the drawing activity. There would be little reason to expect that the award would have had much effect on the behavior of children for whom the drawing activity was already highly salient and pleasurable. On the other hand, the range of initial interest was fairly large, and it might be expected that the award would have had some effect among those children in the present sample with relatively little interest. This was apparently the case. Each experimental group was divided into two groups on the basis of initial interest in the drawing activity. Of the resulting six groups, only the children in the unexpected-award group who were below the median in degree of initial interest showed a substantial increase in interest following the experimental manipulation ($t = 2.35$, $p < .05$). Children above the median in initial interest in the unexpected-award group showed a trivial decrease in interest, and children in the control (no-award) group, whether above or below the median, showed a trivial increase in interest.

It would be of some theoretical interest to know whether the expected-award treatment had a different effect on children high in initial interest than on children low in initial interest. Unfortunately, the data do not allow a clear answer to this question. Both the high group and the low group declined in interest in the drawing activity. The high group declined more than the low group, but this could have occurred either because the manipulation was more effective for the high group or simply because there was a "floor effect" for the group already relatively low in interest. It would be interesting to repeat the present experiment in a context avoiding such an artificial restriction of movement.

Finally, it is important to note that the award manipulation also had an immediate effect on children's performance during the experimental sessions. The pictures drawn by the children for the experimenter were rated on overall quality by three blind judges on a scale from 1 (very poor) to 5 (very good). Although the three conditions did not differ in the number of pictures drawn (2.61 for the expected-award, 2.44 for the unexpected-award, and 2.33 for the no-award children), the quality of pictures drawn in the expected-award condition was lower than in the other groups. The average quality ratings for the expected-award group (2.18) differed significantly from both the unexpected-award (2.85) and no-award (2.69) groups ($t = 3.01$, $p < .01$, and $t = 2.08$, $p < .05$, respectively). Thus the detrimental effects of the expected-award manipulation were apparent during the experimental sessions, as well as later in the classroom setting.

DISCUSSION

The present results indicate that it is possible to produce an overjustification effect. In the expected-award condition, children showed decreased interest in the drawing activity after having undertaken it in order to obtain a goal which was extrinsic to the pleasures and satisfaction of drawing in its own right. In the unexpected-award condition, on the other hand, children receiving the same extrinsic reward showed undiminished or increased interest in the activity. This detrimental effect of the expected-award procedure was manifest both in quality of performance during the experimental sessions and in subsequent unobtrusive measures of intrinsic interest in the classroom setting.

As an empirical proposition, the present findings have important practical implications for situations in which extrinsic incentives are used to enhance or maintain children's interest in activities of some initial interest to the child. Such situations, we would suggest, occur frequently in traditional classrooms where systems of extrinsic rewards—whether grades, gold stars, or the awarding of special privileges—are applied as a matter of course to an entire class of children.

Many of the activities we ask children to attempt in school, in fact, are of intrinsic interest to at least some of the children; one effect of presenting these activities within a system of extrinsic incentives, the present study suggests, is to undermine the intrinsic interest in these activities of at least those children who had some interest to begin with. The quite limited manipulation employed in this study, involving a symbolic reward not unlike those routinely employed in the classroom, was sufficient to produce significant differences in the children's subsequent behavior in a natural preschool classroom. This is consistent with the complaint, from Dewey (1900) and Whitehead (1929) up to the time of Holt (1964) and Silberman (1970), that a central problem with our educational system is its inability to preserve the intrinsic interest in learning and exploration that the child seems to possess when he first enters school. Instead, these authors have suggested, the schooling process seems almost to undermine children's spontaneous interest in the process of learning itself.

At the same time, because the implications of this point of view for social control and socialization are potentially so great, it is important to point immediately to the hazards of overgeneralization from the present experiment. Certainly there is nothing in the present line of reasoning or the present data to suggest that contracting to engage in an activity for an extrinsic reward will always, or even usually, result in a decrement in intrinsic interest in the activity. The present experiment was carefully designed to allow a demonstration of the overjustification effect. The target activity was deliberately chosen to be highly attractive, and subjects were all children who actually manifested some intrinsic interest in the activity. Extrinsic incentives were superfluous. Under such circumstances, there is every reason to believe that it should be relatively easy to manipulate loss of interest and difficult to increase it above its already fairly high level.

The present experiment does not speak to situations which depart very greatly from the present situation. There is considerable evidence from studies of token-economy programs (Fargo, Behrns, & Nolen, 1970; O'Leary & Drabman, 1971) supporting the proposition that extrinsic incentives may often be used effectively to increase interest in certain broad classes of activities. On the present line of reasoning, this proposition should be particularly true when (*a*) the level of initial intrinsic interest in the activity is very low and some extrinsic device is essential for producing involvement with the activity; or (*b*) the activity is one whose attractiveness becomes apparent only through engaging in it for a long time or only after some minimal level of mastery has been attained. In fact, such conditions characterize the prototypical token-economy program in that tangible extrinsic rewards are *necessary* to elicit the desired behavior. Hence, it would be a mistaken overgeneralization from the present study to proscribe broadly the use of token-economy programs to modify children's behavior.

It has already been recommended by some thoughtful proponents of token economies that their use be limited to circumstances in which less powerful techniques have been tried and found inadequate (O'Leary, Poulos, & Devine, 1972)—in other words, only when they are necessary. It has also been stressed that in any case, the successful implementation of powerful reinforcement systems demands considerable sensitivity as well as ingenuity on the part of the practitioner (Bandura, 1969). The present study provides empirical evidence of an undesirable consequence of the unnecessary use of extrinsic rewards, supporting the case for the exercise of discretion in their application (O'Leary & Drabman, 1971).

REFERENCES

Aronson, E. The psychology of insufficient justification: An analysis of some conflicting data. In S. Feldman (Ed.), *Cognitive consistency*. New York: Academic Press, 1966.

Bandura, A. *Principles of behavior modification*. New York: Holt, Rinehart & Winston, 1969.

Bem, D. J. An experimental analysis of self-persuasion. *Journal of Experimental Social Psychology*, 1965, 1, 199–218.

Bem, D. J. Self-perception: An alternative interpretation of cognitive dissonance phenomena. *Psychological Review*, 1967, 74, 183–200.

Bem, D. J. Self-perception theory. In L. Berkowitz (Ed.), *Advances in experimental social psychology*. Vol. 6. New York: Academic Press, 1972.

Brunswik, E. *Perception and the object world*. Leipzig: Deuticke, 1934.

DeCharms, R. *Personal causation*. New York: Academic Press, 1968.

Deci, E. L. Effects of externally mediated rewards on intrinsic motivation. *Journal of Personality and Social Psychology*, 1971, 18, 105–115.

Dewey, J. *The school and society*. Chicago: University of Chicago Press, 1900.

Fargo, G. A., Behrns, C., & Nolen, P. *Behavior modification in the classroom*. Belmont, Calif.: Wadsworth, 1970.

Harter, S., & Zigler, E. Effectance motivation in normal and retarded children. Unpublished manuscript, Yale University, 1972.

Heider, F. *The psychology of interpersonal relations*. New York: Wiley, 1958.

Holt, J. *How children fail*. New York: Dell, 1964.

Jones, E. E., & Davis, K. E. From acts to dispositions: The attribution process in person perception. In L. Berkowitz (Ed.), *Advances in experimental social psychology*. Vol. 2. New York: Academic Press, 1965.

Jones, E. E., Kanouse, D. E., Kelley, H. H., Nisbett, R. E., Valins, S., & Weiner, B. *Attribution: Perceiving the causes of behavior*. New York: General Learning Press, 1972.

Kelley, H. H. Attribution theory in social psychology. In D. Levine (Ed.), *Nebraska symposium on motivation: 1967*. Lincoln: University of Nebraska Press, 1967.

Kruglanski, A. W., Friedman, I., & Zeevi, G. The effects of extrinsic incentive on some qualitative aspects of task performance. *Journal of Personality*, 1971, 39, 606–617.

Lepper, M. R. Dissonance, self-perception, and honesty in children. *Journal of Personality and Social Psychology*, 1973, 25, 63–74.

Michotte, A. E. *The perception of causality*. Paris: Vrin, 1946.

Nisbett, R. E., & Valins, S. *Perceiving the causes of one's own behavior*. New York: General Learning Press, 1971.

O'Leary, K. D., & Drabman, R. Token reinforcement programs in the classroom: A review. *Psychological Bulletin*, 1971, 75, 379–398.

O'Leary, K. D., Poulos, R. W., & Devine, V. T. Tangible reinforcers: Bonuses or bribes? *Journal of Consulting and Clinical Psychology*, 1972, 38, 1–8.

Silberman, C. *Crisis in the classroom*. New York: Random House, 1970.

Whitehead, A. N. *The aims of education*. New York: Mentor, 1929.

Winer, B. J. *Statistical principles in experimental design*. New York: McGraw-Hill, 1962.

NOTES

1. All *p* values reported in this article are based on two-tailed tests of significance.

(Received April 10, 1972)

READING 2

For many years, social psychologists who studied attribution theory assumed that people all over the world perceive each other through the same processes and are subject to the same biases. It was generally assumed, for example, that the tendency to attribute actions to persons relative to situations, known as the Fundamental Attribution Error, was pervasive—and universal. As we discuss in Chapter 4 (Perceiving Persons), it is now clear that cultures shape the way people explain the events of human behavior—and that while westerners tend to see individuals as autonomous and motivated by internal forces, many nonwestern "collectivist" cultures take a holistic view that emphasizes the relationship between individuals and their surroundings. Do these differing worldviews influence the attributions we make? Is it possible that the fundamental attribution error is a uniquely Western phenomenon? In the first study to ask that question, Miller (1984) compared Americans and Asian Indians of varying ages in the way they explained the causes of other people's behavior. As you'll see, Miller's research sheds light on how the invisible hand of cultural upbringing can influence the way we perceive the people in our world.

Culture and the Development of Everyday Social Explanation

Joan G. Miller
Committee on Human Development, Department of Behavioral Sciences, University of Chicago

The impact of cultural meaning systems on the development of everyday social explanation is explored in a cross-cultural investigation undertaken among Indian and American adults and children (ages 8, II, and 15 years). It is demonstrated that at older ages Americans make greater reference to general dispositions and less reference to contextual factors in explanation than do Hindus. References to general dispositions also undergo a much greater developmental increase among Americans than among Hindus, whereas references to contextual factors show the opposite pattern of developmental change. Evidence suggests that these cross-cultural and developmental differences result from contrasting cultural conceptions of the person acquired over development in the two cultures rather than from cognitive, experiential, or informational differences between attributors. Discussion focuses on theoretical implications of such a demonstration for understanding: (a) the importance of integrating semantic with structural considerations in theories of social attribution, (b) the need to develop nonteleological frameworks for interpreting age and cultural diversity in conceptualization, and (c) the role of cultural communication in the acquisition of everyday social knowledge.

This study was funded by National Institute of Mental Health Grant MH 08139-01 and by an East-West Center Research Fellowship.

Thanks are extended to Richard A. Shweder, Donald W. Fiske, Mihaly Csikzentmihalyi, Fred L. Strodtbeck, A. K. Ramanujan, McKim Marriott, Daniel G. Freedrnan, and Geoffrey White for their helpful comments on this research. Appreciation is also expressed to D. P. Pattanayak and the Central Institute of Indian Languages in Mysore, India for their support of the project.

Requests for reprints should be sent to Joan G. Miller, Committee on Human Development, Department of Behavioral Sciences, Univ. of Chicago, Chicago, Illinois 60637.

Cultural influences on attributional diversity have been somewhat neglected by psychological theorists. In most cases, developmental and cross-cultural differences occurring in attribution have been interpreted as arising from differences in attributors' cognitive capacities to process information concerning the covariation structure of experience and/or from differences in the objective experiences to which attributors have been exposed. The purpose of the present research is to demonstrate the impact of cultural meaning systems as a third variable, independent of such subjective and objective determinants, which must be taken into account to explain age and cultural variation occurring in

SOURCE: J.G. Miller. 1984. "Culture and the Development of Everyday Social Explanation," *JOURNAL OF PERSONALITY AND SOCIAL PSYCHOLOGY, 46*, No. 5, 961–978.

attribution. Such a demonstration is offered through a cross-cultural investigation comparing modes of everyday social explanation used by people in the United States, a Western culture emphasizing individualistic notions of the person, and by people in India, a non-Western culture stressing more holistic views of the person. Evidence is presented to suggest that various cross-cultural and developmental differences observed in attribution among Americans and Hindus result from divergent cultural conceptions of the person acquired over development in the two cultures rather than from cognitive or objective experiential differences between attributors. Discussion focuses on theoretical implications of such a demonstration for understanding the impact of cultural meaning systems on social attribution.

INTERPRETATION OF DIVERSITY IN DISPOSITIONAL ATTRIBUTIONS

Marked developmental and cross-cultural differences have been documented to occur in references to general dispositions of the agent in social attribution. References to general dispositions of the agent, it has been observed, increase significantly over development among Western populations (Flapan, 1968; Livesley & Bromley, 1973; Peevers & Secord, 1973; Scarlett, Press, & Crockett, 1971; Waern, Hecht, & Johansson, 1974). American adults typically emphasize dispositional qualities, in particular, personality traits, when making social inferences, for example, "She is friendly and gregarious" (Fiske & Cox, 1979, p. 148). In contrast, young Western children tend to stress actions, interpersonal relationships, and other contextual factors when describing others or giving explanations, for example, "She goes skating every Thursday" or "She has three brothers" (Livesley & Bromley, 1973, p. 123). Although no seminaturalistic data was available on a non-Western child population, evidence suggests that adults from non-Western cultures generally place less emphasis on dispositional properties of the agent and great emphasis on contextual factors than do American and Western European adults (Levy, 1973; Selby, 1974, 1975; Shweder & Bourne, 1982; Strauss, 1973).

Cognitive Interpretation

A dominant interpretation offered to explain such attributional diversity focuses on differences in individuals' cognitive capacities to generate dispositional attributions (e.g., Livesley & Bromley, 1973). It is maintained that young children and certain non-Western attributors fail to emphasize dispositional modes of attribution because they have not developed the abstract classificatory abilities required for summarizing behavioral regularities by means of dispositions. Such attributors are seen as cognitively incapable of classifying diverse behavior observed over time and across situations on the basis of conceptual similarity. Support for such a cognitive interpretation may be seen in early research indicating that young children rely on more concrete modes of classification than do adults (Bruner & Olver, 1963; Inhelder & Piaget, 1964; Olver & Hornsby, 1966; Vygotsky, 1962). Whereas adults tend to classify objects on the basis of conceptual similarity, children show a greater tendency to categorize objects in a holistic structure on the basis of spatiotemporal and/or functional interrelationships obtaining between the objects.

Recent research challenges this cognitive interpretation of the observed attributional variation in dispositional attributions. Some ability to classify objects on the basis of conceptual similarity, for example, has been demonstrated in children as young as 3 years, using a three-member oddity task (Rosch, Mervis, Gray, Johnson, & Boyes-Braem, 1976). Memory studies have documented that children as young as 2 years are able to make use of the categorical structure in lists to facilitate recall (Goldberg, Perlmutter, & Myers, 1974). The research suggests that at least part of the poorer performance of certain subjects on tasks assessing classificatory behavior derives from the complexity or ambiguity of the tasks rather than from deficits in individuals' cognitive capacities (see, e.g., Gelman, 1978).

Experiential Interpretation

A second related explanation that has been applied to explain age and cultural diversity in references to general dispositions emphasizes contrasting objective experiential conditions found cross-culturally and over development to which such modes of attribution are viewed as adapted. It is argued that young children and certain non-Western attributors fail to emphasize dispositional modes of attribution because they lack exposure to the more complex experiential conditions, associated with modernization, which make it functional to use taxonomic modes of categorization and lead to the development of abstract cognitive orientations (Goody & Watt, 1968; Greenfield, 1972; Horton, 1967; Scribner & Cole, 1973). It is asserted, for example, that certain attributors may not be exposed to sufficient diversity to require that they locate dispositional properties by which to distinguish an agent's behavior from that of others in the same context or by which to predict an agent's behavior across contexts (Super, Harkness, & Baldwin, 1977). Support for such an experiential interpretation may be seen in research demonstrating greater use of taxonomic modes of categorization on classification tasks among individuals exposed to modernizing influences, such as schooling, literacy, and urbanization, than among individuals not exposed to such influences (Bruner, Olver, & Greenfield, 1966; Luria, 1976; Stevenson, Parker, Wilkinson, Bonnevaux, & Gonzalez, 1978).

Empirical as well as theoretical considerations suggest, however, that differential exposure to experiential conditions requiring taxonomic categorization cannot fully explain the observed age and cultural diversity in dispositional attributions. Some of the early findings, recent research indicates, may have resulted from the nonequivalence of research situations to individuals from different cultural backgrounds rather than from differences in individuals' cognitive orientations (Labov, 1970; Shweder, Bourne, & Miyamoto, 1978). Recent work suggests that environmental conditions give rise to localized, not to generalized, differences in cognitive performance (Cole, Sharpe, & Lave, 1979; Weisner, 1976). It has been demonstrated that subjects exposed to various modernizing influences, such as schooling or urbanization, display more abstract modes of classification only on the types of tasks emphasized in those settings rather than on all types of tasks. Such results call into question the claim that global differences in cognitive orientation result from exposure to modernizing conditions. It may also be noted that objects or events may be classified as similar because of their prescriptive cultural significance, even though they do not share a particular set of correlated attributes. The claim then that abstract modes of categorizing persons are not required under non-technologically developed experiential conditions may be challenged as overlooking the many nonfunctional purposes underlying social categorization.

Cultural Interpretation

An alternative interpretation of age and cultural diversity in dispositional attributions focuses on contrasting culturally derived conceptions of the person, which influence attributors' interpretations of experience. Cultural differences in dispositional attributions are seen as resulting, in part, from the more individualistic cultural conceptions of the person acquired by individuals over development in Western cultures, as contrasted with the more holistic cultural conceptions of the person adopted by individuals over development in non-Western cultures. Conceptions of the person emphasized in many Western cultures underscore the separation and independence of the agent from the context (Marriott, 1976). The autonomous individual tends to be treated as the primary unit of right and moral responsibility (Lukes, 1973; Sampson, 1977; Weber, 1930). Portraying the agent as inherently asocial if not antisocial, such cultural conceptions tend to view deviance as arising from dispositional factors within the agent (Greenstone, 1982; MacPherson, 1962). In contrast, cultural views stressed in many non-Western cultures emphasize the openness and interdependence characterizing the agent's relations with the surround (Dumont, 1965, 1970; Geertz, 1974). Forwarding a social view of the agent (O'Flaherty & Derrett, 1978), such cultural conceptions tend to approach deviance in interactional terms, as resulting from some disequilibrium in the agent's relations with the environment (Marsella & White, 1982). These contrasting cultural views may be seen expressed, for example, in the "individually centered" cultural practices found in many Western cultures for dealing with mental illness, practices generally absent or given much less emphasis in non-Western cultures (Waxler, 1974, 1977).

Attributors' acquisition of such divergent cultural conceptions, it is asserted, may contribute to the attributional differences observed in use of general dispositions (Shweder & Bourne, 1982; Shweder, Bourne, & Miyamoto, 1978). Adoption of the Western cultural perspective is seen as priming attributors to stress dispositional properties of the agent in making inferences about the determinants of behavior. The Western cultural emphasis on the agent's autonomy from contextual influences and on individual responsibility for action, for example, is viewed as encouraging attributors to search for internal factors predicting behavior across contexts and distinguishing one agent's behavior from that of another. In contrast, it is posited that individuals' acquisition of more relational conceptions of the person in non-Western cultures may lead them to give less weight than Western attributors to general dispositions of the agent when making social inferences. Emphasizing the situational variability of behavior and treating the social role rather than the individual as the primary normative unit, such cultural conceptions are seen as heightening non-Western attributors' sensitivity to the contextual determinants of action (Ramanujan, 1980; Selby, 1975). In maintaining that cultural meaning systems are not merely accommodations to functional constraints, it is argued that the observed cross-cultural variation in dispositional attributions cannot be fully explained by reference to differences in attributors' objective adaptive requirements.

This cultural perspective may be applied to the interpretation of age differences observed in social attribution. The developmental patterning of attributional differences would be viewed as reflecting the time lag required for acquisition of the dominant views of the person held in a culture. In particular, the age increase in references to general dispositions documented to occur in Western cultures would be seen as arising from childrens' relatively gradual adoption, through processes of enculturation, of the individualistic views of the person stressed in such societies. In contrast, it would be anticipated that in non-Western cultures, modes of attribution are modified over development in the direction of the dominant holistic cultural views of the person, views stressing the contextual influences on behavior, not the agent's general dispositions.

HYPOTHESES UNDERLYING PRESENT INVESTIGATION

The present cross-cultural investigation was undertaken to provide a developmental test of this cultural interpretation of attributional diversity. An attempt was made to demonstrate that the development of social inference entails, in part, the acquisition of culturally variable meaning systems and cannot be understood merely by reference to subjective and/or objective determinants. This demonstration proceeded by showing that references to general dispositions by American and Hindu adults and children (a) conformed to patterns hypothesized on the basis of contrasting cultural conceptions of the person emphasized in the two cultures and (b) could not be fully explained by reference to various alternative cognitive and/or experiential factors.

Consideration of the differences in cultural notions discussed led to the hypothesis that Americans at older ages would make greater reference to general dispositions of the agent in explanation than would Hindus. This cross-cultural difference was anticipated to be greater in the explanation of deviant behavior than in the explanation of prosocial behaviors, given the American, but not Hindu, cultural emphasis on the agent-oriented determinants of deviance. Examination of alternative non-cultural interpretations of the anticipated cultural and age diversity in references to general dispositions proceeded by assessing attributors' abilities to classify on the basis of conceptual similarity and by examining the relationship between attributors' references to general dispositions and their exposure to modernizing influences. It was predicted that (a) individuals at all ages tested in both cultures would display the cognitive skills in classification required to generate dispositional attributions and that (b) references to general dispositions would not vary as a function of attributors' exposure to objective conditions identified by theorists as making taxonomic categorization of behavior adaptive.

STUDY 1

Method

Subjects Data were obtained from Indians in Mysore, a city in Southern India, and from Americans in Chicago. The main sample, interviewed in English, included 40 middle-class Hindu adults and 30 middle-class Hindu children in each age group of 8, 11, and 15 years as well as 30 middle-class American adults and 30 middle-class American children in each age group of 8, 11, and 15 years. Each age/cultural subgroup comprised an equal number of males and females. For control purposes, interviews were conducted in the local language (Kannada) among 20 middle-class Hindu adults and 12 middle-class Hindu children in each age group of 8, 11, and 15 years. American and Hindu children sampled had the same number of years of education. No significant differences in education (M = 17.5 years), age (M = 40.5 years), or in occupation (academic or other professional) occurred between adults in the Hindu and American middle-class samples.

To permit assessment of the impact of socioeconomic status as compared with subcultural orientation on attribution, data were obtained in their native language from 30 lower middle-class Anglo-Indian adults and from 10 lower class Hindu adults. The lower middle-class Anglo-Indian adults and lower class Hindu adults were less educated (*Ms* = 31.3 years and 34.7 years respectively), and they held lower status occupations (primarily blue-collar and menial-labor jobs) than the middle-class Hindu and American adults.

Procedure *Explanation procedure.* Subjects were asked to narrate two prosocial behaviors and two deviant behaviors and to explain, immediately after narrating each behavior, why the behavior was undertaken. In the case of deviant behaviors, subjects were instructed to "describe something a person you know well did recently that you considered a wrong thing to have done." In the case of prosocial behaviors, subjects were requested to "describe something a person you know well did recently that you considered good for someone else." The behaviors narrated and explained by subjects had to meet the criteria of being intentional, nonroutine, and performed in each case by a different agent whom the subject had interacted with on at least three separate occasions.

This strategy of specifying in formal terms the types of behaviors for subjects to explain, while allowing subjects to supply the content of such behaviors from their own experiences, was undertaken to maximize the functional equivalence of the behaviors explained across subgroups. Meaning, research suggests, is created through the conceptual assumptions brought to bear in comprehension, not referentially fixed (Bransford & McCarrell, 1974). In the present case, it was anticipated that the contrasting conceptual assumptions held by subjects at different ages would lead them to understand the same stimulus differently. An identical experimental stimulus then, it was judged, would not be equivalent in meaning for all subjects. In contrast, in requesting that subjects make distinctions that are common early in development and cross-culturally, the present alternative methodological approach was judged to produce greater functional comparability in the types of behaviors explained across subgroups. Explanations, for example, are most often offered spontaneously in relation to events experienced as somewhat unusual rather than routine (Hart & Honoré, 1959; Mackie, 1974). Distinctions between intentional versus unintentional behavior and between socially desirable versus deviant action, research also suggests, are evident at early ages and in diverse cultures (Bretherton & Bates, 1979; DiVesta, 1966; Keasey, 1978; Osgood, May, & Miron, 1975; White, 1980).

Half the subjects in each age/cultural subgroup explained the two deviant behaviors followed by the two prosocial behaviors, and the other half explained the behaviors in the reverse order. Interviews were tape-recorded and later transcribed.

A coding scheme, outlined in Table 1, was constructed to enable exhaustive coding of subjects' responses and assessment of the research hypotheses.[1] Based, in part, on a system for analyzing human motivation developed by Burke (1969) and on earlier content analyses (Lewis, 1978; Shweder, Bourne, & Miyamoto, 1978), the scheme offers several advantages. General in nature, it identifies global distinctions that, it may reasonably be assumed, are universal. As a formal system, the scheme is able to accommodate diverse content found among attributors from different age and cultural backgrounds.

TABLE 1

Outline of Scheme for Coding Explanations

- I. Agent
  - A. General dispositions
    - 1. Personality
    - 2. Value, attitude
    - 3. Preference, interest
    - 4. General capability
    - 5. Physical characteristic
  - B. Situationally specific aspects
    - 1. Purpose
    - 2. Feeling
    - 3. End in itself
    - 4. Specific ability
    - 5. Physical state
- II. Context
  - A. Social/spatial/temporal location
    - 1. Social norm, regulation
    - 2. Descriptive references
  - B. Aspects of persons other than agent
    - 1. General aspects
    - 2. Situationally specific aspects
  - C. Impersonal aspects of context
- III. Acts/occurrences
- IV. Agent/context combination
- V. Other
  - A. Reasons mitigating against behavior
  - B. Extraneous comments
  - C. Questionable comments (unscorable)

Major distinctions are made in the scheme between references to (a) aspects of the agent undertaking the behavior, including the agent's general dispositions (e.g., "Agent A is proud") and situationally specific aspects (e.g., "Agent A was tired that day"); to (b) the context, including the social/spatial/temporal location (e.g., "His friends were with him"), aspects of persons other than the agent (e.g., "Agent A's friend was feeling sick"); and to (c) acts or occurrences (e.g., "She hit him" or "He fell down"). Attributions made simultaneously to the agent and to the context are encompassed under a combination category (e.g., "They [the agent and his friend] were annoyed").

Subject's responses were segmented into units for coding purposes by dividing them into independent clauses, each of which included no more than one verb(s)–object sequence, verb(s)–predicate nominative, or verb(s)–predicate adjective; for example, "Sally is considerate / outgoing / and friendly" = 3 units; "I think she always has been jealous of me / because I've always done better in school than her" = 2 units. The proportion of subjects' references to various types of reasons in explaining particular behaviors was calculated by (a) coding all clauses in subjects' responses in terms of one of the categories in the coding scheme, (b) identifying and eliminating any redundant mentions of a particular type of reason, and (c) dividing the proportion of nonredundant mentions of a particular type of reason by the proportion of nonredundant mentions of all reasons. This mode of calculating references to various reasons is illustrated in the following scoring of an explanation given by a Hindu adult: (a) "It was dark" (context: social/spatial/temporal location); (b) "and there was no one else to help" (context: social/spatial/temporal location); (c) "Agent A was the only one there" (context: social/spatial/temporal location, redundant); (d) "Also A is a very kind man" (agent: general dispositions). The response is scored as including three distinct reasons (a, b, and d), with contextual factors accounting for 67% of the distinct reasons mentioned and general dispositions accounting for the remainder.

Reliability in applying the coding scheme was assessed between the author, another American, and an Indian from the Mysore region on a set of American and Hindu protocols. For overall agreement on the proportion of distinct mentions of different types of reasons per protocol, $r = 0.84$. No difference in agreement occurred as a function of the cultural origin of the coders or of the cultural source of the responses. These results, indicating high levels of agreement between American and Hindu coders, may be seen to provide some evidence that the scheme possessed cross-cultural validity.

Classification procedure. A classification test, based on a procedure developed by Flavell and Stedman (1961), was constructed to assess subjects' abilities to classify on the basis of conceptual similarity, a cognitive prerequisite for descriptive use of general dispositions.[2] The task required subjects to distinguish between word pairs related on the basis of conceptual similarity and word pairs related on spatiotemporal and/or functional bases, the types of concrete bases observed to dominate young children's and non-Western adults' social attributions.

In constructing the task, four sets of different word pairs were selected to illustrate each of the following modes of conceptual interrelationship: (a) similarity (e.g., "talk, shout"); (b) contingency (e.g., "happy, smile"); (c) spatial contiguity (e.g., "market, sell"); and (d) linkage in an action sequence (e.g., "wash, hands"). The words selected represented ones relevant to the description of everyday social behavior and familiar to subjects in both cultures. Each word pair was coupled once with each of the other three word pairs in its set to generate a 24-item questionnaire. For each item, subjects were instructed to select the word pair "most similar in meaning." Subsequent scoring of the procedure focused only on word pairs contrasting items related on an abstract basis with items related on one of the three concrete bases. For example, for the item "(market, sell) (talk, shout)," a subject's response of "talk, shout" would be scored as correctly identifying the word pair most similar in meaning. Couplings between concrete word pairs—for example, "(happy, smile) (market, sell)"—were not analyzed.

Results and Discussion

The data were analyzed with repeated measures analysis of variance (ANOVA), with an arc sin transformation applied to all scores involving proportions (Winer, 1962). Assessment of subjects' explanations focused on their use of distinct reasons. Analysis revealed no significant effects of sex or of order of explaining prosocial as contrasted with deviant behaviors on any of the dependent measures. Responses were therefore analyzed with both sexes and orders of responding combined. Due to the low frequency of responses coded under the agent-context combination category, (less than 3% in any age/cultural subgroup), such responses are reported under their respective agent and context categories. Comparisons between the main and the controlling middle-class Hindu samples revealed no significant effects of language on subjects' overall responses to the procedure or on their use of general dispositions or contextual factors in explanation.

Examination of Cross-Cultural and Age Differences in Explanation *Overall responses to explanation procedure.* An average of 85% of the responses in each age/cultural subgroup were scored as reasons explaining the behavior, with an average of 2% scored as reasons mitigating against performance of the behavior (e.g., "It wasn't because she was angry") and an average of 14% scored as extraneous comments (e.g., "I think what happened was funny"). Only a very small percentage of responses were unscorable (a maximum of 2% in any age/cultural subgroup). A 2 × 4 × 2 (culture × age × valence of behavior) ANOVA on the proportion of reason codings revealed no significant effects. No differences occurred across age/cultural subgroups in the proportion of responses coded in terms of some type of reason category (Categories I through V-A in the coding scheme) as compared with responses coded as extraneous comments or as questionable.

A 2 × 4 × 2 (culture × age × valence of behavior) ANOVA on the number of distinct reasons given in explanation revealed only a significant main effect of age, $F(3, 242) = 30.45$, $p < .01$. Adults produced approximately 3.3 distinct reasons per behavior being explained, whereas 8-year-olds averaged slightly under 2 distinct reasons.

These results demonstrate a general comparability across the cultures in subject's responses to the procedure. The bulk of subjects' verbalizations were task focused, with no cultural differences occurring in fluency.

Weighting of general dispositions. A 2 × 4 × 2 (culture × age × valence of behavior) ANOVA on the proportion of references to general dispositions (Category I-A in the coding scheme) revealed significant main effects of culture, $F(1, 242) = 20.98$, $p < .01$, and of age, $F(3, 242) = 22.14$, $p < .01$, as well as significant interactions of Culture × Age, $F(3, 242) = 4.99$, $p < .01$, and Valence × Culture, $F(1, 242) = 15.18$, $p < .01$. As predicted, at older ages Americans gave greater weight to general dispositions in explanation than did Hindus. Also as hypothesized, this cross-cultural difference was more marked in the case of deviant than in the case of prosocial behaviors. Analysis revealed that most of the cross-cultural differences observed in the use of general dispositions resulted from references to personality characteristics (e.g., "Agent A is insecure" or "Agent A is kind").

The upper half of Table 2 contrasts the mean percentage of references to general dispositions in explanation across the age and cultural subgroups. An average of 40% of all reasons mentioned by American adults made reference to general dispositions, in contrast to under 20% of all reasons cited by Hindu adults. This cross-cultural variation was particularly great in explanations of deviant behaviors, with American adults (M = 45%) placing three times as much weight on general dispositions as Hindu adults did (M = 15%).

In contrast to the striking cross-cultural differences observed among adults, little difference distinguished the responses of the youngest subjects. Responses of 8-year-old and 11-year-old American subjects, for example, differed from those of 8-year-old and 11-year-old Hindu subjects by only 2%, on average.

To evaluate within-culture developmental trends, post hoc trend analyses, evaluated by the Scheffé test (Keppel, 1973), were undertaken on the proportion of references to general dispositions. A significant linear age increase in references to general dispositions was observed to occur among Americans, $F(1, 116) = 67.22$, $p < .01$. In contrast, a similar analysis performed on Hindu responses showed no significant linear age effect.

The American emphasis on dispositional characteristics may be illustrated by consideration of explanations offered by American adults of deviant behavior. An American adult subject, for example, cited the following deviant behavior involving an agent cheating on her income tax return:

> A neighbor of mine—she and her husband, they talk to us about a great number of things. She recently told me with a certain amount of even pride how she itemized her taxes to get back even more from the government—really outright cheating. On giving to charity she declared the maximum. And she knows and we know—'cause she tells us—that they didn't give anything to charity at all.

TABLE 2
Proportion of References to General Dispositions and Context Among Main American and Hindu Subgroups

Age group	Deviant behaviors: U.S.	Deviant behaviors: India	Prosocial behaviors: U.S.	Prosocial behaviors: India
General Dispositions				
Adult	.45	.15	.35	.22
15 years	.30	.07	.11	.18
11 years	.13	.07	.15	.15
8 years	.13	.08	.08	.11
Context				
Adult	.14	.32	.22	.49
15 years	.18	.23	.42	.39
11 years	.11	.17	.30	.39
8 years	.11	.12	.36	.34

The subject explained the neighbor's behavior by reference to her personality characteristics: "That's just the type of person she is. She's very competitive." In a second case, a different American subject narrated a deviant act involving an agent's usurping credit for someone else's idea:

> This involved one of the teachers I work with at school. It was a process of scheduling—something to do with scheduling. I came up with an innovative idea of organizing the scheduling, of what we should do. I talked to some of the other faculty members about it, and this first teacher picked it up and quickly went to the principal and presented it as if it were his own idea.

As in the previous example, this behavior was also seen as deriving from the agent's general dispositions: "He was just a very self-absorbed person. He was interested only in himself."

The present results provide support for the predictions based on American and Hindu cultural conceptions of the person. As hypothesized, at older ages Americans gave greater weight to general dispositions in explanation than did Hindus. This cross-cultural difference, also as predicted, was more marked in explanations of deviant than of prosocial behaviors. Consonant with a cultural view of developmental change, within-cultural developmental variation in attribution was observed to parallel cross-cultural adult variation in attribution. Whereas references to general dispositions increased markedly across the age range sampled among Americans, they showed little developmental change among Hindus.

Weighting of contextual factors. Further examination of the data focused on contextual attributions, modes of attribution that, it was anticipated, might be employed more by Hindus than by Americans, given the holistic cultural views of the person emphasized in India. A 2 × 4 × 2 (culture × age × valence of behavior) ANOVA undertaken on the proportion of references to the context (Category II in the coding scheme) revealed significant main effects of culture, $F(1, 242) = 8.63$, $p < .01$; age, $F(3, 242) = 4.89$, $p < .01$, and valence, $F(1, 242) = 112.31$, $p < .01$, as well as a significant Culture × Age interaction, $F(3, 242) = 6.18$, $p < .01$. All subjects made greatest reference to the context in explanation of prosocial behaviors, an effect resulting from the greater number of normative reasons invoked to explain prosocial as compared with deviant behaviors. At older ages Hindus made significantly greater reference to the context than did Americans. Most of this cross-cultural difference resulted from attributions to the social/spatial/temporal location, a category encompassing references to social roles and to patterns of interpersonal relationship (e.g., "She is his aunt" or "He has many enemies") as well as references to the placement of persons, objects, or events in time or space (e.g., "It was early in the morning" or "He lives far away from school"). Such modes of attribution may be seen to be reflective of Indian cultural conceptions in their emphasis on locating a person, object, or event in relation to someone or something else.

The mean percentage of references to the context are compared in the lower half of Table 2. Hindu adults ($M = 40\%$) were observed to give over twice as much weight to contextual factors in explanations as did American adults ($M = 18\%$). Little cross-cultural difference in contextual explanations occurred among children. Unlike the case of general dispositions, however, contextual references were employed frequently at younger ages, accounting for over one third of children's explanations of prosocial behaviors.

Post hoc trend analyses, evaluated by the Scheffè test, indicated a significant linear age increase among Hindus in proportionate references to the context, $F(1, 126) = 22.37$, $p < .01$. In contrast, no significant linear age increase occurred among Americans in contextual explanations.

The Hindu stress on contextual determinants of behavior may be seen in explanations by Hindu adults of deviant behavior. One Hindu adult subject, for example, discussed the following deviant behavior involving an agent's cheating a customer out of money paid for work the agent was to perform:

> I had to construct a house, and for that I had given advance money for Agent A to do that construction work. Agent A had promised—he had given in writing—that he would do that particular work. I gave him an advance of 1,500 rupees. He utilized it for his personal purposes, and then he never did that work or returned the money. That man, he deceived me up to the extent of 1,500 rupees. That's a great injustice. But I can go to the court of law. I have the documents, everything.

The Hindu subject explained the behavior by reference to the agent's socioeconomic position: "The man is unemployed. He is not in a position to give that money." Another Hindu subject cited the following deviant behavior involving an advisor's assuming first authorship on a paper written by someone else:

> This involved a scholar in some other department, and she has got her PhD now. She wanted to publish four or five papers from her thesis. She produced some papers, but the thing is, her advisor, he put his name as first author and this young scholar as the second author. She was very hurt because that means usually the credit goes to the first author.

The Hindu subject attributed the advisor's behavior to social role relations: "She was his student. She would not have the power to do it (publish it) by herself." The deviant behaviors under consideration in these two cases may be seen to involve similar issues as in the earlier American examples (i.e., financial cheating and failure to acknowledge the contributions of a second person). Unlike the American cases, however, the deviant behaviors were attributed to factors in the social surround and not to general dispositions of the agent.

Results observed in references to the context are in the direction suggested by the present cultural theory. Contextual references, modes of attribution more reflective of holistic than of individualistic cultural orientations, were used more at older ages by attributors from the culture maintaining holistic views of the person than by attributors from the culture maintaining more individualistic emphases. Similarly, a significant developmental increase in contextual references occurred only among Hindus and not among Americans.

Evaluation of Cognitive and Experiential Interpretations Although the cultural and age differences observed in the use of general dispositions conform to the patterns hypothesized on the basis of American and Hindu cultural conceptions of the person, they are consonant as well with alternative noncultural effects. In particular, such attributional diversity might be interpreted as resulting from differences in attributors' cognitive capacities to generate dispositional attributions and/or from differences in attributors' exposure to objective conditions that make taxonomic modes of categorization adaptive. Analyses were therefore undertaken to evaluate the adequacy of such alternative explanations of the observed attributional trends.

Cognitive interpretation. To evaluate a cognitive interpretation of the observed cross-cultural and age differences in reference to general dispositions, assessment was undertaken of subjects' abilities to classify on the basis of conceptual similarity in the classification procedure. A 2 × 4 (culture × age) ANOVA was conducted on the number of times that subject selected word pairs related on the basis of conceptual similarity as more similar in meaning than word pairs related on a concrete basis when the two types of word pairs were coupled. No significant effects of culture or age were observed in this analysis.

TABLE 3
Percentage Selections of Conceptually Similar Word Pairs in Classification Task Among Main American and Hindu Subgroups

Age group	U.S.	India
Adult	90.1	91.2
15 years	85.7	89.0
11 years	88.3	84.6
8 years	84.4	82.3

Table 3 contrasts the mean percentage of times that subjects selected word pairs related on the basis of conceptual similarity as more similar in meaning than word pairs related on a concrete basis. It may be seen that all subjects displayed relatively high levels of ability to distinguish abstract from concrete modes of conceptual interrelationship, correctly identifying abstract modes of conceptual interrelationship in all age/cultural subgroups on an average of better than 82% of the time. The analysis indicated that subjects were able to overlook the contextual interrelationships existing between word pairs (e.g., "school, learn") to isolate interrelationships based primarily on conceptual similarity (e.g., "boy, man").

The high levels of performance displayed by all subjects in the present procedure, it may be noted, do not imply the absence of any differences in subjects' classificatory abilities across the age/cultural subgroups. It is possible, for example, that significant age and/or cultural differences might be present on abstract classificatory skills not tapped by the present procedure, such as flexibility in shifting bases of classification, exhaustiveness in classification, and so forth. Given the context specificity of most cognitive abilities, it is also likely that somewhat greater subgroup differences in performance might be observed under contrasting task conditions, for example, utilizing a more difficult set of word items or a response mode making greater demands on subjects' verbal abilities and/or memory capacities.

Although they do not indicate identity in subjects' classificatory capacities, the present results do, however, demonstrate that subjects at all ages tested in both cultures possessed at least some capacity to classify on the basis of conceptual similarity. It was shown that all subjects were able to distinguish relationships of similarity from competing concrete spatiotemporal and/or functional relationships. The trends are consonant with past findings indicating the availability of some capacity in abstract classification early in development (Nelson, 1977). These trends suggest that it is unlikely that the cross-cultural and age variability observed in dispositional attributions reflects a total incapacity of certain subjects to assume an abstract cognitive orientation.

Experiential interpretation. To evaluate an experiential interpretation of the observed cross-cultural and age differences in reference to general dispositions, comparison was undertaken of references to general dispositions by Indian adult subgroups, contrasting in their exposure to modernizing conditions and/or in their subcultural orientation. The following adult subgroups were compared: (a) the main Hindu middle-class sample, (b) the control Hindu middle-class sample, (c) the lower class Hindu sample, and (d) the lower middle-class Anglo-Indian sample. As college graduates with professional occupational backgrounds and extensive mobility, the middle-class Hindus had the greatest exposure to modernizing conditions, whereas the lower class Hindus had the least exposure to modernizing conditions, experiencing 3 years or less of education and having menial-labor occupational backgrounds and virtually no mobility. The lower middle-class Anglo-Indians represented an intermediate subgroup, in their levels of exposure to modernizing conditions, having high school educations, blue-collar occupational backgrounds, and limited mobility. As a Christian community of mixed Euro-Indian descent (Anthony, 1969; Maher, 1962), however, the Anglo-Indians held more Westernized cultural meaning systems than either the middle-class or lower class Hindus.

Contrasting multiple subgroups within the same culture, the present analysis is valuable in providing a controlled test of the research hypotheses. If references to general dispositions reflected merely attributors' exposure to more complex experiential conditions, associated with modernization, middle-class Hindu adults would be anticipated to make the greatest reference to general dispositions; Anglo-Indian adults, slightly less reference; and lower class Hindu adults, the least reference. In contrast, if references to general dispositions reflected attributors' maintenance of Westernized cultural meaning systems, independently of their socioeconomic status, it would be anticipated that the greatest reference to general dispositions would occur among Anglo-Indian adults, with little difference in the use of general dispositions occurring among the Hindu adult subgroups.

A 4 × 2 (Indian adult subgroup × valence of behavior) ANOVA on the proportion of references to general dispositions made by all Indian adults revealed a significant Subgroup × Valence interaction, $F(3, 96) = 3.34$, $p < .05$. Lower middle-class Anglo-Indians were observed to make significantly greater reference to general dispositions in explaining deviant behaviors than did either the middle-class or lower class Hindu subgroups.

Table 4 contrasts the mean percentage of references to general dispositions by the various Indian adult subgroups. It may be seen that explanations of deviant behavior by Hindu middle-class adults differed by less than 2% from those of Hindu lower class adults, despite the marked socioeconomic differences between the two groups. In contrast, even though the Anglo-Indians were slightly lower in socioeconomic status than the middle-class Hindus, they gave approximately twice as much weight to general dispositions in explanation of deviance as did the middle-class Hindus. As in the cross-cultural comparison between Americans and Hindus, subcultural differences between Anglo-Indians and Hindus were much greater in explanations of deviant behaviors than in explanations of prosocial behaviors.

In documenting that references to general dispositions did not vary with attributors' socioeconomic status, a variable closely linked in past research with objective conditions conducive to abstraction, the present results call into question an experiential interpretation of the observed cultural and age variation in references to general dispositions. The use of general dispositions, the results imply, does not represent merely a functional adaptation to the more complex experiential demands associated with modernization.

The results provide direct support for the present alternative cultural interpretation of attributional diversity in documenting that dispositional attributions varied with subcultural orientation within India in the same direction that they varied with cultural orien-

TABLE 4
Proportion of References to General Dispositions Among Indian Adult Subgroups

Adult subgroup	Deviant behaviors	Prosocial behaviors
Anglo-Indian	.29	.16
Hindu middle class (main)	.15	.22
Hindu middle class (control)	.13	.23
Hindu lower class	.13	.15

tation across the United States and India. Consonant with their semi-westernized cultural orientations, Anglo-Indians (M = 29%) were observed to display a pattern of weighting general dispositions in explanations of deviance intermediate between that of Americans (M = 14%). Such results then lend support to the view that attributors' adoption of more individualistic as contrasted with more holistic culturally derived conceptual assumptions underlies the observed attributional diversity in the use of general dispositions.

STUDY 2

The analyses strongly support the present cultural interpretation of attributional diversity in explanation, but it might alternatively be argued that the observed cross-cultural attributional variation resulted from differences in the behaviors explained by subjects in each age and cultural subgroup. The research required subjects to explain deviant and prosocial behaviors, meeting certain formal criteria. Such a methodological strategy, it was judged, resulted in greater functional equivalence in the behaviors explained across subgroups than would have been achieved by having all subjects explain identical behaviors.

The results observed, given use of the present methodology, however, might be interpreted in informational terms. It might be maintained that certain objective events, regardless of culture, are conceptually understood in a certain way and call for a similar type of explanation. Such an assertion, for example, has been made by various developmental theorists in positing that universally certain substantive content (e.g., injury to persons) will be seen as a moral violation (Turiel, 1978, 1979). Applied to the present case, it might be argued that the observed cross-cultural and age variation in references to general dispositions resulted exclusively from objective differences in the information being explained across subgroups and did not depend on subjects' culturally derived conceptual understandings of such information.

In order to evaluate this informational interpretation, a second sample of American adults was asked to explain a set of deviant behaviors generated originally by Hindu adults and explained in ways representative of the dominant Hindu adult pattern of explanation. The explanations of these incidents offered by the original Hindu subjects were not presented to the American subjects. If informational effects represented a major determinant of the observed attributional diversity, it would be anticipated that explanations by this new American sample would more closely resemble the dominant Hindu adult pattern of explanation than the dominant American adult pattern. In contrast, the reverse finding would suggest that attributors' culturally derived conceptual assumptions must be taken into account to explain the observed attributional diversity in explanation.

Method

Subjects Subjects included 10 male and 10 female middle-class American adults, drawn from a university population. They had a mean age of 24.5 years and a mean education of 17.8 years.

Procedure Deviant behaviors were chosen for presentation to subjects because they were the type of behaviors on which greatest cross-cultural differences in attribution had been observed in the original investigation. Selection of these behaviors entailed isolating all deviant behaviors that Hindu adults had explained by (a) some reference to the social/spatial/temporal location and by (b) no reference to the agent's general dispositions. Four behaviors were then randomly and blindly sampled from the set of behaviors meeting these criteria. In no case were two behaviors sampled from the same Hindu adult.

Two minor changes were made in the behaviors narrated by Hindu adults before presenting them to the American subjects to avoid overt identification of the responses as Indian: (a) the word *dollar* was substituted for *rupee*, and (b) nouns were substituted for proper names. Otherwise the exact wording of the original Hindu adult subjects was preserved.

The procedure was introduced to subjects as a task in which they would be asked to explain four nonhypothetical incidents that had been cited originally by other adults as examples of wrong behaviors. The same probe questions used in the cross-cultural investigation were used in this second study. Subjects were asked to explain why they thought each behavior had been undertaken immediately after having the behavior read to them by the interviewer. Subjects' responses were tape-recorded and later transcribed and coded with the coding scheme used in the cross-cultural investigation. In debriefing after the interview, subjects indicated no awareness or suspicion that the deviant behaviors had been generated originally by non-Americans.

Results and Discussion

Results indicated that the explanations by this new sample of American adults more closely resembled the dominant American adult pattern of explanation than the dominant Hindu adult pattern of explanation observed in the cross-cultural investigation. For example, the new sample of American adults made, on the average, 36% of their attributions to general dispositions of the agent, a pattern of weighting general dispositions that is more similar to that displayed by the original American adult sample (M = 45%) than that displayed by the original Hindu adult sample (M = 15%). Similarly, the weight given to contextual reasons by the new American sample (M = 17%) practically matched that given by the original American adult subjects (M = 14%) but was markedly divergent from that observed among the original Hindu adult subjects (M = 32%).

Explanations presented below of the same deviant behavior by the original Hindu subject and by an American in the second study illustrate the type of divergence observed in Hindu as contrasted with American explanations:

> *Deviant behavior cited by Hindu adult subject:* This concerns a motorcycle accident. The back wheel burst on the motorcycle. The passenger sitting in the rear jumped. The moment the passenger fell, he struck his head on the pavement. The driver of the motorcycle—who is an attorney—as he was on his way to court for some work, just took the passenger to a local hospital and went on and attended to his court work. I personally feel the motorcycle driver did a wrong thing. The driver left the passenger there without consulting the doctor concerning the seriousness of the injury—the gravity of the situation—whether the passenger should be shifted immediately—and he went on to the court. So ultimately the passenger died.
>
> *Interview question:*
> Why did the driver leave the passenger at the hospital without staying to consult about the seriousness of the passenger's injury?
>
> *Explanation by Hindu adult subject:*
> It was the driver's duty to be in court for the client whom he's representing (context: social/ spatial/-temporal location); secondly, the driver might have gotten nervous or confused (agent: specific aspects); and thirdly, the passenger might not have looked as serious as he was (context: aspects of persons).
>
> *Explanation by American adult subject:*
>
> The driver is obviously irresponsible (agent: general dispositions); the driver was in a state of shock (agent: specific aspects); the driver is aggressive in pursuing career success (agent: general dispositions).

Although both the Hindu and the American subject considered the driver's emotional state as one determinant of his behavior, the Hindu adult cited additional contextual reasons for the driver's behavior, whereas the American adult made references to dispositional causes. It should be noted that the contextual reasons cited by the Hindu subject (the driver's role obligations as a lawyer and the passenger's physical condition) were explicitly mentioned in the description of the deviant behavior presented to the American subject. The American adult, however, overlooked such available information to concentrate on dispositional properties of the agent, factors that could only be inferred. It may be argued that the American utilized certain culturally derived conceptual premises—that enduring dispositions regulate behavior across contexts and that the autonomous individual is the primary normative unit—to construct his explanation of the event. In contrast, the Hindu's focus on contextual factors appeared to reflect, in part, his culturally derived views of persons as highly vulnerable to situational influences and of the social role as primary locus of moral responsibility.

The results observed in the present study then provide some evidence to suggest that the cross-cultural and age differences in explanation observed in the cross-cultural investigation did not arise merely from variation in the objective behaviors being explained in each age/cultural subgroup. It has been demonstrated that when explaining a set of deviant behaviors generated by Hindu adults, American adults deemphasized contextual reasons emphasized by Hindus and, in turn, emphasized general dispositional factors, reflective of American cultural conceptions of the person, that were neglected by Hindus. Such results may be seen to imply that the cultural and age variability in attribution observed in the larger cross-cultural investigation cannot be fully explained without taking into account the culturally derived conceptual assumptions informing attributors' interpretations of the particular behaviors under consideration.

GENERAL DISCUSSION

The investigation may be seen to contribute to a theoretical understanding of semantic influences on attribution, the patterning of cultural and age diversity in attribution and the role of social transmission in the acquisition of everyday social knowledge.

Importance of Integrating Semantic With Structural Considerations

Theories of attribution developed within psychology have tended to neglect the impact of cultural meaning systems on attribution. This neglect arises, in part, from tendencies to treat the categories underlying veridical attribution as self-evident (see, e.g., Rosch, 1975; Rosch & Mervis, 1975; Rosch, et al., 1976). It tends to be assumed that particular objective information, when processed accurately, gives rise to one true conceptual representation of its causal structure rather than to multiple veridical conceptual representations.

Adoption of such an approach to categorization has led many theorists to focus primarily on structural considerations in attempts to explain the patterning of attribution and to appraise the adequacy of alternative modes of attribution. Objective variables, the information available to the attributor, and/or subjective variables, the cognitive processing of information by the attributor, have been regarded as sufficient to explain the patterning of attribution. Culture, as an intersubjective system of meanings, has generally not been considered an additional necessary and independent influence on the attribution process. Depending on the particular approach, cultural meaning systems have tended to be viewed as (a) subordinate to the operational constructions of the attributor and thus not a source of patterning of individual modes of conceptual representation (e.g., Piaget, 1954, 1966, 1970a, 1970b); as (b) nonessential sources of information concerning the objective covariation structure of experience, providing information to supplement or substitute for that acquired through individual observation (e.g., Kelley, 1972a, 1972b, 1973); or as (c) adapted to objective constraints and thus pot an independent determinant of individual modes of conceptual representation (e.g., Bruner et al., 1966).

Focus similarly has tended to center on structural considerations in appraising the adequacy of alternative modes of attribution. Attribution has been viewed primarily as serving the requirements of adaptation, enabling observers with limited cognitive resources to predict and control the causal structure of experience. Consonant with this perspective, the scientific criteria of predictive power and parsimony have tended to be applied as primary standards for appraising the adequacy of alternative modes of attribution. Such orientations may be seen reflected, for example, in dominant metaphors used to characterize the attributor, such as an "intuitive scientist" (Ross, 1977) or a "cognitive miser" (Taylor, 1981).

The present investigation extends current approaches in providing evidence concerning the independent impact of cultural meaning systems on attribution. It was shown that cross-cultural and developmental variation in references to general dispositions could be predicted based on differences between the more individualistic cultural views of the person stressed in the United States as compared with the more holistic cultural views of the person emphasized in India. Evidence suggested that this attributional diversity could not be fully explained by reference to the structural factors traditionally emphasized within psychological approaches, that is, by reference to differences in attributors' classificatory abilities and/or their objective adaptive requirements.

Such results underscore the importance of recognizing that the conceptual assumptions informing social attribution are discretionary and culturally variable, not self-evident. It cannot be assumed that a given pattern of co-occurrences gives rise to only one veridical conceptual representation. Rather, it must be recognized that the same objective information may give rise to contrasting yet equally adequate conceptual representations, depending on the particular culturally derived conceptual premises brought to bear in interpreting that information by the attributor.

To descriptively represent reality, the properties available in experience, it may be seen, must be given differential weight, not merely inductively processed (Goodman, 1968, 1972; Shweder, Bourne, & Miyamoto, 1978). An infinite number of properties might be considered in any conceptual representation of reality. Taking all properties into account simultaneously would not then result in a determinate classification. As Goodman illustrates in arguing against a "copy" theory of conceptual representation,

> "To make a faithful picture [representation], come as close as possible to copying the object as it is." This simple-minded injunction baffles me; for the object before me is a man, a swarm of atoms, a complex of

> cells, a fiddle, a friend, a fool and much more. If none of these constitute the object just as it is, then none is *the* way the object is. I cannot copy all these at once; and the more nearly I succeeded, the less would the result be a realistic picture. (1968, p. 6)

Which properties of experience are considered in a descriptive representation reflect, in large part, their cultural relevance. In the present investigation, for example, it appeared that the more individualistic cultural views of the person held by older Americans led them to focus on dispositional properties of the agent in explanation, whereas Hindus' more holistic cultural orientations led them to stress contextual influences.

It must also be recognized that the conceptual assumptions informing social attribution may serve prescriptive and not merely descriptive purposes and thus may not be based on patterns of correlated attributes (Geertz, 1973; Schnedier, 1968). A purpose underlying social categorization is to forward rules for conduct, not merely or necessarily to represent patterns of co-occurrences, as in the exclusively inductive categories of science. Social categories, then it may be seen, have no necessary empirical correlates. A category such as *woman,* in referring to "agents who should be paid equal salaries to men" or to "agents who should treat their husbands as Gods," for example, may or may not relate to ways that women actually are treated or behave. This independence of prescriptive categories from objective evidence was reflected in the present study in contrasting normative interpretations placed on the same information by American and Hindu subjects.

The present considerations highlight the need for greater efforts to integrate semantic with structural considerations in current theories of attribution. Attributors' information and mode of information processing must be taken into account to distinguish more rational from less rational weighting of evidence. Such structural considerations alone, however, cannot explain the processes by which a veridical understanding of experience is approached in attribution. It must be recognized that conceptual interpretation, in terms of culturally derived premises, and inductive or deductive processing of evidence constitute independent and essential elements entailed in attaining veridical knowledge of experience.

Equally the investigation demonstrates the need for attention to semantic criteria in appraising the adequacy of alternative modes of attribution. It has been seen that, in encompassing prescriptive considerations, cultural conceptions of the person influencing attribution may not necessarily map correlated attributes. Functional criteria, such as parsimony and predictive power, then represent neither sufficient nor in all cases necessary standards by which to appraise the adequacy of alternative modes of attribution.

Need for Nonteleological Interpretations of Cultural and Age Diversity in Conceptualization

The patterning of attribution across age and culture has been viewed by many psychological theorists as resulting from a closed causal process and as following a progressive developmental course. It tends to be maintained that age and cultural diversity in conceptualization may be predicted by reference to universal laws of psychological and/or societal development. Cognitive-developmental theorists, for example, have linked the emergence of more abstract modes of conceptual representation to the transition to more advanced stages of cognitive development over ontogeny (e.g., Inhelder & Piaget, 1964). Other developmental and cross-cultural theorists have stressed the impact of experiential conditions associated with socioeconomic development, such as schooling, literacy, and urbanization, in promoting the acquisition of more abstract modes of conceptual representation (e.g., Bruner et al, 1966; Greenfield, 1972; Horton, 1967; Luria, 1976; Scribner & Cole, 1973). It is assumed in such approaches then that conceptual diversity observed across age and culture may be comparatively ranked as reflecting more or less advanced levels of cognitive development and/or more or less complex objective conditions, associated with modernization, to which attributors have been exposed.

The present investigation provides evidence suggesting that many of the conceptual changes occurring in attribution cannot be explained in such evolutionary terms. The finding that the patterning of attribution followed contrasting developmental courses between Americans and Hindus challenges the assertion that there is a determinate directionality to conceptual changes occurring over ontogeny. Equally, the demonstration that references to general dispositions among Indian adults varied with subcultural orientation (Anglo-Indian vs. Hindu) independently of socioeconomic status (middle class vs. lower class) calls into question the claim that technological development or modernization is causally related to changes in individuals' conceptual orientations. The observed trends rather suggest that attributors' conceptual orientations are not necessarily isomorphic with their exposure to modernizing conditions.

The present investigation then highlights the need for the adoption of nonteleological frameworks for interpreting age and cultural diversity in conceptualization (Cole & Griffin, 1980; Super, 1980). Changes occurring in conceptualization across cultures with technological development and over ontogency, the results imply, must be regarded in historical and not causal terms. Such changes need to be considered as, at least potentially, cohort specific and liable to variation with a shift in cultural values.

The results also underscore the need to evaluate conceptual diversity in local terms rather than by reference to a universal normative standard. It was observed that the conceptual schemes informing attribution across different age and cultural groups cannot in all cases be comparatively scaled as providing more or less valid representations of the causal structure of experience or as reflecting more or less rational information processing. It must be recognized then that changes in conceptualization with ontogenetic and/or societal development are not necessarily progressive (Kuhn, 1962; Shweder, in press). Conceptual schemes found in different age and cultural groups may represent alternative yet equally rational systems for interpreting experience rather than more or less advanced levels in a single conceptual framework.

Role of Cultural Communication in Knowledge Acquisition

Psychological theories of attribution, particularly, in the Piagetian tradition, have tended to place primary emphasis on processes of self-construction in the acquisition of knowledge (see, e.g., Piaget, 1970a, 1970b). Social transmission tends not to be regarded as an essential component in the acquisition process. Although such approaches portray the attributor as active, it may be argued that they generally do not view the attributor as creative. The attributor's role tends to be seen as entailing solely the rational processing of covariation information and not as equally involving discretionary interpretation of this information in terms of culturally variable criteria.

The present investigation provides evidence showing the need to give greater weight to the social aspects of knowledge (D'Andrade, 1981; Higgins, Ruble, & Hartup, 1983; Schwartz, 1981). What constitutes objective knowledge of the world, it is demonstrated, is framed in terms of culturally variable concepts acquired gradually over development. Such knowledge then cannot be acquired through processes of autonomous individual discovery but requires the communication of culturally derived conceptual premises for interpreting experience.

In demonstrating that the knowledge acquired in attribution is of a culturally constituted and not just culturally interpreted reality, the present investigation also stresses the creative aspects of the acquisition process. The attributor is seen as not merely discovering preexisting patterns of covariation but as becoming initiated into a world created by cultural rules, rules that bear no necessary relationship to objective or subjective determinants (D'Andrade, in press). Such cultural understandings are not static. Enculturation entails processes of change along with processes of continuity. Attributors may be viewed, in part, as creating new cultural understandings through modifications introduced into existing understandings. It must then be recognized that social transmission and active construction of knowledge represent complementary, not necessarily opposed, aspects of knowledge acquisition.

REFERENCES

Anthony, F. (1969). *Britain's betrayal in India.* Bombay: Allied Publishers.

Bransford, J. D., & McCarrell, N. S. (1974). A Sketch of a cognitive approach to comprehension: Some thoughts about understanding what it means to comprehend. In W. B. Weiner & D. S. Palermo (Eds.), *Cognition and the symbolic process* (pp. 189–229). Hillsdale, NJ: Eribaum.

Bretherton, I., & Bates, E. (1979). The emergence of intentional communication. In I. Uzgiris (Ed.), *New directions for child development* (pp. 81–100). San Francisco: Jossey-Bass.

Bruner, J. S., & Olver, R. R. (1963). Development of equivalence transformation in children. In J. Wright & J. Kagan (Eds.), Basic cognitive processes in children. *Monographs of the Society for Research in Child Development, 28*, 125–142.

Bruner, J. S., Olver, R. R., & Greenfield, P. (Eds.) (1966). *Studies in cognitive Growth.* New York: Wiley.

Burke, K. (1969). *A grammar of motives.* Berkeley: University of California Press.

Cole, M., & Griffin, P. (1980). Cultural amplifiers reconsidered. In D. Olson (Ed.), *The social foundations of language and thought* (pp. 343–364). New York: W. W. Norton.

Cole, M., Sharp, D., & Lave, C. (1976). The cognitive consequences of education: Some empirical evidence and theoretical misgivings. *Urban Review, 9*, 218–233.

D'Andrade, R. (1981). The cultural part of cognition. *Cognitive Science, 5*, 179–195.

D'Andrade, R. (in press). Cultural meaning systems. In R. A. Shweder & R. A. Levine (Ed.), *Culture theory: essays on mind, self and emotion.* Cambridge, England: Cambridge University Press.

DiVesta, F. J. (1966). A developmental study of the semantic structures of children. *Journal of Verbal Learning and Verbal Behavior, 5,* 249–259.

Dumont, L. (1965). The modern conception of the individual, notes on it genesis. *Contributions to Indian Sociology, 8,* 13–61.

Dumont, L. (1970). Homo Hierarchicus. Chicago: University of Chicago Press.

Fiske, S. T., & Cox, M. C. (1979). Person concepts: The effect of target familiarity and description purpose on the process of describing others. *Journal of Personality, 47,* 136–161.

Flapan, D. (1968). *Children's understanding of social interaction.* New York: Teachers College Press.

Flavell, J. H., & Stedman, D. J. (1961). A developmental study of judgments of semantic similarity. *Journal of Genetic Psychology, 98,* 279–293.

Geertz, C. (1973). *The interpretation of cultures.* New York: Basic Books.

Geertz, C. (1974). From the native's point of view: On the nature of anthropological understanding. *American Academy of Arts and Sciences Bulletin, 28,* 26–43.

Gelman, R. (1978). Cognitive development. *Annual Review of Psychology, 29,* 297–332.

Goldberg, S., Perlmutter, M., & Myers, N. (1974). Recall of related unrelated lists by 2-year-olds. *Journal of Experimental Child Psychology, 18,* 1–8.

Goodman, N. (1968). *Languages of art.* New York: Bobbs-Merrill.

Goodman, N. (1972). Seven strictures on similarity. In N. Goodman (Ed.), *Problems and projects* (pp. 437–446). New York: Bobbs-Merrill.

Goody, J., & Watt, I. (1968). The consequences of literacy. In J. Goody (Ed.), *Literacy in traditional societies* (pp. 27–68). New York: Cambridge University Press.

Greenfield, P. M. (1972). Oral or written language: the consequences for cognitive development in Africa, the United Stages and England. *Language and Speech, 15,* 169–178.

Greenstone, J. D. (1982). The transient and the permanent in American politics: standards, interests and the concept of "public." In J. D. Greenstone (Ed.), *Public values and private power in American politics* (pp. 3–33). Chicago: Rand McNally.

Hart, H. L., & Honoré, A. (1959). *Causation in the law.* Clarendon, England: Oxford University Press.

Higgins, E. T., Ruble, D. N., & Hartup, W. W. (Eds.) (1983). *Social cognition and social development: A Sociocultural perspective.* Cambridge, England: Cambridge University Press.

Horton, R. (1967). African traditional thought and Western science, part 3. *Africa, 37,* 159–187.

Inhelder, B., & Piaget, J. (1964). *The early growth of logic in the child.* London: Routledge and Kegan Paul.

Keasey, C. B. (1978). Children's developing awareness and usage of intentionality and motives. In C. B. Keasey (Ed.), *Nebraska symposium on motivation* (Vol. 25, pp. 219–260). Lincoln: University of Nebraska Press.

Kelley, H. H. (1972a). Attribution in social interaction. In E. E. Jones, D. E. Kanouse, H. H. Kelley, R. E. Nisbett, S. Valins, & W. Weiner (Eds.), *Attribution: Perceiving the causes of behavior* (pp. 1–26). Morristown, NJ: General Learning Press.

Kelley, H. H. (1972b). Causal schemata and the attribution process. In E. E. Jones, D. E. Kanouse, H. H. Kelley, R. E. Nisbett, S. Valins, & W. Weiner (Eds.), *Attribution: Perceiving the causes of behavior* (pp. 151–174). Morristown, NJ: General Learning Press.

Kelley, H. H. (1973). The process of causal attribution. *American Psychologist, 28,* 107–128.

Keppel, G. (1973). *Design and analysis.* Englewood Cliffs, NJ: Prentice-Hall.

Kuhn, T. (1962). *The structure of scientific revolutions.* Chicago: University of Chicago Press.

Labov, W. (1970). The logic of non-standard English. In F. Williams (Ed.), *Language and poverty* (pp. 153–189). Chicago Markham Press.

Levy, R. I. (1973). *Tahitians.* Chicago: University of Chicago Press.

Lewis, P. (1978). *Modes of explanation in everyday life.* Unpublished manuscript, Committee on Human Development, University of Chicago.

Livesley, W. J., & Bromley, D. B. (1973). *Person perception in childhood and adolescence.* London: Wiley.

Lukes, S. (1973). *Individualism.* Oxford, England: Basil Blackwell.

Luria, A. R. (1976). *Cognitive development: Its cultural and social foundations.* Cambridge, MA: Harvard University Press.

Mackie, J. L. (1974). *The cement of the universe.* London: Oxford University Press.

MacPherson, C. B. (1962). *The political theory of possessive individualism.* New York: Oxford University Press.

Maher, R. (1962). *These are the Anglo-Indians.* Calcutta: Swallow Press.

Mariott, M. (1976). Hindu transactions: Diversity without dualism. In B. Kapferer, (Ed.), *Transaction and meaning.* Philadelphia: Institute for the Study of Human Issues. 109–142.

Marsella, A. J., &. White, G. (Eds.) (1982). *Cultural conceptions of mental health and therapy.* Boston: Reidel.

Nelson, K. (1977). Cognitive development and the acquisition of concepts. In R. Anderson, R. Spiro, & W. Montague (Eds.),

Schooling and the acquisition of knowledge (pp. 215–239). Hillsdale, NJ: Erlbaum.

O'Flaherty, W. D., &. Derrett. J. D. (Eds.) (1978). *The concept of duty in South Asia.* India: Vikas Publishing House.

Oliver, R. R., & Hornsby, J. R. (1966). On equivalence. In J. S. Bruner, R. R Oliver, & P. Greenfield (Eds.), *Studies in cognitive growth* (pp. 68–85). New York: Wiley.

Osgood, C. E., May, W. H., &. Miron, M. S. (1975). *Cross-cultural universals of affective meaning.* Urbana: University of Illinois Press.

Peevers, B. &. Secord, P. (1973). Developmental changes in attribution of descriptive concepts to persons. *Journal of Personality and Social Psychology, 27,* 120–128.

Piaget, J. (1954). *The construction of reality in the child.* New York: Basic Books.

Piaget, J. (1966). Need and significance of cross-cultural studies in genetic psychology. *International Journal of Psychology, 1,* 3–13.

Piaget, J. (1970a). Piaget's theory. In P. Mussen, (Ed.), *Carmichael's manual of child psychology* (Vol. 1, pp. 703–732). New York: Wiley.

Piaget, J. (1970b). *Structuralism.* New York: Basic Books.

Ramanujan, A. K. (1980). *Is there an Indian way of thinking*? Unpublished manuscript, Department of South Asian Languages and Civilization, University of Chicago.

Rosch, E. (1975). Universals and culture specifics in human categorization. In R. W. Brislin, S. Bochner, & W. J. Lonner (Eds.), *Cross-cultural perspectives on learning* (pp. 177–206). New York: Wiley.

Rosch, E., & Mervis, C. B. (1975). Family resemblance: Studies in the internal structure of categories. *Cognitive Psychology, 7,* 573–605.

Rosch, E., Mervis, C. B. Gray, W. D., Johnson, D. M., & Boyes-Braem, P. (1976). Basic objects in natural categories. *Cognitive Psychology, 8,* 382–439.

Ross, L. (1977). The intuitive psychologist and his shortcomings: distortions in the attribution process. In L. Berkowitz (Ed.), *Advances in experimental social psychology* (Vol. 10, pp. 173–220). New York: Academic Press.

Sampson, E. E. (1977). Psychology and the American ideal. *Journal of Personality and Social Psychology, 35,* 767–782.

Scarlett, H., Press, A., & Crockett, W. (1971). Children's descriptions of peers: A Wernerian developmental analysis. *Child Development, 42,* 439–453.

Schneider, D. M. (1968). *American kinship: A cultural account.* Chicago: University of Chicago Press.

Schwartz, T. (1981). The acquisition of culture. *Ethos, 9,* 4–17.

Scribner, S., & Cole, M. (1973). Cognitive consequences of formal and informal education. *Science, 183,* 554–559.

Scribner, S., & Cole, M. (1981). *The psychology of literature.* Cambridge, MA: Harvard University Press.

Selby, H. A. (1974). *Zapotec deviance: The convergence of folk and modern sociology.* Austin: University of Texas Press.

Selby, H. A. (1975). Semantics and causality in the study of deviance. In M. Sanches & B. Blount (Eds.), *Sociocultural dimensions of language use* (pp. 11–24). New York: Academic Press.

Sharp, D., Cole, M., & Lave, C. (1979). Education and cognitive development: the evidence from experimental research. *Monographs of the Society for Research in Child Development, 44* (1–2, Serial No. 178).

Shweder, R. A. (in press). Anthropology's Romantic rebellion against the Enlightenment: Or there's more to thinking than reason and evidence. In R. A. Shweder & R. A. Levine (Eds.), *Culture theory: Essays on mind, self and emotion.* Cambridge, England: Cambridge University Press.

Shweder, R. A., & Bourne, E. (1982). Does the concept of the person vary cross-culturally? In A. J. Marsella & G. White, (Eds.), *Cultural conceptions of mental health and therapy* (pp. 97–137). Boston: Reidel.

Shweder, R. A., Bourne, E. J., & Miyamoto, J. M. (1978). *Concrete thinking and category formation.* Unpublished manuscript, Committee on Human Development, Univ. of Chicago.

Stevenson, H., Parker, T., Wilkinson, A., Bonnevaux, B., & Gonzalez, M. (1978). Schooling environment and cognitive development: A cross-cultural study. *Monographs of the Society for Research in Child Development, 43* (3, Serial No. 175).

Strauss, A. S. (1973). Northern Cheyenne ethnosociology. *Ethos, 1,* 326–357.

Super, C. M. (1980). Cognitive development: Looking across growing up. In C. M. Super & S. Harkness (Eds.), *Anthropological perspectives on child development* (pp. 59–69). San Francisco: Jossey-Bass.

Super, C. M., Harkness., S., & Baldwin, L. M. (1977). Category behavior in natural ecologies in cognitive tests. *The Quarterly Newsletter of the Institute for Comparative Human Development, 4,* No. 1.

Taylor, S. E. (1981). The interface of cognitive and social psychology. In J. H. Harvey (Ed.), *Cognition, social behavior and the environment* (pp. 189–211). Hillsdale, NJ: Erlbaum.

Turiel, E. (1978). Social regulation and domains of social concepts. In W. Damon (Ed.), *New directions for child development: Social cognition* (pp. 45–75). San Francisco: Jossey-Bass.

Turiel, E. (1979). Distinct conceptual and developmental domains. Social convention and morality. In C. B. Keasey (Ed.), *Nebraska symposium on motivation* (Vol. 25, pp. 77–116). Lincoln: University of Nebraska Press.

Vygotsky, L. S. (1962). *Thought and language.* Cambridge, M. I. T. Press.

Waern, Y., Hecht, U., & Johansson, B. (1974, December). How do children interpret others' behavior? *Reports from the psychological laboratories.* University of Stockholm (No. 437, pp. 1–14).

Waxlwer, N. (1974). Culture and mental illness: A social labeling perspective. *Journal of Nervous and Mental Disease,* 379–395.

Waxler, N. (1977). Is mental illness cured in traditional societies? A theoretical analysis. *Culture, Medicine, and Psychiatry, 1,* 233–253.

Weber, M. (1930). The Prostant ethic and the spirit of capitalism. London: G. Allen and Unwin.

Weisner, T. (1976). Urban-rural differences in African childrens's performance on cognitive and memory. *Ethos, 4,* 223–250.

White, G. (1980). Conceptual universals in personal description. *American Anthropologist,* 82, 559–780.

Winer, B. J. (1962). *Statistical principles in experimental design.* New York: McGraw-Hill.

Received July 28, 1985.
Revision received November 14, 1985.

NOTES

1. Instructions for the coding scheme may be obtained by writing to the author.
2. A copy of the classification procedure may be obtained by writing to the author.

READING 3

Using a simple videogame, the effect of ethnicity on shoot/don't shoot decisions was examined. African American or White targets, holding guns or other objects, appeared in complex backgrounds. Participants were told to "shoot" armed targets and to "not shoot" unarmed targets. In Study 1, White participants made the correct decision to shoot an armed target more quickly if the target was African American than if he was White, but decided to "not shoot" an unarmed target more quickly if he was White. Study 2 used a shorter time window, forcing this effect into error rates. Study 3 replicated Study 1's effects and showed that the magnitude of bias varied with perceptions of the cultural stereotype and with levels of contact, but not with personal racial prejudice. Study 4 revealed equivalent levels of bias among both African American and White participants in a community sample. Implications and potential underlying mechanisms are discussed.

The Police Officer's Dilemma: Using Ethnicity to Disambiguate Potentially Threatening Individuals

Joshua Correll, Bernadette Park, and Charles M. Judd
University of Colorado at Boulder

Bernd Wittenbrink
University of Chicago

Joshua Correll, Bernadette Park, and Charles M. Judd, Department of Psychology, University of Colorado at Boulder; Bernd Wittenbrink, Graduate School of Business, University of Chicago.

This material is based on work supported by a National Science Foundation graduate research fellowship awarded to Joshua Correll. Support for this work also came from National Institute of Mental Health Grant R01-45049 awarded to Bernadette Park and Charles M. Judd and from a sabbatical award from the James McKeen Cattell Fund awarded to Bernadette Park. We thank Paul G. Davies for his invaluable contributions to the conceptual development of this project, and Joshua Ingram and David M. Deffenbacher for their assistance in its implementation.

Correspondence concerning this article should be addressed to Joshua Correll, Department of Psychology, University of Colorado, Boulder, Colorado 80309-0345.
E-mail: jcorrell@psych.colorado.edu

In February 1999, around midnight, four plain-clothes police officers were searching a Bronx, New York, neighborhood for a rape suspect. They saw Amadou Diallo, a 22-year-old West African immigrant, standing in the doorway of his apartment building. According to the police, Diallo resembled the suspect they were tracking. When they ordered him not to move, Diallo reached into his pants pocket. Believing he was reaching for a gun, the police fired a total of 41 shots, 19 of which hit and killed Diallo. Diallo was in fact unarmed. All four officers were later acquitted of any wrongdoing in the case.

The police could not have known for certain that Diallo was harmless. In the dark, they had ordered a potentially dangerous man to freeze, and that man reached for something. If Diallo had been armed, their decision to open fire would never have been questioned. But the decision to shoot a man who later proved to be unarmed did raise questions, one fundamental question in particular: Would the police have responded differently if Diallo had been White? Perhaps Diallo would have been given the benefit of the doubt, perhaps the order to freeze would have been repeated, perhaps a slight delay in the decision to fire would have given the officers time to recognize that this suspect was not reaching for a gun. Though it is impossible to reach a definitive answer with respect to Diallo's case, the dilemma faced by these officers has important consequences for cities nationwide and warrants

SOURCE: Correll, J., Park, B., Judd, C. M., & Wittenbrink, B. 2002. "The Police Officer's Dilemma: Using Ethnicity to Disambiguate Potentially Threatening Individuals", *JOURNAL OF PERSONALITY AND SOCIAL PSYCHOLOGY*, *83*, 1314–1329.

a systematic investigation. It seems crucial to understand whether or not the decision to shoot is influenced by the target's ethnicity, and if so, what this bias represents.

Social psychology has long held an interest in the way that schemata, including expectancies about social categories like ethnicity, guide the interpretation of ambiguous information (Duncan, 1976; Hilton & von Hippel, 1990; Jacobs & Eccles, 1992; Rothbart & Birrell, 1977; Sagar & Schofield, 1980). The quick and almost effortless classification of a unique individual into a broad social category (Brewer, 1988; Fiske; Lin, & Neuberg, 1999; Fiske & Neuberg, 1990) may lead people to assume that traits generally associated with the category also apply to this particular member. Either in the absence of individuating information (Darley & Gross, 1983; Locksley, Borgida, Brekke, & Hepburn, 1980; see Hamilton & Sherman, 1994, for a review) or in spite of it (Beckett & Park, 1995; Krueger & Rothbart, 1988), stereotypic associations can influence an observer's perceptions in a top-down fashion. A stereotype, in essence, can function as a schema to help clarify or disambiguate an otherwise confusing situation.

Of particular interest to the question of Diallo's death is the possibility that the officers' decision to fire was influenced by the stereotypic association between African Americans and violence. The ambiguity of Diallo's behavior (what was he reaching for?), which ironically provides a justification for the officers' decision, may have set the stage for bias, prompting the officers to draw on other sources of information, including stereotypes, in an effort to understand what was happening. Duncan (1976) showed that the same mildly aggressive behavior is perceived as more threatening when it is performed by an African American than when it is performed by a White person. A White person's light push seems like a violent shove when performed by an African American. Sagar and Schofield (1980), following Duncan, presented 6th-grade boys with line drawings and verbal accounts of ambiguous dyadic interactions, for example, two boys bumping into one another in the hallway, or one boy borrowing a pencil from a classmate without asking. To manipulate the ethnicity of the people interacting, the researchers simply shaded in the drawings. Like Duncan, they found that when an actor was depicted as African American, rather than White, his behavior seemed more mean and threatening to the participants. Sagar and Schofield further found that this bias in perception was similar for both White and African American participants. That is, the tendency to see an African American's behavior as more mean and threatening than a White person's did not depend on the observer's ethnicity. On the basis of this result, Sagar and Schofield argued that the bias reflects not the internalization of anti-African American attitudes, but rather the application of a widely known and cognitively derived stereotype about the group to the particular target individual.

Devine (1989) went on to demonstrate that the impact of ethnicity on interpretation could occur even without participants' awareness. She asked participants to rate a target's ambiguously hostile behavior after subliminally priming them with words related to both the social category and the stereotype of African Americans (but excluding words directly related to violence). Participants who were primed with a greater number of these words were more likely to interpret the behavior as hostile, even though the target's ethnicity was never mentioned. Lepore and Brown (1997) primed only the social category of African Americans (not the stereotype) and found that the effect of the primes on interpretation of behavior was only evident among the more prejudiced participants. In all of these studies, the association between the social category, African American, and the concept of violence seems to lead participants to interpret an ambiguous target as more dangerous.

Most recently, Payne (2001) demonstrated that participants were faster and more accurate in distinguishing guns from hand tools when they were primed with an African American face, as opposed to a White face. Using Jacoby's (1991; Jacoby, Toth, & Yonelinas, 1993) Process Dissociation Procedure, Payne then separated participants' errors into automatic and controlled components. The magnitude of the automatic estimate represents the degree to which the ethnicity of the prime influences participants' decisions when their ability to control that decision fails. Among participants who were low in motivation to control prejudiced responding, Payne found that greater prejudice was associated with a greater automatic effect.

The primary goal of the current research was to carry this line of inquiry one step further, investigating the effect of a target's ethnicity on participants' decision to "shoot" that target. We present data from a simplified videogame, which roughly simulates the situation of a police officer who is confronted with an ambiguous, but potentially hostile, target, and who must decide whether or not to shoot. In the game, images of people who are either armed or unarmed, and either African American or White, appear unexpectedly in a variety of contexts. Unlike previous research, this game requires participants to make a behavioral shoot/don't shoot decision similar to that of a police officer. And unlike a sequential priming study (such as Payne, 2001), this game simultaneously presents a target person's ethnicity and the object he is holding. A participant need not process ethnicity to determine whether the target is armed. In spite of these differences, the research reviewed above strongly suggests that interpretation of the target as dangerous, and the associated decision to shoot, will vary as a function of the target's ethnicity. In Studies 1 and 2, we test this basic prediction. In Studies 3 and 4, we make an initial effort to understand the processes underlying this bias in the decision to shoot.

STUDY 1

Method

Participants and Design Forty undergraduates (24 female, 16 male) at the University of Colorado at Boulder participated in this experiment in return for either $8 or partial credit toward a class requirement.[1] One of the male participants was Latino. All other participants were White. The study used a 2 × 2 within-subject design, with Target Ethnicity (African American vs. White) and Object Type (gun vs. no gun) as repeated factors.

Materials Using the PsyScope software package (Cohen, MacWhinney, Flatt, & Provost, 1993), we developed a simplistic videogame that presented a series of background and target images. The videogame used a total of 20 backgrounds and 80 target images. Twenty young men, 10 African American and 10 White, were recruited on college campuses to pose as models for the targets. Each of these models appeared in the game four times, twice as a target in the gun condition and twice as a target in the no-gun condition, with a different object and in a different pose each time (five basic poses were used in the game). There were four non-gun objects (a silver-colored aluminum can, a silver camera, a black cell phone, and a black wallet) and two guns (a silver snub-nosed revolver and a black 9-mm pistol). Each of the objects, within condition, appeared equally often in each of the five poses. The four target images for each model were superimposed on randomly determined backgrounds, constrained so that each background was used once in each of the four conditions and no target appeared on the same background more than once. Background images included an intentionally diverse assortment of photographs, such as train station terminals, parks, hotel entrances, restaurant facades, and city sidewalks. No people appeared in any of the original background scenes. Examples of the stimuli appear in Figure 1.

In total, there were 80 trials in the videogame, with 20 trials in each cell of the 2 × 2 design created by crossing the ethnicity of the target with whether the target held a gun or a non-gun. Each of the 80 trials began with the presentation of a fixation point, followed by a series of empty backgrounds, presented in slide-show fashion. The number of backgrounds on a given trial was randomly determined, ranging from 1 to 4. The duration of each was also random, ranging from 500 to 1,000 ms. The final background in the series was replaced by the target image, created by superimposing the target on the final background. From the perspective of the participant, a man seemed to simply appear on the background. The design of the game was intended to ensure that the participant never knew when or where the target would appear in the background or when a response would be required.

To play the game, the participant needed to decide as quickly as possible whether the object the man was holding was a gun or not. If it was a gun, the man posed an imminent danger, and the participant needed to shoot him as quickly as possible by pushing the right button, labeled *shoot*, on a button box. If he was holding some object other than a gun, he posed no danger, and the participant needed to press the left button, labeled *don't shoot*, as quickly as possible. Participants were instructed to use separate hands for each button and to rest their fingers on the buttons between trials. The game awarded and deducted points on the basis of performance. A hit (correctly shooting a target holding a gun) earned 10 points, and a correct rejection (not shooting a target holding some non-gun object) earned 5 points. A false alarm (shooting a target holding a non-gun) was punished by taking away 20 points, and a miss (not shooting a target holding a gun) resulted in our harshest penalty: a loss of 40 points.[2] This payoff matrix represented an effort to partially, if weakly, recreate the payoff matrix experienced by police officers on the street, where shooting an innocent suspect is a terrible mistake (as in the case of Amadou Diallo), but where the stronger motivation is presumably to avoid misidentifying an armed and hostile target, which could result in an officer's death. To minimize nonresponse, the game assessed a timeout penalty of 10 points if participants failed to respond to a target within 850 ms. This time window was selected to force participants to respond relatively quickly, while still allowing enough time such that errors in the game would be minimized. Participants' decisions ("shoot" or "don't shoot") and their reaction times were recorded for each trial. Each trial ended by giving participants feedback on whether they had made the correct decision on that trial and by showing them their cumulative point total.

Figure 1. Target and background example scenes from videogame. Color originals are available at psych.Colorado.edu/~jcorrell/tpod.html.

TABLE 1
Means (and Standard Deviations) for Reaction Times and Error Rates as a Function of Target Ethnicity and Object Type (Studies 1, 2 and 3)

	Reaction times		Errors per 20 trials	
Study	White targets	Afr. Am. targets	White targets	Afr. Am. targets
Study 1				
Armed targets	554(46)	544(39)	0.70(1.07)	0.40(0.78)
Unarmed targets	623(38)	634(39)	1.23(1.29)	1.45(1.04)
Study 2				
Armed targets	449(23)	451(28)	2.46(1.83)	1.48(1.38)
Unarmed targets	513(32)	523(38)	2.40(2.76)	3.29(2.87)
Study 3				
Armed targets	550(40)	539(45)	0.76(0.86)	0.49(0.80)
Unarmed targets	607(38)	620(38)	0.33(0.90)	0.65(1.24)

Note. Afr. Am. = African American.

Procedure Participants, in groups of 1 to 4, were met by a male experimenter who outlined the study as an investigation of perceptual vigilance, or the ability to monitor and quickly respond to a variety of stimuli. A detailed set of instructions for the videogame task followed, including the point values for each of the outcomes. Participants were also informed that the people with the first, second, and third highest scores in the study would receive a prize ($30, $15, and $10, respectively) and that 5 others, randomly selected from participants with scores in the top 30%, would each receive $10. These prizes were intended to make the payoff matrix personally meaningful. Finally, participants were asked to pay attention to the faces of the targets, because they would be tested on their ability to recognize the targets at the end of the game. Participants then moved to individual rooms to play the game.

At the conclusion of the game, participants were presented with a series of 16 recognition trials in a paper-and-pencil task to determine whether facial characteristics of the targets had been attended to. For each of the 16 faces, participants had to indicate whether they believed it was the face of one of the targets that had been seen during the game or not. Half of the presented targets had in fact been seen previously; half had not. Additionally, half of the targets were African American and half were White.

Following the recognition task, participants were given a short questionnaire, which asked whether they valued the monetary incentives, whether they remembered the point values for hits, misses, false alarms, and correct rejections. Participants were then fully debriefed, with the experimenter paying particular attention to alleviate any negative feelings aroused by the game.

Results and Discussion

To analyze the resulting reaction times, we excluded all trials on which the participant had either timed-out (i.e., failed to make a decision in the allotted 850-ms window) or made an incorrect response (e.g., shooting a target holding a non-gun). This resulted in the exclusion of data from 7% of the trials across participants, with a maximum of 20% of the trials for any one participant. Response latencies on the remaining trials were log-transformed and then averaged within subject across trials occurring in the same cell of the 2 × 2 within-subject research design, An analysis of variance (ANOVA) of the resulting mean latencies was then conducted, treating Target Ethnicity (White vs. African American) and Object Type (gun versus no gun) as within-subject factors.

This analysis revealed a significant main effect for Object, $F(1, 39) = 244.16$, $p < .0001$, and a significant Object × Ethnicity interaction, $F(1, 39) = 21.86$, $p < .0001$. The resulting cell means (converted back to the millisecond metric) appear in Table 1. As these means reveal, participants were significantly faster at making the correct decision to shoot, when the target held a gun, than the correct decision to not shoot, when the target did not hold a gun. More central to our predictions, the interaction suggests that the speed of responding on gun versus no-gun trials depended on target ethnicity. We decomposed this interaction by examining the simple effects of ethnicity separately for the gun and no-gun trials. Both were significant: Participants fired at an armed target more quickly if he was African American than if he was White, $F(1, 39) = 10.89$, $p < .005$, and they decided not to shoot an unarmed White target more quickly than an unarmed African American target, $F(1, 39) = 9.77$, $p < .005$.

We intentionally gave participants a long enough response window (850 ms) in this study to maximize correct responses to examine effects on response latencies. And, as we suspected, the proportions of errors were quite low, averaging 4% of the trials across participants. Nonetheless, it is possible to examine the error rates to see if they depended on Target Ethnicity, Object Type, or their interaction (see mean error rates in Table 1). This analysis revealed a main effect for Object, $F(1, 39) = 32.31$, $p < .0001$, such that errors in the no-gun condition (i.e., false alarms) were more frequent than errors in the gun condition (i.e., misses). The interaction between Ethnicity and Object was also significant, suggesting that the tendency to make more false alarms than misses was more pronounced for African American targets than for White targets, $F(1, 39) = 7.68$, $p < .01$. That is, whereas participants tended to shoot unarmed targets more frequently than they decided not to shoot armed targets, in general, this tendency was stronger when the target was African American than when the target was White. The simple effects were in the correct direction, but not statistically significant. Participants were marginally more likely to miss an armed target when he was White than when he was African American, $F(1, 39) = 3.66$, $p = .06$, but errors in response to unarmed targets did not seem to depend on ethnicity, $F(1, 39) = 1.68$, $p = .20$.

Both the latency and error results attest to the role of target ethnicity in disambiguating potentially threatening stimuli. Clearly, the responses of participants to these stimuli depended at some level on the ethnic category of the target, with potentially hostile targets identified as such more quickly if they were African American rather than White and benign targets identified as such more quickly if they were White rather than African American. Although these results are certainly consistent with our expectations, they are also somewhat surprising given the fact that the target ethnicity appeared at exactly the same time as the object that had to be identified as a gun or not. Certainly participants could have performed perfectly on the task by attending only to the object held in the target's hand and by completely ignoring the target's ethnicity or any other individuating information.

To examine whether a target's features, other than the object he held, were attended to by participants, we examined their ability to recognize the faces of the targets they had seen during the game. A signal detection analysis revealed that sensitivity to old versus new faces was not above chance level in these recognition data (mean $d' = 0.15$), $t(39) = 1.15$, $p = .26$. Separate analyses within target ethnicity revealed that participants were unable to recognize African American targets at a better than chance level (mean $d' = -0.08$), $t(39) = -0.48$, $p = .63$, although recognition sensitivity for the White targets did exceed chance levels (mean $d' = 0.33$), $t(39) = 2.26$, $p < .05$. Our data suggest, then, that target ethnicity affected participants' judgments even while participants remained largely incapable of recognizing the faces of the targets they had seen.

STUDY 2

Our first study allowed participants a sufficient response window so that they made correct decisions in the case of nearly all targets. That is, error rates were very low. As a result, the strongest results from the first study were found with decision latencies on correct responses, with faster decisions to armed African American targets than to armed Whites, and faster decisions to unarmed White targets than to unarmed African Americans. Although significant, the interactive effects of Target Ethnicity and Object Type on response errors were substantially weaker (and, the relevant simple comparisons were not significant).

In the second study, we sought to replicate the basic pattern of results from the first study, but this time to make the task substantially harder by shortening the amount of time during which participants had to respond. Clearly, if the effects that we are exploring are to be relevant to more real-life scenarios, such as those encountered by police officers, then we would like to show our effects on actual responses (and errors in responses) rather than simply on the speed with which correct responses are made. Additionally, to increase the importance of performance in the task, we recruited participants exclusively for pay in this study and we offered them incentives directly tied to the quality of their performance, paying up to $20 for a study taking well less than an hour.

Method

Participants and Design Forty-four undergraduates (33 female, 11 male) participated in this experiment in return for a minimum payment of $10, with the opportunity to earn additional money (up to a total of $20) by scoring points in the game. This incentive was intended to increase the personal significance of the rewards and penalties. One male participant was Latino, and 1 female was Asian. All other participants were White. We used the same 2 × 2 design, with Target Ethnicity (African American vs. White) and Object Type (gun vs. no gun) as within-subject factors.

Materials and Procedure The materials and procedure were identical to those of Study 1, with the exception of the following modifications. First, we made clear to participants that they would be paid as a function of their performance. They were told that they started with an initial sum of $14 to their credit. Each point earned or lost (according to the same payoff matrix used in Study 1) was worth 1 cent. It was made clear that if they performed perfectly across all 80 trials, they would earn $20. If they lost points, they could lose up to $4, but they were guaranteed a base pay of $10. Second, we adjusted the game's response window from 850 ms to

630 ms to force participants to make decisions more quickly, with the goal of increasing error rates. Although a 630-ms response window may provide ample time to process simple stimuli such as faces or isolated objects, our images were fairly complex, and the shortened window proved a challenge for our participants. A pretest indicated that the shortened response window had the desired effect, increasing errors, but also dramatically increasing the proportion of trials on which participants failed to respond in time. Because the meaning of a timeout is ambiguous, a third change we made was to discourage timeouts by increasing their associated penalty from 10 to 50 points (i.e., 50 cents) and stressing the importance of responding quickly in the instructions. As participants' point totals directly affected the amount they were paid, this provided a considerable incentive. We also set an a priori limit, such that any participant with more than 10 timeouts would be excluded from the analysis. A final change we made was to the program used to record participants' data. In Study 1, for each trial, the program only recorded the response, response latency, target ethnicity, and target object (gun vs. no-gun), but the exact target and background for the trial were not recorded. We modified this in Study 2 so that we could identify particular stimuli that were associated with a greater number of errors.

Results and Discussion

Before conducting the primary analysis of error rates, we eliminated 5 participants (all female) who exceeded our a priori threshold of 10 timeouts (one eighth of all trials). Additionally, we examined error rates for particular targets to determine if correct responses were particularly difficult for some. In fact, there were a number of targets that were outliers in the overall distribution, inducing many more errors than the other targets. For instance, one unarmed African American target was shot by more than 90% of our participants. Additionally, one armed African American target and four unarmed White targets resulted in errors for more than one third of the participants. In each of these target images, some detail seemed potentially misleading. For example, one target had a stripe in his shorts that could be mistaken for a gun given the position of his arm. We suspect the substantially shorter time-out window was responsible for producing the unusually high error rates for these six targets. To deal with these outliers, we conducted all analyses twice, once with the full dataset and once deleting the six outlying targets. The analyses that we report are based on the partial dataset. However, with only one exception, as noted below, the results were unaffected by their inclusion/exclusion.

Participants' error rates (number of errors divided by the total number of valid trials) were subjected to a 2 × 2 ANOVA, with Target Ethnicity (White vs. African American) and Object Type (gun vs. no gun) as the independent variables. The relevant cell means are given in Table 1. The analysis revealed a significant effect for Object, such that the proportion of errors when a gun was present (i.e., misses) was lower than the proportion of errors when a gun was absent (i.e., false alarms), $F(1, 38) = 6.42$, $p < .02$. We also found the predicted interaction between Ethnicity and Object, $F(1, 38) = 17.83$, $p < .0001$. A test of the simple effects revealed that, when the target was unarmed, participants mistakenly shot him more often if he was African American than if he was White, $F(1, 38) = 6.53$, $p < .02$, though this effect was not significant when all targets were analyzed. When the target was armed, however, participants mistakenly decided not to shoot more often if he was White than if he was African American, $F(1, 38) = 13.31$, $p < .001$.

In addition to the analyses of the error rates, we also analyzed the decision latencies for correct responses, as in Study 1. Not surprisingly, given the considerably shorter response window in this study, there were no effects in the latencies. It seems that Study 1's interaction in response speed was, in this study, pushed over into error rates, due to the tightened response window.

As in Study 1, participants were unable to recognize presented targets above chance level. An analysis of the mean sensitivity to old versus new faces revealed a nonsignificant overall $d' = -0.02$, $t(38 = -0.15$, $p = .88$. Sensitivity was not above chance for either the White targets (mean $d' = 0.12$), $t(38) = 0.74$, $p = .46$, or for the African American targets (mean $d' = -0.16$), $t(38) = -0.97$, $p = .34$.

To understand the error rate results in greater detail, further analyses were conducted using the signal detection model (Green & Swets, 1966/1974; MacMillan & Creelman, 1991). Applied to the present context, the signal detection analysis assumes that targets encountered, both those with a gun and those without a gun, vary on a judgment-relevant dimension. For example, in the present studies, the extent to which the targets appeared to be threatening might have served as a critical dimension. On average, targets with guns are more threatening than targets who possess other objects (to the extent that they are discriminated at all), but nevertheless, there is a distribution of targets within each set, and these vary in how threatening they subjectively appear to be. Thus, we have two distributions of targets, one of targets with guns and one of targets without guns, and the signal detection model assumes that these are both normal distributions with equal variances. To some extent, of course, these two distributions overlap and the question of sensitivity is the question of the extent to which this is true. That is, if participants are relatively sensitive or accurate, shooting those targets who have guns and not shooting those targets who don't have guns, then the two distributions are largely separated from each other.

Additionally, because participants make a choice between shooting and not shooting a target on the basis of the subjective sense of how threatening the target appears to be, they set a decision threshold somewhere along the continuum that underlies the two distributions. Above that threshold, they shoot the target; below threshold they do not. Where that threshold is set is commonly referred to as the *decision criterion.*

From the two kinds of errors (false alarms: shooting an unarmed target; misses: not shooting an armed target), one can derive estimates of both sensitivity, commonly defined as d', and decision criterion, in this case defined as c. We estimated both of these parameters for our participants, once for the White targets and once for the African American targets. Unsurprisingly, given the relatively low percentages of errors, participants showed considerable accuracy (i.e., high levels of d') for both the White and African American targets (White $M = 2.47$ [$SD = 0.87$]; African American $M = 2.48$ [$SD = 0.85$]). A test of differential sensitivity between the two kinds of targets failed to reject the null hypothesis, $F(1, 38) = 0.01$, $p = .93$. There were differences, however, between the two kinds of targets in the response criterion (White $M = 0.03$ [$SD = 0.30$]; African American $M = -0.24$ [$SD = 0.31$]), such that a significantly lower decision criterion to shoot the target was found for African American targets, $F(1, 38) = 22.21$, $p < .0001$. These results are depicted graphically in Figure 2. In sum, from the perspective of the signal detection model, the differences between responses to the African American and White targets arose not from differences in the underlying accuracy with which the two kinds of targets, those with a gun and those without a gun, can be discriminated. Rather, in the case of the African American targets, participants simply set a lower threshold for the decision to shoot, being willing to shoot targets who seemed less threatening.[3]

STUDY 3

Studies 1 and 2 provide evidence that the decision to shoot an armed target is made more quickly and more accurately if that target is African American than if he is White, whereas the decision not to shoot is made more quickly and more accurately if the target is White. This pattern of results is fundamentally consistent with research suggesting that participants may use ethnicity to interpret an ambiguously threatening target. When ambiguous behavior is performed by an African American, it seems more hostile, more mean, and more threatening than when it is performed by a White person (Duncan, 1976; Sagar & Schofield, 1980). Participants also recognize a weapon more quickly and more accurately after seeing an African American face, rather than a White face (Payne, 2001). Here, we have shown that ethnicity can also influence a behavioral judgment with serious consequences for both target and shooter.

Simply documenting the existence of this bias does not clarify the mechanism by which ethnicity influences the decision to shoot. We suggested earlier that participants may use the stereotypic association between the social category, African American, and concepts like violence or danger as a schema to help interpret ambiguous behavior on the part of any given African American target. Through deductive inference, traits associated with the category may be applied to the individual category member. It is important to recognize that the proposed process does not require a participant to dislike African Americans, or to hold any explicit prejudice against them, nor does it require that the participant endorse the stereotype; it simply requires that, at some level, the participant associates the two concepts "African American" and "violent." Previous research is equivocal in its support of this possibility, suggesting that bias in the interpretation of an ambiguous stimulus may depend on both stereotypic associations and on prejudice. Sagar and Schofield (1980), for example, provide evidence for a stereotype-driven effect. Recall that these researchers found that both White and African American participants interpreted behavior as more threatening if it had been performed by an African American target. Reasoning that bias among the African American participants is not likely to reflect prejudice against African Americans, they concluded that it reflects instead a common belief, or stereotype, that African Americans are more violent than Whites. A culturally

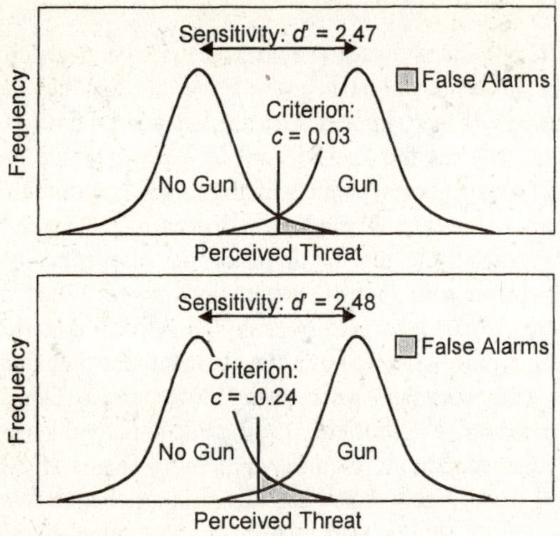

Figure 2. Hypothetical normal distributions representing unarmed and armed targets for signal detection analyses: White (top panel) and African Americans (bottom panel) targets.

communicated stereotypic association may influence interpretations even if the observer does not personally endorse the stereotype or hold a prejudiced attitude (Devine, 1989). Data presented by both Lepore and Brown (1997) and Payne (2001), however, have shown that more prejudiced participants show greater bias in their interpretations of ambiguous stimuli (for Payne, 2001, this relationship was moderated by motivation to control prejudice). Of course, the effect of prejudice on perceptions may be indirect, operating chiefly through the stronger negative stereotypic associations that accompany prejudiced attitudes. The question is whether stereotypic associations predict bias over and above prejudice. To be clear, we hypothesize that although the magnitude of the bias evident in our videogame may covary with participants' prejudice against African Americans, it is not a function of that prejudice, per se, but rather reflects the deductive application of stereotypic associations (often associated with prejudice) between African Americans and violence. Because participants can use traits associated with the group to disambiguate a particular African American target, they may inappropriately perceive that target as threatening or hostile.

Study 3 represents a first attempt to test these predictions. After playing the videogame, participants completed a questionnaire designed to measure prejudice and two forms of the association between African Americans and violence. The first measure of this association assessed stereotypes that the participant personally endorses or believes. We refer to this as the *personal stereotype*. The second measure, called the *cultural stereotype*, is designed to assess the participant's awareness that a stereotype of African Americans as violent is present in U.S. culture, generally. Though we use the terms *personal stereotype* and *cultural stereotype*, this distinction maps cleanly on to the endorsement/knowledge distinction suggested by Devine (Devine, 1989; Devine & Elliot, 1995), who has shown that, although people often personally disavow negative stereotypes about African Americans, they are well aware that those stereotypes exist. Because this knowledge represents a psychological link between the social category and the trait, activating the concept of the group may predispose a participant to make use of the stereotypic trait in interpretations of an ambiguous target—even if he or she does not personally endorse the stereotype. Both personal and cultural forms of the stereotypic association, then, may influence interpretation of an ambiguous target.

Method

Participants and Design Forty-eight undergraduates (26 female, 22 male) participated in this experiment in return for either $10 or partial credit toward a class requirement. Two male participants were Latino, and 1 female was Asian. Another female was African American and was excluded from our analyses. All other participants were White. Two White females were also removed from the dataset, one because the game's *shoot* and *don't shoot* labels were reversed, and one because she was working as a research assistant on a different study of African American stereotypes. The final sample included 45 students. This study used the same 2 × 2 within-subject design, with Target Ethnicity (African American vs. White) and Object Type (gun vs. no gun) as repeated factors.

Materials

Videogame. In this study, we used the videogame parameters we had used in Study 1. The response window was set at 850 ms, and we expected effects primarily in the latency of correct responses, rather than in error rates.

Questionnaire. Study 3 added a battery of individual difference measures. First, participants completed the Modern Racism Scale (MRS; McConahay, Hardee, & Batts, 1981), the Discrimination (DIS) and Diversity Scales (DIV) (both from Wittenbrink, Judd, & Park, 1997), all of which are designed to measure prejudice against African Americans, as well as the Motivation to Control Prejudiced Responding Scale (MCP; Dunton & Fazio, 1997; Fazio, Jackson, Dunton, & Williams, 1995), which assesses participants willingness to express any prejudice they may feel. Items from these scales were intermixed (presented in a single, randomly determined, order) and responses were given on 5-point scales, ranging from *strongly disagree* to *strongly agree.* The items were intermingled with filler items from the Right-Wing Authoritarianism Scale (RWA, Altemeyer, 1988) and the Personal Need for Structure Scale (PNS; Thompson, Naccarato, Parker, & Moskowitz, 2001), which are addressed below. Second, to examine the degree to which participants endorsed a negative stereotype of African Americans as aggressive and dangerous, we asked them to estimate, on the basis of their personal beliefs, the percentage of both African Americans and Whites who are dangerous, violent, and aggressive (separate estimates were made for each trait by filling in a value from 0% to 100%). Third, we included a measure of participants' perceptions of the cultural stereotype that African Americans are aggressive and dangerous. Participants were asked to again consider the three attributes (dangerous, violent, and aggressive), giving prevalence estimates, not on the basis of their own personal beliefs, but rather on the basis of their perceptions of what most White Americans would estimate. These estimates were made by marking a 130-mm line anchored with the adjective (e.g., *dangerous*) on the right, and its negation (e.g., *not dangerous*) on the left.

In addition to these primary measures, the questionnaire included several exploratory components. We included the RWA scale (Altemeyer, 1988), which measures an individual's predisposition to think of social relations in terms of dominance and submission; the PNS scale (Thompson et al., 2001), which measures differences in the desire for a simple structure; and a five-item measure of contact with African Americans. These measures were included partly as filler items designed to mask the questionnaire's focus on prejudice and stereotyping, but also because these constructs have been shown to be related to prejudice or stereotyping in previous research (Neuberg & Newson, 1993; Pettigrew & Tropp, 2000; Pratto, Sidanius, Stallworth, & Malle, 1994). Responses to the contact items were made on 7-point scales. The first contact question asked participants to rate how many African Americans they know, using a scale anchored with *don't know any African Americans* and *know* a lot of African Americans. The second item asked for a rating of how well they know their African American acquaintances on a scale from *don't know well* to *know very well.* The third item asked about the degree of contact with African Americans in their neighborhood, when growing up. The fourth item asked about the number of African American friends they had while growing up. And the fifth item asked about the number of African Americans who had attended their high school. The last three items used a scale ranging from *none* to *many.*

Procedure As before, a male experimenter greeted participants, in groups of 1 to 4, and introduced the study as an investigation of perceptual vigilance. He went on to note that, because the vigilance task did not require the entire time period, participants would work on a separate questionnaire study afterward. After learning about the rules of the game, participants moved to computer terminals in private rooms and played the videogame. As each participant completed the game, the experimenter moved him or her to a table (still in the private room) and administered the short questionnaire, from Studies 1 and 2, assessing basic reactions to the game. The experimenter subsequently announced that the videogame study was over and provided another consent form, ostensibly for the separate questionnaire study. After collecting the consent form, he handed the participant an envelope containing the questionnaire. We made every effort to stress the confidentiality of the responses on the questionnaire. The experimenter told participants not to put any identifying information on the forms, not even a code number, and to seal the packet in the envelope when they had finished. He then left them alone to complete the questions. As in Studies 1 and 2, participants were fully debriefed. During this process, the experimenter probed for suspicion about the relationship between the game and the subsequent questionnaire.

Results and Discussion

In the debriefing, 6 participants reported that they had noticed that both the game and the questionnaire involved ethnicity, and that this awareness had prompted them to wonder if the two were related. Two of the 6 reported strong suspicion. The following results are based on the complete dataset, but exclusion of the 6 participants does not affect the analyses in either direction or significance. To analyze the videogame data, we submitted the log-transformed reaction times from correct trials to a 2 × 2 ANOVA, with Target Ethnicity and Object Type as the independent variables (see Table 1 for means converted back to milliseconds). The targets that had proved problematic in Study 2 were excluded from this analysis, though their inclusion does not substantially affect the results. Replicating the results from the first study, we found both a pronounced effect for Object, such that armed targets were responded to more quickly than unarmed targets, $F(1, 44) = 171.33, p < .0001$, and an Ethnicity × Object interaction, $F(1, 44) = 22.44, p < .0001$. Simple effects tests revealed that, when the target was armed, participants, on average, fired more quickly if he was African American than if he was White, $F(1, 44) = 4.15, p < .05$. When presented with an unarmed target, participants chose the "don't shoot" alternative more quickly if he was White than if he was African American, $F(1, 44) = 22.72, p < .0001$.

Mean scores on the error rates were largely consistent with those from Study 1. The Ethnicity × Object interaction was significant, $F(1, 44) = 7.20, p = .01$. Simple effects tests showed an ethnicity effect only among targets without guns, $F(1, 44) = 5.76, p = .02$, such that these were incorrectly shot more often if they were African American. The simple effect for armed targets was not significant, $F(1, 44) = 2.31, p = .14$. A test of the mean recognition sensitivity for the presented targets was significant in this study (mean $d' = 0.25$), $t(44) = 2.51, p = .016$. As in Study 1, however, sensitivity was above chance only for the White targets (mean $d' = 0.62$), $t(44) = 4.71, p < .0001$, and not for the African American targets (mean $d' = -0.15$), $t(44) = -1.14, p = .26$.

Having replicated the Ethnicity × Object interaction in the response latency scores, we wanted to examine its correlates. Accordingly, for each participant we computed a within-subject contrast score, assessing the magnitude of the Ethnicity × Object interaction for that particular participant. Higher scores on this variable, which we refer to as *Shooter Bias*, indicate faster responses to unarmed White than to unarmed African American targets, and to armed African American than armed White targets.

Table 2 reports the correlations between this Shooter Bias measure and the various questionnaire measures. Table 2 also reports the means, standard deviations, and internal consistency (coefficient alpha) statistics for the various attitude scales in our data. With the exception of contact and the personal and cultural stereotype measures, all measures were collected on 5-point scales with higher numbers indicating greater endorsement of the construct. None of the explicit prejudice scales—MRS, DIS, and DIV—show significant correlations with the Shooter Bias from the videogame. That is, those who reported higher levels of prejudice on these scales did not show a stronger ethnicity bias in the videogame. Because these three measures are highly intercorrelated, we also combined them, averaging all items together. This composite scale was similarly uncorrelated with Shooter Bias.

To compute the personal stereotype measure of African Americans as aggressive, we calculated the degree to which participants rated African Americans as more violent than Whites, more dangerous than Whites, and more aggressive than Whites. These three difference scores were averaged together to form the personal stereotype index. The measure reflects perceptions of the prevalence of the negative stereotypic attributes among African Americans relative to Whites. Because this measure is based on percentage estimates, it can potentially range from −100 to 100. One participant chose not to complete the relevant items, so all tests of the personal stereotype are based on a sample of 44, rather than 45. The same process was followed in computing the extent to which participants believed there is a negative cultural stereotype of African Americans as dangerous and aggressive. Because the raw scores on the cultural stereotype items were made on 130-mm lines, the index potentially ranges from − 130 to 130. As is clear in Table 2, the measure of personal endorsement of the negative stereotype of African Americans as aggressive and violent did not correlate with the Shooter Bias. However, the perception of a parallel negative cultural stereotype did correlate with the magnitude of the Shooter Bias in the videogame.

Of the exploratory measures (RWA, PNS, and contact), only contact was related to Shooter Bias. Contact scores were calculated by averaging participants' responses to the five 7-point contact items. This measure showed a significant and somewhat surprising correlation with the bias: Participants who reported more contact with African Americans exhibited a more pronounced Shooter Bias in the videogame. We discuss this intriguing effect in the General Discussion when we consider potential mechanisms that may give rise to Shooter Bias.

We suggested that the Shooter Bias evident in this videogame might be a consequence of participants using stereotypic associations about African Americans to help interpret ambiguous African American targets. The data from Study 3 suggest that the magnitude of the bias was related to participants' perceptions of the cultural stereotype about African Americans. The bias was not, however, related to either personally endorsed stereotypes or to prejudice. This is somewhat surprising, because, to the extent that people personally endorse the violent

TABLE 2
Correlations of Shooter Bias in Videogame With Questionnaire Measures (Study 3)

Variable	*M*	*SD*	α	Shooter Bias	MRS	DIS	DIV	Prejudice comp	Personal stereo	Cultural stereo	MCP	Contact	RWA
MRS	1 63	66	86	.15									
DIS	2 09	.73	87	16	80**								
DIV	2 43	64	64	05	46**	59**							
Prejudice comp.	2 09	.60	.91	.14	.85**	95**	78**						
Personal stereo	1.43	7 56	54	05	.38**	38**	.38**	43**					
Cultural stereo.	41 37	24 15	.88	37**	- 06	- 07	- 21	- 12	- 06				
MCP	3.23	.48	.72	.03	-.35*	- 29*	- 27†	- 34*	- 31*	06			
Contact	2 56	1 00	.72	38**	-.18	- 02	11	- 03	-.07	09	15		
RWA	2.16	61	.72	- 04	.26†	.24	.37**	33*	02	- 25†	25†	11	
PNS	2 78	55	77	- 15	16	.00	- 16	- 01	- 04	15	17	- 06	.29*

Note. For all measures except personal stereotype, $n = 45$. All comparisons involving personal stereotype are based on $n = 44$. MRS = Modern Racism Scale; DIS = Discrimination Scale; DIV = Diversity Scale; Prejudice comp. = prejudice composite; stereo. = stereotype; MCP = Motivation to Control Prejudiced Responding Scale; RWA = Right-Wing Authoritarianism Scale; PNS = Personal Need for Structure Scale.
†$p \leq .10$. *$p \leq .05$. **$p \leq 5$ .01.

stereotype or hold prejudices against African Americans, we might suppose the negative associations to be stronger and more likely to influence their interpretations of, and behavior toward, an ambiguous target.

There are well-documented social desirability concerns associated with expressing prejudice or negative stereotypic beliefs about African Americans (Dunton & Fazio, 1997; McConahay et al., 1981; Plant & Devine, 1998), so it may be that participants simply refused to express their personal views. In his research, Payne (2001) found no zero-order correlation between prejudice (as measured by the MRS) and the automatic component in his weapon identification task. He did find a moderated relationship between the two variables, though, such that a positive correlation emerged only among participants who were low in MCP. A similar test in our data yielded no significant interaction between MRS and MCP, $F(1, 41) = 0.00$, $p < .95$, or between personal stereotype and MCP, $F(1, 40) = 0.95$, $p < .34$, when predicting Shooter Bias.

Unlike prejudice and personal stereotypes, our measure of cultural stereotype should be generally free from social desirability concerns. It involves participants' estimates of the stereotype held by American society. The fact that cultural stereotype correlates with Shooter Bias suggests that awareness of the stereotype, itself, even though a person may not believe that stereotype, can be sufficient to produce bias. One might argue, however, that our cultural stereotype measure was just another way of measuring personal prejudice, in a manner that allowed participants to express their own prejudices relatively free from normative constraints. That is, by attributing prejudicial beliefs to others, participants were now able to express more freely the prejudice that they themselves felt.

The bivariate correlation between the cultural stereotype measure and our composite personal prejudice scale was –.12 (p = .41), suggesting that this cultural stereotype measure is not a simple proxy for personal prejudice levels. However, it might be the case that the relationship between the cultural stereotype measure and personal prejudice depends on the participant's level of motivation to control prejudice, again following the theoretical arguments of Fazio et al. (1995). To examine this possibility, we regressed the cultural stereotype measure on our composite personal prejudice measure, MCP, and their interaction. The interaction proved to be a significant predictor, $F(I, 41) = 4.67$, $p < .05$, The direction of this interaction was as predicted: there was a more positive relationship between personal prejudice levels and the cultural stereotype measure among those who were lower in motivation to control prejudice.

We were interested in whether cultural stereotype would continue to predict Shooter Bias once we removed the extent to which the cultural stereotype variable is a measure of personal prejudice, particularly among those low in motivation to control prejudice. Accordingly, we estimated a model with Shooter Bias as the criterion, regressing it on the cultural stereotype measure while controlling for our personal prejudice composite, MCP, and the interaction between personal prejudice and MCP. In this model, again, only the cultural stereotype measure related significantly to bias in the videogame, $F(l, 40) = 5.24$, $p < .03$. Thus, even removing personal prejudice levels from the cultural stereotype, and controlling for the fact that personal prejudice levels were more strongly related to the cultural stereotype among those low in MCP, the cultural stereotype measure continued to predict bias in our videogame.[4] This suggests that it is truly knowledge of the cultural stereotype that is at work here, rather than simply an indirect measure of personal prejudice. We consider this a sobering prospect because it suggests that the bias may be endemic in American society.

A number of studies have shown that cultural stereotypes can be automatically activated even when a perceiver does not endorse them (Banaji & Greenwald, 1995; Devine, 1989; Gilbert & Hixon, 1991; Macrae, Milne, & Bodenhausen, 1994). Cultural influences, including television, movies, music, and newspapers provide a constant barrage of information that often depicts African Americans as violent (Cosby, 1994; Gray, 1989), and those depictions may shape our understanding of the world (Gerbner, Gross, Morgan, & Signorielli, 1986). Popular culture, including Gangsta Rap songs like the Notorious B.I.G.'s "Somebody's Gotta Die," Snoop Dogg's "Serial Killa," or Dr. Dre's "Murder Ink," and movies like *Colors* or *Training Day* may foster bias by enhancing detrimental stereotypic associations, in spite of the fact that the audience knows the characters and events are fictitious.

If cultural stereotypes associating African Americans with violence do, in fact, lead to Shooter Bias, any person exposed to American culture should be liable to demonstrate the bias, regardless of his or her personal views about African Americans. Research suggests that the very people who are targeted by cultural stereotypes are influenced by the media representations they see (Berry & Mitchell-Kernan, 1982; Stroman, 1986; SuberviVelez & Necochea, 1990), know full well that the stereotypes exist (Steele & Aronson, 1995), and even activate those stereotypes automatically (Banaji & Greenwald, 1995). Sagar and Schofield (1980), as noted above, found similar levels of bias among their African American and White participants using their interpretation task. To examine further the possibility that knowledge of the cultural stereotype may, in and of itself, lead to Shooter Bias, we sought to test for bias in a more diverse sample that included African American participants.

STUDY 4

Method

Participants and Design Fifty-two adults from bus stations, malls, and food courts in Denver, Colorado, were recruited to participate in this study in return for $5. The study followed the same 2 × 2 within-subject design used in Studies 1–3, with Target Ethnicity (African American vs. White) and Object Type (gun vs. no gun) as repeated factors, but in Study 4 we added a between-subject factor, namely Participant Ethnicity (African American vs. White). The final sample included 25 African Americans (6 females, 19 males) and 21 Whites (8 females, 13 males). One Asian and 4 Hispanic or Latino participants, and 1 participant who did not indicate his ethnicity, were excluded from the analyses, though the results do not differ if they are included in the White sample.

TABLE 3
Means (and Standard Deviations) for Reaction Times and Error Rates as a Function of Target Ethnicity, Object Type, and Participant Ethnicity (Study 4)

Participants	Reaction times: White targets	Reaction times: Afr. Am. targets	Errors per 20 trials: White targets	Errors per 20 trials: Afr. Am. targets
White participants				
Armed targets	590(43)	578(36)	1.38(1.36)	0.76(0.77)
Unarmed targets	652(40)	665(41)	1.19(0.93)	1.29(1.49)
Afr. Am. participants				
Armed targets	578(42)	567(47)	2.00(1.53)	1.52(1 58)
Unarmed targets	645(47)	659(41)	1.64(1.80)	1.44(1.47)

Note. Afr. Am. = African American.

Materials In this study, we used the videogame parameters from Studies 1 and 3. The response window was set at 850 ms and, again, we expected effects in the latency of correct responses; rather than in error rates. Before beginning this study, the targets identified as problematic in Study 2 were edited in Photoshop, to clarify the object in the picture.

Procedure At each location, two male experimenters set up 2–3 laptop computers equipped with the videogame program and earphones, to minimize distractions inherent in the nonlaboratory environment. Without a button box, participants pressed the *k* key on the laptop keyboard to indicate *shoot,* and the *d* key to indicate *don't shoot.* While one experimenter circulated and recruited participants, the other oversaw the experiment, giving instructions to each participant individually. After completing the videogame, participants were paid and debriefed. In this study, we did not include instructions to attend to target faces, nor did we test for recognition after the game.

Results and Discussion

Before analyzing the videogame data, we reexamined the targets that were problematic in Study 2. The targets no longer induced unusually high numbers of errors, and they were therefore included in the analyses reported below. The results reported do not change in direction or magnitude if the targets are excluded. We submitted the log-transformed reaction times from correct trials to a 2 × 2 × 2 mixed-model ANOVA, with Participant Ethnicity as a between-subject factor, and Target Ethnicity and Object Type as within-subject factors (see Table 3 for means converted back to milliseconds). Across all participants, we again found a pronounced effect for Object, such that armed targets evoked responses more quickly than unarmed targets, $F(1, 45) = 347.82$, $p < .0001$. The Target Ethnicity × Object interaction, or Shooter Bias, was also significant, $F(1, 45) = 14.75$, $p < .001$. Crucially, though, the magnitude of the bias did not depend on Participant Ethnicity, $F(1, 44) = 0.10$, $p = .75$. Examining the African American and White samples separately, we found that the Target Ethnicity × Object interaction was significant for both, $F(1, 24) = 6.55$, $p = .017$ and $F(1, 20) = 8.01$, $p = .01$, respectively.

Simple effects tests again showed that, when the target was armed, participants decided to shoot more quickly if he was African American than if he was White, $F(1, 45) = 7.62$, $p = .008$. When the target was unarmed, participants pressed the *don't shoot* button more quickly if he was White than if he was African American, resulting in an identical test statistic, $F(1, 45) = 7.62$, $p = .008$. Neither simple effect depended on Participant Ethnicity, $F(1, 44) = 0.07$, $p = .79$, for the unarmed targets, and $F(1, 44) = 0.42$, $p = .52$, for the unarmed targets.

An analysis of the error rates revealed that the Target Ethnicity × Object interaction was only marginal, $F(1, 45) = 3.24$, $p = .08$, and its magnitude did not depend on Participant Ethnicity, $F(1, 44) = 0.66$, $p = .42$.

GENERAL DISCUSSION

In four studies, we attempted to recreate the experience of a police officer who, confronted with a potentially dangerous suspect, must decide whether or not to shoot. Our goal was to examine the influence of the suspect's ethnicity on that decision. We used a simplified videogame to present African American and White male targets, each holding either a gun or a nonthreatening object. Participants were instructed to shoot only armed targets. We reasoned that participants might use the stereotype, or schema, that African Americans are violent to help disambiguate the target stimuli, and would therefore respond with greater speed and accuracy to stereotype-consistent targets (armed African Americans and unarmed Whites) than to stereotype-inconsistent targets (armed Whites and unarmed African Americans).

In Study 1, participants fired on an armed target more quickly when he was African American than when he was White, and decided not to shoot an unarmed target more quickly when he was White than when he was African American. In Study 2, we attempted to increase error rates by forcing participants to make decisions very quickly. Participants in this study failed to shoot an armed target more often when that target was White than when he was African American. If the target was unarmed, participants mistakenly shot him more often when he was African American than when he was White. A signal detection analysis of these data revealed that, although participants' ability to distinguish between armed and unarmed targets did not depend on target ethnicity, participants set a lower decision criterion to shoot for African American targets than for Whites. That is, if a target was African American, participants generally required less certainty that he was, in fact, holding a gun before they decided to shoot him. In Study 3, we returned to an analysis of reaction times, replicating the Ethnicity × Object Type interaction (Shooter Bias) obtained in Study 1, and examining individual difference measures associated with the magnitude of that effect. Shooter Bias was more pronounced among participants who believed that there is a strong stereotype in American culture characterizing African Americans as aggressive, violent and dangerous; and among participants who reported more contact with African Americans. Prejudice and personal endorsement of the stereotype that African Americans are violent failed to predict Shooter Bias in the simple correlations, and their predictive power was no stronger among participants low in motivation to control prejudice. The fact that Shooter Bias in Study 3 was related to perceptions of the cultural stereotype, rather than prejudice or personally endorsed stereotypes, suggests that mere knowledge of the stereotype is enough to induce this bias. In Study 4, we obtained additional support for this prediction. Testing both White and African American participants, we found that the two groups display equivalent levels of bias.

The results of these studies consistently support the hypothesized effect of ethnicity on shoot/don't shoot decisions. Both in speed and accuracy, the decision to fire on an armed target was facilitated when that target was African American, whereas the decision not to shoot an unarmed target was facilitated when that target was White. This Shooter Bias effect is consistent with the results reported by Payne (2001). Payne primed participants with African American and White faces, and asked them to identify subsequent target objects as either hand tools or weapons. His results suggest that responses to hand tools were faster (and, in a second study, more accurate) when preceded by White, relative to African American, primes, whereas responses to weapons were faster (but no more accurate) when preceded by African American primes. This priming effect maps nicely onto our results. The consistency between our results and those obtained by Payne is particularly striking given methodological differences between the two paradigms. Four primary differences stand out. Payne used small, decontextualized and relatively simple images of faces (the center portion of the face) and objects, whereas our stimuli were very complex, with target individuals appearing against realistic backgrounds. Payne used a sequential priming task, whereas we used simultaneous presentation of ethnicity and object. A consequence of Payne's priming task, which used a constant 200-ms stimulus onset asynchrony, is that the appearance of a prime in his task should have clearly indicated to participants that a target was imminent. Our task, however, presented targets at random intervals, with no prime, so that participants were never certain about when they would appear. Finally, whereas Payne asked his participants to identify a target object as a tool or a weapon, we asked our participants to decide whether or not to shoot a target person. Although both decisions depend on the presence of a weapon, the psychological implications of the two tasks are quite different. Payne's task was framed as a categorization judgment, whereas our task was characterized as a behavioral response. In spite of these distinctions, both paradigms reveal a pronounced effect of target ethnicity on reactions to weapons.

In line with Sagar and Schofield (1980), we have argued that ethnicity influences the shoot/don't shoot decision primarily because traits associated with African Americans, namely "violent" or "dangerous," can act as a schema to influence perceptions of an ambiguously threatening target. The relationship between cultural stereotype and Shooter Bias obtained in Study 3 provides support for this hypothesis. The subsequent finding that African Americans and Whites, alike, display this bias further buttresses the argument. It is unlikely that participants in our African American sample held strong prejudice against their own ethnic group (Judd, Park, Ryan, Brauer, & Kraus, 1995), but as members of U.S. society, they are, presumably, aware of the cultural stereotype that African Americans are violent (Devine & Elliot, 1995; Steele & Aronson, 1995). These associations, we suggest, may influence reactions to the targets in our videogame. Though ambient cultural associations may impact most members of U.S. society, it is certainly plausible that personal endorsement of stereotypes, and perhaps prejudice, will lead to even stronger negative associations with African Americans, potentially magnifying bias. (Though the data in Study 3, specifically the lack of a relationship between Shooter Bias and personal stereotype, offer little support for this argument, at present.)

It seems appropriate at this juncture to speculate on mechanisms that may underlie Shooter Bias. Our basic findings indicate that a target's ethnicity, though technically irrelevant to the decision task at hand, somehow interferes with participants' ability to react appropriately to the object in the target's hand. This interference seems roughly analogous to a Stroop effect, and research on this extensively studied phenomenon may provide a useful perspective from which to consider our results. The common Stroop experiment presents participants with a word, and requires them to identify the color of the ink in which that word is written (e.g., green ink). Performance on this simple task can be disrupted when the word, itself, refers to a different color than the ink (e.g., *RED* printed in green ink), relative to performance when the color of the ink and the referent of the word are the same (e.g., *GREEN* printed in green ink) or when the word does not refer to a color at all (e.g., *EGGS* printed in green ink). The Stroop paradigm, like our videogame, simultaneously presents participants with information that is relevant to the judgment at hand (ink color and object, respectively) as well as information that is irrelevant (word name and ethnicity, respectively). Participants need not process the irrelevant information to perform the task, but in both cases, the presence of incongruent information on the irrelevant dimension interferes with participants' ability to process the relevant information. Researchers have suggested that, because we so frequently read the words that we see, reading occurs quickly. Ink naming, though, is an unusual and relatively cumbersome task. If these two processes occur in parallel, the quicker word reading may produce interference by winning a kind of horse race, getting to the finish line and influencing responses ahead of the slower ink-naming process, which eventually provides the definitive answer (Cohen, Dunbar, & McClelland, 1990; Posner & Snyder, 1975). Similarly, the speedy categorization of people into ethnic categories, described by Brewer (1988) and Fiske and Neuberg (1990), should quickly activate stereotypes and interfere with the unfamiliar and less automatic gun/no-gun judgment (see Figure 3). This analogy is not perfect, of course. Although it may be natural to read the word *RED* when it appears, the typical day-to-day response to an African American does not involve gunfire. However, to the extent that a person spontaneously associates an African American target with violence, the ethnicity of the target should conflict with the judgment that he is unarmed, and it may therefore inhibit the "don't shoot" response.

Cohen et al. (1990) characterized Stroop interference as an interaction between two variables: attention to the irrelevant dimension and the strength of the association between the incongruent information and the incorrect response. Both of these variables can moderate Stroop effects independently (see Walley, McLeod, & Khan, 1997; Walley, McLeod, & Weiden, 1994, for research on attention; see Lu & Proctor, 2001, for research on the strength of association). Though it is only speculation at present, we suggest that the two significant predictors of Shooter Bias in Study 3, cultural stereotype and contact, are important because they capture these two components of Stroop interference. We have already presented the argument that a cultural stereotype represents an associative link between African Americans and traits related to violence and danger. We further suggest that the role of contact in predicting Shooter Bias may reflect, at least in part, the other component of Stroop interference: attention to irrelevant ethnic cues. People who have had extensive contact with African Americans may have, over the course of that experience, learned to naturally parse the world in terms of ethnic categories. They may be essentially schematic for ethnicity. Greater attention to ethnicity combined with an association between African Americans and violence should, from the Stroop perspective, magnify Shooter Bias. In line with this prediction, Payne (Payne, Lambert, & Jacoby, in press) has shown that asking participants to use ethnic cues in their judgments (like a person engaged in racial profiling) increases the magnitude of the automatic component in error responses in his task, relative to control participants who receive no special instructions. Of greater interest, asking participants to avoid using ethnicity in their judgments also increases the magnitude of the automatic component. This suggests that attention to the irrelevant ethnic cue may produce interference.

The Stroop conceptualization offers another, perhaps more hopeful, prediction. If Shooter Bias is, in part, a function of the automaticity with which ethnic cues are processed relative to the automaticity of the object cues (i.e., ethnicity's ability to win the horse race against the relevant dimension), the bias should be minimized by interventions that speed up the gun/no-gun decision. As the relevant decision becomes more automatic, the effect of the irrelevant dimension should weaken. Experimental research (MacLeod, 1998; MacLeod & Dunbar, 1988) as well as computer simulations (Cohen et al., 1990) have demonstrated that repeated training on ink-naming tasks, which should render that process more automatic, reduces Stroop interference. Similarly, training participants to quickly and effortlessly distinguish guns from cell phones may reduce Shooter Bias.

Though we have characterized Shooter Bias as a result of distorted interpretations of an ambiguous target, there are several stages at which this bias may actually be functioning. Before shooting, a participant must (a) *perceive* the object, (b) *interpret* the object as a gun with some degree of certainty, and (c) *decide* to press the "shoot" button once a criterion of certainty has been reached. Stereotypic schemata may theoretically affect any or all of these processes, and it is difficult to disentangle them theoretically, let alone empirically. Figure 3 depicts the three processing stages and how faster, more automatic processing along the irrelevant dimension (as suggested by the Stroop research) might bias each stage of relevant processing (the solid arrows). Throughout this article, we have argued that bias impacts the second stage of this process, changing the interpretation of an ambiguous object. A participant who catches a glimpse of some elongated shape in the target's hand may draw on stereotypic associations, interpreting the shape as a gun if the target is African American but as a cell phone if he is White. Participants may almost "see" different objects.

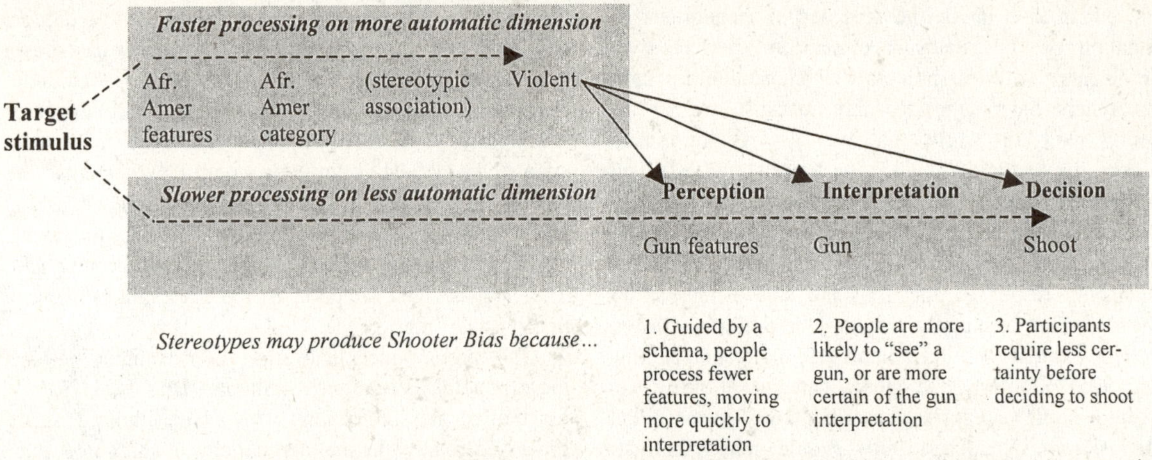

Figure 3. Faster, more automatic processing on the irrelevant ethnic dimension may bias participants' (a) perception of targets, (b) interpretation of targets, or (c) the criterion of certainty required for the "shoot" response.
Afr Amer = African American

One problem with this perspective is that we took pains to ensure that the objects presented in our target images were clearly identifiable. Even under time pressure, is it fair to characterize these objects as ambiguous? Certainly, very few of our participants actually misperceived the objects: our primary effects were in reaction times, not errors, and errors were consistently quite low. It is possible that the bias in reaction time represents the effects of stereotypes on actual perception of the object, not on its interpretation. von Hippel and his associates (von Hippel, Jonides, Hilton & Narayan, 1993) showed that when a participant has a relevant schema, he or she can infer the gist of a stimulus with very few perceptual details. Without a schema, though, more detailed perceptual encoding may be necessary. In the context of the current research, the stereotype of African Americans may influence the number features a participant must process to make the correct object identification. An African American target provides a schema relevant to guns, so participants who see just a few features of a gun quickly identify it and decide to shoot. A White target, perhaps, provides no useful schema, and participants must attend to more features of the gun in his hand before they recognize it, causing them to respond more slowly. von Hippel's research provides an elegant rationale for the differential speed required to shoot an armed target, but we are less confident that perceptual differences underlie reactions to the unarmed targets. Perceptual processes can only account for the simple effect of ethnicity among unarmed targets if we assume that White people stereotypically carry cell phones, wallets, coke cans, and cameras, and that this stereotype reduces the number of perceptual cues necessary to identify these objects relative to African Americans, where no cell phone stereotype exists. Empirically, it should be possible to test the viability of a perceptual encoding account of Shooter Bias. If perceptual differences drive ethnic bias, then memory for trivial details, such as the kind of gun or the color of the cell phone, which should reflect the extent of perceptual encoding, should differ as a function of target ethnicity.

Another, more macroscopic, alternative to our interpretation-based account is that Shooter Bias may reflect changes in the decision criterion that participants use. Bias would clearly emerge if participants require one level of certainty that the object is a gun when deciding to shoot African American targets, but have another, more stringent, criterion for Whites. Even if the perception and interpretation of an object do not differ as a function of target ethnicity (e.g., the participant is 75% certain that the object is a gun for both African American and White targets), a participant who requires 60% certainty for African American targets, but 80% certainty for Whites, will show Shooter Bias. Unfortunately, the current studies do not allow us to discern between the interpretation and decision criterion explanations. Though the signal detection terms, *sensitivity* and *criterion*, might foster an expectation that Study 2 should be able to resolve this question, that is not the case. Study 2 suggested that sensitivity was equal for African American and White targets, and that only the criterion differed. The criterion may differ, though, either because the certainty needed to make the shoot/don't shoot decision differs with target ethnicity (bias in the decision stage), or because a given object in the hand of an African American target is *simultaneously* more likely to be perceived as a gun and less likely to be perceived as a non-gun, than the same object in a White target's hand (bias in the interpretation stage). The signal detection theory figure from Study 2 assumes that the average armed White target and the average armed African American target seem equally threatening, that the two gun distributions fall at the same point on the *x*-axis. As we have graphed it, the figure suggests that the criterion to shoot shifts down for African American targets. However, it is also possible that participants use the same criterion for White and African American targets, but generally perceive African Americans as more threatening. If this were the case, the criterion line in the chart for African American targets would have the same *x*-coordinate as the White criterion line, but the mean of the two African American distributions (both armed and unarmed) would seem to shift up on the dimension of perceived threat. Even using signal detection theory, we have no way to statistically disentangle these two possibilities in the current data.

Bias in the decision-making stage may be seen as consistent with ideomotor effects. Bargh, Chen, and Burrows (1996, Study 3), for example, found that participants primed with African American faces exhibited more aggressive behavior in response to a rude request from an experimenter. It is possible that the participants' behavior was still driven by bias in their interpretation, that those primed with African American actually perceived the experimenter as more hostile (along the lines of Devine, 1989). But Bargh and others (e.g., Chartrand & Bargh, 1996; Dijksterhuis, Aarts, Bargh, & van Knippenberg, 2000; Stapel & Koomen, 2001) have demonstrated direct behavioral priming effects in a number of situations designed to preclude interpretation-based bias. It is not unreasonable to suppose that participants in our studies were cued by a target's ethnicity to behave aggressively toward African American targets, shooting them more often and more quickly than Whites. Payne (2001), though, did not require a behavioral response. Because his task required that participants classify objects as guns or hand tools, rather than react violently, ideomotor effects cannot account for his findings. In the absence of more definitive evidence, and given the consistency between Payne's results and ours, parsimony argues for an interpretation-based explanation of Shooter Bias, rather than a criterion-based or ideomotor explanation.

These studies have demonstrated that the decision to shoot may be influenced by a target person's ethnicity. In four studies, participants showed a bias to shoot African American targets more rapidly and/or more frequently than White targets. The implications of this bias are clear and disturbing. Even more worrisome is the suggestion that mere knowledge of the cultural stereotype, which depicts African Americans as violent, may produce Shooter Bias, and that even African Americans demonstrate the bias. We understand that the demonstration of bias in an African American sample is politically controversial given the nature of this task, and we offer two considerations. First, the results of a single study are not definitive. Our findings should be replicated by researchers in other labs with different materials before generalizations are made. Second, our goals as psychologists include understanding, predicting, and controlling behavior. Ultimately, efforts to control (i.e., reduce or eliminate) any ethnic bias in the decision to shoot must be based on an accurate understanding of how target ethnicity influences that decision, even if that understanding is politically or personally distasteful.

Though these studies suggest that bias in the decision to shoot may be widespread, it is not yet clear that Shooter Bias actually exists among police officers. The studies we report use exclusively lay samples, and there is no reason to assume that this effect will generalize beyond this population. There is even a possibility, suggested by literature on the Stroop effect, that police training may actually reduce Shooter Bias by rendering the gun/no-gun decision more automatic for officers. If this is the case, police might show less bias than the average college sophomore. Examining these sorts of effects in a sample of police officers is of the utmost importance.

The studies reported here suggest that Shooter Bias is present among White college students (Studies 1–3) and among a community sample that consists of both Whites and African Americans (Study 4). The effect is robust and clearly a cause for concern, no matter the underlying cause. On the basis of our data, though, bias does not seem to simply reflect prejudice toward African Americans, and there is reason to believe the effect is present simply as a function of stereotypic associations that exist in our culture. That these associations can have such potentially profound consequences for members of stigmatized groups is a finding worthy of great concern. Since the death of Amadou Diallo, New York has witnessed a number of similar, though less publicized, cases, and Cincinnati, Ohio, has added Timothy Thomas's name to the list of unarmed African American men killed by police officers. Social psychological theory and research may prove invaluable in the effort to identify, understand and eventually control processes that bias decisions to shoot (and possibly kill) a person, as a function of his or her ethnicity.

REFERENCES

Altemeyer, B. (1988). *Enemies of freedom: Understanding right-wing authoritarianism.* San Francisco: Jossey-Bass.

Banaji, M. R., & Greenwald, A. G. (1995). Implicit gender stereotyping in judgments of fame. *Journal of Personality and Social Psychology, 68,* 181–198.

Bargh, J. A., Chen, M., & Burrows, L. (1996). Automaticity of social behavior: Direct effects of trait construct and stereotype activation on action. *Journal of Personality and Social Psychology, 71,* 230–244.

Beckett, N. E., & Park, B. (1995). Use of category versus individuating information: Making base-rates salient. *Personality and Social Psychology Bulletin, 21,* 21–31.

Berry, G. L., & Mitchell-Kernan, C. (1982) Introduction. In G. L. Berry & C. Mitchell-Kernan (Eds.), *Television and the socialization of the minority child* (pp. 1–11). New York: Academic Press.

Brewer, M. B. (1988). A dual process model of impression formation. In T. K. Srull & R. S. Wyer (Eds.), *Advances in social cognition* (Vol. 1, pp. 1–36). Hillsdale, NJ: Erlbaum.

Chartrand, T. L., & Bargh, J. A. (1996). Automatic activation of impression formation and memorization goals: Nonconscious goal priming reproduces effects of explicit task instructions. *Journal of Personality and Social Psychology, 71,* 464–478.

Cohen, J. D., Dunbar, K., & McClelland, J. L. (1990). On the control of automatic processes: A parallel distributed processing account of the Stroop effect. *Psychological Review, 97,* 332–361.

Cohen, J. D., MacWhinney, B., Flatt, M., & Provost, J. (1993). PsyScope: An interactive graphic system for designing and controlling experiments in the psychology laboratory using Macintosh computers. *Behavior Research Methods, Instruments & Computers, 25,* 257–271.

Cosby, C. O. (1994). *Television's imageable influences: The self-perceptions of young African-Americans.* Lanham, MD: University Press of America.

Darley, J. M., & Gross, P. G. (1983). A hypothesis-confirming bias in labeling effects. *Journal of Personality and Social Psychology, 44,* 20–33.

Devine, P. G. (1989). Stereotypes and prejudice: Their automatic and controlled components. *Journal of Personality and Social Psychology, 56,* 5–18.

Devine, P. G., & Elliot, A. J. (1995). Are racial stereotypes really fading? The Princeton trilogy revisited. *Personality and Social Psychology Bulletin, 21,* 1139–1150.

Dijksterhuis, A., Aarts, H., Bargh, J. A., & van Knippenberg, A. (2000). On the relation between associative strength and automatic behavior. *Journal of Experimental Social Psychology, 36,* 531–544.

Duncan, B. L. (1976). Differential social perception and attribution of intergroup violence: Testing the lower limits of stereotyping of blacks. *Journal of Personality and Social Psychology 34,* 590–598.

Dunton, B. C., & Fazio, R. H. (1997). An individual difference measure of motivation to control prejudiced reactions. *Personality and Social Psychology Bulletin, 23,* 316–326.

Fazio, R. H., Jackson, J. R., Dunton, B. C., & Williams, C. J. (1995). Variability in automatic activation as an unobtrusive measure of racial attitudes: A bona fide pipeline? *Journal of Personality and Social Psychology, 69,* 1013–1027.

Fiske, S. T., Lin, M., & Neuberg, S. L. (1999). The continuum model: Ten years later. In S. Chaiken & Y. Trope (Eds.), *Dual-process theories in social psychology* (pp. 231–254). New York: Guilford Press.

Fiske, S. T., & Neuberg, S. L. (1990). A continuum of impression formation, from category-based to individuating processes: Influences of information and motivation on attention and interpretation. In M. P. Zanna (Ed.), *Advances in experimental social psychology* (Vol. 23, pp. 1–74). New York: Academic Press.

Gerbner, G., Gross, L., Morgan, M., & Signorielli, N. (1986). Living with television: The dynamics of the cultivation process. In J. Bryant & D. Zillman (Eds.), *Perspectives of media effects* (pp. 14–40). Hillsdale, NJ: Erlbaum.

Gilbert, D. T., & Hixon, J. G. (1991). The trouble of thinking: Activation and application of stereotypic beliefs. *Journal of Personality and Social Psychology, 60,* 509–517.

Gray, H. (1989) Television, Black Americans, and the American dream. *Critical Studies in Mass Communication, 6,* 376–386.

Green, D. M., & Swets, J. A. (1966). *Signal detection theory and psychophysics.* New York: Wiley. (Reprinted 1974, Huntington, NY: Krieger).

Hamilton, D. L., & Sherman, J. W. (1994). Stereotypes. In R. S. Wyer & T. K. Srull (Eds.), *Handbook of social cognition* (pp. 1–68). Hillsdale, NJ: Erlbaum.

Hilton, J. L., & von Hippel, W. (1990). The role of consistency in the judgment of stereotype-relevant behaviors. *Personality and Social Psychology Bulletin 16,* 430–448.

Jacobs, J. E., & Eccles, J. S. (1992). The impact of mothers' gender-role stereotypic beliefs on mothers' and children's ability perceptions. *Journal of Personality and Social Psychology 63,* 932–944.

Jacoby, L. L. (1991). A process dissociation framework: Separating automatic from intentional uses of memory. *Journal of Memory and Language, 30,* 513–541.

Jacoby, L. L., Toth, J. P., & Yonelinas, A. P. (1993). Separating conscious and unconscious influences of memory: Measuring recollection. *Journal of Experimental Psychology: General, 122,* 139 –154.

Judd, C. M., Park, B., Ryan, C. S., Brauer, M., & Kraus, S. (1995). Stereotypes and ethnocentrism: Diverging interethnic perceptions of African American and White American youth. *Journal of Personality and Social Psychology, 69,* 460–481.

Krueger, J., & Rothbart, M. (1988). The use of categorical and individuating information in making inferences about personality. *Journal of Personality and Social Psychology, 55,* 187–195.

Lepore, L., & Brown, R. (1997). Category and stereotype activation: Is prejudice inevitable? *Journal of Personality and Social Psychology, 72,* 275–287.

Locksley, A., Borgida, E., Brekke, N., & Hepburn, C. (1980). Sex stereotypes and social judgment. *Journal of Personality and Social Psycho*logy, *39,* 821–831.

Lu, C.-H., & Proctor, R. W. (2001). Influence of irrelevant information on human performance: Effects of S-R association strength and relative timing. *Quarterly Journal of Experimental Psychology: Human Experimental Psychology, 54*(A), 95–136.

MacLeod, C. M. (1998). Training on integrated versus separated Stroop tasks: The progression of interference and facilitation. *Memory & Cognition, 26,* 201–211.

MacLeod, C. M., & Dunbar, K. (1988). Training and Stroop-like interference: Evidence for a continuum of automaticity. *Journal of Experimental Psychology: Learning, Memory, and Cognition, 14,* 126–135.

MacMillan, N. A., & Creelman, C. D. (1991). *Detection theory: A users guide.* Cambridge, England: Cambridge University Press.

Macrae, C. N., Milne, A. B., & Bodenhausen, G. V. (1994). Stereotypes as energy-saving devices: A peek inside the cognitive toolbox. *Journal of Personality and Social Psychology, 66,* 37–47.

McConahay, J. B., Hardee, B. B., & Batts, V. (1981). Has racism declined in America? It depends on who is asking and what is asked. *Journal of Conflict Resolution, 25,* 563–579.

Neuberg, S. L., & Newson, J. T. (1993). Personal need for structure: Individual differences in the desire for simpler structure. *Journal of Personality and Social Psychology, 65,* 113–131.

Payne, B. K. (2001). Prejudice and perception: The role of automatic and controlled processes in misperceiving a weapon. *Journal of Personality and Social Psychology, 81,* 181–192.

Payne, B. K., Lambert, A. J., & Jacoby, L. L. (in press). Best laid plans: Effects of goals on accessibility bias and cognitive control in race-based misperceptions of weapons. *Journal of Experimental Social Psychology.*

Pettigrew, T. F., & Tropp, L. R. (2000). Does intergroup contact reduce prejudice: Recent meta-analytic findings. In S. Oskamp (Ed.), *Reducing prejudice and discrimination* (pp. 93–114). Mahwah, NJ: Erlbaum.

Plant, E. A., & Devine, P. G. (1998). Internal and external motivation to respond without prejudice. *Journal of Personality and Social Psychology, 75,* 811–832.

Posner, M. I., & Snyder, C. R. R. (1975). Attention and cognitive control. In R. L. Solo (Ed.), *Information processing and cognition: The Loyola symposium* (pp. 55–85). Hillsdale, NJ: Erlbaum.

Pratto, F., Sidanius, J., Stallworth, L. M., & Malle, B. F. (1994). Social dominance orientation: A personality variable predicting social and political attitudes. *Journal of Personality and Social Psychology, 67,* 741–763.

Rothbart, M., & Birrell, P. (1977). Attitude and perception of faces. *Journal of Research in Personality 11,* 209–215.

Sagar, H. A., & Schofield, J. W. (1980). Racial and behavioral cues in black and white children's perceptions of ambiguously aggressive acts. *Journal of Personality and Social Psychology,* 39, 590–598.

Stapel, D. A., & Koomen, W. (2001). The impact of interpretation versus comparison mindsets on knowledge accessibility effects. *Journal of Experimental Social Psychology, 37,* 134–149.

Steele, C. M., & Aronson, J. (1995). Stereotype threat and the intellectual test performance of African Americans. *Journal of Personality and Social Psychology, 69,* 797–811.

Stroman, C. A. (1986). Television viewing and self-concept among Black children. *Journal of Broadcasting and Electronic Media,* 30, 87–93.

SuberviVelez, F. A., & Necochea, J. (1990). Television viewing and self-concept among Hispanic American children—A pilot study. *Howard Journal of Communications, 2,* 315–329.

Thompson, M. M., Naccarato, M. E., Parker, K. C. H., & Moskowitz, G. B. (2001). The personal need for structure and personal fear of invalidity measures: Historical perspectives, current applications, and future directions. In G. B. Moskowitz (Ed.), *Cognitive social psychology: The Princeton symposium on the legacy and future of social cognition* (pp. 19–39). Mahwah, NJ: Erlbaum.

von Hippel, W., Jonides, J., Hilton, J. L., & Narayan, S. (1993). Inhibitory effect of schematic processing on perceptual encoding. *Journal of Personality and Social Psychology, 64,* 921–935.

Walley, R. E., McLeod, B. E., & Khan, M. (1997). Tests of a translational model of Stroop interference: Translation or attention? *Canadian Journal of Experimental Psychology, 51,* 10–19.

Walley, R. E., McLeod, B. E., & Weiden, T. D. (1994). Increased attention to the irrelevant dimension increases interference in a spatial Stroop task. *Canadian Journal of Experimental Psychology, 48,* 467–492.

Wittenbrink, B., Judd, C. M., & Park, B. (1997). Evidence for racial prejudice at the implicit level and its relationship with questionnaire measures. *Journal of Personality and Social Psychology, 72,* 262–274.

NOTES

1. Gender did not moderate any of the effects we report in this or subsequent studies. In Study 3, there was a main effect of gender, such that men had faster reaction times for all targets than did women, $t(43) = 2.31$, $p = .03$, but this effect did not replicate in the other studies.
2. These point values should, objectively, create a bias to shoot: The two "don't shoot" options yield an average reward of –17.5 points, whereas the "shoot" options yield a less aversive average of –5 points.
3. The same pattern of signal detection results emerges both for Study 1 and for Study 3. For Study 1, sensitivity did not differ: African American $d' = 3.30$, White $d' = 3.28$, $F(1, 39) = 0.10$, $p = .75$; but the decision criterion did: African American $c = -0.17$, White, $c = -0.09$, $F(1, 39) = 10.07$, $p = .003$. In Study 3, sensitivity did not differ: African American $d' = 3.54$, White $d' = 3.56$, $F(1, 44) = 0.12$, $p = .73$; but the decision criterion did: African American $c = -0.02$, White $c = 0.07$, $F(1, 44) = 6.96$, $p = .02$.
4. The attempt to control for the prejudice composite measure, MCP, and their interaction only removes variance based on personal prejudice to the extent that these scales reliably measure that variance. There is reason to assume that these measures only partially assess prejudice, particularly for participants high in MCP. Thus, although the analysis represents our best attempt to examine the effects of cultural stereotypes over and above prejudice in the current dataset, it is nonetheless imperfect. Our thanks to Keith Payne for this insight.

Received February 11, 2002
Revision received July 5, 2002
Accepted July 5, 2002

READING 4

This article by Steele and Aronson (1995) triggered a wave of research and interest in what soon came to be known as *stereotype threat*—a predicament in which members of stereotyped groups face situations in which they have reason to fear being seen through the lens of negative stereotypes about their abilities in some domain. Many of the studies inspired by this article are discussed in Chapter 5 (Perceiving Groups). In the research presented here, Steele and Aronson test the provocative hypothesis that African American students may perform below their potential on intellectual tests because of this kind of threat. That is, the testing situation may bring to mind negative stereotypes and low expectations concerning African Americans' abilities on these kinds of tests, which makes African American students vulnerable to being undermined by these concerns. What's particularly exciting about this research is how a relatively simple change in the way the test is introduced to the students can eliminate this threat and allow African American students to perform to their potential.

Stereotype Threat and the Intellectual Test Performance of African Americans

Claude M. Steele
Stanford University

Joshua Aronson
University of Texas, Austin

Stereotype threat *is being at risk of confirming, as self-characteristic, a negative stereotype about one's group. Studies 1 and 2 varied the stereotype vulnerability of Black participants taking a difficult verbal test by varying whether or not their performance was ostensibly diagnostic of ability, and thus, whether or not they were at risk of fulfilling the racial stereotype about their intellectual ability. Reflecting the pressure of this vulnerability, Blacks underperformed in relation to Whites in the ability-diagnostic condition but not in the nondiagnostic condition (with Scholastic Aptitude Tests controlled). Study 3 validated that ability-diagnosticity cognitively activated the racial stereotype in these participants and motivated them not to conform to it, or to be judged by it. Study 4 showed that mere salience of the stereotype could impair Blacks' performance even when the test was not ability diagnostic. The role of stereotype vulnerability in the standardized test performance of ability-stigmatized groups is discussed.*

Claude M. Steele, Department of Psychology, Stanford University; Joshua Aronson, School of Education, University of Texas, Austin. This research was supported by National Institutes of Health Grant MH51977, Russell Sage Foundation Grant 879.304, and by Spencer Foundation and James S. McDonnell Foundation postdoctoral fellowships, and its completion was aided by the Center for Advanced Study in the Behavioral Sciences.

We thank John Butner, Emmeline Chen, and Matthew McGlone for assistance and helpful comments on this research.

Correspondence concerning this article should be addressed to Claude M. Steele, Department of Psychology, Stanford University, Stanford, California 94305, or Joshua Aronson, School of Education, University of Texas, Austin, Texas 78712.

Not long ago, in explaining his career-long preoccupation with the American Jewish experience, the novelist Philip Roth said that it was not Jewish culture or religion per se that fascinated him, it was what he called the Jewish "predicament." This is an apt term for the perspective taken in the present research. It focuses on a social-psychological predicament that can arise from widely-known negative stereotypes about one's group. It is this: the existence of such a stereotype means that anything one does or any of one's features that conform to it make the stereotype more plausible as a self-characterization in the eyes of others, and perhaps even in one's own eyes. We call this predicament *stereotype threat* and argue that it is experienced, essentially, as a self-evaluative threat. In form, it is a predicament that can beset the members of any group about whom negative stereotypes exist. Consider the stereotypes elicited by the terms *yuppie, feminist, liberal,* or *White male*. Their prevalence in society raises the possibility for potential targets that the stereotype is true of them and, also, that other people will see them that way. When the allegations of the stereotype are importantly negative, this predicament may be self-threatening enough to have disruptive effects of its own.

The present research examined the role these processes play in the intellectual test performance of African Americans. Our reasoning is this: whenever African American students perform an explicitly scholastic or intellectual task, they face the threat of confirming or being judged by a negative societal stereotype—a suspicion—about their group's intellectual ability and competence. This threat is not borne by people not stereotyped in this way. And the self-threat it causes—through a variety of mechanisms—may interfere with the intellectual functioning of these students, particularly during standardized tests. This is the principal hypothesis examined in the present research. But as this threat persists over time, it may have the further effect of pressuring these students to protectively disidentify with achievement in school and related intellectual domains. That is, it may pressure the person to define or redefine the self-concept such that school achievement is neither a basis of self-evaluation nor a personal identity. This protects the person against the self-evaluative threat posed by the stereotypes but may have the byproduct of diminishing interest, motivation, and, ultimately, achievement in the domain (Steele, 1992).

The anxiety of knowing that one is a potential target of prejudice and stereotypes has been much discussed: in classic social science (e.g., Allport, 1954; Goffman, 1963), popular books (e.g., Carter, 1991) and essays, as, for example, S. Steele's (1990) treatment of what he called *racial vulnerability*. In this last analysis, S. Steele made a connection between this experience and the school life of African Americans that has similarities to our own. He argued that after a lifetime of exposure to society's negative images of their ability, these students are likely to internalize an "inferiority anxiety"—a state that can be aroused by a variety of race-related cues in the environment. This anxiety, in turn, can lead them to blame others for their troubles (for example, White racism), to underutilize available opportunities, and to generally form a victim's identity. These adaptations, in turn, the argument goes, translate into poor life success.

The present theory and research do not focus on the internalization of inferiority images or their consequences. Instead they focus on the immediate situational threat that derives from the broad dissemination of negative stereotypes about one's group—the threat of possibly being judged and treated stereotypically, or of possibly self-fulfilling such a stereotype. This threat can befall anyone with a group identity about which some negative stereotype exists, and for the person to be threatened in this way, he need not even believe the stereotype. He need only know that it stands as a hypothesis about him in situations where the stereotype is relevant. We focused on the stereotype threat of African Americans in intellectual and scholastic domains to provide a compelling test of the theory and because the theory, should it be supported in this context for this group, would have relevance to an important set of outcomes.

Gaps in school achievement and retention rates between White and Black Americans at all levels of schooling have been strikingly persistent in American society (e.g., Steele, 1992). Well publicized at the kindergarten through 12th grade level, recent statistics show that they persist even at the college level where, for example, the national drop-out rate for Black college students (the percentage who do not complete college within a 6-year window of time) is 70% compared to 42% for White Americans (American Council on Education, 1990). Even among those who graduate, their grades average two thirds of letter grade lower than those of graduating Whites (e.g., Nettles, 1988). It has been most common to understand such problems as stemming largely from the socioeconomic disadvantage, segregation, and discrimination that African Americans have endured and continue to endure in this society, a set of conditions that, among other things, could produce racial gaps in achievement by undermining preparation for school.

Some evidence, however, questions the sufficiency of these explanations. It comes from the sizable literature examining racial bias in standardized testing. This work, involving hundreds of studies over several decades, generally shows that standardized tests predict subsequent school achievement as well for Black students as for White students (e.g., Cleary, Humphreys, Kendrick, & Wesman, 1975; Linn, 1973; Stanley, 1971). The slope of the lines regressing subsequent school achievement on entry-level standardized test scores is essentially the same for both groups. But embedded in this literature is another fact: At every level of preparation as measured by a standardized test—for example, the Scholastic Aptitude Test (SAT)—Black students with that score have poorer subsequent achievement—GPA, retention rates, time to graduation, and so on—than White students with that score (Jensen, 1980). This is variously known as the overprediction or underachievement phenomenon, because it indicates that, relative to Whites with the same score, standardized tests actually overpredict the achievement that Blacks will realize. Most important for our purposes, this evidence suggests that Black-White achievement gaps are not due solely to group differences in preparation. Blacks achieve less well than Whites even when they have the same preparation, and even when that preparation is at a very high level. Could this underachievement, in some part, reflect the stereotype threat that is a chronic feature of these students' schooling environments?

Research from the early 1960s—largely that of Irwin Katz and his colleagues (e.g., Katz, 1964) on how desegregation affected the intellectual performance of Black students—shows the sizable influence on Black intellectual performance of factors that can be interpreted as manipulations of stereotype threat. Katz, Roberts, and Robinson (1965), for example, found that Black participants performed better on an IQ subtest when it was presented as a test of eye-hand coordination—a nonevaluative and thus threat-negating test representation—than when it was said to be a test of intelligence. Katz, Epps, and Axelson (1964) found that Black students performed better on an IQ test when they believed their performance would be compared to other Blacks as opposed to Whites. But as evidence that bears on our hypothesis, this literature has several limitations. Much of the research was conducted in an era when American race relations were different in important ways than they are now. Thus, without their being replicated, the extent to which these findings reflect enduring processes of stereotype threat as opposed to the racial dynamics of a specific historical era is not clear. Also, this research seldomly used White control groups. Thus it is difficult to know the extent to which some of the critical effects were mediated by the stereotype threat of Black students as opposed to processes experienced by any students.

Other research supports the present hypothesis by showing that factors akin to stereotype threat—that is, other factors that add self-evaluative threat to test taking or intellectual performance—are capable of disrupting that performance. The presence of observers or coactors, for example, can interfere with performance on mental tasks (e.g., Geen, 1985; Seta, 1982). Being a "token" member of a group—the sole representative of a social category—can inhibit one's memory for what is said during a group discussion (Lord & Saenz, 1985; Lord, Saenz, & Godfrey, 1987). Conditions that increase the importance of performing well—prizes, competition, and audience approval—have all been shown to impair performance of even motor skills (e.g., Baumeister, 1984). The stereotype threat hypothesis shares with these approaches the assumption that performance suffers when the situation redirects attention needed to perform a task onto some other concern—in the case of stereotype threat, a concern with the significance of one's performance in light of a devaluing stereotype.

For African American students, the act of taking a test purported to measure intellectual ability may be enough to induce this threat. But we assume that this is most likely to happen when the test is also frustrating. It is frustration that makes the stereotype—as an allegation of inability—relevant to their performance and thus raises the possibility that they have an inability linked to their race. This is not to argue that the stereotype is necessarily believed; only that, in the face of frustration with the test, it becomes more plausible as a self-characterization and thereby more threatening to the self. Thus for Black students who care about the skills being tested—that is, those who are identified with these skills in the sense of their self-regard being somewhat tied to having them—the stereotypeloads the testing situation with an extra degree of self-threat, a degree not borne by people not stereotyped in this way. This additional threat, in turn, may interfere with their performance in a variety of ways: by causing an arousal that reduces the range of cues participants are able to use (e.g., Easterbrook, 1959), or by diverting attention onto task-irrelevant worries (e.g., Sarason, 1972; Wine, 1971), by causing an interfering self-consciousness (e.g., Baumeister, 1984), or overcautiousness (Geen, 1985). Or, through the ability-indicting interpretation it poses for test frustration, it could foster low performance expectations that would cause participants to withdraw effort (e.g., Bandura, 1977, 1986). Depending on the situation, several of these processes may be involved simultaneously or in alternation. Through these mechanisms, then, stereotype threat might be expected to undermine the standardized test performance of Black participants relative to White participants who, in this situation, do not suffer this added threat.

STUDY 1

Accordingly, Black and White college students in this experiment were given a 30-min test composed of items from the verbal Graduate Record Examination (GRE) that were difficult enough to be at the limits of most participants' skills. In the stereotype-threat condition, the test was described as diagnostic of intellectual ability, thus making the racial stereotype about intellectual ability relevant to Black participants' performance and establishing for them the threat of fulfilling it. In the nonstereotype-threat condition, the same test was described simply as a laboratory problem-solving task that was nondiagnostic of ability. Presumably, this would make the racial stereotype about ability irrelevant to Black participants' performance and thus preempt any threat of fulfilling it. Finally, a second nondiagnostic condition was included which exhorted participants to view the difficult test as a challenge. For practical reasons we were interested in whether stressing the challenge inherent in a difficult test might further increase participants' motivation and performance over what would occur in the nondiagnostic condition. The primary dependent measure in this experiment was participants' performance on the test adjusted for the influence of individual differences in skill level (operationalized as participants' verbal SAT scores).

We predicted that Black participants would underperform relative to Whites in the diagnostic condition where there was stereotype threat, but not in the two nondiagnostic conditions—the non-diagnostic-only condition and the non-diagnostic-plus-challenge condition—where this threat was presumably reduced. In the non-diagnostic-challenge condition, we also expected the additional motivation to boost the performance of both Black and White participants above that observed in the non-diagnostic-only condition. Several additional measures were included to assess the effectiveness of the manipulation and possible mediating states.

Method

Design and Participants This experiment took the form of a 2 × 3 factorial design. The factors were race of the participant, Black or White, and a test description factor in which the test was presented as either diagnostic of intellectual ability (the diagnostic condition), as a laboratory tool for studying problem solving (the non-diagnostic-only condition), or as both a problem-solving tool and a challenge (the non-diagnostic-challenge condition). Test performance was the primary dependent measure. We recruited 117 male and female, Black and White Stanford undergraduates through campus advertisements which offered $10.00 for 1 hr of participation. The data from 3 participants were excluded from the analysis because they failed to provide their verbal SAT scores. This left a total of 114 participants randomly assigned to the three experimental conditions with the exception that we ensured an equal number of participants per condition.

Procedure Participants who signed up for the experiment were contacted by telephone prior to their experimental participation and asked to provide their verbal and quantitative SAT scores, to rate their enjoyment of verbally oriented classes, and to provide background information (e.g., year in school, major, etc.). When participants arrived at the laboratory, the experimenter (a White man) explained that for the next 30 min they would work on a set of verbal problems in a format identical to the SAT exam, and end by answering some questions about their experience.

The participant was then given a page that stated the purpose of the study, described the procedure for answering questions, stressed the importance of indicating guessed answers (by a check), described the test as very difficult and that they should expect not to get many of the questions correct, and told them that they would be given feedback on their performance at the end of the session. We included the information about test difficulty to, as much as possible, equate participants' performance expectations across the conditions. And, by acknowledging the difficulty of the test, we wanted to reduce the possibility that participants would see the test as a miscalculation of their skills and perhaps reduce their effort. This description was the same for all conditions with the exception of several key phrases that comprised the experimental manipulation.

Participants in the diagnostic condition were told that the study was concerned with "various personal factors involved in performance on problems requiring reading and verbal reasoning abilities." They were further informed that after the test, feedback would be provided which "may be helpful to you by familiarizing you with some of your strengths and weaknesses" in verbal problem solving. As noted, participants in all conditions were told that they should not expect to get many items correct, and in the diagnostic condition, this test difficulty was justified as a means of providing a "genuine test of your verbal abilities and limitations so that we might better understand the factors involved in both." Participants were asked to give a strong effort in order to "help us in our analysis of your verbal ability."

In the non-diagnostic-only and non-diagnostic-challenge conditions, the description of the study made no reference to verbal ability. Instead, participants were told that the purpose of the research was to better understand the "psychological factors involved in solving verbal problems. . . ." These participants too were told that they would receive performance feedback, but it was justified as a means of familiarizing them "with the kinds of problems that appear on tests [they] may encounter in the future." In the non-diagnostic-only condition, the difficulty of the test was justified in terms of a research focus on difficult verbal problems and in the non-diagnostic-challenge condition it was justified as an attempt to provide "even highly verbal people with a mental challenge. . . ." Last, participants in both conditions were asked to give a genuine effort in order to "help us in our analysis of the problem solving process." As the experimenter left them to work on the test, to further differentiate the conditions, participants in the non-diagnostic-only condition were asked to try hard "even though we're not going to evaluate your ability." Participants in the non-diagnostic-challenge condition were asked to "please take this challenge seriously even though we will not be evaluating your ability."

Dependent Measures The primary dependent measure was participants' performance on 30 verbal items, 27 of which were difficult items taken from GRE study guides (only 30% of earlier samples had gotten these items correct) and 3 difficult anagram problems. Both the total number correct and an accuracy index of the number correct over the number attempted were analyzed.

Participants next completed an 18-item self-report measure of their current thoughts relating to academic competence and personal worth (e.g., "I feel confident about my abilities," "I feel self-conscious," "I feel as smart as others," etc.). These were measured on 5-point scales anchored by the phrases *not at all* (1) and *extremely* (5). Participants also completed a 12-item measure of cognitive interference frequently used in test anxiety research (Sarason, 1980) on which they indicated the frequency of several distracting thoughts during the exam (e.g., "I wondered what the experimenter would think of me," "I thought about how poorly I was doing," "I thought about the difficulty of the problems," etc.) by putting a number from 1 (*never*) to 5 (*very often*) next to each statement. Participants then rated how difficult and biased they considered the test on 15-point scales anchored by the labels *not at all* (1) and *extremely* (15). Next, participants evaluated their own performance by estimating the number of problems they correctly solved, and by comparing their own performance to that of the average Stanford student on a 15-point scale with the end points *much worse* (1) and *much better* (15). Finally, as a check on the manipulation, participants responded to the question:

> The purpose of this experiment was to: (a) provide a genuine test of my abilities in order to examine personal factors involved in verbal ability; (b) provide a challenging test in order to examine factors involved in solving verbal problems; (c) present you with unfamiliar verbal problems to measure verbal learning.

Participants were asked to circle the appropriate response.

Results

Because there were no main or interactive effects of gender on verbal test performance or the self-report measures, we collapsed over this factor in all analyses.

Manipulation Check Chi-square analyses performed on participants' responses to the postexperimental question about the purpose of the study revealed only an effect of condition, x^2 (2) = 43.18, $p < .001$. Participants were more likely to believe the purpose of the experiment was to evaluate their abilities in the diagnostic condition (65%) than in the nondiagnostic condition (3%), or the challenge condition (11%).

Test Performance The ANCOVA on the number of items participants got correct, using their self-reported SAT scores as the covariate (Black mean = 592, White mean = 632) revealed a significant condition main effect, $F(2, 107) = 4.74$, $p < .02$, with participants in the non-diagnostic-challenge condition performing higher than participants in the non-diagnostic-only and diagnostic conditions, respectively, and a significant race main effect, $F(1, 107) = 5.22$, $p < .03$, with White participants performing higher than Black participants.[1] The race-by-condition interaction did not reach conventional significance ($p < .19$). The adjusted condition means are presented in Figure 1.

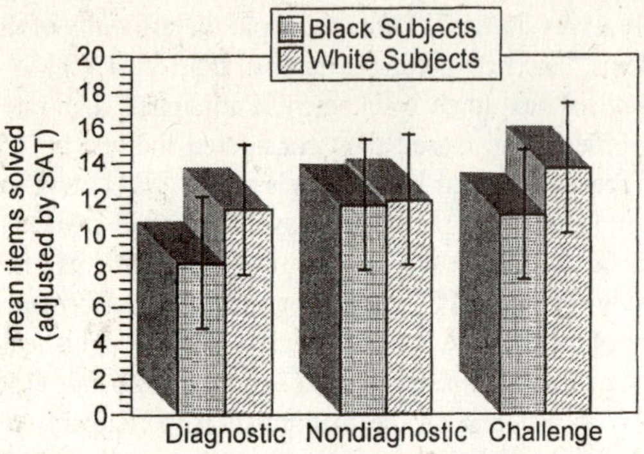

Figure 1. Mean test performance Study 1.

If making the test diagnostic of ability depresses the performance of Black students through stereotype threat, then their performance should be lower in the diagnostic condition than in either the non-diagnostic-only or non-diagnostic-challenge conditions which presumably lessened stereotype threat, and it should be lower than that of Whites in the diagnostic condition. Bonferroni contrasts[2] with SATs as a covariate supported this reasoning by showing that Black participants in the diagnostic condition performed significantly worse than Black participants in either the nondiagnostic condition, $t(107) = 2.88$, $p < .01$, or the challenge condition, $t(107) = 2.63$, $p < .01$, as well as significantly worse than White participants in the diagnostic condition $t(107) = 2.64$, $p < .01$.

But, as noted, the interaction testing the differential effect of test diagnosticity on Black and White participants did not reach significance. This may have happened, however, because an incidental pattern of means—Whites slightly outperforming Blacks in the nondiagnostic-challenge condition—undermined the overall interaction effect. To pursue a more sensitive test, we constructed a weighted contrast that compared the size of the race effect in the diagnostic condition with that in the nondiagnostic condition and assigned weights of zero to the White and Black non-diagnostic-challenge conditions. This analysis (including the use of SATs as a covariate) reached marginal significance, $F(1, 107) = 3.27$, $p < .08$. In sum, then, the hypothesis was supported by the pattern of contrasts, but when tested over the whole design, reached only marginal significance.

Accuracy An ANCOVA on accuracy, the proportion correct of the number attempted, with SATs as the covariate, found that neither condition main effect nor the interaction reached significance, although there was a marginally significant tendency for Black participants to evidence less accuracy, $p < .10$. This tendency was primarily due to Black participants in the diagnostic condition who had the lowest adjusted mean accuracy of any group in the experiment, .420. The adjusted means for the White diagnostic, White non-diagnostic-only, White non-diagnostic-challenge, Black non-diagnostic-only, and Black diagnostic-challenge conditions were, .519, .518, .561, .546, and .490, respectively. Bonferroni tests revealed that Black participants in the diagnostic condition were reliably less accurate than Black participants in the non-diagnostic-only condition and While participants in the diagnostic condition, $t(107) = 2.64$, $p < .01$, and $t(107) = 2.13$, $p < .05$, respectively.

No condition or interaction effects reached significance for the number of items completed or the number of guesses participants recorded on the test (all Fs < 1). The overall means for these two measures were 22.9 and 4.1, respectively.

Self-Report Measures There were no significant condition effects on the self-report measure of academic competence and personal worth or on the self-report measure of disruptive thoughts and feelings during the test. Analysis of participants' responses to the question about test bias yielded a main effect of race, $F(1, 107) = 10.47$, $p < .001$. Black participants in all conditions thought the test was more biased than White participants.

Perceived Performance Participants' estimates of how many problems they solved correctly and of how they compared to other participants both showed significant condition main effects, $F(2, 106) = 7.91$, $p < .001$, and $F(2, 107) = 3.17$, $p < .05$, respectively. Performance estimates were higher in the non-diagnostic-only condition ($M = 11.81$) than in either the diagnostic ($M = 9.20$) or non-diagnostic-challenge conditions ($M = 8.15$). Bonferroni tests showed that Black participants in the diagnostic condition ($M = 4.89$) saw their relative performance as poorer than Black participants in the non-diagnostic-only condition ($M = 6.54$), $t(107) = 2.81$, $p < .01$, and than Black participants in the nondiagnostic-challenge condition ($M = 6.30$), $t(107) = 2.40$, $p < .02$., while test description had no effect on the ratings of White participants. The overall mean was 5.86.

Discussion

With SAT differences statistically controlled, Black participants performed worse than White participants when the test was presented as a measure of their ability, but improved dramatically, matching the performance of Whites, when the test was presented as less reflective of ability. Nonetheless, the race-by-diagnosticity interaction testing this relationship reached only marginal significance, and then, only when participants from the nondiagnostic-challenge condition were excluded from the analysis. Thus there remained some question as to the reliability of this interaction.

We had also reasoned that stereotype threat might undermine performance by increasing interfering thoughts during the test. But the conditions affected neither self-evaluative thoughts nor thoughts about the self in the immediate situation (Sarason, 1980). Thus to further test the reliability of the predicted interaction and explore the mediation of the stereotype threat effect, we conducted a second experiment.

STUDY 2

We argued that the effect of stereotype threat on performance is mediated by an apprehension over possibly conforming to the negative group stereotype. Could this apprehension be detected as a higher level of general anxiety among stereotype-threatened participants? To test this possibility, participants in all conditions completed a version of the Spielberger State Anxiety Inventory (STAI) immediately after the test. This scale has been successfully used in other research to detect anxiety induced by evaluation apprehension (e.g., Geen, 1985). We also measured the amount of time they spent on each test item to learn whether greater anxiety was associated with more time spent answering items.

Method

Participants Twenty Black and 20 White Stanford female undergraduates were randomly assigned (with the exception of attaining equal cell sizes) to either the diagnostic or the nondiagnostic conditions as described in Study 1, yielding 10 participants per condition. Female participants were used in this experiment because, due to other research going on, we had considerably easier access to Black female undergraduates than to Black male undergraduates. This decision was justified by the finding of no gender differences in the first study, or, as it turned out, in any of the subsequent studies reported in this article—all of which used both men and women.

Procedure This experiment used the same test used in Study 1, with several exceptions; the final three anagram problems were deleted and the test period was reduced from 30 to 25 min. Also, the test was presented on a Macintosh computer (LCII). Participants controlled with the mouse how long each item or item component was on the screen and could, at their own pace, access whatever item material they wanted to see. The computer recorded the amount of time the items, or item components were on the screen as well as the number of referrals between item components (as in the reading comprehension items)—in addition to recording participants' answers.

Following the exam, participants completed the STAI and the cognitive interference measure described for Study 1. Also, on 11-point scales (with end-points *not at all* and *extremely*) participants indicated the extent to which they guessed when having difficulty, expended effort on the test, persisted on problems, limited their time on problems, read problems more than once, became frustrated and gave up, and felt that the test was biased.

Results and Discussion

The ANCOVA performed on the number of items correctly solved yielded a significant main effect of race, $F(1, 35) = 10.04$, $p < .01$, qualified by a significant Race × Test Description interaction, $F(1, 35) = 8.07$, $p < .01$. The mean SAT score for Black participants was 603 and for White participants 655. The adjusted means are presented in Figure 2. Planned contrasts on the adjusted scores revealed that, as predicted, Blacks in the diagnostic condition performed significantly worse than Blacks in the nondiagnostic condition $t(35) = 2.38$, $p < .02$, than Whites in the diagnostic condition $t(35) = 3.75$, $p < .001$, and than Whites in the nondiagnostic condition $t(35) = 2.34$, $p < .025$.

For accuracy—the number correct over the number attempted—a similar pattern emerged: Blacks in the diagnostic condition had lower accuracy ($M = .392$) than Blacks in the nondiagnostic condition ($M = .490$) or than Whites in either the diagnostic condition ($M = .485$) or the nondiagnostic condition ($M = .435$). The diagnosticity-by-race interaction testing this pattern reached significance, $F(1, 35) = 4.18$, $p < .05$. But the planned contrasts of the Black diagnostic condition against the other conditions did not reach conventional

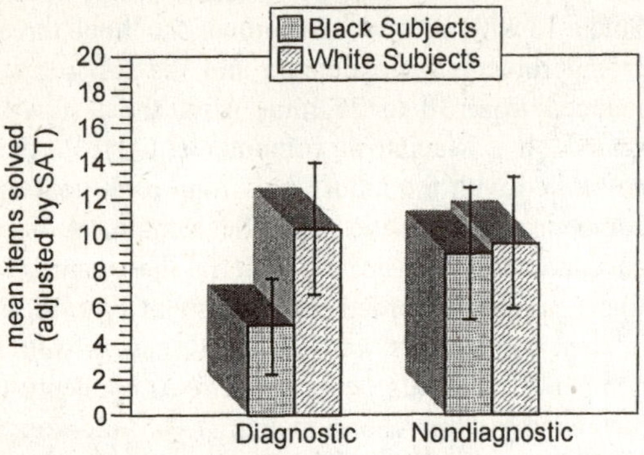

Figure 2. Mean test performance Study 2.

significance, although its contrasts with the Black nondiagnostic and White diagnostic conditions were marginally significant, with *ps* of .06 and .09 respectively.

Blacks completed fewer items than Whites, $F(1, 35) = 9.35$, $p < .01$, and participants in the diagnostic conditions tended to complete fewer items than those in the nondiagnostic conditions, $F(1, 35) = 3.69$, $p < .07$. The overall interaction did not reach significance. But planned contrasts revealed that Black participants in the diagnostic condition finished fewer items ($M = 12.38$) than Blacks in the nondiagnostic condition ($M = 18.53$), $t(35) = 2.50$, $p < .02$; than Whites in the diagnostic condition ($M = 20.93$), $t(35) = 3.39$, $p < .01$; and than Whites in the nondiagnostic condition ($M = 21.45$), $t(35) = 3.60$, $p < .01$.

These results establish the reliability of the diagnosticity-by-race interaction for test performance that was marginally significant in Study 1. They also reveal another dimension of the effect of stereotype threat. Black participants in the diagnostic condition completed fewer test items than participants in the other conditions. Test diagnosticity impaired the rate, as well as the accuracy of their work. This is precisely the impairment caused by evaluative pressures such as evaluation apprehension, test anxiety, and competitive pressure (e.g., Baumeister, 1984). But one might ask why this did not happen in the near-identical Study 1. Several factors may be relevant. First, the most involved test items—reading comprehension items that took several steps to answer—came first in the test. And second, the test lasted 25 min in the present experiment whereas it lasted 30 min in the first experiment. Assuming, then, that stereotype threat slowed the pace of Black participants in the diagnostic conditions of both experiments, this 5-min difference in test period may have made it harder for these participants in the present experiment to get past the early, involved items and onto the more quickly answered items at the end of the test, a possibility that may also explain the generally lower scores in this experiment.

This view is reinforced by the ANCOVA (with SATs as a covariate) on the average time spent on each of the first five test items—the minimum number of items that all participants in all conditions answered. A marginal effect of test presentation emerged, $F(1, 35) = 3.52$, $p < .07$, but planned comparisons showed that Black participants in the diagnostic condition tended to be slower than participants in the other conditions. On average they spent 94 s answering each of these items in contrast to 71 for Black participants in the nondiagnostic condition, $t(35) = 2.39$, $p < .05$; 73 s for Whites in the diagnostic condition, $t(35) = 2.12$, $p < .05$, and 71 s for Whites in the nondiagnostic condition, $t(35) = 2.37$, $p < .05$. Like other forms of evaluative pressure, stereotype threat causes an impairment of both accuracy and speed of performance.

No differences were found on any of the remaining measures, including self-reported effort, cognitive interference, or anxiety. These measures may have been insensitive, or too delayed. Nonetheless, we lack an important kind of evidence. We have not shown that test diagnosticity causes in Black participants a specific apprehension about fulfilling the negative group stereotype about their ability—the apprehension that we argue disrupts their test performance. To examine this issue we conducted a third experiment.

STUDY 3

Taking an intellectually diagnostic test and experiencing some frustration with it, we have assumed, is enough to cause stereotype threat for Black participants. In testing this reasoning, the present experiment examines several specific propositions.

First, if taking or expecting to take a difficult, intellectually diagnostic test makes Black participants feel threatened by a specifically racial stereotype, then it might be expected to activate that stereotype in their thinking and information processing. That is, the racial stereotype, and perhaps also the self-doubts associated with it, should be more cognitively activated for these participants than for Black participants in the nondiagnostic condition or for White participants in either condition (e.g., Dovidio, Evans, & Tyler, 1986; Devine, 1989; Higgins, 1989). Accordingly, in testing whether test diagnosticity arouses this state, the present experiment measured the effect of conditions on the activation of this stereotype and of related self-doubts about ability.

Second, if test diagnosticity makes Black participants apprehensive about fulfilling and being judged by the racial stereotype, then these participants, more than participants in the other conditions, might be motivated to disassociate themselves from the stereotype. Brent Staples, an African American editorialist for the *New York Times*, offers an example of this in his recent autobiography, *Parallel Time*. He describes beginning graduate school at the University of Chicago and finding that as he walked the streets of Hyde Park he made people uncomfortable. They grouped more closely when he walked by, and some even crossed the street to avoid him. He eventually realized that in that urban context, dressed as a student, he was being perceived through the lens of a race-class stereotype as a potentially menacing Black man. To deflect this perception he learned a trick; he would whistle Vivaldi. It worked. Upon hearing him do this, people around him visibly relaxed and he felt out of suspicion. If it is apprehension about being judged in light of the racial stereotype that interferes with the performance of Black participants in the diagnostic condition, then these participants, like Staples, might be motivated to deflect such a perception by showing that the broader racial stereotype is not applicable to them. To test this possibility, the present experiment measured the effect of conditions on participants' stated preferences for such things as activities and styles of music, some of which were stereotypic of African Americans.

Third, by adding to the normal evaluative risks of test performance the further risk of self-validating the racial stereotype, the diagnostic condition should also make Black participants more apprehensive about their test performance. The present experiment measured this apprehension as the degree to which participants self-handicapped their expected performance, that is, endorsed excuses for poor performance before the test.

The experiment took the form of a 2 × 3 design in which the race of participants (African American or White) was crossed with diagnostic, nondiagnostic, and control conditions. The diagnostic and nondiagnostic conditions were the same as those described for Study 2, while in the control condition participants completed the critical dependent measures without expecting to take a test of any sort. In the experimental conditions, the dependent measures were administered immediately after the diagnosticity instructions and just before the test was ostensibly to be taken. These included measures of stereotype activation, stereotype avoidance, and, as a measure of general performance apprehension, participants' willingness to self-handicap. Participants in this experiment never took the test. The measures of stereotype activation and stereotype avoidance, we felt, could activate the racial stereotype and stereotype threat among Black participants in both the diagnostic and nondiagnostic conditions, making performance results difficult to interpret.

If test diagnosticity threatens Black participants with a specifically racial stereotype, then Black participants in the diagnostic condition, more than participants in the other conditions, should show greater cognitive activation of the stereotype and ability-related self-doubts, greater motivation to disassociate themselves from the stereotype, and greater performance apprehension as indicated by the endorsement of self-handicapping excuses.

Method

Participants Thirty-five Black (9 male, 26 female) and 33 White (20 male, 13 female) Stanford undergraduates were randomly assigned to either a diagnostic, nondiagnostic, or control condition, yielding from 10 to 12 participants per experimental group.

Procedure A White male experimenter gave a booklet to participants as they arrived that explained that the study was examining the relationship between two types of cognitive processes: lexical access processing (LAP) and higher verbal reasoning (HVR). They were told that they would be asked to complete two tasks, one of which measured LAP—"the visual and recognition processing of words"—and the other of which measured HVR—"abstract reasoning about the meaning of words." Test diagnosticity was manipulated as in Study 1 with the following written instructions to further differentiate the conditions:

> *Diagnostic:* Because we want an accurate measure of your ability in these domains, we want to ask you to try as hard as you can to perform well on these tasks. At the end of the study, we can give you feedback which may be helpful by pointing out your strengths and weaknesses.

> *Nondiagnostic:* Even though we are not evaluating your ability on these tasks, we want to ask you to try as hard as you can to perform well on these tasks. If you want to

know more about your LAP and HVR performance, we can give you feedback at the end of the study.

Finally, participants were shown one sample item from the LAP (an item of the same sort as used in the fragment completion task) and three sample items from the HVR—difficult verbal GRE problems. The purpose of the HVR sample items was to alert participants to the difficulty of the test and the possibility of poor performance, thus occasioning the relevance of the racial stereotype in the diagnostic condition.

Participants in the control condition arrived at the laboratory to find a note on the door from the experimenter apologizing for not being present. The note instructed them to complete a set of measures lying on the desk in an envelope with the participant's name on it. The envelope contained the LAP word fragment measure and the stereotype avoidance measure (described below) with detailed instructions. No mention of verbal ability evaluation was made.

Measures *Stereotype activation.* Participants first performed a word-fragment completion task, introduced as the "LAP task," versions of which have been shown to measure the cognitive activation of constructs that are either recently primed or self-generated (Gilbert & Hixon, 1991; Tulving, Schacter, & Stark, 1982). The task was made up of 80 word fragments with missing letters specified as blank spaces (e.g., _ _ C E). Twelve of these fragments had as one possible solution a word reflecting either a race-related construct or an image associated with African Americans. The list was generated by having a group of 40 undergraduates (White students from the introductory psychology pool) generate a set of words that reflected the image of African Americans. From these lists, the research team identified the 12 most common constructs (e.g., lower class, minority) and selected single words to represent those constructs on the task. For example, the word "race" was used to represent the construct "concerned with race" on the task. Then, for each of the words placed on the task, at least two letter spaces were omitted and the word was checked again to determine whether other, non-stereotype-related associations to the word stem were possible. Leaving at least two letter spaces blank in each word fragment greatly unconstrains the number of word completions possible for each fragment when compared to leaving only one letter space blank. This reduces the chance of ceiling effects in which virtually all participants would think of the race-related fragment completion. The complete list was as follows: _ _ C E (RACE); L A _ _ (LAZY); _ _ A C K (BLACK); _ _ O R (POOR); C L _ S _ (CLASS); B R _ _ _ _ _ (BROTHER); _ _ _ T E (WHITE); M I _ _ _ _ _ _ (MINORITY); W E L _ _ _ _ (WELFARE); C O _ _ _ (COLOR); T O _ _ _ (TOKEN).

We included a fairly high number (12) of target fragments so that if ceiling or floor effects occurred on some fragments it would be less likely to damage the sensitivity of the overall measure. To reduce the chance that participants would become aware of the racial nature of the target fragments, they were spaced with at least three filler items between them, and there were only two target fragments per page in the task booklet. Participants were instructed to work quickly, spending no more than 15 s on each item.

Self-doubt activation. Seven word fragments reflecting self-doubts about competence and ability were included in the 80-item LAP task: L O _ _ _ (LOSER); D U _ _ (DUMB); S H A _ _ (SHAME); _ _ _ E R I O R (INFERIOR); F L _ _ _ (FLUNK); _ A R D (HARD); W _ _ K (WEAK). These were generated by the research team, and again included at least two blank letter spaces in each fragment. As with the racial fragments, these were separated from one another (and from the racial fragments) by at least three filler items.

Stereotype avoidance. This measure asked participants to rate their preferences for a variety of activities and to rate the self-descriptiveness of various personality traits, some of which were associated with images of African Americans and African American life. Participants in the diagnostic and nondiagnostic conditions were told that these ratings were taken to give us a better understanding of the underpinnings of LAP and HVR processes. Control participants were told that these measures were being taken to assess the typical interests and personality traits of Stanford undergraduates. The measure contained 57 items asking participants to rate the extent to which they enjoyed a number of activities (e.g., pleasure reading, socializing, shopping, traveling, etc.), types of music (e.g., jazz, rap music, classical music), sports (e.g., baseball, basketball, boxing), and finally, how they saw themselves standing on various personality dimensions (e.g., extroverted, organized, humorous, etc.). All ratings were made on 7-point Likert scales with 1 indicating the lowest preference or degree of trait descriptiveness. Some of these activities and traits were stereotypic of African Americans. For an item to be selected as stereotypic, 65% of our pretest sample of 40 White participants had to have generated the item when asked to list activities and traits they believed to be stereotypic of African Americans. In the activities category, the stereotype-relevant items were: "How much do you enjoy sports?" and "How much do you enjoy being a lazy 'couch potato'?" The stereotype-relevant music preference item was *rap music;* the stereotype-relevant sports preference item was *basketball;* and the stereotype-relevant trait ratings were *lazy* and *aggressive/belligerent.*

Participants also completed a brief demographic questionnaire (asking their age, gender, major, etc.) just before they expected to begin the test. As another measure of participants' motivation to distance themselves from the stereotype, the second item of this questionnaire gave them the option of recording their race. We reasoned that participants who wanted to avoid having their performance viewed through the lens of a racial stereotype would be less willing to indicate their race.

Self-handicapping measure. This measure just preceded the demographic questionnaire. The directions stated "as you know, student life is sometimes stressful, and we may not always get enough sleep, etc. Such things can affect cognitive functioning, so it will be necessary to ask how prepared you feel." Participants then indicated the number of hours they slept the night before in addition to responding, on 7-point scales (with 7 being the higher rating on these dimensions) to the following questions: "How able to focus do you feel?;" "How much stress have you been under lately?;" "How tricky/unfair do you typically find standardized tests?"

Results

Stereotype Activation A 2 (race) × 3 (condition: diagnostic, nondiagnostic, or control) ANCOVA (with verbal SAT as the covariate: Black mean = 581, White mean = 650) was performed on the number of target word fragments filled in with stereotypic completions. This analysis yielded significant main effects for both race, $F(1, 61) = 13.77$, $p < .001$, and for experimental condition, $F(2, 61) = 5.90$, $p < .005$. These main effects, however, were qualified by a significant Race × Condition interaction, $F(2, 61) = 3.30$, $p < .05$. Figure 3 shows that as expected, the diagnostic condition significantly increased the number of race-related completions of Black participants but not of White participants. Black participants in the diagnostic condition produced more race-related completions ($M = 3.70$) than Black participants in the nondiagnostic condition ($M = 2.10$), $t(61) = 3.53$, $p < .001$, or for that matter, more than participants in any of other conditions, all $ps < .05$.

Self Doubt Activation It did the same for their self doubts. The number of self-doubt-related completions of self-doubt target fragments were submitted to an ANCOVA (as described above) yielding a main effect of experimental condition, $F(2, 61) = 4.33$, $p < .02$, and a Race × Condition interaction, $F(2, 61) = 3.34$, $p < .05$. As Figure 3 shows, Black participants in the diagnostic condition, as predicted, generated the most self-doubt-related completions, significantly more than Black participants in the nondiagnostic condition, $t(61) = 3.52$, $p < .001$, and more than participants in any of the other conditions as well, all $ps < .05$.

Stereotype Avoidance The six preference and stereotype items described above were summed to form an index of stereotype avoidance that ranged from 6 to 42 with 6 indicating high avoidance and 42 indicating low avoidance (Cronbach's alpha = .65). When these scores were submitted to the ANCOVA they yielded a significant effect of condition, $F(2, 61) = 4.73$, $p < .02$, and a significant Race × Condition interaction, $F(2, 61) = 4.14$, $p < .03$. As can be seen in Figure 3, Black participants in the diagnostic condition were the most avoidant of conforming to stereotypic images of African Americans ($M = 20.80$), more so than Black participants in the nondiagnostic condition ($M = 29.80$), $t(61) = 3.61$, $p < .001$, and/or White participants in either condition, all $ps < .05$.

Indicating Race Did the ability diagnosticity of the test affect participants' tendency to indicate their race on the demographic questionnaire? Among Black participants in the diagnostic condition, only 25% would indicate their race on the questionnaire, whereas 100% of the participants in each of the other conditions would do so. Using a 0/1 conversion of the response frequencies (with 0 = refusal to indicate race and 1 = indication of race) the standard ANCOVA performed on this measure revealed a marginally significant effect of race, $F(1, 61) = 3.86$, $p < .06$, a significant effect of condition, $F(2.61) = 3.40$, $p < .04$, and a significant Race X Condition interaction, $F(1, 61) = 6.60$, $p < .01$, all due, of course, to the unique unwillingness of Black participants in the diagnostic condition to indicate their race.

Self-Handicapping Four measures assessed participants' desire to claim impediments to performance. Because participants in the control conditions did not complete this measure, these responses were submitted to separate 2(race) × 2(diagnosticity) ANCOVAs. Cell means are presented in Table 1. Framing the verbal

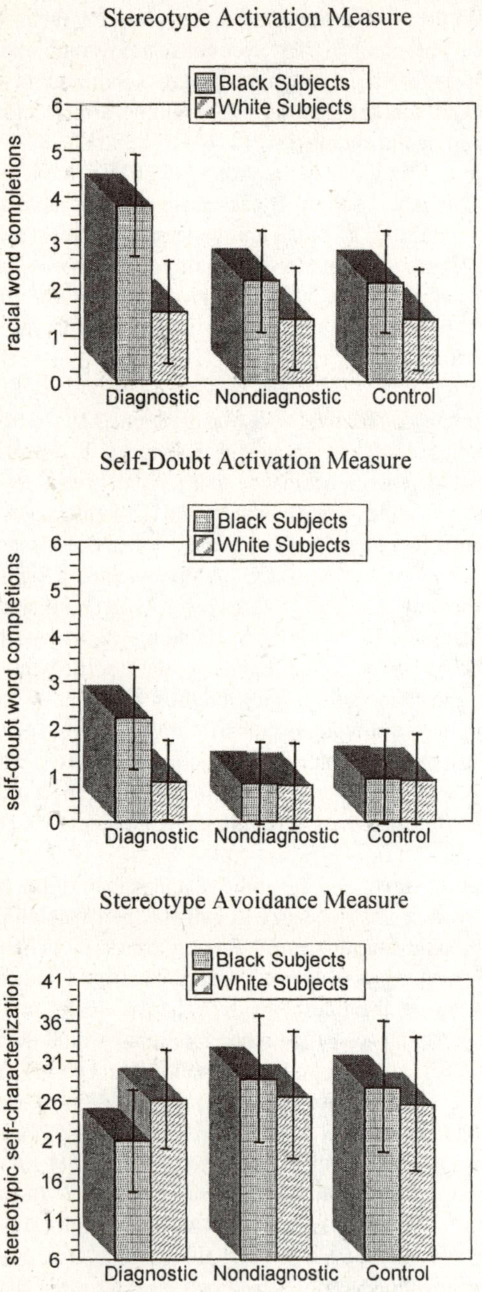

Figure 3. Indicators of stereotype threat.

tasks as diagnostic of ability had significant effects on three of the four measures. For the number of hours of sleep, the ANCOVA yielded a significant effect of race, $F(1, 39) = 8.22$, $p < .01$, and a significant effect of condition, $F(1, 39) = 6.53$, $p < .02$. These effects were qualified by a significant Race × Condition interaction, $F(1, 39) = 4.1$, $p < .01$. For participants' ratings of their ability to focus, a similar result emerged: main effects of race, $F(1, 39) = 7.26$, $p < .02$, and condition, $F(1, 39) = 10.67$, $p < .01$, and a significant qualifying interaction, $F(1, 39) = 5.73$, $p < .03$. And finally, the same pattern of effects emerged for participants' ratings of how tricky or unfair they generally find standardized tests to be: a race main effect, $F(1, 39) = 13.24$, $p < .001$, a condition main effect, $F(1, 39) = 13.42$, $p < .001$, and a marginally significant, qualifying interaction, $F(1, 39) = 3.58$, $p < .07$. No significant effects emerged on participants' ratings of their current stress.

Discussion

We had assumed that presenting an intellectual test as diagnostic of ability would arouse a sense of stereotype threat in Black participants. The present results dramatically support this assumption. Compared to participants in the other conditions—that is, Blacks in the nondiagnostic condition and Whites in either condition—Black participants expecting to take a difficult, ability-diagnostic test showed significantly greater cognitive activation of stereotypes about Blacks, greater cognitive activation of concerns about their ability, a greater tendency to avoid racially stereotypic preferences, a greater tendency to make advance excuses for their performance, and finally, a greater reluctance to have their racial identity linked to their performance even in the pedestrian way of recording it on their questionnaires. Clearly the diagnostic instructions caused these participants to experience a strong apprehension, a distinct sense of stereotype threat.

TABLE 1
Self-Handicapping Responses in Study 3

	Experimental condition			
	Diagnostic		Nondiagnostic	
Measure	Blacks ($n = 12$)	Whites ($n = 11$)	Blacks ($n = 11$)	Whites ($n = 10$)
Hours of sleep	5.10_a	7.48_b	7.05_b	7.70_b
Ability to focus	4.03_a	5.88_b	5.85_b	6.16_b
Current stress	5.51_a	5.24_a	5.00_a	5.02_a
Tests unfair	5.46_a	2.78_b	3.14_b	2.04_b

Note. Means not sharing a common subscript differ at the .01 level according to Bonferroni procedure. Means sharing a common subscript do not differ.

So far, then, we have shown that representing a difficult test as diagnostic of ability can undermine the performance of Black participants, and that it can cause in them a distinct sense of being under threat of judgment by a racial stereotype. This manipulation of stereotype threat—in terms of test diagnosticity—is important because it establishes the generality of the effect to a broad range of real-life situations.

But two questions remain. The first is whether stereotype threat itself—in the absence of the test being explicitly diagnostic of ability—is sufficient to disrupt the performance of these participants on a difficult test. That is, we do not know whether mere activation of the stereotype in the test situation—without the test being explicitly diagnostic of ability—would be enough to cause such effects. A second question is whether the disruptive effect of the diagnosticity manipulation was in fact mediated by the stereotype threat it caused. Showing first that test diagnosticity disrupts Black participants' performance and then, separately, that it causes in these participants to be threatened by the stereotype, does not prove that the effect of test diagnosticity on performance was mediated by the stereotype threat it caused. The performance effect could have been mediated by some other effect of the diagnosticity manipulation. We conducted a fourth experiment to address these questions, and thereby, to test the replicability of the stereotype threat effect under different conditions.

STUDY 4

This experiment again crossed a manipulation of stereotype threat with the race of participants in a 2 × 2 design with test performance as the chief dependent measure. We addressed the first question above by representing the test in this experiment as nondiagnostic of ability. If stereotype threat then depressed Black participants' performance, we would know that stereotype threat is sufficient to cause this effect even when the test is not represented as diagnostic of ability. We addressed the second question by taking from Study 3 a dependent measure of stereotype threat that had bee significantly affected by the diagnosticity manipulation, and manipulating that variable as an independent variable in the present experiment. If this manipulation then affects Black participants' performance, we would know that at least one aspect of the stereotype threat caused by the diagnosticity manipulation was able to impair performance. This would mean that the effect of that manipulation on performance was, or could have been, mediated by the stereotype threat it caused.

The variable that we manipulated in the present study was whether or not participants were required to list their race before taking the test. Recall that in Study 3, 75% of the Black participants in the diagnostic condition refused to record their race on the questionnaire when given the option, whereas all of the participants in the other conditions did. On the assumption that this was a sign of their stereotype avoidance, we reasoned that having participants record their race just prior to the test should prime the racial stereotype about ability for Black participants, and thus make them stereotype threatened. If this threat alone is sufficient to impair their performance, then, with SATs covaried, these participants should perform worse than White participants in this condition.

In the non-stereotype-threat conditions, the demographic questionnaire simply omitted the item requesting participants' race and, otherwise, followed the nondiagnostic procedures of Studies 1 and 2. Without raising the specters of ability or race-relevant evaluation, we expected Black participants in this condition to experience no stereotype threat and to perform (adjusted for SATs) on par with White participants.

Method

Design and Participants This experiment took the form of a 2 × 2 design in which participants' race was crossed with whether or not they recorded their ethnicity on a preliminary questionnaire. Twenty-four Black (6 male, 18 female) and 23 White (11 male, 12 female) Stanford undergraduates were randomly assigned to either the race-prime condition or the no-race-prime condition. Data from two Black participants were discarded because they arrived with suspicions about the racial nature of the study. One White student failed to provide her SAT score and was discarded from data analyses. These participants were replaced to bring the number of participants in each of the four conditions to 11.

Procedure The procedure closely paralleled that of the nondiagnostic conditions in Studies 1 and 2. After explaining the purpose and format of the test, the experimenter (White man) randomly assigned the participant to the race-prime or no-race-prime condition by drawing a brief questionnaire (labeled "personal information") from a shuffled stack. This questionnaire comprised the experimental manipulation. It was identical for all participants—asking them to provide their age, year in school, major, number of siblings, and parents' education—except that in the race-prime condition the final item asked participants to indicate their race. Because this questionnaire was given to the participant immediately prior to the test, the experimenter remained blind to the participant's condition throughout the pretest interaction. After ensuring that the participant had completed the questionnaire, the experimenter started the test and left the room. Twenty-five minutes later he returned, collected the test, and gave the participant a dependent measure questionnaire.

Dependent Measures This experiment used the same 25-min test used in Study 2, but in this experiment it was administered on paper. During the test, participants marked their guesses, and after the test, they indicated on 11-point scales (with end points *not at all* and *extremely*) the extent to which they guessed when they were having difficulty, expended effort on the test, persisted on problems, limited their time on problems, read problems more than once, became frustrated and gave up, and felt that the test was biased.

Participants also completed a questionnaire aimed at measuring their stereotype threat, by expressing their agreement on 7-point scales (with endpoints *strongly disagree* and *strongly agree*) with each of eight statements (e.g., "Some people feel I have less verbal ability because of my race," "The test may have been easier for people of my race," "The experimenter expected me to do poorly because of my race," "In English classes people of my race often face biased evaluations," "My race does not affect people's perception of my verbal ability").

As a measure of academic identification, nine further items explored the effect of conditions on participants' perceptions of the importance of verbal and math skills to their education and intended career (e.g., "verbal skills will be important to my career," "I am a verbally oriented person," "I feel that math is important to me," etc.). Participants responded to these items on 11-point scales with end-points labeled *not at all* and *extremely*.

Results

Test Performance A 2 (race) × 2 (race prime vs. no race prime) ANCOVA on test performance with self-reported SATs as a covariate (Black mean = 591, White

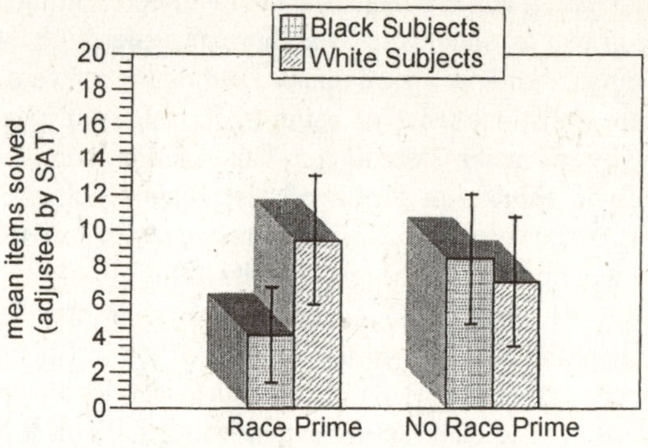

Figure 4. Mean test performance Study 4.

mean = 643) revealed a strong condition interaction in the predicted direction. As Figure 4 shows, Blacks in the race-prime condition performed worse than virtually all of the other groups, yet in the no-race-prime condition their performance equaled that of Whites, $F(1, 39) = 7.82$, $p < .01$. Planned contrasts on these adjusted scores revealed that, as predicted, Blacks in the race-prime condition performed significantly worse than Blacks in the no-race-prime condition, $t(39) = 2.43$, $p < .02$, and significantly worse than Whites in the race-prime condition, $t(39) = 2.87$, $p < .01$. Black participants in the race-prime condition performed worse than Whites in the no-race-prime condition, but not significantly so. Nonetheless, the comparison pitting the Black race-prime condition against the three remaining conditions was highly significant, $F(1, 39) = 8.15$, $p < .01$.

Accuracy The ANCOVA for this index—the percent correct of the items attempted for each participant—with participants' SATs as the covariate revealed a significant tendency for participants in the race-prime condition to have poorer accuracy, $F(1, 39) = 4.07$, $p = .05$. The adjusted means for the Black and White participants in the race-prime condition were .402 and .438 respectively, while those for the Black and White participants in the no-race-prime condition were .541 and .520 respectively. Condition contrasts did not reach significance, although the difference between the Black participants in the race-prime and no-race-prime conditions was marginally significant, $p < .08$. Again, these data suggest that lessened accuracy is part of the process through which stereotype threat impairs performance.

Number of Items Completed An ANCOVA (again with SATs removed as a covariate) revealed only a significant Race × Race Prime interaction for the number of test items participants completed, $F(1, 39) = 12.13$, $p < .01$. In the race-prime condition Blacks completed fewer items than Whites, $t(39) = 3.83$, $p < .001$. The adjusted means were 11.58 and 20.15 respectively. In the no-race-prime condition, however, Blacks and Whites answered roughly the same number of problems. The adjusted means were 15.32 and 13.03, respectively.

Performance-Relevant Measures Although participants' postexam ratings revealed no differences in the degree to which they thought they guessed on the test ($F < 1$), the ANCOVA performed on the actual number of guesses participants indicated on their test sheet revealed a Race × Race Prime interaction, $F(1, 39) = 5.56$, $p < .03$. Black participants made fewer guesses when race was primed ($M = 1.99$) than when it was not ($M = 2.74$), whereas White participants tended to guess more when race was primed ($M = 4.23$) than when it was not ($M = 1.58$). No significant condition effects emerged for participants' self-reported effort where, on an 11-point scale with 11 indicating *extremely hard* work, the overall mean was 8.84.

Participants' estimates of how well they had performed, taken after the test, showed no condition effects (the overall mean was 7.4 items). Neither were there condition effects on participants' ratings (made during the postexperimental debriefing) of how much having to indicate their ethnicity bothered them during the test (or *would* have bothered them in the case of participants in the no-race-prime condition). The overall mean was 3.31 on an 11-point scale for which 11 indicated the most distraction. Participants often stated in postexperimental interviews that they found recording their race unnoteworthy because they had to do it so often in everyday life. Of the items bearing on participants' experience taking the test, only one effect emerged: Black participants reported reading test items more than once to a greater degree than did White participants, $F(1, 39) = 8.62$, $p < .01$.

Stereotype Threat and Academic Identification Measures A MANOVA of the stereotype threat scale revealed that Black participants felt more stereotype threat than White participants, $F(9, 31) = 8.80$, $p < .01$. No other effects reached significance. Analyses of participants' responses to questions regarding the personal importance of math, verbal skills, and athletics revealed that Black participants reported valuing sports less than Whites, $F(1, 39) = 4.11$, $p < .05$. As in Study 3, this result may reflect Black participants distancing themselves from the stereotype of the academically untalented Black athlete. Correlations between participants' numerical performance estimates and their ratings of the importance of sports, showed that for Blacks, the worse they believed they performed, the more they devalued sports—in the no-race-prime condition ($r = .56$), and particularly in the race-prime condition ($r = .70$).

Discussion

Priming racial identity depressed Black participants' performance on a difficult verbal test even when the test was not presented as diagnostic of intellectual ability. It did this, we assume, by directly making the stereotype mentally available and thus creating the self-threatening predicament that their performance could prove the stereotype self-characteristic. In Studies 1, 2 and 3, the stereotype was evoked indirectly by describing the test as diagnostic of an ability to which it was relevant. What this experiment shows is that mere cognitive availability of the racial stereotype is enough to depress Black participants' intellectual performance, and that this is so even when the test is presented as not diagnostic of intelligence. Also—because we know from Study 3 that the diagnosticity manipulation strongly affects participants' willingness to record their race—this finding shows that the performance-depressing effect of the diagnosticity manipulation in the earlier experiments was, or could have been, mediated by the effect of that manipulation on stereotype threat—as opposed to some other aspect of the manipulation.

Still, we had expected Black participants in the race-prime condition to show more stereotype threat (as measured by the stereotype threat and stereotype avoidance measures) than Black participants in the no-race-prime condition—reflecting the effect of the manipulation. Instead, while Blacks showed more stereo type threat than Whites, Blacks in the race-prime condition showed no more stereotype threat than Blacks in the no-race-prime condition. Nor did these groups differ on the identification measures. This may have happened for several reasons. These measures came after the test in this experiment, not before it as in Study 3. Thus, after experiencing the difficult, frustrating exam, all Black participants may have been somewhat stereotype threatened and stereotype avoidant (more so than the White participants) regardless of their condition.

Also, the lack of a condition difference between Black participants on the stereotype threat and identification items may have occurred because these items asked participants to respond in reference to settings (e.g., English classes) and attitudes (e.g., about how one's race is generally regarded) that are beyond their immediate experience in the experiment.

Compared to participants in the other conditions, Black participants in the race-prime condition did not report expending less effort on the test; they were not more disturbed at having to list their race; and they did not guess more than other participants. Also, Black participants in both conditions reread the test items more than White participants. Such findings do not fit the idea that these participants underperformed because they withdrew effort from the experiment.

To establish the replicability of the race-prime effect and to explore the possible mediational role of anxiety, we conducted a two-condition experiment which randomly assigned only Black participants to either the race-prime or no-race-prime conditions described in Study 4. We also administered the test on computer to enable a measure of the time participants spent on the items, and gave participants an anxiety measure at the end of the experiment. Replicating Study 4, race-prime participants got significantly fewer items correct ($M = 4.4$) than no-race-prime participants ($M = 7.7$), $t(18) = 2.34$, $p < .04$; they were marginally less accurate ($M = .334$) than no-race-prime participants ($M = .395$), $p = .10$; and they answered fewer items ($M = 13.2$) than no-race-prime participants ($M = 20.1$), $t(18) = 2.89$, $p < .01$. Race-prime participants spent more time on the first five test items (the number which all participants completed) ($M = 79$ s) than no-race-prime participants ($M = 61$ s), $t(18) = 2.27$, $p < .04$, and they were significantly more anxious than no-race-prime participants, $t(18) = 2.34$, $p < .04$. The means on the STAI were 48.5 and 40.5 respectively, on a scale that ranged from 20 (indicating *low anxiety*) to 80 (*extreme anxiety*). These results show that a race prime reliably depresses Black participants' performance on this difficult exam, and that it causes reactions that could be a response to stereotype threat—namely, an anxiety-based perseveration on especially the early test items, items that, as reading comprehension items, required multiple steps.

GENERAL DISCUSSION

The existence of a negative stereotype about a group to which one belongs, we have argued, means that in situations where the stereotype is applicable, one is at risk of confirming it as a self-characterization, both to one's self and to others who know the stereotype. This is what is meant by stereotype threat. And when the stereotype involved demeans something as important as intellectual ability, this threat can be disruptive enough, we hypothesize, to impair intellectual performance.

In support of this reasoning, the present experiments show that making African American participants vulnerable to judgment by negative stereotypes about their group's intellectual ability depressed their standardized test performance relative to White participants, while conditions designed to alleviate this threat, improved their performance, equating the two groups once their differences in SATs were controlled. Studies 1 and 2 produced this pattern by varying whether or not the test was represented as diagnostic of intellectual ability—a procedure that varied stereotype threat by varying the relevance of the stereotype about Blacks' ability to their performance. Study 3 provided direct evidence that this manipulation aroused stereotype threat in Black participants by showing that it activated the racial stereotype and stereotype-related self-doubts in their thinking, that it led them to distance themselves from African American stereotypes. Study 4 showed that merely recording their race—presumably by making the stereotype salient—was enough to impair Black participants' performance even when the test was not diagnostic of ability. Taken together these experiments show that stereotype threat—established by quite subtle instructional differences—can impair the intellectual test performance of Black students, and that lifting it can dramatically improve that performance.

Mediation: How Stereotype Threat Impairs Performance

Study 3 offers clear evidence of what being stereotype threatened is like—as well as demonstrating that the mere prospect of a difficult, ability-diagnostic test was enough to do this to our sample of African American participants. But how precisely did this state of self-threat impair performance, through what mechanism or set of mechanisms did the impairment occur?

There are a number of possibilities: distraction, narrowed attention, anxiety, self-consciousness, withdrawal of effort, over-effort, and so on (e.g., Baumeister, 1984). In fact, several such mechanisms may be involved simultaneously, or different mechanisms may be involved under different conditions. For example, if the test were long enough to solidly engender low performance expectations, then withdrawal of effort might play a bigger mediational role than, say, anxiety, which might be more important with a shorter test. Such complexities notwithstanding, our findings offer some insight into how the present effects were mediated.

Our best assessment is that stereotype threat caused an inefficiency of processing much like that caused by other evaluative pressures. Stereotype-threatened participants spent more time doing fewer items more inaccurately—probably as a result of alternating their attention between trying to answer the items and trying to assess the self-significance of their frustration. This form of debilitation—reduced speed and accuracy—has been shown as a reaction to evaluation apprehension (e.g., Geen, 1985); test anxiety (e.g., Wine, 1971; Sarason, 1972); the presence of an audience (e.g., Bond, 1982); and competition (Baumeister, 1984). Several findings, by suggesting that stereotype-threatened participants were both motivated and inefficient, point in this direction. They reported expending as much effort as other participants. In those studies that included the requisite measures—Study 2 and the replication study reported with Study 4—they actually spent more time per item. They did not guess more than non-stereotype-threatened participants, and, as Black participants did generally, they reported rereading the items more. Also, as noted, these participants were strong students, and almost certainly identified with the material on the test. They may even have been more anxious. Stereotype threat increased Black participants' anxiety in the replication study, although not significantly in Study 2. Together then, these findings suggest that stereotype threat led participants to try hard but with impaired efficiency.

Still, we note that lower expectations may have also been involved, especially in real-life occurrences of stereotype threat. As performance falters under stereotype threat, and as the stereotype frames that faltering as a sign of a group-based inferiority, the individual's expectations about his or her ability and performance may drop—presumably faster than they would if the stereotype were not there to credit the inability interpretation. And lower expectations, as the literature has long emphasized (e.g., Bandura, 1977, 1986; Carver, Blaney, & Scheier, 1979; Pyszczynski & Greenberg, 1983) can further undermine performance by undermining motivation and effort. It is precisely a process of stereotype threat fostering low expectations in a domain that we suggest leads eventually to disidentification with the domain. We assume that this process did not get very far in the present research because the tests were short, and because our participants, as highly identified students, were unlikely to give up on these tests—as their self-reports tell us. But we do assume that lower expectations can play a role in mediating stereotype threat effects.

There is, however, strong evidence against one kind of expectancy mediation. This is the idea that lowered performance or self-efficacy expectations alone mediated the effects of stereotype threat. Conceivably, the stereotype threat treatments got Black participants to expect that they would perform poorly on the test—presumably by getting them to accept the image of themselves inherent in the racial stereotype. The stereotype threat condition did activate participants' self-doubts. This lower expectation, then, outside of any experience these participants may have had with the test itself, and outside of any apprehension they may have had about self-confirming the stereotype, may have directly weakened their motivation and performance. Of course it would be important to show that stereotype threat effects are mediated in African American students by expectations implicit in the stereotype, expectations powerful enough to more or less automatically cause their underperformance.

But there are several reasons to doubt this view. For one thing, it isn't clear that our stereotype threat manipulations led Black participants to accept lower expectations and then to follow them unrevisedly to lower performance. For example, they resisted the self-applicability of the stereotype. But most important, as noted, it is almost certain that any expectation formed prior to the test would be superseded by the participants' actual experience with the test items; rising with success and falling with frustration. In fact, another experiment in our lab offered direct evidence of this by showing that expectations manipulated before the test had no effect on performance. Its procedure followed, in all conditions, that of the standard diagnostic condition used in Studies 1 and 2—with the exception that it directly manipulated efficacy and performance expectations before participants took the test. After being told that the test was ability diagnostic, and just before taking the test, the experimenter (an Asian woman) asked participants what their SAT scores were. After hearing the score, in the positive expectation condition, she commented that the participant should have little trouble with the test. In the negative expectation condition, this comment indicated that the participant would have trouble with the test, and nothing was said in a no-expectation condition. Both White and Black participants were run in all three expectation conditions. While the experiment replicated the standard effect of Whites outperforming Blacks under these stereotype threat conditions (participants' SATs were again used as a covariate) $F(1, 32) = 5.12$, $p < .03$, this personalized expectation manipulation had no effect on the performance of either group. For Blacks, the means were 4.32, 6.38, and 6.55, for the positive, negative and no-expectations conditions, respectively, and for Whites, for the same conditions, they were 8.24, 9.25, and 11.23, respectively. Thus in an experiment that was sensitive enough to replicate the standard stereotype threat effect, expectations explicitly manipulated before the test had no effect on performance. They are unlikely, then, to have been the medium through which stereotype threat affected performance in this research.

Finally, participants in all conditions of these experiments were given low performance expectations by telling them that they should expect to get few items correct due to the difficulty of the test. Importantly, this instruction did not depress the performance of participants in the non-stereotype-threat conditions. Thus it is not likely that a low performance expectation, implied by the stereotype, would have been powerful enough, by itself, to lower performance among these participants when a direct manipulation of the expectation could not.

The Emerging Picture of Stereotype Threat

In the social psychological literature there are other constructs that address the experience of potential victims of stereotypes. For clarity's sake, we briefly compare the construct of stereotype threat to these.

"Token" Status and Cognitive Functioning Lord & Saenz (1985) have shown that token status in a group—that is, being the token minority in a group that is otherwise homogeneous—can cause deficits in cognitive functioning and memory, presumably as an outgrowth of the self-consciousness it causes. Although probably in the same family of effects as stereotype threat, token status would be expected to disrupt cognitive functioning even when the token individual is not targeted by a performance-relevant stereotype, as with, for example, a White man in a group of women solving math problems. Nor do stereotype threat effects require token status, as was shown in the present experiments. In real life, of course, these two processes may often co-occur, as for the Black in an otherwise non-Black classroom. They are nonetheless, distinct processes.

Attributional Ambiguity Another important theory, and now extensive program of research by Crocker and Major (e.g., Crocker & Major, 1989; Crocker, Voelkl, Testa, & Major, 1991) examined how people contend with the self-evaluative implications of having a stigmatized identity. Both their theory and ours focus on the psychology of contending with social devaluation and differ most clearly in which aspect of this psychology they attend to. The work of Crocker and Major focused on the implications of this psychology for self-esteem maintenance (for example, the strategies available for protecting self-esteem against stigmatized status) and we have focused on its implications for intellectual performance. There is also a conceptual difference. Attributional ambiguity refers to the confusion a potential target of prejudice might have over whether or not he is being treated prejudicially. Stereotype threat, of course, refers to his apprehension over confirming, or eliciting the judgment that the stereotype is self-characteristic. Again, the two processes can co-occur—as for the woman who gets cut from the math team, for example—but are distinct.

The Earlier Research of the Katz Group We also note that stereotype threat may explain the earlier findings of Katz and his colleagues. They found in the 1960s that the intellectual performance of Black participants rose and fell with conditions that seemed to vary in stereotype threat—for example, whether the test was represented as a test of intelligence or as one of psychomotor skill. A stereotype threat interpretation of these findings was foiled, however, by the lack of White participant control groups. Thus, the finding that manipulations very similar to Katz's depressed Black participants' performance while not depressing White participants' performance makes stereotype threat a parsimonious account of all these findings.

Test Difficulty and Racial Differences in Standardized Test Performance The test used in these experiments is quite difficult, as the low performance scores indicate. As we argued, it may have to be at least somewhat demanding for stereotype threat to be occasioned. But acknowledging this parameter raises a question: Does stereotype threat significantly undermine the performance of Black students on the SAT? And if it does, is it appropriate to use the SAT as the standard for equating Black and White participants on skill level within our experiments? The answer to the first question has to be that it depends on how much frustration is experienced on the SAT. If the student perceives that a significant portion of the test is within his or her competence, it may preempt or override stereotype threat by proving the stereotype inapplicable. When the student cannot gain this perception, however, the group stereotype becomes relevant as an explanation and may undermine performance. Thus we surmise that over the entire range of Black student test takers, stereotype threat causes a significant depression of scores.

And, of course, this point holds more generally. An important implication of this research is that stereotype threat is an underappreciated source of classic deficits in standardized test performance (e.g., IQ) suffered by Blacks and other stereotype-threatened groups such as those of lower socioeconomic status and women in mathematics (Herrnstein, 1973; Jensen, 1969, 1980; Spencer & Steele, 1994). In addition to whatever environmental or genetic endowments a person brings to the testing situation, this research shows that this situation is not group-neutral—not even, quite possibly, when the tester and test content have been accommodated to the test-taker's background. The problem is that stereotypes afoot in the larger society establish a predicament in the testing situation—aside from test content—that still has the power to undermine standardized test performance, and, we suspect, contribute powerfully to the pattern of group differences that have characterized these tests since their inception.

But, for several reasons, we doubt that this possibility compromises the interpretation of the present findings. First, it is unlikely that stereotype threat had much differential effect on the SATs of our Black and White participants since both groups, as highly selected students, are not likely to have experienced very great frustration on these tests. Second, even if our Black participants' SATs were more depressed in this way, using such depressed scores as a covariate in the present analyses would only adjust Black performance more in the direction of reducing the Black-White difference in the stereotype threat conditions. Thus, while a self-threateningly difficult test is probably a necessary condition for stereotype threat, and while stereotype threat may commonly depress the standardized test performance of Black test takers, these facts are not likely to have compromised the present results.

In conclusion, our focus in this research has been on how social context and group identity come together to mediate an important behavior. This approach is Lewinian; it is also hopeful. Compared to viewing the problem of Black underachievement as rooted in something about the group or its societal conditions, this analysis uncovers a social psychological predicament of race, rife in the standardized testing situation, that is amenable to change—as we hope our manipulations have illustrated.

REFERENCES

Allport, G. (1954). *The nature of prejudice*, New York: Addison-Wesley. American Council on Education. (1990). *Minorities in higher education.* Washington, DC: Office of Minority Concerns.

Bandura, A. (1977). Self-efficacy: Toward a unifying theory of behavioral change. *Psychological Review, 84*, 191–215.

Bandura, A. (1986). Fearful expectations and avoidant actions as coeffects of perceived self-inefficacy. *American Psychologist, 41*, 1389–1391.

Baumeister, R. F. (1984). Choking under pressure: Self-consciousness and paradoxical effects of incentives on skillful performance. *Journal of Personality and Social Psychology, 46*, 610–620.

Bond, C. F. (1982). Social facilitation: A self-presentational view. *Journal of Personality and Social Psychology, 42*, 1042–1050.

Carter, S. L. (1991). *Reflections of an affirmative action baby.* New York: Basic Books.

Carver, C. S., Blaney, P. H., & Scheier, M. F. (1979). Reassertion and giving up: The interactive role of self-directed attention and outcome expectancy. *Journal of Personality and Social Psychology, 37*, 1859–1870.

Cleary, T. A., Humphreys, L. G., Kendrick, S. A., & Wesman, A. (1975). Educational uses of tests with disadvantaged students. *American Psychologist, 30*, 15–41.

Crocker, J., & Major, B. (1989). Social stigma and self-esteem: The self-protective properties of stigma. *Psychological Review, 96*, 608–630.

Crocker, J., Voelkl, K., Testa, M., & Major, B. (1991). Social stigma: The affective consequences of attributional ambiguity. *Journal of Personality and Social Psychology, 60*, 218–228.

Devine, P. G. (1989). Stereotypes and prejudice: Their automatic and controlled components. *Journal of Personality and Social Psychology, 56*, 5–18.

Dovidio, J. F., Evans, N., & Tyler, R. B. (1986). Racial stereotypes: The contents of their cognitive representations. *Journal of Experimental Social Psychology, 22*, 22–37.

Easterbrook, J. A. (1959). The effect of emotion on cue utilization and the organization of behavior. *Psychological Review, 66*, 183–201.

Geen, R. G. (1985). Evaluation apprehension and response withholding in solution of anagrams. *Personality and Individual Differences, 6*, 293–298.

Geen, R. G. (1991). Social motivation. *Annual Review of Psychology, 42*, 377–399.

Gilbert, D. T., & Hixon, J. G. (1991). The trouble of thinking: Activation and application of stereotypic beliefs. *Journal of Personality and Social Psychology, 60*, 509–517.

Goffman, I. (1963). *Stigma*. New York: Simon & Shuster, Inc.

Herrnstein, R. (1973). *IQ in the meritocracy*. Boston: Little Brown.

Higgins, E. T. (1989). Knowledge accessibility and activation: Subjectivity and suffering from unconscious sources. In J. S. Uleman & J. A. Bargh (Eds.), *Unintended Thoughts* (pp. 75–123). New York: Guilford.

Jensen, A. R. (1969). How much can we boost IQ and scholastic achievement? *Harvard Educational Review, 39*, 1–123.

Jensen, A. R. (1980). *Bias in mental testing*. New York: Free Press.

Katz, I. (1964). Review of evidence relating to effects of desegregation on the intellectual performance of Negroes. *American Psychologist, 19*, 381–399.

Katz, I., Epps, E. G., & Axelson, L. J. (1964). Effect upon Negro digit symbol performance of comparison with Whites and with other Negroes. *Journal of Abnormal and Social Psychology, 69*, 963–970.

Katz, I., Roberts, S. O., & Robinson, J. M. (1965). Effects of task difficulty, race of administrator, and instructions on digit-symbol performance of Negroes. *Journal of Personality and Social Psychology, 2*, 53–59.

Linn, R. L. (1973). Fair test use in selection. *Review of Educational Research, 43*, 139–161.

Lord, C. G., & Saenz, D. S. (1985). Memory deficits and memory surfeits: Differential cognitive consequences of tokenism for tokens and observers. *Journal of Personality and Social Psychology, 49*, 918–926.

Lord, C. G., Saenz, D. S., & Godfrey, D. K. (1987). Effects of perceived scrutiny on participant memory for social interactions. *Journal of Experimental Social Psychology, 23*, 498–517.

Nettles, M. T (1988). *Toward undergraduate student equality in American higher education*. New York: Greenwood.

Pyszczynski, T., & Greenberg, J. (1983). Determinants of reduction in effort as a strategy for coping with anticipated failure. *Journal of Research in Personality, 17*, 412–422.

Sarason, I. G. (1972). Experimental approaches to test anxiety: Attention and the uses of information. In C. D. Spielberger (Ed.), Anxiety: *Current trends in theory and research* (Vol. 2). New York: Academic Press.

Seta, J. J. (1982). The impact of coactors' comparison processes on task performance. *Journal of Personality and Social Psychology, 42*, 281–291.

Spencer, S. J., & Steele, C. M. (1994). *Under suspicion of inability: Stereotype vulnerability and women's math performance.* Unpublished manuscript, State University of New York at Buffalo and Stanford University.

Stanley, J. C. (1971). Predicting college success of the educationally disadvantaged. *Science, 171*, 640–647.

Steele, C. M. (1992, April). Race and the schooling of black Americans. *The Atlantic Monthly*.

Steele, S. (1990). *The content of our character*. New York: St. Martin's Press.

Tulving, E., Schacter, D. L., & Stark, H. A. (1982). Priming effects in word-fragment completion are independent of recognition memory. *Journal of Experimental Psychology: Learning, Memory, and Cognition, 8*, 336–342.

Wine, J. (1971). Test anxiety and direction of attention. *Psychological Bulletin, 76*, 92–104.

NOTES

1. Because we did not warn participants to avoid guessing in these experiments, we do not report the performance results in terms of the index used by Educational Testing Service, which includes a correction for guessing. This correction involves subtracting from the number correct, the number wrong adjusted for the number of response options for each wrong item and dividing this by the number of items on the test. Because 27 of our 30 items had the same number of response options (5), this correction amounts to adjusting the number correct almost invariably by the same number. All analyses are the same regardless of the index used.
2. All comparisons of adjusted means reported hereafter used the Bonferroni procedure.

Received August 9, 1994
Revision received May 9, 1995
Accepted May 18, 1995

PART II

Social Influence

READING 5

Festinger's cognitive dissonance theory states that people seek to maintain a consistency between their beliefs and their actions—and that this motive can give rise to some irrational and sometimes maladaptive behavior. As discussed in Chapter 6 (Attitudes), this theory predicts that under certain conditions, people who find themselves behaving in ways that contradict their beliefs experience an unpleasant state of tension known as cognitive dissonance. To reduce this tension, they often change their attitude to bring it in line with their behavior, exhibiting a process of self-persuasion. The following study by Festinger and Carlsmith (1959) represents the first controlled test of this important theory. In this study, as you will see, people who were given little inducement to lie—compared to those who were highly paid for it—come to believe that lie as a way to justify their behavior.

Cognitive Consequences of Forced Compliance

Leon Festinger and James M. Carlsmith
Stanford University

What happens to a person's private opinion if he is forced to do or say something contrary to that opinion? Only recently has there been any experimental work related to this question. Two studies reported by Janis and King (1954; 1956) clearly showed that, at least under some conditions, the private opinion changes so as to bring it into closer correspondence with the overt behavior the person was forced to perform. Specifically, they showed that if a person is forced to improvise a speech supporting a point of view with which he disagrees, his private opinion moves toward the position advocated in the speech. The observed opinion change is greater than for persons who only hear the speech or for persons who read a prepared speech with emphasis solely on elocution and manner of delivery. The authors of these two studies explain their results mainly in terms of mental rehearsal and thinking up new arguments. In this way, they propose, the person who is forced to improvise a speech convinces himself. They present some evidence, which is not altogether conclusive, in support of this explanation. We will have more to say concerning this explanation in discussing the results of our experiment.

Kelman (1953) tried to pursue the matter further. He reasoned that if the person is induced to make an overt statement contrary to his private opinion by the offer of some reward, then the greater the reward offered, the greater should be the subsequent opinion change. His data, however, did not support this idea. He found, rather, that a large reward produced less subsequent opinion change that did a smaller reward. Actually, this finding by Kelman is consistent with the theory we will outline below but, for a number of reasons, is not conclusive. One of the major weaknesses of the data is that not all subjects in the experiment made an overt statement contrary to their private opinion in order to obtain the offered reward. What is more, as one might expect, the percentage of subjects who complied increased as the size of the offered reward increased. Thus, with self-selection of who did and who did not make the required overt statement and with varying percentages of subjects in the different conditions who did make the required statement, no interpretation of the data can be unequivocal.

Recently, Festinger (1957) proposed a theory concerning cognitive dissonance from which come a number of derivations about opinion change following forced compliance. Since these derivations are stated in detail by Festinger (1957, Ch. 4), we will here give only a brief outline of the reasoning.

Let us consider a person who privately holds opinion "X" but has, as a result of pressure brought to bear on him, publicly stated that he believes "not X."

1. This person has two cognitions which, psychologically, do not fit together: one of these is the knowledge that he believes "X," the other the knowledge that he has publicly stated that he believes "not X." If no factors other than his private opinion are considered, it would follow, at least in our culture, that

SOURCE: Leon Festinger and James M. Carlsmith. 1959. *JOURNAL OF ABNORMAL AND SOCIAL PSYCHOLOGY, 58,* 203–210.

our culture, that if he believes "X" he would publicly state "X." Hence, his cognition of his private belief is dissonant with his cognition concerning his actual public statement.

2. Similarly, the knowledge that he has said "not X" is consonant with (does fit together with) those cognitive elements corresponding to the reasons, pressures, promises of rewards and/or threats of punishment which induced him to say "not X."
3. In evaluating the total magnitude of dissonance, one must take account of both dissonances and consonances. Let us think of the sum of all the dissonances involving some particular cognition as "D" and the sum of all the consonances as "C." Then we might think of the total magnitude of dissonance as being a function of "D" divided by "D" plus "C."

   Let us then see what can be said about the total magnitude of dissonance in a person created by the knowledge that he said "not X" and really believes "X." With everything else held constant, this total magnitude of dissonance would decrease as the number and importance of the pressures which induced him to say "not X" increased.

   Thus, if the overt behavior was brought about by, say, offers of reward or threats of punishment, the magnitude of dissonance is maximal if these promised rewards or threatened punishments were just barely sufficient to induce the person to say "not X." From this point on, as the promised rewards or threatened punishment become larger, the magnitude of dissonance becomes smaller.
4. One way in which the dissonance can be reduced is for the person to change his private opinion so as to bring it into correspondence with what he has said. One would consequently expect to observe such opinion change after a person has been forced or induced to say something contrary to his private opinion. Furthermore, since the pressure to reduce dissonance will be a function of the magnitude of the dissonance, the observed opinion change should be greatest when the pressure used to elicit the overt behavior is just sufficient to do it.

The present experiment was designed to test this derivation under controlled, laboratory conditions. In the experiment we varied the amount of reward used to force persons to make a statement contrary to their private views. The prediction [from 3 and 4 above] is that the larger the reward given to the subject, the smaller will be the subsequent opinion change.

PROCEDURE

Seventy-one male students in the introductory psychology course at Stanford University were used in the experiment. In this course, students are required to spend a certain number of hours as subjects (*Ss*) in experiments. They choose among the available experiments by signing their names on a sheet posted on the bulletin board which states the nature of the experiment. The present experiment was listed as a two-hour experiment dealing with "Measures of Performance."

During the first week of the course, when the requirement of serving in experiments was announced and explained to the students, the instructor also told them about a study that the psychology department was conducting. He explained that, since they were required to serve in experiments, the department was conducting a study to evaluate these experiments in order to be able to improve them in the future. They were told that a sample of students would be interviewed after having served as *Ss*. They were urged to cooperate in these interviews by being completely frank and honest. The importance of this announcement will become clear shortly. It enabled us to measure the opinions of our *Ss* in a context not directly connected with our experiment and in which we could reasonably expect frank and honest expressions of opinion.

When the *S* arrived for the experiment on "Measures of Performance" he had to wait for a few minutes in the secretary's office. The experimenter (*E*) then came in, introduced himself to the *S* and, together, they walked into the laboratory room where the *E* said:

> This experiment usually takes a little over an hour but, of course, we had to schedule it for two hours. Since we have that extra time, the introductory psychology people asked if they could interview some of our subjects. [Offhand and conversationally.] Did they announce that in class? I gather that they're interviewing some people who have been in experiments. I don't know much about it. Anyhow, they may want to interview you when you're through here.

With no further introduction or explanation the *S* was shown the first task, which involved putting 12 spools onto a tray, emptying the tray, refilling it with spools, and so on. He was told to use one hand and to work at his own speed. He did this for one-half hour. The *E* then removed the tray and spools and placed in front of the *S* a board containing 48 square pegs. His task was to turn each peg a quarter turn clockwise, then another quarter turn, and so on. He was told again to use one hand and to work at his own speed. The *S* worked at this task for another half hour.

While the *S* was working on these tasks, the *E* sat, with a stopwatch in his hand, busily making notations on a sheet of paper. He did so in order to make it convincing that this was what the *E* was interested in and that these tasks, and how the *S* worked on them, was the total experiment. From our point of view the experiment had hardly started. The hour which the *S* spent working on the repetitive, monotonous tasks was intended to provide, for each *S* uniformly, an experience about which he would have a somewhat negative opinion.

After the half hour on the second task was over, the *E* conspicuously set the stop watch back to zero, put it away, pushed his chair back, lit a cigarette, and said:

> O.K. Well, that's all we have in the experiment itself. I'd like to explain what this has been all about so you'll have some idea of why you were doing this. [*E* pauses.] Well, the way the experiment is set up is this. There are actually two groups in the experiment. In one, the group you were in, we bring the subject in and give him essentially no introduction to the experiment. That is, all we tell him is what he needs to know in order to do the tasks, and he has no idea of what the experiment is all about, or what it's going to be like, or anything like that. But in the other group, we have a student that we've hired that works for us regularly, and what I do is take him into the next room where the subject is waiting—the same room you were waiting in before—and I introduce him as if he had just finished being a subject in the experiment. That is, I say: "This is so-and-so, who's just finished the experiment, and I've asked him to tell you a little of what it's about before you start." The fellow who works for us then, in conversation with the next subject, makes these points [The *E* then produced a sheet headed "For Group B" which had written on it: It was very enjoyable, I had a lot of fun, I enjoyed myself, it was very interesting, it was intriguing, it was exciting. The *E* showed this to the *S* and then proceeded with his false explanation of the purpose of the experiment.] Now, of course, we have this student do this, because if the experimenter does it, it doesn't look as realistic, and what we're interested in doing is comparing how these two groups do on the experiment—the one with this previous expectation about the experiment, and the other, like yourself, with essentially none.

Up to this point the procedure was identical for *Ss* in all conditions. From this point on they diverged somewhat. Three conditions were run, Control, One Dollar, and Twenty Dollars, as follows:

Control Condition

The *E* continued:

> Is that fairly clear? [Pause.] Look, that fellow [looks at watch] I was telling you about from the introductory psychology class said he would get here a couple of minutes from now. Would you mind waiting to see if he wants to talk to you? Fine. Why don't we go into the other room to wait? [The *E* left the *S* in the secretary's office for four minutes. He then returned and said:] O.K. Let's check and see if he does want to talk to you.

One and Twenty Dollar Conditions

The *E* continued:

> Is that fairly clear how it is set up and what we're trying to do? [Pause.] Now, I also have a sort of strange thing to ask you. The thing is this. [Long pause, some confusion and uncertainty in the following, with a degree of embarrassment on the part of the *E*. The manner of the *E* contrasted strongly with the preceding unhesitant and assured false explanation of the experiment. The point was to make it seem to the *S* that this was the first time the *E* had done this and that he felt unsure of himself.] The fellow who normally does this for us couldn't do it today—he just phoned in, and something or other came up for him—so we've been looking around for someone that we could hire to do it for us. You see, we've got another subject waiting [looks at watch] who is supposed to be in that other condition. Now Professor _________, who is in charge of this experiment, suggested that perhaps we could take a chance on your doing it for us. I'll tell you what we had in mind: the thing is, if you could do it for us now, then of course you would know how to do it, and if something like this should ever come up again, that is, the regular fellow couldn't make it, and we had a subject scheduled, it

> would be very reassuring to us to know that we had somebody else we could call on who knew how to do it. So, if you would be willing to do this for us, we'd like to hire you to do it now and then be on call in the future, if something like this should ever happen again. We can pay you a dollar (twenty dollars) for doing this for us, that is, for doing it now and then being on call; do you think you could do that for us?

If the S hesitated, the E said things like, "It will only take a few minutes," "The regular person is pretty reliable; this is the first time he has missed," or "If we needed you we could phone you a day or two in advance; if you couldn't make it, of course, we wouldn't expect you to come." After the S agreed to do it, the E gave him the previously mentioned sheet of paper headed "For Group B" and asked him to read it through again. The E then paid the S one dollar (twenty dollars), made out a hand-written receipt form, and asked the S to sign it. He then said;

> O.K., the way we'll do it is this. As I said, the next subject should be here by now. I think the next one is a girl. I'll take you into the next room and introduce you to her, saying that you've just finished the experiment and that we've asked you to tell her a little about it. And what we want you to do is just sit down and get into a conversation with her and try to get across the points on that sheet of paper. I'll leave you alone and come back after a couple of minutes. O.K.?

The *E* then took the *S* into the secretary's office where he had previously waited and where the next *S* was waiting. (The secretary had left the office.) He introduced the girl and the *S* to one another saying that the *S* had just finished the experiment and would tell her something about it. He then left saying he would return in a couple of minutes, the girl, an undergraduate hired for this role, said little until the *S* made some positive remarks about the experiment and then said that she was surprised because a friend of hers had taken the experiment the week before and had told her that it was boring and that she ought to try to get out of it. Most *Ss* responded by saying something like "Oh, no, it's really very interesting. I'm sure you'll enjoy it." The girl, after this listened quietly, accepting and agreeing to everything the *S* told her. The discussion between the *S* and the girl was recorded on a hidden tape recorder.

After two minutes the *E* returned, asked the girl to go into the experimental room, thanked the *S* for talking to the girl, wrote down his phone number to continue the fiction that we might call on him again in the future and then said: "Look, could we check and see if that fellow from introductory psychology wants to talk to you?"

From this point on, the procedure for all three conditions was once more identical. As the *E* and the *S* started to walk to the office where the interviewer was, the *E* said: "Thanks very much for working on those tasks for us. I hope you did enjoy it. Most of our subjects tell us afterward that they found it quite interesting. You get a chance to see how you react to the tasks and so forth," This short persuasive communication was made in all conditions in exactly the same way. The reason for doing it, theoretically, was to make it easier for anyone who wanted to persuade himself that the tasks had been, indeed, enjoyable.

When they arrived at the interviewer's office, the *E* asked the interviewer whether or not he wanted to talk to the *S*. The interviewer said yes, the *E* shook hands with the *S*, said good-bye, and left. The interviewer, of course, was always kept in complete ignorance of which condition the *S* was in. The interview consisted of four questions, on each of which the *S* was first encouraged to talk about the matter and was then asked to rate his opinion or reaction on an 11-point scale. The questions are as follows:

1. Were the tasks interesting and enjoyable? In what way? In what way were they not? Would you rate how you feel about them on a scale from 5 to +5 where –5 means they were extremely dull and boring, +5 means they were extremely interesting and enjoyable, and zero means they were neutral, neither interesting nor uninteresting.
2. Did the experiment give you an opportunity to learn about your own ability to perform these tasks? In what way? In what way not? Would you rate how you feel about this on a scale from 0 to 10 where 0 means you learned nothing and 10 means you learned a great deal.
3. From what you know about the experiment and the tasks involved in it, would you say the experiment was measuring anything important? That is, do you think the results may have scientific value? In what way? In what way not? Would you rate your opinion on this matter on a scale from 0 to 10 where 0 means the results have no scientific value or importance and 10 means they have a great deal of value and importance.
4. Would you have any desire to participate in another similar experiment? Why? Why not? Would you

rate your desire to participate in a similar experiment again on a scale from –5 to +5, where –5 means you would definitely dislike to participate, +5 means you would definitely like to participate, and 0 means you have no particular feeling about it one way or the other.

As may be seen, the questions varied in how directly relevant they were to what the *S* had told the girl. This point will be discussed further in connection with the results.

At the close of the interview the *S* was asked what he thought the experiment was about and, following this, was asked directly whether or not he was suspicious of anything and, if so, what he was suspicious of. When the interview was over, the interviewer brought the *S* back to the experimental room where the *E* was waiting together with the girl who had posed as the waiting *S*. (In the control condition, of course, the girl was not there.) The true purpose of the experiment was then explained to the *S* in detail, and the reasons for each of the various steps in the experiment were explained carefully in relation to the true purpose. All experimental *S*s in both One Dollar and Twenty Dollar conditions were asked, after this explanation, to return the money they had been given. All *S*s, without exception, were quite willing to return the money.

The data from 11 of the 71 *S*s in the experiment had to be discarded for the following reasons:

1. Five *S*s (three in the One Dollar and two in the Twenty Dollar condition) indicated in the interview that they were suspicious about having been paid to tell the girl the experiment was fun and suspected that that was the real purpose of the experiment.
2. Two *S*s (both in the One Dollar condition) told the girl that they had been hired, that the experiment was really boring but they were supposed to say it was fun.
3. Three *S*s (one in the One Dollar and two in the Twenty Dollar condition) refused to take the money and refused to be hired.
4. One *S* (in the One Dollar condition), immediately after having talked to the girl, demanded her phone number saying he would call her and explain things, and also told the *E* he wanted to wait until she was finished so he could tell her about it.

These 11 *S*s were, of course, run through the total experiment anyhow and the experiment was explained to them afterwards. Their data, however, are not included in the analysis.

Summary of Design

There remain, for analysis, 20 *S*s in each of the three conditions. Let us review these briefly: 1. *Control condition.* These *S*s were treated identically in all respects to the *S*s in the experimental conditions, except that they were never asked to, and never did, tell the waiting girl that the experimental tasks were enjoyable and lots of fun. 2. *One Dollar condition.* These *S*s were hired for one dollar to tell a waiting *S* that tasks, which were really rather dull and boring, were interesting, enjoyable, and lots of fun. 3. *Twenty Dollar condition.* These *S*s were hired for twenty dollars to do the same thing.

RESULTS

The major results of the experiment are summarized in Table 1 which lists, separately for each of the three experimental conditions, the average rating which the *S*s gave at the end of each question on the interview. We will discuss each of the questions on the interview separately, because they were intended to measure different things. One other point before we proceed to examine the data. In all the comparisons, the Control condition should be regarded as a baseline from which to evaluate the results in the other two conditions. The Control condition gives us, essentially, the reactions of *S*s to the tasks and their opinions about the experiment as falsely explained to them, without the experimental introduction of dissonance. The data from the other conditions may be viewed, in a sense, as changes from this baseline.

How Enjoyable the Tasks Were

The average ratings on this question, presented in the first row of figures in Table 1, are the results most important to the experiment. These results are the ones most directly relevant to the specific dissonance which was experimentally created. It will be recalled that the tasks were purposely arranged to be rather boring and monotonous. And, indeed, in the Control condition the average rating was –.45, somewhat on the negative side of the neutral point.

In the other two conditions, however, the *S*s told someone that these tasks were interesting and enjoyable. The resulting dissonance could, of course, most directly be reduced by persuading themselves that the tasks were, indeed, interesting and enjoyable. In the One Dollar condition, since the magnitude of dissonance was high,

TABLE 1
Average Ratings on Interview Questions for Each Condition

	Experimental Condition		
Question on Interview	Control ($N = 20$)	One Dollar ($N = 20$)	Twenty Dollars ($N = 20$)
How enjoyable tasks were (rated from −5 to +5)	−.45	+1.35	−.05
How much they learned (rated from 0 to 10)	3.08	2.80	3.15
Scientific importance (rated from 0 to 10)	5.60	6.45	5.18
Participate in similar exp. (rated from −5 to +5)	−.62	+1.20	−.25

the pressure to reduce this dissonance would also be high. In this condition, the average rating was +1.35, considerably on the positive side and significantly different from the Control condition at the .02 level[1] ($t = 2.48$).

In the Twenty Dollar condition, where less dissonance was created experimentally because of the greater importance of the consonant relations, there is correspondingly less evidence of dissonance reduction. The average rating in this condition is only −.05, slightly and not significantly higher than the Control condition. The difference between the One Dollar and Twenty Dollar conditions is significant at the .03 level ($t = 2.22$). In short, when an *S* was induced, by offer of reward, to say something contrary to his private opinion, this private opinion tended to change so as to correspond more closely with what he had said. The greater the reward offered (beyond what was necessary to elicit the behavior) the smaller was the effect.

Desire to Participate in a Similar Experiment

The results from this question are shown in the last row of Table 1. This question is less directly related to the dissonance that was experimentally created for the *S*s. Certainly, the more interesting and enjoyable they felt the tasks were, the greater would be their desire to participate in a similar experiment. But other factors would enter also. Hence, one would expect the results on this question to be very similar to the results on "how enjoyable the tasks were" but weaker. Actually, the result, as may be seen in the table, are in exactly the same direction, and the magnitude of the mean differences is fully as large as on the first question. The variability is greater, however, and the differences do not yield high levels of statistical significance. The difference between the One Dollar condition (+1.20) and the Control condition (−.62) is significant at the .08 level ($t = 1.78$). The difference between the One Dollar condition and the Twenty Dollar condition (−.25) reaches only the .15 level of significance ($t = 1.46$).

The Scientific Importance of the Experiment

This question was included because there was a chance that differences might emerge. There are, after all, other ways in which the experimentally created dissonance could be reduced. For example, one way would be for the *S* to magnify for himself the value of the reward he obtained. This, however, was unlikely in this experiment because money was used for the reward and it is undoubtedly difficult to convince oneself that one dollar is more than it really is. There is another possible way, however. The *S*s were given a very good reason, in addition to being paid, for saying what they did to the waiting girl. The *S*s were told it was necessary for the experiment. The dissonance could, consequently, be reduced by magnifying the importance of this cognition. The more scientifically important they considered the experiment to be, the less was the total magnitude of dissonance. It is possible, then, that the results on this question, shown in the third row of figures in Table 1, might reflect dissonance reduction.

The results are weakly in line with what one would expect if the dissonance were somewhat reduced in this manner. The One Dollar condition is higher than the other two. The difference between the One and Twenty Dollar conditions reaches the .08 level of significance on a two-tailed test ($t = 1.79$). The difference between the One Dollar and Control conditions is not impressive at all ($t = 1.21$). The result that the Twenty Dollar condition is actually lower than the Control condition is undoubtedly a matter of chance ($t = 0.58$).

How Much They Learned From the Experiment

The results on this question are shown in the second row for figures in Table 1. The question was included because, as far as we could see, it had nothing to do with the dissonance that was experimentally created and could not be used for dissonance reduction. One would then expect no differences at all among the three conditions. We felt it was important to show that the effect was not a completely general one but was specific to the content of the dissonance which was created. As can be readily seen in Table 1, there are only negligible differences among conditions. The highest *t* value for any of these differences is only 0.48.

DISCUSSION OF A POSSIBLE ALTERNATIVE EXPLANATION

We mentioned in the introduction that Janis and King (1954; 1956) in explaining their findings, proposed an explanation in terms of the self-convincing effect of mental rehearsal and thinking up new arguments by the person who had to improvise a speech. Kelman (1953), in the previously mentioned study, in attempting to explain the unexpected finding that the persons who complied in the moderate reward condition changed their opinion more than in the high reward condition, also proposed the same kind of explanation. If the results of our experiment are to be taken as strong corroboration of the theory of cognitive dissonance, this possible alternative explanation must be dealt with.

Specifically, as applied to our results, this alternative explanation would maintain that perhaps, for some reason, the *S*s in the One Dollar condition worked harder at telling the waiting girl that the tasks were fun and enjoyable. That is, in the One Dollar condition they may have rehearsed it more mentally, thought up more ways of saying it, may have said it more convincingly, and so on. Why this might have been the case is, of course, not immediately apparent. One might expect that, in the Twenty Dollar condition, having been paid more, they would try to do a better job of it than in the One Dollar condition. But nevertheless, the possibility exists that the *S*s in the One Dollar condition may have improvised more.

Because of the desirability of investigating this possible alternative explanation, we recorded on a tape recorder the conversation between each *S* and the girl. These recordings were transcribed and then rated, by two independent raters, on five dimensions. The ratings were, of course, done in ignorance of which condition each *S* was in. The reliabilities of these ratings, that is, the correlations between the two independent raters, ranged from .61 to .88, with an average reliability of .71. The five ratings were:

1. The content of what the *S* said *before* the girl made the remark that her friend told her it was boring. The stronger the *S*'s positive statements about the tasks, and the more ways in which he said they were interesting and enjoyable, the higher the rating.
2. The content of what the *S* said *after* the girl made the above-mentioned remark. This was rated in the same way as for the content before the remark.
3. A similar rating of the over-all content of what the *S* said.
4. A rating of how persuasive and convincing the *S* was in what he said and the way in which he said it.
5. A rating of the amount of time in the discussion that the *S* spent discussing the tasks as opposed to going off into irrelevant things.

The mean ratings for the One Dollar and Twenty Dollar conditions, averaging the ratings of the two independent raters, are presented in Table 2. It is clear from examining the table that, in all cases, the Twenty Dollar condition is slightly higher. The differences are small, however, and only on the rating of "amount of time" does the difference between the two conditions even approach significance. We are certainly justified in concluding that the *S*s in the One Dollar condition did not improvise more nor act more convincingly. Hence, the alternative explanation discussed above cannot account for the findings.

SUMMARY

Recently, Festinger (1957) has proposed a theory concerning cognitive dissonance. Two derivations from this theory are tested here. These are:

1. If a person is induced to do or say something which is contrary to his private opinion, there will be a tendency for him to change his opinion so as to bring it into correspondence with what he has done or said.
2. The larger the pressure used to elicit the overt behavior (beyond the minimum needed to elicit it) the weaker will be the above-mentioned tendency.

A laboratory experiment was designed to test these derivations. Subjects were subjected to a boring experience and then paid to tell someone that the experience had been interesting and enjoyable. The amount of money paid the subject was varied. The private opinions of the subjects concerning the experiences were then determined.

The results strongly corroborate the theory that was tested.

TABLE 2
Average Ratings of Discussion Between Subject and Girl

	Condition		
Dimension Rated	One Dollar	Twenty Dollar	Value of *t*
Content before remark by girl (rated from 0 to 5)	2.26	2.62	1.08
Content after remark by girl (rated from 0 to 5)	1.63	1.75	0.11
Over-all content (rated from 0 to 5)	1.89	2.19	1.08
Persuasiveness and conviction (rated from 0 to 10)	4.79	5.50	0.99
Time spent on topic (rated from 0 to 10)	6.74	8.19	1.80

REFERENCES

Festinger, L. A. *Theory of cognitive dissonance.* Evanston, Ill: Row Peterson, 1957.

Janis, I. L., & King, B. T. The influence of role-playing on opinion change. *J. Abnorm. Soc. Psychol.*, 1954, 49, 211–218.

Kelman, H. Attitude change as a function of response restriction. *Hum. Relat.*, 1953, 6, 185–214.

King, B. T., & Janis, I. L. Comparison of the effectiveness of improvised versus non-improvised role-playing in producing opinion changes. *Hum. Relat.*, 1956, 9, 177–186.

NOTES

1 All statistical tests referred to in this paper are two-tailed.

Received November 18, 1957

READING 6

Over the years, research has shown that as social animals, people are highly influenced by the judgments and behaviors of others, which is an essential theme of much of the research presented throughout the textbook, and most specifically in Chapter 7 (Conformity). Sometimes we conform because we are uncertain of how to react and so we turn to others for guidance. At other times, we conform in our public behavior to avoid standing out as different. But is conformity always the result of a calculated decision, or are people also vulnerable to subtle, almost reflex-like influences—as when we yawn in response to the sight of others yawning or laugh when we hear others laughing? Can this type of mimicry be demonstrated in a controlled experiment? In the following series of studies, Chartrand and Bargh (1999) had participants interact with a partner who exhibited certain motor habits and found that, without even realizing it, the participants imitated these behaviors, a phenomenon they called the "the chameleon effect" after the lizard that changes colors according to its physical environment. Why does this nonconscious form of influence occur? Read on and you will see.

The Chameleon Effect: The Perception–Behavior Link and Social Interaction

Tanya L. Chartrand and John A. Bargh
New York University

The chameleon effect *refers to nonconscious mimicry of the postures, mannerisms, facial expressions, and other behaviors of one's interaction partners, such that one's behavior passively and unintentionally changes to match that of others in one's current social environment. The authors suggest that the mechanism involved is the perception–behavior link, the recently documented finding (e.g., J. A. Bargh, M. Chen, & L. Burrows, 1996) that the mere perception of another's behavior automatically increases the likelihood of engaging in that behavior oneself. Experiment 1 showed that the motor behavior of participants unintentionally matched that of strangers with whom they worked on a task. Experiment 2 had confederates mimic the posture and movements of participants and showed that mimicry facilitates the smoothness of interactions and increases liking between interaction partners. Experiment 3 showed that dispositionally empathic individuals exhibit the chameleon effect to a greater extent than do other people.*

> He looked about his surroundings. They had become so familiar to him that, without realizing it, he was beginning to take on some of the mannerisms of the people who lived there.
>
> —Georges Simenon, *Maigret and the Toy Village*

As the saying goes, "Monkey see, monkey do." Primates, including humans, are quite good at imitation. Such imitation, in all primates, has generally been considered to be an intentional, goal-directed activity—for instance, mimicry helps one to learn vicariously from the experience of conspecifics or to ingratiate oneself to the other person (see Bandura, 1977; Galef, 1988; Heyes, 1993; Piaget, 1946; Tomasello, Savage-Rumbaugh, & Kruger, 1993).

This research was supported in part by National Science Foundation Grants SBR-9409448 and SBR-9809000.

We thank Vinnie Chawla, Catherine Cordova, Elina Geskin, Nora Guerra, Peter Karp, Marianna Moliver, and Christina Ungerer for serving as experimenters and confederates and Annette Lee Chai, Ap Dijksterhuis, Peter Gollwitzer, Katelyn McKenna, and Dan Wegner for helpful suggestions on an earlier version of this article.

Correspondence concerning this article should be addressed to Tanya L. Chartrand, who is now at the Department of Psychology, Ohio State University, 1885 Neil Avenue Mall, Columbus, Ohio 43210, or to John A. Bargh, Department of Psychology, New York University, 6 Washington Place, Seventh Floor, New York, New York 10003. Electronic mail may be sent to tanyac@psych.nyu.edu or to bargh@psych.nyu.edu.

SOURCE: Chartrand, T.L., & Bargh, J.A. 1999. The Chameleon Effect: The Perception-behavior Link and Social Interaction. *JOURNAL OF PERSONALITY AND SOCIAL PSYCHOLOGY, 76,* 893–910.

Recently, however, several studies have documented a passive, direct effect of social perception on social behavior, an effect that is unintended and not in the service of any discernible purpose (Bargh, Chen, & Burrows, 1996; Chen & Bargh, 1997; Dijksterhuis, Spears, et al., 1998; Dijksterhuis & van Knippenberg, 1998; Macrae et al., 1998; Mussweiler & Foerster, 1998). These findings suggest that imitation and mimicry effects in humans might often be unintentional (Chen, Chartrand, Lee Chai, & Bargh, 1998). As the popular meaning of the phrase "to ape" is "to intentionally imitate," perhaps the monkey metaphor may not be the most appropriate animal metaphor for the phenomenon.

We believe that the chameleon is a better one. In the motion picture *Zelig*, Woody Allen plays a human chameleon who cannot help but take on the behavior, personality, and values of whomever he is with. Like a chameleon changing its color to match its current surroundings, Zelig's behavior changes to match the norms and values of the group with which he is currently involved. Although Allen's film took this phenomenon to laughable extremes, it is nevertheless a common experience to discover, after the fact, that one has taken on the accent, speech patterns, and even behavioral mannerisms of one's interaction partners. The naturalness and nonconsciousness of this process was frequently commented on by the author Georges Simenon, whose fictional Inspector Maigret (the subject of the opening epigraph) routinely immersed himself in the lives of murder victims as a favorite method for solving the crimes.

Such a "chameleon effect" may manifest itself in different ways. One may notice using the idiosyncratic verbal expressions or speech inflections of a friend. Or one may notice crossing one's arms while talking with someone else who has his or her arms crossed. Common to all such cases is that one typically does not notice doing these things—if at all—until after the fact.

PERCEIVING IS FOR DOING

The Perception–Behavior Link

Throughout the history of psychology, many have argued that the act of perceiving another person's behavior creates a tendency to behave similarly oneself. To begin with, William James's principle of *ideomotor action* held that merely thinking about a behavior increases the tendency to engage in that behavior (James, 1890). This principle is in harmony with the proposed existence of a perception–action link, if one assumes perceptual activity to be one source of behavior-relevant ideation. Making just this assumption, Berkowitz (1984) invoked the principle of ideomotor action in his revised theory of how violence portrayed in the mass media increases the probability of aggression in the viewer. He argued that activation spread automatically in memory from representations of the perceived violent acts to other aggressive ideas of the viewer. This spreading activation to aggressive behavioral representations, he asserted, automatically led the viewer to behave in a more aggressive manner.

Carver, Ganellen, Froming, and Chambers (1983) tested Berkowitz's ideomotor account of modeling effects. They posited that individuals use *interpretive schemas* for perceiving and interpreting behaviors and *behavioral schemas* for producing behaviors. Because these two schemas are assumed to have substantial overlap in their semantic features, they should tend to become active at the same times. Carver et al. predicted that perceiving a hostile behavior in the environment would activate not only one's hostile interpretive schema, but one's hostile behavioral schema as well, so that the mere act of interpreting the behavior as hostile would make the perceiver more likely to behave in a hostile manner. Participants first were primed (or not) with hostile-related stimuli and then, in an ostensibly unrelated study, were to give shocks to another participant each time the latter made an error in a learning task. Results supported the hypothesis: Relative to the control group, participants who had been previously exposed to hostility-related priming stimuli gave longer shocks to the "learner."

Researchers in the area of language acquisition have also posited a "common-coding" principle to account for rapid language acquisition in young children. In a seminal paper, Lashley (1951) asserted that "the processes of language comprehension and language production have too much in common to depend on wholly different mechanisms" (p. 120). Following Lashley, Prinz (1990) hypothesized a common, or shared, representational system for language comprehension and action codes. He further suggested that the coding system for perceiving behaviors in others is the same as for performing those behaviors—and if so, he argued, that code cannot be used simultaneously in the service of perception and of behavior.

In an experimental demonstration of Prinz's (1990) thesis, Muesseler and Hommel (1997) instructed participants to reproduce certain sequences of four left and right arrow key presses as quickly as they could on each trial (the keys were labeled "<" and ">" respectively; thus, on one trial the sequence might be "< < > <" and on another trial "> < > <"). Participants practiced the sequence until they were ready to perform it rapidly. As soon as they made the first keypress of the sequence, however, the computer display briefly presented an additional left or right arrow key that they had been instructed to append to the end of their practiced sequence. The timing of this presentation was such that it occurred precisely when the participant was pressing the second of the four keys in the sequence. Which of the two keys ("<" or ">") was to be pressed at the end of the practiced sequence was manipulated to be either the same or the opposite of the key actually being pressed at that moment. As hypothesized, participants made more errors (i.e., more often pressed the wrong extra key) if the presented symbol corresponded to the one they were pressing at that moment than when it was different. Apparently, the behavior of pressing the right (or left) arrow key interfered with the ability to perceive the right (or left) arrow key symbol, consistent with Prinz's position that the same representation is used for perceiving as for behaving, and cannot be used for both at the same moment in time.

Priming of Social Behavior

The existence of an automatic, unintended, and passive effect of perception on behavior has important ramifications for whether social behavior can occur nonconsciously and without intention. If the effect of perception on behavior is automatic, then direct environmental causation of social behavior could be produced in a two-step process. The first would involve automatic (i.e., not effortful or consciously guided) perceptual categorization and interpretation of social behavior (environment to perception), with this perceptual activation continuing on to activate corresponding behavioral representations (perception to behavior). In this way, the entire sequence from environment to behavior would occur automatically, without conscious choice or guidance playing a role (see Bargh & Chartrand, 1999).

Regarding the first stage of this hypothetical sequence, it is now widely accepted that much of social perceptual activity is automated (i.e., immediate, efficient, and not consciously guided). Many years of research have demonstrated the variety of ways in which (a) behaviors are encoded spontaneously and without intention in terms of relevant trait concepts (e.g., Bargh & Thein, 1985; Carlston & Skowronski, 1994; Uleman, Newman, & Moskowitz, 1996; Winter & Uleman, 1984), (b) contextual priming of trait concepts changes the perceiver's interpretation of an identical behavior through temporarily increasing their accessibility or readiness to be used (see Bargh, 1989; Higgins, 1989, 1996; Wyer & Srull, 1989, for reviews), and (c) stereotypes of social groups become activated automatically upon the mere perception of the distinguishing features of a group member (e.g., Bargh, 1994, 1999; Brewer, 1988; Devine, 1989).

Thus, if the automatic activation of perceptual representations continuously activates behavioral representations, the same priming manipulations that have been shown to influence social perception should also influence social behavior. In support of this prediction, Bargh, Chen, et al. (1996) found that when stereotypes or trait constructs were "primed," or nonconsciously activated in the course of an unrelated task, the participant subsequently was more likely to act in line with the content of the primed trait construct or stereotype. In Experiment 1, in what was ostensibly a language test, participants were exposed to words related to either rudeness (e.g., "rude," "impolite," and "obnoxious"), politeness (e.g., "respect," "considerate," and "polite"), or neither (in the control condition); considerable previous work on impression formation using the same priming method (but with varying trait content; e.g., Banaji, Hardin, & Rothman, 1993; Srull & Wyer, 1979, 1980) had shown it to activate the corresponding perceptual trait constructs. On the basis of the hypothesized perception–behavior link, this activation was expected to continuously activate the behavioral constructs of rudeness or politeness, increasing the likelihood of such behavior.

After completing this priming task, participants encountered a situation in which they could either behave in a rude fashion and interrupt an ongoing conversation or behave in a polite fashion and wait for the conversation to end on its own—without the participant's intervention, the conversation would continue on for 10 min. Results showed that significantly more participants in the rude priming condition (67%) interrupted the conversation than did those in the control condition (38%), whereas only 16% of those primed with the polite condition interrupted it—in other words, fully 84% of participants in the politeness priming condition waited the entire 10 min without interrupting.

Experiment 2 of Bargh, Chen, et al. (1996) extended these findings to the case of stereotype (collections of group-related traits, as opposed to single-trait concepts) activation. Participants were first primed either with words related to the stereotype of the elderly (e.g., "Florida," "sentimental," "wrinkle") or with words unrelated to the stereotype. Importantly, none of the primes was semantically related to slowness or weakness, though these concepts are components of the stereotype. As predicted, priming the stereotype caused participants to subsequently behave in line with the stereotype content; specifically, they walked more slowly down the hallway after leaving the experiment. Experiment 3 conceptually replicated this effect by subliminally presenting faces of young male African Americans to some participants, who then reacted to a provocation with greater hostility (a component of the African American stereotype; see, e.g., Devine, 1989) than did control participants. This latter effect was replicated and extended by Chen and Bargh (1997).

Dijksterhuis and van Knippenberg (1998) have conceptually replicated these findings by demonstrating that priming a stereotype or trait can affect subsequent performance on an intellectual task. In several studies, these researchers primed participants with a positive stereotype ("professor"), a negative stereotype ("soccer hooligans"), a positive trait ("intelligent"), or a negative trait ("stupid"). Those participants primed with either the professor stereotype or the "intelligent" trait showed enhanced performance on a general knowledge scale (similar to Trivial Pursuit), whereas those primed with the hooligan stereotype or the "stupid" trait showed decreased performance.

Mediational Evidence

The Bargh, Chen, et al. (1996) and Dijksterhuis and van Knippenberg (1998) studies showed that priming techniques produce changes in behavior based on the hypothesis of an automatic perception–behavior link. However, these studies (as well as that of Carver et al., 1983) did not provide evidence that perceptual activity mediated the effect of priming on behavior, because perception itself was never manipulated (or measured). It remains possible that environmental events (which priming manipulations simulate) directly activate perception and separately directly activate behavioral tendencies.

One way to show that passive perceptual activity automatically causes behavior would be to show that manipulations known to cause changes in perception and judgment produce corresponding changes in behavior. Dijksterhuis and his colleagues (Dijksterhuis, Aarts, Bargh, & van Knippenberg, 1998; Dijksterhuis, Spears, et al., 1998) have conducted a series of such studies.

Assimilation and contrast effects in automatic behavior Research in social perception has documented two main forms of representation that moderate social judgments: trait categories (e.g., honesty) and exemplars (representations of specific people who exemplify the trait, such as Einstein for intelligence). In general, the evidence shows that activated trait categories usually produce assimilation effects; ambiguously relevant behavior is assimilated into the category rather than contrasted against it. A person whose trait category of honesty is in a heightened state of accessibility or activation is more likely than the average person to consider someone generous when he or she gives money to a charity following his or her boss's request to do so (e.g., Higgins, Rholes, & Jones, 1977; Srull & Wyer, 1979). But if a person is thinking about exemplars of a given trait, such as Einstein for the "intelligent" trait, then ambiguously relevant behaviors (getting a B on a test) are seen as less, not more representative of that trait (Herr, Sherman, & Fazio, 1984; Smith & Zarate, 1992; Stapel, Koomen, & van der Pligt, 1997). The exemplar sets a high standard against which mundane trait-consistent behaviors pale in comparison.

If perception mediates the ideomotor effects of the environment on behavior, then one should find assimilation effects on behavior with category priming and contrast effects on behavior with exemplar priming—the same effects one obtains on perceptual and judgmental dependent measures. Confirming this prediction, Dijksterhuis, Spears, et al. (1998) showed that priming (without specific examples) the stereotype of professors versus that of supermodels (the latter group being stereotypically viewed as unintelligent by the participant population) produced assimilation effects on behavior. Those participants primed with the professor stereotype gave more correct answers on a subsequent knowledge test than did those primed with the supermodel stereotype. But when specific exemplars of the two categories served as the priming stimuli (e.g., Albert Einstein and Claudia Schiffer), the opposite pattern was obtained; that is, contrast effects on behavior were observed.

Amount of experience mediates perception–behavior effects Another approach to gaining positive evidence of mediation by perceptual activity is to assess individual differences regarding how much contact the individual has had with that group. The more contact, the stronger and more automatic the perceptual representation, and thus the stronger and more likely the behavioral effect. Dijksterhuis, Aarts, et al. (1998) assessed how much contact college-age experimental participants had per week with the elderly. It was assumed that greater amounts of contact with the elderly would correspond to stronger perceptual associations between being elderly and having relatively poor memory. In the course of a lexical decision task, it was shown that the greater the participant's amount of contact with the elderly, the stronger the association between the concepts of the elderly and of forgetfulness. Moreover, a subsequent memory test for all of the target stimuli in the lexical decision task showed that greater amounts of contact with the elderly were related to poorer memory performance. Most importantly, however, the effect of contact on memory was entirely mediated by the strength of the perceptual association between the concepts *elderly* and *forgetful.* There was no direct effect of amount of contact on behavior that was not mediated by the strength of the perceptual representation.

RESEARCH ON BEHAVIORAL COORDINATION

Observations of and theories about nonconscious mimicry have a long history (see Bandura, 1977; Bavelas, Black, Lemery, & Mullett, 1987; Koffka, 1925; Piaget, 1946). Interestingly, most of the early writers on the topic conceptualized mimicry in terms of empathy. Adam Smith (1759/1966), for example, posited that reflexive imitation occurs after one takes the perspective of the other and realizes what he or she must feel, and Charles Darwin (1872/1965) used the term sympathy to refer to imitation based on reflex or habit. In fact, according to Gordon Allport (1968), the original meaning of the term empathy was "objective motor mimicry"; it was only in the latter half of the 20th century that it came to be used as a global term encompassing vicarious emotion, role taking, and the ability to understand others.

Research on nonconscious mimicry began after a seminal paper by Scheflen in 1964. He observed that postural configurations were a source of information about an ongoing social interaction, as they communicated messages about liking and understanding. Moreover, individuals were said to utilize this postural information unconsciously to orient themselves within a group. Three basic lines of research on behavioral coordination developed thereafter (see Bernieri & Rosenthal, 1991). Research on rhythmic synchrony has included work on the precise synchronization between the speech and body movements of the two interaction partners (Bernieri, 1988; Condon & Ogston, 1966; Condon & Sander, 1974; Dittmann & Llewellyn, 1968, 1969; Kendon, 1970; cf. McDowall, 1978). Facial mimicry research has focused on neonates' mimicry of adult facial expressions (Meltzoff & Moore, 1977, 1979, 1983; cf. Kaitz, Meschulach-Sarfaty, Auerbach, & Eidelman, 1988). However, no consensus developed from this research as to the mechanisms responsible for the effect (Anisfeld, 1979; Jacobson & Kagan, 1979; Masters, 1979).

Facial mimicry has also been found in adults (Dimberg, 1982; Vaughan & Lanzetta, 1980; Zajonc, Adelmann, Murphy, & Niedenthal, 1987), although it is not clear from these studies whether the observers actually experience the same emotions as the other person or simply mimic his or her facial expressions. The Zajonc et al. finding that couples grow to resemble each other the longer they are together is especially intriguing given the present hypothesis of a perception–behavior link, because one reason for the increased resemblance could be the similar facial lines left by many years of unconsciously mimicking the perceived facial expressions of the partner.

The third type of behavioral coordination research, and the one that most closely resembles the chameleon effect, is that on behavior matching, which occurs when people mimic behavior patterns by adopting similar postures or showing similar body configurations (La France, 1979, 1982; La France & Broadbent, 1976). The main focus of this research has been to link posture similarity in naturalistic settings to rapport, which (though rarely operationalized the same way twice) often includes measures of involvedness, togetherness, being "in step," and compatibility (see also Bavelas, Black, Chovil, Lemery, & Mullett, 1988; Bavelas, Black, Lemery, & Mullett, 1986, 1987).

Despite the considerable amount of research on mimicry and behavioral coordination, there has been relatively little attention given to the mechanism responsible for it. The consensus position appears to be that behavioral coordination is in some way related to empathy, rapport, and liking, although some see mimicry as the cause and others see it as the effect of empathic understanding. That mimicry and behavioral coordination are said to serve the adaptive function of facilitating social interaction and interpersonal bonding does not, however, answer the question of how these effects are produced.

Four critical elements are missing from these observational studies. First, although moderate posture sharing has been reported, there has been no baseline or control group with which to compare the amount of mimicry observed; without this, one cannot determine whether it occurs more often than chance would predict. In fact, La France (1982) has stated that "posture mirroring is not constant nor ubiquitous" (p. 290), and the results of one statistical test of its existence suggested that it did not occur more often than would be predicted by chance (Bernieri, 1988). Although there is wide agreement that posture and body movement mimicking do occur, it nonetheless remains an experimentally unproven observation.

Second, there has been no test of the minimal conditions under which behavior matching occurs. As noted before, research has shown that there is greater posture similarity when the interactants like each other and feel more rapport (Charney, 1966; La France, 1979; La France & Broadbent, 1976; Scheflen, 1964). However, there has been no compelling test of whether there is significant mimicry among unacquainted interaction partners. If the perception–behavior link is the mechanism underlying behavior matching, then it should occur even among strangers. Furthermore, the chameleon effect is hypothesized to be an entirely passive and preconsciously automatic process (i.e., it does not depend on the concurrent operation of an intentional goal, such as ingratiation, during the interaction; see Bargh, 1989). Thus, not only should it occur among strangers, but it should occur even without an active goal to get along with and be liked by the interaction partner. To date, there have been no tests of whether posture and behavior mimicry occur under such minimal conditions.

Third, the previous studies were correlational and did not manipulate the postures and mannerisms of either interactant.[1] This lack of experimental control over which mannerisms are done and how long they are engaged in precludes one from inferring causation. That is, one cannot conclude from these studies that Person X was mimicking Person Y; rather, one can only say that Persons X and Y were displaying the same mannerisms or postures at a given time. For one thing, there could be other, third factors that could spuriously lead to these shared behaviors (e.g., a hot room causing all present to fan their face). For a valid demonstration of the chameleon effect, one would need to show that Person X first engages in a particular behavior, and then Person Y mimics that behavior, without intending or having any reason to do so.

Finally, just as chameleons change their coloring to blend in with their current environment, an experimental demonstration of a behavioral chameleon effect should incorporate, as a within-subjects factor, variability in the behavior of interaction partners, to show that the participant's behavior changes accordingly. Again, to date, there has been no demonstration of such passive behavior adaptations to multiple interaction partners.

THE CHAMELEON EFFECT AS CAUSE OF INTERPERSONAL RAPPORT AND EMPATHY

We propose that the chameleon effect is the mechanism behind mimicry and behavioral coordination and thereby is the source of the observed smoother social interaction and interpersonal bonding produced by the (nonconscious) mimicry. In relating these formerly disparate areas of research, we hypothesize that the perception of another's behavior (be it facial expression, body posture, mannerism, etc.) increases the tendency for the perceiver to behave in a similar manner, and that this is an entirely passive and nonconscious phenomenon. Thus, we argue that the perception of another's behavior does not require or depend on the perceiver having any interpersonal goal, such as ingratiation, toward the person being perceived, nor does perception require the two interaction partners to have an already established relationship (i.e., a preexisting state of rapport). Unlike the prior correlational accounts of mimicry and rapport, we posit a directional causal sequence: Perception causes similar behavior, and the perception of the similar behavior on the part of the other creates shared feelings of empathy and rapport. In short, the widely documented automatic link between perception and behavior exists, at least in pan, as a kind of natural "social glue" that produces empathic understanding and even greater liking between people, without their having to intend or try to have this happen.

As noted above, the studies that showed that the same priming manipulations that influence social perception also influence social behavior are suggestive, but not conclusive, evidence for automatic effects of perception on behavior. What is needed is a demonstration, within a social interaction context, that the perceiver's behavior changes as a function of the behavior of the interaction partner, and that these changes occur without conscious choice or guidance.

Thus, our first goal (Experiment 1) was to provide an experimental test of the existence of nonconscious-mimicry of behavioral mannerisms in a way that (a) determines whether it occurs at greater-than-chance levels, (b) tests whether it occurs among strangers when no affiliation goal is operating, (c) manipulates mannerisms and behaviors of interaction partners (confederates of the experimenter) to determine the direction of causality of the effect, and (d) tests for a chameleon-type change in behavior as a function of the behavior of the current interaction partner. Unlike previous researchers, we did not observe individuals who were already engaged in an interaction; rather, we created dyadic interactions between participants and confederates during which confederates varied their facial expressions and behavioral mannerisms. In Experiments 2 and 3, we sought to verify that these automatic effects of social perception on social interaction produce greater empathy and liking between the interaction partners; in Experiment 3, we examined this issue by testing whether individual differences in empathy covary with individual differences in the chameleon tendency.

EXPERIMENT 1: A TEST OF UNINTENTIONAL MIMICRY BETWEEN STRANGERS

Method

Overview Students participated in two consecutive dyadic sessions. Session 1 consisted of a 10-min interaction with 1 other "participant" (Confederate 1; C1), during which they took turns describing various photographs. Participants then repeated this photograph description task in Session 2 with a 2nd "participant" (Confederate 2; C2).

Confederates varied their mannerisms throughout the interactions. During Session 1, C1 either rubbed his or her face or shook his or her foot. During Session 2, C2 did whichever behavior C1 did not do. Facial expressions varied as well; C1 either smiled or had a neutral expression (i.e., did not smile) throughout Session 1. During Session 2, C2 smiled if C1 had not smiled, and did not smile if C1 had smiled. The order of mannerisms and facial expressions was counterbalanced, and C2 always did the mannerism and facial expression that C1 did not do. A video camera recorded participants during both sessions so that coders could later judge the extent to which participants mimicked the mannerisms and facial expressions of the 2 confederates.

Participants Thirty-nine male and female students enrolled in an introductory psychology course at New York University participated in the experiment in partial fulfillment of a course requirement. Data from 4 of these participants were excluded from subsequent analyses for the following reasons: (a) 3 participants chose to not sign the consent form giving us permission to code and analyze their videotape, and (b) during debriefing, 1 participant expressed suspicion that the other participant was in fact a confederate. However, neither she nor any of the other participants accurately guessed our hypothesis.

Thus, we computed all analyses on responses from a final sample of 35 participants. For 14 participants, C1 smiled and shook his or her foot and C2 did not smile and rubbed his or her face. Because the possibility existed that encountering the smiling confederate first would affect participants' interactions with the nonsmiling C2, it was important to counterbalance the order of facial expressions by having the nonsmiling confederate interact first with some of the participants. Thus, C1 did not smile with 21 participants (of these, C1 rubbed his or her face with 8 and shook his or her foot with 13).

Apparatus and materials Two male and two female assistants served as experimenters and confederates, rotating in the roles of experimenter or confederate. The experiment room had one chair for the experimenter at the front of the room, behind a desk in which the materials and stimuli for the experiment were kept. The room also contained two chairs for the participant and confederate that were placed approximately 1.2 m apart. These two chairs were half-facing each other and half-facing the experimenter's desk. With this arrangement, the participants could see the confederates' mannerisms during the interaction but could not see the experimenter's, whose body was effectively hidden by the desk.

Participants were videotaped throughout both sessions by means of a video camera on a shelf in the corner of the room. The camera was focused on the participant's chair, resulting in a clear view of the participant's entire seated body. To ensure that coders of the videos were blind to condition, we did not videotape the confederates. Thus, when judging a particular participant's responses, the raters did not know the corresponding mannerisms or facial expressions of the 2 confederates.

Color photographs for the experiment were chosen from magazines such as *Newsweek*, *Time*, and *Life*. The photos were cut out of the magazines and mounted on heavy black cardboard. Twelve photos were chosen that ranged somewhat in emotional content, amount of action involved, and ambiguity of what was being portrayed in the photo.[2] These variables were not manipulated systematically, but the photographs were rotated so that participants did not always describe the same type of photo when with the smiling or nonsmiling confederate (e.g., only describing somewhat "happy" photos when with the smiling confederate). Thus, although 6 of the 12 photos were reserved for the confederates (so they could memorize a prepared script for each) and the other 6 were reserved for the participant, the order of the photos within each set varied.

Procedure Each participant completed the experiment individually. Prior to each session, the experimenter turned on the video camera that would record the participant throughout the session. The experimenter then brought the participant into the laboratory room and seated him or her in the participant's chair. The experimenter then left the participant alone in the room for 1 min (ostensibly to retrieve copies of a needed form from another room), during which time the participant was videotaped to obtain a baseline measure. This baseline period was later coded to determine the extent to which the participant was already rubbing his or her face, shaking his or her foot, or smiling before interacting with any confederate.

The experimenter reentered the room and delivered the cover story. It was explained that the purpose of the study was to test a new projective measure being created by some psychologists in the department. (The assumptions underlying the use of projective measures were briefly explained to those participants unfamiliar with them.) The participant was informed that some researchers were trying to develop a revised version of one of the more common measures (the Thematic Apperception Test) that (a) could be administered to more than one person at a time and (b) would use photographs instead of picture drawings.

The participant was told that the researchers were in the initial stage of creating working sets of photographs to serve as the stimuli for the projective test. Toward this end, they were first testing various sets of photos on a "normal" (i.e., nonpatient) population. Specifically, college students were being recruited to describe what they saw in the various photographs. Participants could discuss the visual aspects of the photo, or free associate and say whatever came to mind (including what the people in the photos were thinking or feeling), or both. Importantly, the experimenter emphasized to the participant that responses would not be analyzed by any of the psychologists (or anyone else), so there was no need to be concerned about the content of his or her responses. Instead, the ease with which the students described and generated responses to the photos would ostensibly be taken as the indicator of the usefulness of those particular photos. Accordingly, the participant was told that at the conclusion of the experiment, he or she would be asked about the experience of describing the photographs (e.g., how easy it was to generate responses for them).

The participant was further informed that several sets of photographs had already been gathered and tested on students 1 at a time in individual sessions. The photos were now being tested in group settings, beginning with groups of 2 students at a time. The participant was then given a consent form to sign and told that he or she would be involved in two separate group sessions, each with 1 other participant. It was explained that another session was being conducted concurrently in another room, and that 1 of the participants from a previous session there would be the 1st partner. The experimenter then brought in the 1st other participant (C1) and seated him or her in the confederate's chair. The participant and C1 were each given a set of three photos facing down. The experimenter explained that the two sets of photos were different and reminded them that their task was to take turns describing what they saw in each photograph. They were told to describe each photo in any way they wished for approximately 1 min.

The experimenter suggested that C1 turn over the first photo and begin. C1 described the photograph, following a memorized script to ensure that responses were standardized across different confederates find different experimental sessions. It should be noted that the confederates were trained to deliver the responses with natural hesitation, including pauses, *umms*, and *hmms*. One example of a scripted response refers to a photo of a man holding in his arms a small dog with a leg cast:

> This is a picture of a man holding a small dog—maybe a chihuahua but I'm not sure. The dog's leg is in a cast, so I guess it's broken. I don't know how dogs' legs get broken, but maybe it got stuck somewhere, like in those gutters outside or something. So then it was probably crying or making a lot of noise and this man heard it. The man looks like a pretty nice guy, so he probably felt sorry for the dog and wanted to help it. This picture looks like it's taken at a vet's office, so the man probably brought the dog to the vet and then they put the cast on the leg, And then this picture was taken right after that. The man didn't know who the dog belonged to, so he's having people take pictures of the dog so that the owner can come pick him up.

The experimenter then asked the participant to turn over his or her first photo and begin describing it. After the participant finished, C1 and the participant continued alternating turns until both completed their sets of three photographs. During the interaction, C1 made minimal eye contact with the participant to minimize the possibility that any personal relationship between the two would be established. C1 was either smiling or not smiling and either rubbing his or her face or shaking his or her foot. Behaviors were always performed throughout the interactions.

After all photographs had been described, the experimenter told participants that they would now be switching partners. One of the participants would be brought to the other laboratory room to join another participant, and the other would stay in the current room to meet a new partner. The experimenter escorted C1 out of the laboratory room and approximately 1 min later brought in C2 to join the participant. The experimenter gave the participant and C2 a different set of three photographs each, and once again they alternated taking turns describing them. This time, however, C2 was displaying the mannerism (rubbing his or her face or shaking his or her foot) and facial expression (smiling or not smiling) that C1 had not.

Following the session with C2, the experimenter said that the debriefing would take place individually, and that C2 would be taken to the other laboratory room where he or she would be debriefed by the other experimenter. The experimenter escorted C2 out of the room and returned alone approximately 30 s later. The experimenter then queried the participant in a "funneled" question sequence (i.e., from general to increasingly specific questions about awareness of hypotheses; see Bargh & Chartrand, in press) to determine if he or she (a) was suspicious that the other participants were in fact confederates, (b) noticed that the confederates each displayed certain mannerisms throughout the session, or (c) thought that the purpose of the experiment was anything other than what the cover story indicated. Finally, the hypotheses and purpose of the study were explained to the participant. The participant was asked to sign a video release form allowing the researchers to examine the data and was thanked for his or her participation in the study.

Results

Interjudge reliability Videotapes were coded by two independent judges blind to the condition of participants. Three time periods were coded for each participant: 1 min of baseline before interacting with confederates (BL), the time spent with C1 (T1), and the time spent with C2 (T2). The coding procedure yielded the following dependent variables: (a) the number of times the participant smiled, (b) the number of times the participant robbed his or her face, and (c) the number of times the participant shook his or her foot.[3]

The following are the interjudge reliabilities: For the number of times smiling, the reliability for the three ratings (BL, TI, and T2) ranged from r = .79 to 1.00, with mean r = .89. For number of times participants shook their foot, the three ratings ranged from r = .53 to .79, with mean r = .68. For number of times participants robbed their face, the interjudge reliabilities ranged from r = .33 to .60, mean r = .50.[4] All reliabilities were significant at $p < .001$.

The mean of the two judges' ratings was taken to form a single rating for each behavior. Ratings for T1 and T2 were then divided by the number of minutes (to the nearest second) that the interaction lasted to arrive at a rate per minute. (This method had the further advantages of equating T1 and T2 with BL so that the numbers would all be in the same metric and ensuring that any differences would not be artifactually due to somewhat longer or shorter interactions in T1 vs. T2.)

For both the smiling and behavioral measures, a repeated measures analysis of variance (ANOVA) was conducted on the number of times each action occurred per minute. For each analysis, we included the baseline rating as a covariate to adjust for individual differences in performing the key behaviors in the absence of another person. Neither the participant's gender nor the order in which the confederates enacted the various behaviors affected the results, so neither of these variables is discussed further.

Facial expression As predicted, there was a significant effect of confederate expression, $F(1, 34) = 20.31$, $p < .0001$. Participants smiled more times per minute when with the smiling confederate ($M = 1.03$) than with the neutral confederate ($M = 0.36$). This result suggests that participants did indeed mimic the facial expression of the confederates.

Behavioral measures We next conducted a repeated measures ANOVA on the number of times participants engaged in the mannerisms per minute. Confederate behavior (foot shaking vs. face rubbing) and participant behavior (foot shaking vs. face rubbing) were the two within-subject variables. Whereas there were no main effects for confederate behavior ($F < 1$) or participant behavior ($p > .25$), the predicted interaction between the two was, in fact, reliable, $F(1, 34) = 9.36$, $p = .004$ (see Figure 1). Our hypothesized chameleon effect specifically predicts that participants should engage in face rubbing (or foot shaking) more in the presence of the confederate engaging in that behavior than in the presence of the confederate not engaging in that behavior. Consistent with this prediction are our findings that participants rubbed their face more times in the presence of the face-rubbing confederate than when with the foot-shaking confederate, $F(1, 34) = 5.71$, $p < .025$, and shook their foot more times when with the foot-shaking confederate than with the face-rubbing confederate, $F(1, 34) = 3.76$, $p = .06$. These results, in conjunction with the facial expression findings, support our hypothesis that individuals passively take on the mannerisms and facial expressions of those around them without the intention or reason to do so.

Liking as potential mediator If the perception–behavior link is, as we argue, a completely nonconscious, non-goal-dependent mechanism that produces the chameleon effect, mimicry of others should occur even in the absence of a reason to do so, such as pursuing an affiliation goal. In the present study, with one smiling and one nonsmiling confederate, it is reasonable to suppose that participants would be more likely to have an affiliation goal—if they had one at all, which the de sign of the experiment attempted to minimize—with the smiling than with the nonsmiling confederate. Thus, one could conceptualize the smiling and nonsmiling confederates as a likeability manipulation.

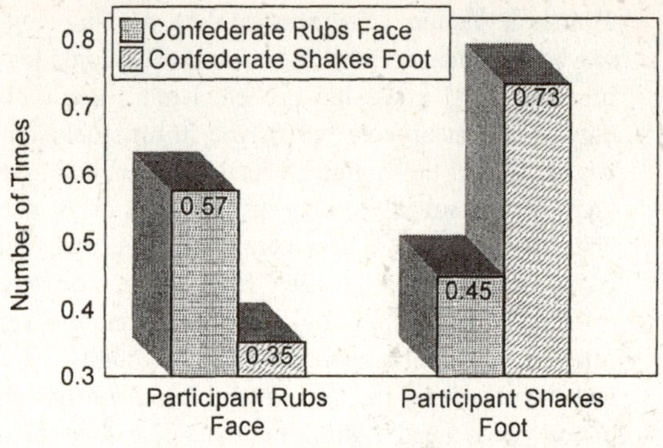

Figure 1. Number of times participants rubbed their face and shook their foot per minute when with a confederate who was rubbing his or her face and a confederate who was shaking his or her foot.

The question becomes, did the participants mimic the foot-shaking and face-rubbing behaviors of the nonsmiling confederate or only those of the smiling confederate?

In the following analysis, whichever of the two behaviors the nonsmiling confederate performed was the key behavior for a given participant. We compared how much participants engaged in the key behavior with the nonsmiling confederate with how much they engaged in that same behavior with the smiling confederate (who was doing the other behavior). A repeated measures ANOVA was conducted on the number of times the action occurred per minute. A significant effect of confederate behavior was obtained, $F(1, 34) = 4.16$, $p = .05$. Participants performed the key action more times with the nonsmiling confederate doing that key behavior ($M = .56$) than with the smiling, likable confederate doing the other behavior ($M = .40$). It was not the case that participants only mimicked the behavior of the smiling, apparently friendly confederate and not the nonsmiling, apparently less friendly confederate.

Were the mimicry effects greater in the presence of the smiling confederate? We next compared the extent to which participants mimicked the behavior (either foot shaking or face rubbing) of the smiling confederate more than the behavior of the nonsmiling confederate. Behavior mimicked (face rubbing or foot shaking) when the participant was with the smiling confederate was the between-subjects variable, and confederate expression (smiling versus nonsmiling) was the within-subjects variable. There was no significant main effect for confederate expression across the two behaviors being mimicked, nor was the interaction significant ($Fs < 1$). Thus, there was no evidence in our study that the obtained effects were goal dependent.

Participants' awareness of having engaged in behavioral mimicry For the chameleon effect to be considered passive and automatic, it must be demonstrated that participants were not aware of having mimicked the confederates. Although intuitively it seems unlikely that participants would want to purposefully mimic the confederates' mannerisms, it is possible that participants believed that shaking their foot or rubbing their face simultaneously with the confederate would be beneficial for the interaction in some way, and they mimicked for these conscious, motivated reasons. However, we have evidence that this was not the case. Participants were asked during the funneled debriefing at the conclusion of the experiment whether anything about either of the confederates stood out to them. Participants were then asked whether either of the confederates had any particular mannerisms or ways of speaking that they noticed or that seemed distinctive. One participant (out of 35) mentioned that 1 of the confederates made hand motions while speaking, and 2 others commented on the slouching posture of 1 confederate. However, none of the participants mentioned noticing that the confederates were shaking their foot or rubbing their face. (When asked, most reported that they "hadn't noticed" the mannerisms of the confederate.) Thus, it seems that not only were participants not consciously trying to imitate the mannerisms of the confederates, but they did not even pay attention to these mannerisms in the first place.

Discussion

Researchers have long been interested in nonconscious mimicry, yet there has been little attention given to identifying the mechanism underlying the phenomenon. We have argued that the perception–behavior link can provide such a mechanism. The perception–behavior link posits the existence of a natural and nonconscious connection between the act of perceiving and the act of behaving, such that perceiving an action being done by another makes one more likely to engage in that same behavior. This mechanism can account for the chameleon effect, the tendency of people to take on the postures and mannerisms of those around them.

In Experiment 1, we sought to provide an experimental test of the chameleon effect in which the mannerisms and facial expressions of interaction partners were manipulated and standardized across participants. Analyses revealed that behavioral mimicry did in fact occur at significantly greater than chance levels. Significant mimicry was found for facial expressions and for two different behavioral mannerisms, after controlling for BL measures of each behavior. Furthermore, the design of the experiment, in which the confederates' behavior was predetermined and standardized and so it was clear who was mimicking whom, enables conclusions to be drawn for the first time about the causal direction of the effect. Unlike previous studies, this one showed that the similarity in mannerisms between participants and confederates could not have been due to any third factor.

Moreover, because participants interacted with 2 different partners, each of whom engaged in different facial expressions and behavioral mannerisms, the results demonstrated the true chameleon-like nature of the perception–behavior effect, as the participants' behavior changed as a function of the behavior of their current interaction partner. Thus, they rubbed their face when interacting with the face-rubbing confederate but then reduced face rubbing and increased foot shaking during their interaction with the foot-shaking confederate. No previous study had demonstrated how an individual's behavior naturally adapts to changes in social environmental settings by blending in to each of them successively.

Because the perception–behavior link is preconscious and not goal dependent, for it to be the cause of the chameleon effect, the effect should occur among strangers when no affiliation goal is present. This was found to be the case; participants mimicked the behavior of strangers, even nonsmiling ones who never made eye contact with them. In designing the experiment, we sought to minimize the possibility that participants would choose to pursue an affiliation or other social goal toward the confederates that would cause them, in pursuit of that goal, to engage in behavioral mimicry (even at a nonconscious, goal-dependent, automatic level). Thus, confederates were instructed to not make eye contact with the participants, and when serving as the smiling confederate, to never smile at the participants. Finally, that the obtained behavioral mimicry occurred just as much in the presence of the nonsmiling as the smiling confederate is further evidence against the goal-dependent alternative account.

EXPERIMENT 2: THE ADAPTIVE FUNCTION OF THE CHAMELEON EFFECT

What is the adaptive function served by the chameleon effect, the nonconscious tendency to behave with others as those others are behaving? As reviewed above, there is consensus among researchers that behavior matching is related to greater liking and rapport between the interactants. Our second goal for the present research was to test whether behavior matching does in fact increase liking and create a sense of smoother interactions. Our hypothesis that automatic effects of perception on behavior serve adaptive functions is part of a larger research effort that traces the "downstream" consequences of a variety of immediate, preconscious reactions to the social environment. For example, recent research on the downstream effect of the tendency to automatically evaluate perceived stimuli as either good or bad (e.g., Bargh, Chaiken, Govender, & Pratto, 1992; Bargh, Chaiken, Raymond, & Hymes, 1996; Fazio, Sanbonmatsu, Powell, & Kardes, 1986) has demonstrated direct effects on behavioral predispositions toward those stimuli (Chen & Bargh, 1999), as well as mood effects that reflect the average valence of automatic evaluations made over time in a given environment (Chartrand & Bargh, 1999). The chameleon effect, as another variety of a preconscious automatic process, also likely exists for a useful, adaptive reason.

It is plausible that the chameleon effect serves the basic human need to belong. In a recent review, Baumeister and Leary (1995) argued that according to the existing evidence, the human need to belong is a powerful, fundamental, and extremely pervasive motivation.[5] We desire frequent, nonaversive interactions with others and want to form and maintain strong, stable interpersonal relationships. We try to orient toward fellow human beings in a way that is relatively free from conflict and negative affect. To the extent that two interactants are similar to each other and have things in common (even at the level of behavioral mannerisms), such a smooth, conflict-free interaction will be more likely to occur. Moreover, automatically behaving in a manner similar to other group members—including having similar facial reactions to events—helps prevent an individual member from standing out as different, and so it would help to prevent ostracism and social distance from other group members (see Brewer, 1991).

Researchers of elementary motor mimicry have posited a very specific function served by motor mimicry that is consistent with this analysis. Recall that motor mimicry is a subset of behavior matching that refers to an individual reacting to another person going through a specific, emotion-laden incident (e.g., wincing at the other's pain). The individual reacts as if he or she were experiencing and feeling the same thing as the other person. Bavelas and her colleagues (Bavelas et al., 1988; Bavelas, Black, Lemery, & Mullett, 1986, 1987) take a strong stand that motor mimicry is not an overt manifestation of an intrapersonal process, such as vicarious emotion or cognitive role taking, but rather is an important communication tool that relays the message "I am like you" or "I feel as you do" to the other person.

Over 20 years earlier, Scheflen (1964) similarly suggested that mimicry might serve a communicative function without a person's awareness or intent: "Human behavior can be communicative whether or not it is *intended* to communicate . . . . *The intent of an interactant and the function that a behavior actually has in a group process must be conceptually distinguished* (italics in original; p. 318). We suggest that behavior matching serves this same function, and individuals use behavior mimicry as a communication tool on a completely nonconscious level.

Although behavior-matching researchers have not discussed its use as a communication tool per se, the notion is consistent with the proposed link between behavior matching and rapport. Scheflen (1964) originally posited that people in a group often mirror one another's posture and that this reflects a shared viewpoint. Bernieri and Rosenthal (1991) pointed out that people seem to get along better when their behaviors are well coordinated: "Interpersonal coordination and synchrony may eventually explain how it is that we 'hit it off' immediately with some people and never 'get it together' with others" (p. 429). Tickle-Degnen and Rosenthal (1987) also reviewed the evidence for a link between interpersonal coordination and rapport and suggested that it is quite strong.

Empirical evidence supporting the link between social rapport and interpersonal coordination comes primarily from the work on posture mirroring. In a typical study, La France (1982) found that students frequently displayed the same postural configuration as that of the teacher, and the extent of posture similarity was positively correlated with the students' ratings of rapport, involvement, and togetherness. Interestingly, La France has discovered that posture mirroring (e.g., one person lifting his or her right arm and another person lifting his or her left arm in a "mirror image") is related to rapport, although posture mimicking (e.g., both individuals lifting their right arm) is not (La France & Broadbent, 1976). Additional studies have found a relationship between behavior matching and self-reported rapport and involvement (Charney, 1966; La France, 1979; Trout & Rosenfeld, 1980). Hatfield, Cacioppo, and Rapson (1994) also argued that behavioral mimicry leads to emotional convergence between interaction partners.

Thus, there is consensus among researchers that behavior matching is related to greater liking and rapport. However, there has been disagreement over the causal direction. Some researchers have conceptualized various types of behavioral coordination as by-products or outgrowths of preexisting emotional rapport or liking (Levenson & Ruef, 1997; Scheflen, 1964). However, others have argued for the reverse causal direction. La France (1982), for instance, suggested that posture mirroring may not only reflect shared viewpoints and harmony but may actually be instrumental to achieving them.

Evidence for the mimicry-to-rapport causal direction has been mixed. In a correlational study, La France (1979) used a cross-lag technique to assess causality and found that posture similarity seems to lead to rapport slightly more than vice versa, although there was some evidence that the effect was bidirectional. In a study of the impact of gesture similarity on persuasion and interpersonal influence, Dabbs (1969) manipulated movement similarity by having a confederate "interviewee" mimic the gestures and mannerisms of 1 of 2 participant "interviewers" in the room. Results were equivocal; whereas the participant who was mimicked did not report liking the confederate more than did the participant who was not mimicked, mimicry did cause the confederate to be evaluated more favorably on other dimensions (e.g., he was considered to be well informed and to have sound ideas). In a second experiment, some participants were trained to be confederates 10 min before the start of the experiment and were told to either mimic a 2nd participant or to "antimimic" him (i.e., do the opposite of what he did). Results were again unclear as to the effect of mimicry, but they did suggest that antimimicry could have a negative effect in certain circumstances. Finally, Maurer and Tindall (1983) focused on whether perceptions of a counselor's empathy partially depend on nonverbal cues such as having similar behavioral mannerisms. They found that when counselors mimicked the body positions of their clients, the clients perceived a greater level of expressed empathy on the part of the counselor.

In Experiment 2, we sought to test whether manipulated variations in posture similarity produce variations in liking between interaction partners. We especially wanted to test the extent to which posture similarity affects liking when there is no overarching interpersonal goal held by the interactants toward each other. In both the Dabbs (1969, Experiment 1) and Maurer and Tindall (1983) experiments, there was a role-power differential between the confederate and participant, and so interpersonal goals (e.g., ingratiation) may have affected their results. Our hypothesis, however, is that the chameleon effect operates in a passive, non-goal-dependent manner to create greater liking and ease of interaction. Hence, mimicry of one interaction partner by the other should cause the former to like the partner more and to experience greater ease of interacting, even when the two are strangers or new acquaintances who are not seeking to establish a relationship.

Method

Overview Participants had one 15-min session with another "participant" (a confederate). During this session, the participant and confederate took turns describing what they saw in various photographs. Confederates either mirrored the behavioral mannerisms of the participant throughout the interaction (the experimental condition) or engaged in neutral, nondescript mannerisms (the control condition). When the interaction was over, participants completed a questionnaire on which they were asked to report (a) how much they liked the confederate and (b) how smoothly the interaction had gone.

Participants Seventy-eight male and female students enrolled in an introductory psychology course participated in the experiment in partial fulfillment of a course requirement. Data from 6 of these participants were excluded from analyses for the following reasons: 2 participants in the control condition sat in the same neutral position as the confederates, making it equivalent to the experimental condition in which body language and mannerisms are in synchrony. Four participants suspected that the other participant was in fact a confederate. It should be noted, however, that none of these participants were able to guess our hypothesis. Thus, we computed all analyses on responses from a final sample of 72 participants, with 37 in the mimicking (mirroring) condition and 35 in the control condition.

Apparatus and materials The experiment room was the same as used in Experiment 1. The same color photographs from Experiment 1 were also used for Experiment 2. There were 4 female assistants who served as confederate and experimenter, and they alternated roles. All assistants were trained to mirror the body language and mannerisms of the participants.

Although the confederates were kept blind to the specific hypothesis of the experiment, they were necessarily aware of the manipulation involved and of the participant's assigned experimental condition. It is therefore possible that they could have, intentionally or unintentionally, behaved differently toward the participants who were in the experimental condition (e.g., acted more friendly or likable toward them). To address this possibility, 22 of the sessions (11 of the control condition and 11 of the experimental condition) were videotaped in their entirety to later assess, through the ratings of outside judges, whether the confederates were behaving differently (other than in the mimicry itself) toward participants in the mimicry versus no-mimicry conditions. Both the participant and confederate were visible through the lens of the camera so that judges would be able to see and code the confederate's behavior toward the participant.

The dependent measures were ratings from participants on liking for the confederate and smoothness of the interaction. The key items read, "How likable was the other participant?" and "How smoothly would you say your interaction went with the other participant?" To help camouflage the hypothesis of the study, we embedded these two items among eight other questions that asked about the task itself and the group format (e.g., how easy or difficult it was for them to generate responses to the photos, and whether they thought the various photographs went well together as a single "set"). All items were rated on 9-point scales (for the smoothness item, 1 = *extremely awkward*, 9 = *extremely smooth*; for the likeability item, 1 = *extremely dislikable*, 9 = *extremely likable*).

Procedure The procedure was the same as for Experiment 1, with participants working with confederates to ostensibly help develop the projective measure involving sets of photographs, except that the confederates no longer smiled (or not), shook their foot, or rubbed their face. Instead, during the interaction, the confederate avoided eye contact with the participant and maintained a neutral facial expression. Furthermore, in the mimicry condition, the confederate mirrored the posture, movements, and mannerisms displayed by the participant. In the control condition, the confederate sat in a neutral relaxed position, with both feet on the floor and both hands holding the photos (or resting in the lap).[6]

When the participant and confederate had completed the photograph descriptions, the experimenter explained that they would next complete the questionnaire about the task. Because it was necessary to complete it independently and privately, they would be separated and seated in different rooms. The experimenter asked the confederate to complete the survey in an adjoining room and escorted her there. Then, the experimenter returned to the laboratory room, gave the participant the questionnaire to complete, and told him or her to come to the hallway outside when finished. At this point, the experimenter queried the participant to determine whether he or she was suspicious that (a) the other participant was in fact a confederate, (b) the confederate was mirroring his or her own behaviors, or (c) the purpose of the experiment was anything other than what the cover story indicated. Finally, the purpose and hypotheses of the study were explained to the participant. (Those who were videotaped were asked to sign a video consent form.) The participant was thanked for his or her participation.

Results

Liking and smoothness as a function of being mimicked We predicted that relative to those in the control condition, participants in the experimental condition would report (a) finding the confederate more likable and (b) having smoother interactions with her. To test these hypotheses, a multivariate analysis of variance (MANOVA) was conducted on the liking and smoothness variables, with mimicking of participants by confederates (yes vs. no) as the between-subjects variable. Gender was also included as a between-subjects variable in this and all subsequent analyses, but no reliable main effect for gender or interaction between gender and mimicking emerged, and so the gender variable is not discussed further. In addition, we initially included as an additional between-subjects variable in the MANOVA whether the experimental session had been videotaped, but this variable also did not interact with any of the effects, *F*s < 1. Therefore, the sessions that were videotaped were representative of the larger sample; the liking and smoothness ratings of the participants in these sessions did not differ from the ratings of the participants who were not videotaped.

As predicted, there was an overall effect of mimicking across the two dependent measures, $F(2, 69) = 3.47$, $p = .04$. This effect was not moderated by type of dependent measure, interaction $F < 1$. We also conducted separate univariate tests on the liking and smoothness ratings. Participants in the experimental condition reported liking the confederate more ($M = 6.62$) than did those in the control condition ($M = 5.91$), $F(1, 70) = 5.55$, $p = .02$. Furthermore, they reported that the interaction went more smoothly ($M = 6.76$) than did those in the control condition ($M = 6.02$), $F(1, 70) = 4.08$, $p = .05$. Thus, the results support the hypothesis that mimicry increases liking and fosters smooth, harmonious interactions. Although previous, correlational research showed liking and rapport to be related to posture similarity, this is the fast demonstration that mimicry causes greater liking and smoother interactions.

Confederates' behavior toward participants It is important to consider an alternative explanation for these findings. Although we believe that mimicry by the confederate produced the greater liking and smoothness ratings by participants in that condition, relative to the no-mimicry condition, it is possible that some associated difference in the behavior of the confederates in the two conditions produced the effects. For obvious reasons, it was not possible to keep the confederates blind to the participant's assigned condition (mimicry vs. no-mimicry). Although confederates were kept blind to the specific hypothesis in the study, it remains possible that they unwittingly behaved differently toward the participants in the mimicry versus no-mimicry conditions; for example, they may have behaved in a more friendly manner toward those they mimicked or, more subtly, engaged in greater smiling or made more eye contact with them. If so, this would provide an alternative reason for the participants liking the confederates more in this condition—one having nothing to do with mimicry. Hence, we sought to determine whether there were any such differences in confederate behavior in the two conditions.

As described in the *Method* section, we videotaped a sample ($n = 22$) of the experimental sessions for precisely this reason—to collect evidence germane to this alternative explanation. These videotapes were then independently coded by two judges blind to the experimental hypothesis. For each interaction, the following behaviors were coded: (a) how much eye contact the confederate made with the participant, (b) how much the confederate smiled at the participant, (c) how friendly the confederate acted toward the participant, and (d) how much the confederate appeared to like the participant. All items were rated on a 6-point scale (1 = *low*, 6 = *high*). The reliability between the two judges for the four items combined was quite high, $r = .96$. (The interjudge correlations for each of the individual scale items ranged from $r = .72$ to $r = .91$.) Accordingly, ratings from the two coders were averaged to form a single index for each measure.

TABLE 1
Outside Judges' Ratings (1 = Low, 6 = High) of Confederate's Openness and Friendliness to Participant as a Function of Experimental Condition (Experiment 2)

	No mimicking		Mimicking	
Measure	*M*	*SD*	*M*	*SD*
Eye contact	1.63	0.52	1.41	0.49
Smiling	1.75	0.53	1.45	0.52
Friendliness	2.94	0.18	3.00	0.00
Liking participant	3.25	0.46	3.23	0.41

The means of each of the four ratings are presented in Table 1. No significant differences in eye contact, smiling, friendliness, or liking were observed between the experimental and control conditions (all *ps* > .20). In fact, three of the four measures were actually (but nonsignificantly) lower in the mimicking than the no-mimicking condition. It does not appear that confederates behaved differently toward the participants in the mimicry versus no-mimicry conditions, other than in the mimicry manipulation itself, and so we can more confidently attribute the observed differences in liking for the confederate and for the rated level of smoothness of the interaction to the effects of mimicry.[7]

Participants' awareness of having been mimicked Participants were asked during the funneled debriefing whether they noticed anything in particular about the confederate's behavior or mannerisms and whether anything about the confederate's behavior made them feel awkward or uncomfortable. One participant reported that the confederate kept her head down and did not make eye contact with her. A 2nd participant reported that the confederate was crossing her legs (as was the participant), but she remarked that it "seemed normal and did not make me feel uncomfortable." Thus, only 1 out of

37 participants in the mimicking condition noticed that the confederate had a similar mannerism, but it was not interpreted by that participant as mimicry.

Discussion

After it was demonstrated in Experiment 1 that the perception–behavior link produced chameleon-like passive behavioral mimicry of interaction partners, we sought in Experiment 2 to assess the possible adaptive value of this effect. On the basis of past research linking mimicry to rapport, we hypothesized that the chameleon effect serves the adaptive function of fostering liking between people and creating smooth, harmonious interactions. It follows that if an individual's movements and postures are purposefully mirrored by an interaction partner, that individual should report that the interaction went more smoothly and that the partner was more likable compared with individuals whose movements were not mirrored. The results of Experiment 2 confirmed that, compared with control condition participants, those participants whose movements were mirrored by the confederate both experienced the interaction as having gone more smoothly and liked the confederate significantly more.

It should be noted that this link between mimicking and liking contradicts some previous findings. For instance, La France found that posture similarity and rapport were positively correlated when the interactants were acquainted with each other and involved in an ongoing interaction (La France, 1979, 1982; La France & Broadbent, 1976) but negatively correlated when the interactants were unacquainted (La France & Ickes, 1981; see Bernieri, 1988, for a similar finding). This latter finding implies that the relation between mimicry and rapport should hold only for people involved in an ongoing interaction. The most crucial difference between the La France and Ickes study and ours is that in the former, participants were not interacting at all; rather, they were simply sitting in the same waiting room at the same time. Thus, the positive effects of chameleon-like mimicry for ease of interaction and liking may only accrue within the context of a social interaction and not between strangers who do not interact at all. To us, however, this is an inconsequential constraint that would not diminish the adaptive value of the chameleon effect as a kind of social glue that helps to bind interaction partners together.

EXPERIMENT 3: INDIVIDUAL DIFFERENCES IN NONCONSCIOUS MIMICRY

Although we believe nonconscious behavior mimicry to be a pervasive and ubiquitous phenomenon, we also expect there to be individual differences in the extent to which an individual engages in such behavioral and posture mimicry. Certainly not everyone engages in the chameleon effect to the same degree as did Woody Allen's Zelig. What might determine whether one is more or less likely to nonconsciously mimic others? Surprisingly, no one has thus far posited any personality or individual difference variables as moderators of the chameleon effect, to our knowledge. In Experiment 3, we focused on one such potential moderator.

On the basis of the relation established in Experiment 2 between behavior mimicry on the one hand and liking and interaction smoothness on the other, one individual difference likely to be related to the chameleon effect is empathy. Theoretical distinctions have been made between various components of the empathic response, but research has distilled two major forms. The first is based on cognitive, intellectual reactions, such as the ability to take and understand the other person's perspective. The second is based on visceral, emotional reactions to the others' situation (see Davis, 1983).

We suggest that the cognitive facet of empathy (i.e., perspective taking) is more relevant to the chameleon effect, because, as was demonstrated in Experiment 1, the mechanism that produces the effect is the perception–behavior link. The cause of the chameleon effect is therefore a purely passive, cognitive mechanism that is not associated with or dependent on any particular affective or emotional state. Thus, the most likely candidate for an individual-difference moderator of the chameleon effect would be one concerned with differences in how much attention and thought are paid to one's interaction partners. In other words, a person will be more susceptible to the effects of perception on behavior if he or she engages in greater perceptual activity directed at the other person. Taking the perspective of others is a perceptual, cognitive process that is likely to lead to greater perception of an interaction partner, which in turn leads to more mimicking. Moreover, if it is, as we argue, the passive perception–behavior link that produces the chameleon effect and its consequent benefits for social interaction, then individual differences in the emotional or affective-based form of empathy should not be related to differences in the chameleon effect.

In harmony with this argument is Davis's (1983) finding that perspective taking but not empathic concern (the affective component of empathy) was consistently related to various measures of interpersonal functioning: "Perspective-taking ability should allow an individual to anticipate the behavior and reactions of others, therefore facilitating *smoother* [italics added] and more rewarding interpersonal relationships" (p. 115). Given that (a) we believe social functioning to be one of the adaptive consequences of the chameleon effect, and (b) in Experiment 2 it was demonstrated that mimicry led to smoother interactions, individual differences in perspective taking should be related to individual differences in the extent of the chameleon effect.

We note that many theorists, Mead (1934) and Piaget (1932) among them, have argued that possessing and using an ability to take another's perspective is responsible for much of human social capacity. Among other benefits, well-developed perspective-taking abilities help an individual gain more satisfying interpersonal relations. In a similar vein, Cialdini, Brown, Lewis, Luce, and Neuberg (1997) asserted that the merging of self with other is influenced by perspective taking. It is likely no coincidence that these consequences of frequent perspective taking parallel the consequences of behavioral mimicry we found in Experiment 2. That is, both behavioral mirroring and perspective taking lead to smoother interactions and greater liking. Perhaps, then, one of the reasons why those with a greater tendency to take the perspective of others have greater social functioning and compassion for others is because they engage in more behavioral mimicry; that was our prediction in Experiment 3.

Method

Participants Fifty-five students in an introductory psychology course participated in this study in partial fulfillment of a course requirement. Three of these participants suspected that the confederate was part of the experimental setup, 1 had general suspicions regarding the study, and 1 was not videotaped because of equipment malfunction (again, none of the participants accurately guessed our hypothesis). Data from these 5 participants were excluded from further analysis. Thus, data from 50 participants remained in final analyses.

Apparatus and materials The experiment room was the same as that used in Experiments 1 and 2. Four female assistants alternated serving as confederate and experimenter. Assistants were trained to continually shake their foot and rub their face throughout each interaction as the confederate.

The same color photographs from Experiments 1 and 2 were used. The same video camera setup was used as in Experiment 1, such that only the participants (and not the confederates) were visible through the camera lens.

To measure perspective taking, we used the perspective-taking subscale of Davis's (1980) Interpersonal Reactivity Index (IRI). The IRI also conveniently includes a subscale for empathic concern, which represents the emotional concern-for-others facet of empathy. Thus, administering the IRI allowed us to test our hypothesis that it is the cognitive, perspective-taking component of empathy and not the emotional, empathic-concern facet that moderates the perception–behavior link.

The perspective-taking subscale assesses the tendency to spontaneously adopt the psychological point of view of others. Sample items include "When I'm upset at someone, I usually try to 'put myself in his/her shoes' for a while," "I believe that there are two sides to every question and try to look at them both," and "I sometimes try to understand my friends better by imagining how things look from their perspective." The empathic concern subscale assesses "other-oriented" feelings of sympathy and concern for unfortunate others, and sample items include "I often have tender, concerned feeling for people less fortunate than me"; "I am often quite touched by things that I see happen"; and "Other people's misfortunes do not usually disturb me a great deal." All items are rated on a 5-point scale (A = *does not describe me well;* E = *describes me very well*). There are seven items on each subscale, some of which are reverse-coded. The alpha coefficient for perspective taking is .71 for men and .75 for women; for empathic concern, the alpha is .68 for men and .73 for women.

Procedure Each participant completed the experiment individually. The confederate was always sitting in the waiting area before the participant arrived. The experimenter brought them both into the laboratory room, seating them in the two chairs reserved for them.

The procedure was essentially the same photograph-description task used in Experiments 1 and 2. The major change was that the confederate engaged in two different mannerisms throughout the interaction:

rubbing her face and shaking her foot. As in Experiment 2, the confederate avoided eye contact with the participant whenever possible and maintained a neutral facial expression.

As soon as the participant and confederate completed the photograph descriptions, the experimenter asked if they would mind completing a questionnaire that another psychologist in the department was planning to use in a future experiment. All participants agreed to fill out the questionnaire (the IRI). The experimenter explained that because it was necessary to complete the scale independently, they would be separated from each other at this time and seated in separate rooms. The experimenter chose the confederate to complete the survey in an adjoining room and escorted her there. Then the experimenter returned to the laboratory room, gave the participant the IRI scale, and told him or her to come to the hallway outside when the questionnaire was completed. At that point, the experimenter queried the participant as to any suspicions that (a) the other participant was in fact a confederate or (b) the purpose of the experiment was anything other than what the cover story indicated. Next, the purpose and hypotheses of the study were divulged to the participant. The participant was asked to sign a video consent form. Finally, the participant was thanked for his or her participation.

Results

Interjudge reliability Videotapes were coded by a judge for the number of times participants rubbed their face and shook their foot. Approximately half (23) of the videotapes were then coded by a second judge. Reliability between the two judges was very high: for the number of times participants rubbed their face, $r = .97$, and for the number of times they shook their foot, $r = .82$, both significant at $p < .001$. Ratings between the two judges were averaged to form a single rating for face rubbing and foot shaking. Ratings were then divided by the time duration of the interaction (to the nearest second) to arrive at a rate for behavior per minute.

Perspective taking To test the hypothesis that individuals who are high perspective-takers nonconsciously mimic others to a greater extent, we categorized participants into those who scored high and those who scored low on perspective taking. We computed the median on the perspective-taking subscale of the IRI (median = 19) and classified those participants above the median ($n = 28$) into the *high-perspective-taking* category and those below it ($n = 22$) into the *low-perspective-taking* category.

A repeated measures ANOVA was performed with number of times participants rubbed their face and number of times participants shook their foot as a within-subject variable and perspective taking (high vs. low) as a between-subjects variable. Gender was included as an additional between-subjects variable in this and all subsequent analyses, but no significant main effect for gender or interaction between gender and perspective taking was revealed. Thus, the gender variable is not discussed further. As predicted, however, there was a significant main effect of perspective taking across the two types of mimicking, $F(1, 48) = 3.85, p = .05$. This main effect was not moderated by an interaction with type of behavior (face rubbing vs. foot shaking), $p > .20$. Specifically, high-perspective takers rubbed their face ($M = 1.30$) and shook their foot ($M = 0.40$) more times per minute than did low-perspective takers (Ms = 0.85 and 0.29, respectively). These results support our hypothesis that those individuals who have a greater tendency to take the perspective of others also are more likely to engage in behavioral mimicry.

Empathic concern To test our hypothesis that the emotional facet of empathy would not moderate the chameleon effect, we also performed a median split on the Empathic Concern subscale scores (median = 21). Participants with scores above the median ($n = 28$) were classified into the *high-empathic-concern* category, and those with scores below it ($n = 22$) were placed in the *low-empathic-concern* category.

A repeated measures ANOVA was performed with number of times participants rubbed their face and number of times participants shook their foot as a within-subject variable and empathic concern (high vs. low) as a between-subjects variable. As predicted, there was no main effect of empathic concern across the two types of mimicking, $F < 1$, nor was there an interaction between empathic concern and type of behavior (face rubbing vs. foot shaking), $F < 1$. In fact, the means showed a slight trend for there to be more mimicry of foot shaking and face rubbing among those low in empathic concern than those high on this subscale.

Discussion

Our third goal in this research was to test a personality variable that may moderate the extent to which one engages in behavior mimicry. Because of the link among perspective taking and social skills, empathy with others, and compassion for others, individuals who often take the perspective of others are more likely to have positive, smooth interactions. High-perspective takers may be the ones who are better at nonconsciously guiding social interactions and automatically doing the things that ensure smooth and easy interactions. Part of this may entail mimicking the behavioral mannerisms of interaction partners.

In Experiment 3, we tested whether those who take the perspective of others have more strongly developed this covert mechanism for attaining smooth, positive interactions. Specifically, we predicted that high-perspective takers would be more likely to mimic the mannerisms of another person. We also predicted that the emotional facet of empathy (operationalized as the Empathic Concern subscale of the IRI) would not similarly moderate the cognitive perception–behavior link. As predicted, high-perspective takers mimicked the mannerisms of a confederate more so than did low-perspective takers, and, also as predicted, participants who scored low and participants who scored high on empathic concern did not significantly differ in the extent to which they mimicked the confederate. This supports our prediction that chronic differences in perspective taking would be related to chronic differences in nonconscious mimicking tendencies.

GENERAL DISCUSSION

We have argued that the perception–behavior link, through which merely perceiving an action performed by another can lead one to perform that action, is the mechanism behind the often observed behavior mimicry and consequent empathic understanding within social interactions. In Experiment 1, we tested the existence of the chameleon effect in an experimental demonstration that supported the perception–behavior link as its proximal cause: Changes in a confederate's behavior caused changes in the participant's behavior, in the absence of the participant's awareness of this influence. Experiment 2 provided an explicit test of the commonly held belief that nonconscious mimicry serves the adaptive function of facilitating smooth interactions and fostering liking. In line with this prediction is the finding that individuals whose postures and movements were mirrored by a confederate liked that partner more and thought the interaction went more smoothly compared with those whose behaviors were not mirrored, again without being aware of the true source of this increased empathic understanding and liking. Finally, in Experiment 3, we tested perspective taking as a individual difference that moderates the extent to which one engages in behavior mimicry. As hypothesized, those who frequently take the perspective of interaction partners mimicked the mannerisms of a confederate to a greater extent than did those who less often take the perspective of others, as would be expected if social–perceptual activity mediated the effect.

The present experiments go beyond other recent perception–behavior studies in showing, for the first time, automatic behavioral effects mediated by actual, in-person perception of the partner's behavior (as opposed to priming manipulations that could have influenced behavior directly). They also represent an advance over existing mimicry–empathy research by providing an experimental instead of a correlational demonstration of the effect, by ruling out the need for a purposive interaction goal in order for the effect to occur, and by providing for the first time a mechanism for the effect (viz., the perception–behavior link). Finally, the present investigation shows that two formerly separate effects, previously studied in isolation from one another, are actually outcomes of the same underlying process.

Our conclusion that the effect of perception on behavior is an automatic process that does not depend on conscious choice is consistent with recent neuropsychological findings as well. One telling piece of evidence is the fact that the frequency of direct effects of perception on action is increased in pathological states in which strategic conscious control over behavior is impaired or nonexistent (Prinz, 1990, p. 176). Such "echo-reactions" as the unintentional repetition of the words used by another (*echolalia*) or unintentional imitation of another's actions (*echopraxia*) are commonly observed in patients with aphasia, apraxia, mental retardation, and brain damage whose ability to consciously and intentionally self-regulate is severely impaired. Thus, in the absence of intentional forms of action control, the perception–behavior link remains intact, arguing against the role of conscious choice as a mediator.

Our conclusion is also in harmony with Hilgard's (1965) account of hypnotic suggestion. According to Hilgard, the directives given by the hypnotist are first perceived by the person being hypnotized, and then, because of the suspension of the will that is characteristic of the hypnotic state, passive effects of perception on action are left free to operate. In other words, the suggestions made by the hypnotist have a direct automatic effect on behavior because of the abdication of conscious control by the hypnotized person; in other words, it is an instance of James's (1890) ideomotor action effect in which the ideation is externally induced by the hypnotist (see also Wegner & Wheatley, 1999).

Preconscious Automatic Processes as Adaptive and Beneficial

The perception–behavior link is one of several routes through which the environment can influence behavior without one's awareness, intent, or control. With this particular route, perceptual activity nonconsciously spreads to behavioral representations, increasing the likelihood of behaving similarly to others in the current environment. There has also been research on automatic routes from environment to behavior via the nonconscious activation of motivations and goals (see Bargh, 1990, 1997; Bargh & Gollwitzer, 1994; Chartrand & Bargh, 1996) and via nonconscious evaluation of environmental stimuli (see Bargh, Chaiken, et al., 1996; Chen & Bargh, 1999). Uncovering the adaptive purpose of the perception–behavior link is in harmony with a recent trend in social automaticity research of identifying the adaptive purposes of these various preconscious determinants of behavior; at the same time, it stands in contrast with those theorists who hold that such nonconscious effects are uniformly negative and maladaptive (e.g., Bandura, 1986; Langer, 1989, 1997; Locke & Latham, 1990; Mischel, Cantor, & Feldman, 1996).

For instance, a person's chronic goals within a situation become linked in memory to the representation of that situation, such that entering that environment automatically causes that goal to become active and to operate without the individual's awareness of its activation or guiding role in subsequent behavior (Bargh, 1990; Chartrand & Bargh, 1996). This nonconscious reaction has been conceptualized as an adaptive mechanism because it reflects the individual's history of goal choice within the situation and increases the probability of goal pursuit. It also eliminates the need to consciously choose the goal on each occasion, when attention and thought may be on other matters at the time. Positive, self-actualizing goals, such as achievement, and positive aspects of motivational states, such as persistence and overcoming obstacles to attain the desired goal, have all been shown to occur with nonconscious goal activation and pursuit just as they do with conscious goal pursuit (Bargh & Chartrand, 1999; Bargh, Gollwitzer, Lee Chai, & Barndollar, 1998).

Automatic evaluation research has documented the pervasive tendency for people to classify all environmental stimuli as either positive or negative. This process, too, has been shown to produce adaptive consequences. For one thing, it alerts us to what is beneficial and helpful and what is dangerous in our environment when conscious attention and thought are elsewhere, and it signals the valence of the current environment by automatically affecting the individual's mood (Chartrand & Bargh, 1999). Moreover, approach and avoidance behavioral tendencies are put into motion immediately by positive instead of negative automatic evaluations (Chen & Bargh, 1999), readying the individual to react in an appropriate manner, yet through an entirely nonconscious mechanism.

In the present research we have continued this trend by focusing on the adaptive function of the chameleon effect. Nonconscious behavior mimicry was found to increase liking for the partner and the reported smoothness of the interactions, and individuals who often take the perspective of others engage in it more than do other people.

It should be acknowledged that previous demonstrations of the perception–behavior link did not produce such positive social effects. For instance, in the original Bargh, Chen, et al. (1996) studies, individuals engaged in stereotype-consistent behavior (e.g., hostility) following automatic activation of that stereotype (e.g., for African Americans). Subsequent research has found that such nonconsciously produced stereotype-consistent behavior can produce a self-fulfilling prophecy (Chen & Bargh, 1997), in that one's interaction partner reacts to one's behavior in kind, yet one is not aware of the effect of one's own behavior in causing that stereotype-confirming behavioral response.

That the stereotype version of the perception–behavior effect can produce negative outcomes should come as no surprise, because stereotype effects on perception and judgment are also largely negative. But stereotypes are categories gone awry—they take the perceiver beyond the information actually present in the other person's behavior. This does not mean that categories per se are maladaptive or problematic; to the contrary, they are absolutely essential for normal, moment-to-moment functioning, to simplify the world, to give it meaning, and to furnish anticipations about what is likely to happen next (e.g., Barsalou, 1992; Smith & Medin, 1981). It follows that the typical form of the chameleon effect—behavior tendencies generated nonconsciously from the perceived behavior of one's interaction partner—is, unlike the stereotype version, largely adaptive and of high social utility. This is what we sought to demonstrate in Experiments 2 and 3. The usual form of the chameleon effect, we assert, is to enhance the positivity of social interactions.

Individual Differences in Nonconscious Mimicry

In Experiment 3, we focused on one personality variable that moderated the chameleon effect; however, we do not mean to suggest that no other moderators exist. Further research may well uncover additional individual difference variables that can increase or decrease the extent to which individuals nonconsciously mimic those around them. One such possibility is the *communal/exchange orientation* dimension proposed by Clark and colleagues (Clark & Mills, 1979; Clark, Mills, & Powell, 1986). Individuals with a *communal* orientation towards others might exhibit more nonconscious mimicry than those with an *exchange* orientation, because communally oriented people are, by definition, more perceptually attuned to the needs of others. Moreover, by the same logic, there may be greater frequency of chameleon-like social behavior in collectivistic versus individualistic societies, because the former more than the latter are characterized by interdependence (e.g., Markus & Kitayama, 1991). Therefore, collectivistic cultures are likely to be characterized by a relatively intensified attentional and perceptual focus by individuals on the behavior of others, and in light of the present experimental findings, this increased perception of others' behavior would be expected to produce greater rapport and smoother social interactions.

Implications for Group Processes

At the level of the social group, then, to the extent that members are mimicking each others' facial expressions, postures, mannerisms, and other behaviors, there is likely to be greater cohesion and liking within the group. In Experiment 1, we found that mimicry occurred even in the most minimal circumstances in which the interactants were unacquainted and had no goal to affiliate; thus, it may be that newly formed groups would benefit from nonconscious mimicry and imitation as well as would established groups. We suspect that the chameleon effect contributes to effective behavior coordination among members of a group. The synchrony and immediacy of such behavior coordination in moving schools of fish or flocks of birds, for example, are the result of an automatic, direct effect of perception on behavior (Breder, 1976; Pitcher, 1979; Reynolds, 1987, 1993)—one that clearly does not require conscious choice or reflection to operate. Moreover, the positive effects of empathy, liking, and bonding that occur automatically because of the chameleon effect would likely benefit most newly formed groups in which relationships among the members do not yet exist or are fragile—it would also tend to shape initial feelings among group members in a positive direction.

Such speculations aside, the chameleon effect is clearly a basic and important social psychological phenomenon, one to which all can relate on a personal level. It is our hope that research will continue to elucidate the conditions under which the effect is augmented or diminished. Extending the paradigms into more complex and dynamic group settings seems to us to be an important next step to this end. It seems unlikely to us that such pervasive, nonconscious effects on social behavior as the chameleon effect arose by accident, and such effects are more likely than not to have positive, desirable effects for the individual and for the groups to which he or she belongs.

REFERENCES

Allport, G. W. (1968). The historical background of modern social psychology. In G. Lindzey & E. Aronson (Eds.), *Handbook of social psychology* (2nd ed., Vol. 1, pp. 1–80). Reading, MA: Addison-Wesley.

Anisfeld, M. (1979, July 13). Response to Meltzoff and Moore (1977). *Science, 205*, 214.

Banaji, M. R., Hardin, C., & Rothman, A. J. (1993). Implicit stereotyping in person judgment. *Journal of Personality and Social Psychology, 65*, 272–281.

Bandura, A. (1977). *Social learning theory*. Englewood Cliffs, NJ: Prentice Hall.

Bandura, A. (1986). *Social foundations of thought and action: A social cognitive theory*. Englewood Cliffs, NJ: Prentice Hall.

Bargh, J. A. (1989). Conditional automaticity: Varieties of automatic influence in social perception and cognition. In J. S. Uleman & J. A. Bargh (Eds.), *Unintended thought* (pp. 3–51). New York: Guilford Press.

Bargh, J. A. (1990). Automotives: Preconscious determinants of thought and behavior. In E. T. Higgins & R. M. Sorrentino (Eds.), *Handbook of motivation and cognition* (Vol. 2, pp. 93–130). New York: Guilford Press.

Bargh, J. A. (1994). The four horsemen of automaticity: Awareness, efficiency, intention, and control in social cognition. In R. S. Wyer, Jr., & T. K. Stall (Eds.), *Handbook of social cognition* (2nd ed., pp. 1–40). Hillsdale, NJ: Erlbaum.

Bargh, J. A. (1997). The automaticity of everyday life. In R. S. Wyer, Jr. (Ed.), *Advances in social cognition* (Vol. 10, pp. 1–61). Mahwah, NJ: Erlbaum.

Bargh, J. A. (1999). The cognitive monster. In S. Chaiken & Y. Trope (Eds.), *Dual process theories in social psychology* (pp. 361–382). New York: Guilford Press.

Bargh, J. A., Chaiken, S., Govender, R., & Pratto, F. (1992). The generality of the automatic attitude activation effect. *Journal of Personality and Social Psychology, 62*, 893–912.

Bargh, J. A., Chaiken, S., Raymond, P., & Hymes, C. (1996). The automatic evaluation effect: Unconditionally automatic attitude activation with a pronunciation task. *Journal of Experimental Social Psychology, 32*, 104–128.

Bargh, J. A., & Chartrand, T. L. (1999). The unbearable automaticity of being. *American Psychologist, 54*, 462–479.

Bargh, J. A., & Chartrand, T. L. (in press). Studying the mind in the middle: A practical guide to priming and automaticity research. In H. Reis & C. Judd (Eds.), *Research methods for the social sciences*. New York: Cambridge University Press.

Bargh, J. A., Chen, M., & Burrows, L. (1996). Automaticity of social behavior: Direct effects of trait construct and stereotype activation on action. *Journal of Personality and Social Psychology, 71*, 230–244.

Bargh, J. A., & Gollwitzer, P. (1994). Environmental control of goal-directed action: Automatic and strategic contingencies between situations and behavior. In W. D. Spaulding (Ed.), *Nebraska Symposium on Motivation* (Vol. 41, pp. 71–124). Lincoln: University of Nebraska Press.

Bargh, J. A., Gollwitzer, P., Lee Chai, A., & Barndollar, K. (1998). *Bypassing the will: Nonconscious self-regulation through automatic goal pursuit.* Manuscript submitted for publication, New York University.

Bargh, J. A., & Thein, R. D. (1985). Individual construct accessibility, person memory, and the recall–judgment link: The case of information overload. *Journal of Personality and Social Psychology, 46*, 1129–1146.

Barsalou, L. W. (1992). Cognitive psychology: *An overview for cognitive scientists*. Hillsdale, NJ: Erlbaum.

Baumeister, R. F., & Leary, M. R. (1995). The need to belong: Desire for interpersonal attachments as a fundamental human motivation. *Psychological Bulletin, 117*, 497–529.

Bavelas, J. B., Black, A., Chovil, N., Lemery, C. R., & Mullett, J. (1988). Form and function in motor mimicry: Topographic evidence that the primary function is communication. *Human Communication Research, 14*, 275–299.

Bavelas, J. B., Black, A., Lemery, C. R., & Mullett, J. (1986). "I show how you feel": Motor mimicry as a communicative act. *Journal of Personality and Social Psychology, 50*, 322–329.

Bavelas, J. B., Black, A., Lemery, C. R., & Mullett, J. (1987). Motor mimicry as primitive empathy. In N. Eisenberg & J. Strayer (Eds.), *Empathy and its development* (pp. 317–338). Cambridge, England: Cambridge University Press.

Berkowitz, L. (1984). Some effects of thoughts on anti- and prosocial influences of media events: A cognitive–neoassociation analysis. *Psychological Bulletin, 95*, 410–427.

Bernieri, F. J. (1988). Coordinated movement and rapport in teacher-student interactions. *Journal of Nonverbal Behavior, 12*, 120–138.

Bernieri, F. J., & Rosenthal, R. (1991). Interpersonal coordination: Behavior matching and interactional synchrony. In R. S. Feldman & B. Rimé, (Eds.), *Fundamentals of nonverbal behavior* (pp. 401–432). Cambridge, England: Cambridge University Press.

Breder, C. M. (1976). Fish schools as operational structures. *Fishery Bulletin, 74*, 471–502.

Brewer, M. B. (1988). A dual process model of impression formation. In R. S. Wyer, Jr., and T. K. Srull (Eds.), *Advances in social cognition* (Vol. 1, pp. 1–36). Hillsdale, NJ: Erlbaum.

Brewer, M. B. (1991). The social self: On being the same and different at the same time. *Personality and Social Psychology Bulletin, 17*, 475–482.

Carlston, D. E., & Skowronski, J. J. (1994). Savings in the relearning of trait information as evidence for spontaneous inference generation. *Journal of Personality and Social Psychology, 66*, 840–856.

Carver, C. S., Ganellen, R. J., Froming, W. J., & Chambers, W. (1983). Modeling: An analysis in terms of category accessibility. *Journal of Experimental Social Psychology, 19*, 403–421.

Charney, E. J. (1966). Psychosomatic manifestations of rapport in psychotherapy. *Psychosomatic Medicine, 28*, 305–315.

Chartrand, T. L., & Bargh, J. A. (1996). Automatic activation of impression formation and memorization goals: Nonconscious goal priming reproduces effects of explicit task instructions. *Journal of Personality and Social Psychology, 71*, 464–478.

Chartrand, T. L., & Bargh, J. A. (1999). *Consequences of automatic evaluation for mood.* Manuscript in preparation, New York University.

Chen, M., & Bargh, J. A. (1997). Nonconscious behavioral confirmation processes: The self-fulfilling consequences of automatic stereotype activation. *Journal of Experimental Social Psychology, 33*, 541–560.

Chen, M., & Bargh, J. A. (1999). Consequences of automatic evaluation: Immediate behavioral predispositions to approach or avoid the stimulus. *Personality and Social Psychology Bulletin, 25*, 215–224.

Chen, M., Chartrand, T. L., Lee Chai, A., & Bargh, J. A. (1998). Priming primates: Human and otherwise. *Behavioral and Brain Sciences, 21*, 685–686.

Cialdini, R. B., Brown, S. L., Lewis, B. P., Luce, C., & Neuberg, S. L. (1997). Reinterpreting the empathy–altruism relationship: When one into one equals oneness. *Journal of Personality and Social Psychology, 73*, 481–494.

Clark, M. S., & Mills, J. (1979). Interpersonal attraction in exchange and communal relationships. *Journal of Personality and Social Psychology, 37*, 12–24.

Clark, M. S., Mills, J., & Powell, M. C. (1986). Keeping track of needs in communal and exchange relationships. *Journal of Personality and Social Psychology, 51*, 333–338.

Condon, W. S., & Ogston, W. D. (1966). Sound film analysis of normal and pathological behavior patterns. *Journal of Nervous and Mental Disease, 143*, 338–347.

Condon, W. S., & Sander, L. W. (1974). Synchrony demonstrated between movements of the neonate and adult speech. *Child Development, 45*, 456–462.

Dabbs, J. M. (1969). Similarity of gestures and interpersonal influence. *Proceedings of the 77th Annual Convention of the American Psychological Association, 4*, 337–339.

Darwin, C. (1965). *The expression of the emotions in man and animals.* Chicago: University of Chicago Press. (Original work published 1872)

Davis, M. H. (1980). A multidimensional approach to individual differences in empathy. *Catalog of Selected Documents in Psychology, 10*, 85.

Davis, M. H. (1983). Measuring individual differences in empathy: Evidence for a multidimensional approach. *Journal of Personality and Social Psychology, 44*, 113–126.

Devine, P. G. (1989). Stereotypes and prejudice: Their automatic and controlled components. *Journal of Personality and Social Psychology, 56*, 5–18.

Dijksterhuis, A., Aarts, H., Bargh, J. A., & van Knippenberg, A. (1998). *Intergroup contact and automatic behavior.* Manuscript submitted for publication, University of Nijmegen, the Netherlands.

Dijksterhuis, A., Spears, R., Postmes, T., Stapel, D. A., Koomen, W., van Knippenberg, A., & Scheepers, D. (1998). Seeing one thing and doing another: Contrast effects in automatic behavior. *Journal of Personality and Social Psychology, 75*, 862–871.

Dijksterhuis, A., & van Knippenberg, A. (1998). The relation between perception and behavior, or how to win a game of Trivial Pursuit. *Journal of Personality and Social Psychology, 74*, 865–877.

Dimberg, U. (1982). Facial reactions to facial expressions. *Psychophysiology, 19*, 643–647.

Dittmann, A. T., & Llewellyn, L. G. (1968). Relationship between vocalizations and head nods as listener responses. *Journal of Personality and Social Psychology, 9*, 79–84.

Dittmann, A. T., & Llewellyn, L. G. (1969). Body movement and speech rhythm in social conversation. *Journal of Personality and Social Psychology, 11*, 98–106.

Fazio, R. H., Sanbonmatsu, D. M., Powell, M. C., & Kardes, F. R. (1986). On the automatic activation of attitudes. *Journal of Personality and Social Psychology, 50*, 229–238.

Galef, B. G. (1988). Imitation in animals: History, definition and interpretation of data from the psychological laboratory. In T. Zentall & B. G. Galef (Eds.), *Comparative social learning* (pp. 3–28). Hillsdale, NJ: Erlbaum.

Hatfield, E., Cacioppo, J. T., & Rapson, R. L. (1994). *Emotional contagion.* Cambridge, England: Cambridge University Press.

Herr, P. M., Sherman, S. J., & Fazio, R. H. (1984). On the consequences of priming: Assimilation and contrast effects. *Journal of Experimental Social Psychology, 19*, 323–340.

Heyes, C. M. (1993). Imitation, culture and cognition. *Animal Behaviour, 46*, 999–1010.

Higgins, E. T. (1989). Knowledge accessibility and activation: Subjectivity and suffering from unconscious sources. In J. S. Uleman & J. A. Bargh (Eds.), *Unintended thought* (pp. 75–123). New York: Guilford Press.

Higgins, E. T. (1996). Knowledge activation: Accessibility, applicability, and salience. In E. T. Higgins & A. W. Kruglanski (Eds.), *Social psychology: Handbook of basic principles* (pp. 133–168). New York: Guilford Press.

Higgins, E. T., Rholes, W. S., & Jones, C. R. (1977). Category accessibility and impression formation. *Journal of Experimental Social Psychology, 13*, 141–154.

Hilgard, E. R. (1965). *Hypnotic susceptibility.* New York: Harcourt, Brace & World.

Jacobson, S. W., & Kagan, J. (1979, July 13). Response to Meltzoff and Moore (1977). *Science, 205*, 215.

James, W. (1890). *Principles of psychology.* New York: Holt.

Kaitz, M., Meschulach-Sarfaty, O., Auerbach, J., & Eidelman, A. (1988). A reexamination of newborns' ability to imitate facial expressions. *Developmental Psychology, 24*, 3–7.

Kendon, A. (1970). Movement coordination in social interaction: Some examples described. *Acta Psychologica, 32*, 1–25.

Koffka, K. (1925). *Die grundlagen der psychischen entwicklung* [The foundations of psychological development]. Osterwieck, Germany: Zickfeldt.

La France, M. (1979). Nonverbal synchrony and rapport: Analysis by the cross-lag panel technique. *Social Psychology Quarterly, 42*, 66–70.

La France, M. (1982). Posture mirroring and rapport. In M. Davis (Ed.), *Interaction rhythms: Periodicity in communicative behavior* (pp. 279–298). New York: Human Sciences Press.

La France, M., & Broadbent, M. (1976). Group rapport: Posture sharing as a nonverbal indicator. *Group and Organization Studies, 1*, 328–333.

La France, M., & Ickes, W. (1981). Posture mirroring and interactional involvement: Sex and sex typing effects. *Journal of Nonverbal Behavior, 5*, 139–154.

Langer, E. (1989). *Mindfulness.* Reading, MA: Addison-Wesley.

Langer, E. (1997). *The power of mindful learning.* Reading, MA: Addison-Wesley.

Lashley, K. S. (1951). The problem of serial order in behavior. In L. A. Jeffress (Ed.), *Cerebral mechanisms in behavior: The Hixon Symposium* (pp. 112–136). New York: Wiley & Sons.

Levenson, R. W., & Ruef, A. M. (1997). Physiological aspects of emotional knowledge and rapport. In W. Ickes (Ed.), *Empathic accuracy* (pp. 44–73). New York: Guilford Press.

Locke, E. A., & Latham, G. P. (1990). *A theory of goal setting and task performance*. Englewood Cliffs, NJ: Prentice Hall.

Macrae, C. N., Bodenhausen, G. V., Milne, A. B., Castelli, L., Schloerscheidt, A. M., & Greco, S. (1998). On activating exemplars. *Journal of Experimental Social Psychology, 34*, 330–354.

Markus, H. R., & Kitayama, S. (1991). Culture and the self: Implications for cognition, emotion, and motivation. *Psychological Review, 98*, 224–253.

Masters, J. C. (1979, July 13). Response to Meltzoff and Moore (1977). *Science, 205*, 215.

Maurer, R. E., & Tindall, J. H. (1983). Effect of pastural congruence on client's perception of counselor empathy. *Journal of Counseling Psychology, 30*, 158–163.

McDowall, J. J. (1978). Interactional synchrony: A reappraisal. *Journal of Personality and Social Psychology, 36*, 963–975.

Mead, G. H. (1934). *Mind, self, and society*. Chicago: University of Chicago Press.

Meltzoff, A. N., & Moore, M. K. (1977, October 7). Imitation of facial and manual gestures by human neonates. *Science, 198*, 75–78.

Meltzoff, A. N., & Moore, M. K. (1979, July 13). Note responding to Anisfeld, Masters, and Jacobson and Kagan's comments on Meltzoff and Moore (1977). *Science, 205*, 217–219.

Meltzoff, A. N., & Moore, M. K. (1983). Newborn infants imitate adult facial gestures. *Child Development, 54*, 702–709.

Mischel, W., Cantor, N., & Feldman, S. (1996). Principles of self-regulation: The nature of willpower and self-control. In E. T. Higgins & A. W. Kruglanski (Eds.), *Social psychology: Handbook of basic principles* (pp. 329–360). New York: Guilford Press.

Muesseler, J., & Hommel, B. (1997). Blindness to response-compatible stimuli. *Journal of Experimental Psychology: Human Perception and Performance, 23*, 861–872.

Mussweiler, T., & Foerster, J. (1998). *The sex→aggression link: A perception–behavior dissociation.* Manuscript submitted for publication, Universitat Wurzburg.

Piaget, J. (1932). *The moral judgment of the child.* London: Kegan, Paul, Trench, Trubner.

Piaget, J. (1946). *La formation du symbole chez l'enfant* [Symbol formation in the child]. Paris: Delachaux & Niestlé.

Pitcher, T. J. (1979). Sensory information and the organization of behavior in a shoaling cyprinid fish. *Animal Behavior, 27*, 126–149.

Prinz, W. (1990). A common coding approach to perception and action. In O. Neumann & W. Prinz (Eds.), *Relationships between perception and action* (pp. 167–201). Berlin: Springer-Verlag.

Reynolds, C. W. (1987). Flocks, herds, and schools: A distributed behavioral model. *Computer Graphics, 21*, 25–34.

Reynolds, C. W. (1993). An evolved, vision-based behavioral model of coordinated group motion. In J.-A. Meyer, H. L. Roitblat, & S. W. Wilson (Eds.), *From animals to animats 2* (pp. 384–392). Cambridge, MA: MIT Press.

Scheflen, A. E. (1964). The significance of posture in communication systems. *Psychiatry, 27*, 316–331.

Smith, A. (1966). *The theory of moral sentiments.* New York: Augustus M. Kelley. (Original work published 1759.)

Smith, E. R., & Medin, D. L. (1981). *Categories and concepts.* Cambridge, MA: Harvard University Press.

Smith, E. R., & Zarate, M. A. (1992). Exemplar-based model of social judgment. *Psychological Review, 99*, 3–21.

Srull, T. K., & Wyer, R. S., Jr. (1979). The role of category accessibility in the interpretation of information about persons: Some determinants and implications. *Journal of Personality and Social Psychology, 37*, 1660–1672.

Srull, T. K., & Wyer, R. S., Jr. (1980), Category accessibility and social perception: Some implications for the study of person memory and interpersonal judgment. *Journal of Personality and Social Psychology, 38*, 841–856.

Stapel, D. A., Koomen, W., & van der Pligt, J. (1997). Categories of category accessibility: The impact of trait versus exemplar priming on person judgments. *Journal of Personality and Social Psychology, 74*, 878–893.

Tickle-Degnen, L., & Rosenthal, R. (1987). Group rapport and nonverbal behavior. *Review of Personality and Social Psychology, 9*, 113–136.

Tomasello, M., Savage-Rumbaugh, E. S., & Kruger, A. C. (1993). Imitative learning of actions on objects by children, chimpanzees, and enculturated chimpanzees. *Child Development, 64*, 1688–1705.

Trout, D., & Rosenfeld, H. M. (1980). The effect of postural lean and body congruence on the judgment of psychotherapeutic rapport. *Journal of Nonverbal Communication, 4*, 176–190.

Uleman, J. S., Newman, L. S., & Moskowitz, G. B. (1996). People as flexible interpreters: Evidence and issues from spontaneous trait inference. In M. P. Zanna (Ed.), *Advances in experimental social psychology* (Vol. 28, pp. 211–279). New York: Academic Press.

Vaughan, K. B., & Lanzetta, J. T. (1980). Vicarious instigation and conditioning of facial expressive and autonomic responses to a model's expressive display of pain. *Journal of Personality and Social Psychology, 38*, 909–923.

Wegner, D. M., & Wheatley, T. P. (1999). Apparent mental causation: Sources of the experience of will. *American Psychologist, 54*, 480–492.

Winter, L., & Uleman, J. S. (1984). When are social judgments made? Evidence for the spontaneousness of trait inferences. *Journal of Personality and Social Psychology, 47*, 237–252.

Wyer, R. S., Jr., & Stall, T. K. (1989). *Memory and cognition in its social context.* Hillsdale, NJ: Erlbaum.

Zajonc, R. B., Adelmann, K. A., Murphy, S. T., & Niedenthal, P. M. (1987). Convergence in the physical appearance of spouses. *Motivation and Emotion, 11*, 335–346.

Received April 30, 1998
Revision received December 17, 1998
Accepted December 17, 1998

NOTES

1. Although motor-mimicry researchers have manipulated confederates' behaviors, they were not interested in (and therefore did not manipulate) general postures or behavioral mannerisms. Instead, the experimenters created situations in which participants observed a confederate experiencing a specific event and emotion and then tested whether participants reacted as if the experience were happening to them (e.g., Bavelas et al., 1988; Bavelas, Black, Lemery, & Mullett, 1987).
2. Although an effort was made to avoid photographs with strong emotional content, at the same time we needed to choose photos that would (a) be convincing as stimuli for a projective measure and (b) be able to stimulate 1–2 min of description as well as conjecture as to what was being thought or felt by the people in the photographs.
3. We also coded number of seconds participants spent smiling, rubbing their face, and shaking their foot. The correlations between these seconds measures and the number of times measures was high (for smiling, $r = .92$; for face rubbing, $r = .88$; for foot shaking, $r = .94$). Because of this redundancy, we report only the number of times analyses in the text. However, we computed all analyses on the number of seconds as well, and the results showed the identical pattern and significance level as the number of times analyses.
4. Reliability between judges was higher for the foot-shaking than for the face-rubbing measures. Because there are many physical gestures that can be made in the facial area (e.g., scratching an itch, playing with an earring, fixing hair), a detailed coding key was created and used by both raters. However, judgment calls had to be made, which reduced reliability. It should be noted that in Experiment 2 the reliability for this measure was substantially higher.
5. Brewer's (1991) model of optimal distinctiveness is consistent with this argument and puts it in a larger framework by bringing in a second, opposing need. In this model, social identity is viewed as a reconciliation between the two needs: On the one hand, we have a need for validation, similarity to others, and a sense of belonging, and on the other, we have a need for uniqueness, individuation, and a sense of distinctiveness.
6. It was important that the confederates in the nonmimicking condition not come across as stiff and awkward, while the mimicking confederates came across as relaxed, mobile, and animated. This potential confounded difference in behavior might provide an alternative explanation for our results: The participants liked the confederate in the mimicking condition more not because they were being mimicked by her, but rather because she seemed more relaxed, at ease, animated, and interesting than the confederate in the neutral condition. Consequently, we instructed all confederates to sit in a relaxed (i.e., not stiff and upright) position in both the mimicking and nonmimicking conditions; the only difference was that in the mimicking condition the relaxed position happened to mirror the participant's position, whereas in the nonmimicking condition it did not.
7. Ideally, one would obtain the judges' blind ratings of the likeability of the confederates per se—that is, how likeable a person who is not being mimicked considers the confederate to be. Such a rating would correspond more directly to the liking ratings made by the participants. However, the same confederate interacted with many different participants—sometimes mimicking them and sometimes not. Thus, an overall likeability rating for a given confederate would necessarily include both mimicking and nonmimicking sessions. To avoid this problem and to obtain separate ratings for the mimicking versus nonmimicking conditions, we opted instead to have judges rate the confederates' likeableness toward each individual participant.

READING 7

Milgram's research on obedience to authority is the best known, most dramatic, and most controversial in the history of social psychology. Inspired by the events of World War II Nazi Germany, Milgram constructed a laboratory setting that called upon ordinary people, in response to commands issued by a psychology experimenter, to inflict increasing amounts of pain against an innocent man. Would anyone do it? If so, under what conditions? And what could be done to empower individuals to resist? The following article is Milgram's account of the first of many experiments he would go on to conduct on this subject. Read it, try to put yourself into the shoes of those who took part, and consider what it says about human nature and the way in which each of us can be overwhelmed by powerful situations. Then read in Chapter 7 (Conformity) about the numerous variations on this study that Milgram performed and ask yourself why some factors made little or no difference on the rates of obedience and why other factors did have a significant impact on these results.

Behavioral Study of Obedience

Stanley Milgram
Yale University

This article describes a procedure for the study of destructive obedience in the laboratory. It consists of ordering a naive S to administer increasingly more severe punishment to a victim in the context of a learning experiment. Punishment is administered by means of a shock generator with 30 graded switches ranging from Slight Shock to Danger: Severe Shock. The victim is a confederate of the E. The primary dependent variable is the maximum shock the S is willing to administer before he refuses to continue further. 26 Ss obeyed the experimental commands fully, and administered the highest shock on the generator. 14 Ss broke off the experiment at some point after the victim protested and refused to provide further answers. The procedure created extreme levels of nervous tension in some Ss. Profuse sweating, trembling, and stuttering were typical expressions of this emotional disturbance. One unexpected sign of tension—yet to be explained—was the regular occurrence of nervous laughter, which in some Ss developed into uncontrollable seizures. The variety of interesting behavioral dynamics observed in the experiment, the reality of the situation for the S, and the possibility of parametric variation within the framework of the procedure, point to the fruitfulness of further study.

Obedience is as basic an element in the structure of social life as one can point to. Some system of authority is a requirement of all communal living, and it is only the man dwelling in isolation who is not forced to respond, through defiance or submission, to the commands of others.

Obedience, as a determinant of behavior, is of particular relevance to our time. It has been reliably established that from 1933–45 millions of innocent persons were systematically slaughtered on command. Gas chambers were built, death camps were guarded, daily quotas of corpses were produced with the same efficiency as the manufacture of appliances. These inhumane policies may have originated in the mind of a single person, but they could only be carried out on a massive scale if a very large number of persons obeyed orders.

Obedience is the psychological mechanism that links individual action to political purpose. It is the dispositional cement that binds men to systems of authority. Facts of recent history and observation in daily life suggest that for many persons obedience may be a deeply ingrained behavior tendency, indeed, a prepotent impulse overriding training in ethics, sympathy, and moral conduct. C. P. Snow (1961) points to its importance when he writes:

> When you think of the long and gloomy history of man, you will find more hideous crimes have been committed in the name of obedience than have ever been committed in the name of rebellion. If you doubt that, read William Shirer's "Rise and Fall of the Third

SOURCE: Milgram, Stanley. 1963. "Behavioral Study of Obedience," *JOURNAL OF ABNORMAL AND SOCIAL PSYCHOLOGY,* Vol. *67*, No. 4, 371–378.

Reich." The German Officer Corps were brought up in the most rigorous code of obedience . . . in the name of obedience they were party to, and assisted in, the most wicked large scale actions in the history of the world [p. 24].

While the particular form of obedience dealt with in the present study has its antecedents in these episodes, it must not be thought all obedience entails acts of aggression against others. Obedience serves numerous productive functions. Indeed, the very life of society is predicated on its existence. Obedience may be ennobling and educative and refer to acts of charity and kindness, as well as to destruction.

General Procedure

A procedure was devised which seems useful as a tool for studying obedience (Milgram, 1961). It consists of ordering a naive subject to administer electric shock to a victim. A simulated shock generator used, with 30 clearly marked voltage levels that range from 15 to 450 volts. The instrument bears verbal designations that range from Slight Shock to Danger: Severe Shock. The responses of the victim, who is a trained confederate of the experimenter, are standardized. The orders to administer shocks are given to the naive subject in the context of a "learning experiment" ostensibly set up to study the effects of punishment on memory. As the experiment proceeds the naive subject is commanded to administer increasingly more intense shocks to the victim, even to the point of reaching the level marked Danger: Severe Shock. Internal resistances become stronger, and at a certain point the subject refuses to go on with the experiment. Behavior prior to this rupture is considered "obedience," in that the subject complies with the commands of the experimenter. The point of rupture is the act of disobedience. A quantitative value is assigned to the subject's performance based on the maximum intensity shock he is willing to administer before he refuses to participate further. Thus for any particular subject and for any particular experimental condition the degree of obedience may be specified with a numerical value. The crux of the study is to systematically vary the factors believed to alter the degree of obedience to the experimental commands.

The technique allows important variables to be manipulated at several points in the experiment. One may vary aspects of the source of command, content and form of command, instrumentalities for its execution, target object, general social setting, etc. The problem, therefore, is not one of designing increasingly more numerous experimental conditions, but of selecting those that best illuminate the *process* of obedience from the sociopsychological standpoint.

Related Studies

The inquiry bears an important relation to philosophic analyses of obedience and authority (Arendt, 1958; Friedrich, 1958; Weber, 1947), an early experimental study of obedience by Frank (1944), studies in "authoritarianism" (Adorno, Frenkel-Brunswik, Levinson, & Stanford, 1950; Rokeach, 1961), and a recent series of analytic and empirical studies in social power (Cartwright, 1959). It owes much to the long concern with *suggestion* in social psychology, both in its normal forms (e.g., Binet, 1900) and in its clinical manifestations (Charcot, 1881). But it derives, in the first instance, from direct observation of a social fact; the individual who is commanded by a legitimate authority ordinarily obeys. Obedience comes easily and often. It is a ubiquitous and indispensable feature of social life.

METHOD

Subjects

The subjects were 40 males between the ages of 20 and 50, drawn from New Haven and the surrounding communities. Subjects were obtained by a newspaper advertisement and direct mail solicitation. Those who responded to the appeal believed they were to participate in a study of memory and learning at Yale University. A wide range of occupations is represented in the sample. Typical subjects were postal clerks, high school teachers, salesmen, engineers, and laborers. Subjects ranged in educational level from one who had not finished elementary school, to those who had doctorate and other professional degrees. They were paid $4.50 for their participation in the experiment. However, subjects were told that payment was simply for coming to the laboratory, and that the money was theirs no matter what happened after they arrived. Table 1 shows the proportion of age and occupational types assigned to the experimental condition.

Personnel and Locale

The experiment was conducted on the grounds of Yale University in the elegant interaction laboratory. (This detail is relevant to the perceived legitimacy of the ex-

TABLE 1
Distribution of Age and Occupational Types in the Experiment

Occupations	20–29 years *n*	30–39 years *n*	40–50 years *n*	Percentage of total (occupations)
Workers, skilled and unskilled	4	5	6	37.5
Sales, business, and white collar	3	6	7	40.0
Professional	1	5	3	22.5
Percentage of total (Age)	20	40	40	

Note: Total $N = 40$

periment. In further variations, the experiment was dissociated from the university with consequences for performance.) The role of experimenter was played by a 31-year-old high school teacher of biology. His manner was impassive, and his appearance somewhat stern throughout the experiment. He was dressed in a gray technician's coat. The victim was played by a 47-year-old accountant, trained for the role; he was of Irish-American stock, whom most observers found mild-mannered and likable.

Procedure

One naive subject and one victim (an accomplice) performed in each experiment. A pretext had to be devised that would justify the administration of electric shock by the naive subject. This was effectively accomplished by the cover story. After a general introduction on the presumed relation between punishment and learning, subjects were told:

> But actually, we know *very little* about the effect of punishment on learning, because almost no truly scientific studies have been made of it in human beings.
>
> For instance, we don't know *how much* punishment is best for learning—and we don't know how much difference it makes as to who is giving the punishment, whether an adult learns best from a younger or an older person than himself—or many things of that sort.
>
> So in this study we are bringing together a number of adults of different occupations and ages. And we're asking some of them to be teachers and some of them to be learners. We want to find out just what effect different people have on each other as teachers and learners, and also what effect *punishment* will have on learning in this situation.
>
> Therefore, I'm going to ask one of you to be the teacher here tonight and the other one to be the learner.
>
> Does either of you have a preference?

Subjects then drew slips of paper from a hat to determine who would be the teacher and who would be the learner in the experiment. The drawing was rigged so that the naive subject was always the teacher and the accomplice always the learner. (Both slips contained the word "Teacher.") Immediately after the drawing, the teacher and learner were taken to an adjacent room and the learner was strapped into an "electric chair" apparatus.

The experimenter explained that the straps were to prevent excessive movement while the learner was being shocked. The effect was to make it impossible for him to escape from the situation. An electrode was attached to the learner's wrist, and electrode paste was applied "to avoid blisters and burns." Subjects were told that the electrode was attached to the shock generator in the adjoining room.

In order to improve credibility the experimenter declared, in response to a question by the learner: "Although the shocks can be extremely painful, they cause no permanent tissue damage."

Learning task The lesson administered by the subject was a paired-associate learning task. The subject read a series of word pairs to the learner, and then read the first word of the pair along with four terms. The learner was to indicate which of the four terms had originally been paired with the first word. He communicated his answer by pressing one of four switches in front of him, which in turn lit up one of four numbered quadrants in an answerbox located atop the shock generator.

Shock generator The instrument panel consists of 30 lever switches set in a horizontal line. Each switch is clearly labeled with a voltage designation that ranges from 15 to 450 volts. There is a 15-volt increment from one switch to the next going from left to right. In addition, the following verbal designations are clearly indicated for groups of four switches going from left to right: Slight Shock, Moderate Shock, Strong Shock, Very Strong Shock, Intense Shock, Extreme Intensity Shock, Danger: Severe Shock. (Two switches after this last designation are simply marked XXX.)

Upon depressing a switch: a pilot light corresponding to each switch is illuminated in bright red; an electric buzzing is heard; an electric blue light, labeled "voltage energizer," flashes; the dial on the voltage meter swings to the right; various relay clicks are sounded.

The upper left-hand corner of the generator is labeled Shock Generator, Type ZLB, Dyson Instrument Company, Waltham, Mass. Output 15 Volts–450 Volts.

Details of the instrument were carefully handled to insure an appearance of authenticity. The panel was engraved by precision industrial engravers, and all components were of high quality. No subject in the experiment suspected that the instrument was merely a simulated shock generator.[1]

Sample shock Each naive subject is given a sample shock on the shock generator, prior to beginning his run as teacher. This shock is always 45 volts, and is applied by pressing the third switch of the generator. The shock is applied to the wrist of the naive subject, and has its source in a 45-volt battery wired into the generator. This further convinces the subject of the authenticity of the generator.

Shock instructions The subject is told to administer a shock to the learner each time he gives a wrong response. Moreover—and this is the key command—the subject is instructed to "move one level higher on the shock generator each time the learner flashes a wrong answer." He is also instructed to announce the voltage level before administering a shock. This serves to continually remind subjects of the increasing intensity of shocks administered to the learner.

Preliminary and regular run Pretests revealed that the procedure of reading words and administering shocks requires some practice before it can be handled smoothly. Therefore, immediately preceding the regular run," the teacher is given a preliminary series of 10 words to read to the learner. There are 3 neutral words in the practice series (i.e., words that the learner answers correctly), so that shocks are administered for 7 of the words, with the maximum shock at 105 volts (moderate shock). Almost all subjects master the procedure by the time the preliminary run is over.

Subjects are then presented with a second list, and are told that the procedure is the same as for the first list; the experimenter adds, however:

> When you get to the bottom of the list, repeat it over again, and continue giving shocks, until the learner has learned all the pairs correctly.

The experimenter instructs the subject to,

> start from 15 volts and increase the shock level one step each time the learner gives a wrong answer.

Feedback from the victim In all conditions the learner gives a predetermined set of responses to the word pair test, based on a schedule of approximately three wrong answers to one correct answer. In the present experimental condition no vocal response or other sign of protest is heard from the learner until Shock Level 300 is reached. When the 300-volt shock is administered, the learner pounds on the wall of the room in which he is bound to the electric chair. The pounding can be heard by the subject. From this point on, the learner's answers no longer appear on the four-way panel.

At this juncture, subjects ordinarily turn to the experimenter for guidance. The experimenter instructs the subject to treat the absence of a response as a wrong answer, and to shock the subject according to the usual schedule. He advises the subjects to allow 5–10 seconds before considering no response as a wrong answer, and to increase the shock level one step each time the learner fails to respond correctly. The learner's pounding is repeated after the 315-volt shock is administered; afterwards he is not heard from, nor do his answers reappear on the four-way signal box.

Experimenter feedback At various points in the experiment the subject may turn to the experimenter for advice on whether he should continue to administer shocks. Or he may indicate that he does not wish to go on. It was important to standardize the experimenter's responses to these inquiries and reactions.

If the subject indicated his unwillingness to go on, the experimenter responded with a sequence of "prods," using as many as necessary to bring the subject into line.

> Prod 1: Please continue, *or* Please go on.
> Prod 2: The experiment requires that you continue.
> Prod 3: It is absolutely essential that you continue.
> Prod 4: You have no other choice, you *must* go on.

The prods were always made in sequence; Only if Prod 1 had been unsuccessful, could Prod 2 be used. If the subject refused to obey the experimenter after Prod 4, the experiment was terminated. The experimenter's tone of voice was at all times firm, but not impolite. The sequence was begun anew on each occasion that the subject balked or showed reluctance to follow orders.

Special prods. If the subject asked if the learner was liable to suffer permanent physical injury, the experimenter said:

> Although the shocks may be painful, there is no permanent tissue damage, so please go on. [Followed by Prods 2, 3, and 4 if necessary.]

If the subject said that the learner did not want to go on, the experimenter replied:

> Whether the learner likes it or not, you must go on until he has learned all the word pairs correctly. So please go on, [Followed by Prods 2, 3, and 4 if necessary.)

Dependent Measures

The primary dependent measure for any subject is the maximum shock he administers before he refuses to go any further. In principle this may vary from 0 (for a subject who refuses to administer even the first shock) to 30 (for a subject who administers the highest shock on the generator). A subject who breaks off the experiment at any point prior to administering the thirtieth shock level is termed a *defiant* subject. One who complies with experimental commands fully, and proceeds to administer all shock levels commanded, is termed an *obedient* subject.

Further records With few exceptions, experimental sessions were recorded on magnetic tape. Occasional photographs were taken through one-way mirrors. Notes were kept on any unusual behavior occurring during the course of the experiments. On occasion, additional observers were directed to write objective descriptions of the subjects' behavior. The latency and duration of shocks were measured by accurate timing devices.

Interview and dehoax Following the experiment, subjects were interviewed; open-ended questions, projective measures, and attitude scales were employed. After the interview, procedures were undertaken to assure that the subject would leave the laboratory in a state of well being. A friendly reconciliation was arranged between the subject and the victim, and an effort was made to reduce any tensions that arose as a result of the experiment.

RESULTS

Preliminary Notions

Before giving an account of the experimental results, it is instructive to consider how persons predict others will perform when commanded to administer powerful shocks to another person. Fourteen Yale seniors, all psychology majors, were provided with a detailed description of the experimental situation. They were asked to reflect carefully on it, and to predict the behavior of 100 hypothetical subjects. More specifically, they were instructed to plot the distribution of obedience of "100 Americans of diverse occupations, and ranging in age from 20 to 50 years," who were placed in the experimental situation.

There was considerable agreement among the respondents on the expected behavior of hypothetical subjects. All respondents predicted that only an insignificant minority would go through to the end of the shock series. (The estimates ranged from 0 to 3%; i.e., the most "pessimistic" member of the class predicted that of 100 persons, 3 would continue through to the most potent shock available on the shock generator—450 volts.) The class mean was 1.2%. The question was also posed informally to colleagues of the author, and the most general feeling was that few if any subjects would go beyond the designation Very Strong Shock.

Results of Experiment I

Subjects accept situation With few exceptions subjects were convinced of the reality of the experimental situation, that they were administering shocks to another person, and the most potent shocks were extremely painful. In the post-experimental interview subjects were asked: "How painful to the learner were the last few shocks that you administered to him?" Subjects were instructed to indicate their answers on a printed 14-point scale ranging from "Not at all painful" to "Extremely painful." The modal response was 14 (Extremely painful) with the mean at 13.42.

Signs of extreme tension Many subjects showed signs of nervousness in the experimental situation, and especially upon administering the more powerful shocks. In a large number of cases the degree of tension reached extremes that are rarely seen in sociopsychological laboratory studies. Subjects were observed to sweat, tremble, stutter, bite their lips, groan, and dig their fingernails into their flesh. These were characteristic rather than exceptional responses to the experiment.

One sign of tension was the regular occurrence of nervous laughing fits. Fourteen of the 40 subjects showed definite signs of nervous laughter and smiling. The laughter seemed entirely out of place, even bizarre. Full-blown, uncontrollable seizures were observed for 3 subjects. On one occasion we observed a seizure so violently convulsive that it was necessary to call a halt to the experiment. The subject, a 46-year-old encyclopedia salesman, was seriously embarrassed by his untoward and uncontrollable behavior. In the post-experimental interviews subjects took pains to point out that they were not sadistic types, and that the laughter did not mean they enjoyed shocking the victim.

Distribution of scores It had been conjectured that persons would not, in general, agree to administer shocks beyond the level designated as Very Strong Shock. The distribution of maximum shocks for this experiment is shown in Table 2. The obtained distribution of scores deviates radically from the prediction.

Upon command of the experimenter, each of the 40 subjects went beyond the expected breakoff point. No subject stopped prior to administering Shock Level 20. (At this level—300 volts—the victim kicks on the wall and no longer provides answers to the teacher's multiple-choice questions.)

Of the 40 subjects, 5 refused to obey the experimental commands beyond the 300-volt level. Four more subjects administered one further shock, and then refused to go on. Two broke off at the 330-volt level, and 1 each at 345, 360, and 375 volts. Thus a total of 14 subjects defied the experimenter. It is instructive to reprint their remarks at the point of defiance, as transcribed from the tape recordings:

[0124] I think he's trying to communicate, he's knocking. . . . Well it's not fair to shock the guy . . . these are terrific volts. I don't think this is very humane. . . . Oh, I can't go on with this; no, this isn't right. It's a hell of an experiment. The guy is suffering in there. No, I don't want to go on. This is crazy. [Subject refused to administer more shocks.]

TABLE 2
Distribution of Breakoff Points

Verbal designation and voltage indication	Number of subjects for whom this was maximum shock
Slight Shock	
15	0
30	0
45	0
60	0
Moderate Shock	
75	0
90	0
105	0
120	0
Strong Shock	
135	0
150	0
165	0
180	0
Very Strong Shock	
195	0
210	0
225	0
240	0
Intense Shock	
255	0
270	0
285	0
300	5
Extreme Intensity Shock	
315	4
330	2
345	1
360	1
Danger: Severe Shock	
375	1
390	0
405	0
420	0
XXX	
435	0
450	26

[0123] He's banging in there. I'm gonna chicken out. I'd like to continue, but I can't do that to a man. . . .I'm sorry I can't do that to a man. I'll hurt his heart. You take your check. . . . No really, I couldn't do it.

These subjects were frequently in a highly agitated and even angered state. Sometimes, verbal protest was at a minimum, and the subject simply got up from his chair in front of the shock generator, and indicated that he wished to leave the laboratory.

Of the 40 subjects, 26 obeyed the orders of the experimenter to the end, proceeding to punish the victim until they reached the most potent shock available on the shock generator. At that point, the experimenter called a halt to the session. (The maximum shock is labeled 450 volts, and is two steps beyond the designation: Danger: Severe Shock.) Although obedient subjects continued to administer shocks, they often did so under extreme stress. Some expressed reluctance to administer shocks beyond the 300-volt level, and displayed fears similar to those who defied the experimenter; yet they obeyed.

After the maximum shocks had been delivered, and the experimenter called a halt to the proceedings, many obedient subjects heaved sighs of relief, mopped their brows, rubbed their fingers over their eyes, or nervously fumbled cigarettes. Some shook their heads, apparently in regret. Some subjects had remained calm throughout the experiment, and displayed only minimal signs of tension from beginning to end.

DISCUSSION

The experiment yielded two findings that were surprising. The first finding concerns the sheer strength of obedient tendencies manifested in this situation. Subjects have learned from childhood that it is a fundamental breach of moral conduct to hurt another person against his will. Yet, 26 subjects abandon this tenet in following the instructions of an authority who has no special powers to enforce his commands. To disobey would bring no material loss to the subject; no punishment would ensue. It is clear from the remarks and outward behavior of many participants that in punishing the victim they are often acting against their own values. Subjects often expressed deep disapproval of shocking a man in the face of his objections, and others denounced it as stupid and senseless. Yet the majority complied with the experimental commands. This outcome was surprising from two perspectives: first, from the standpoint of predictions made in the questionnaire described earlier. (Here, however, it is possible that the remoteness of the respondents from the actual situation, and the difficulty of conveying to them the concrete details of the experiment, could account for the serious underestimation of obedience.)

But the results were also unexpected to persons who observed the experiment in progress, through one-way mirrors. Observers often uttered expressions of disbelief upon seeing a subject administer more powerful shocks to the victim. These persons had a full acquaintance with the details of the situation, and yet systematically underestimated the amount of obedience that subjects would display.

The second unanticipated effect was the extraordinary tension generated by the procedures. One might suppose that a subject would simply break off or continue as his conscience dictated. Yet, this is very far from what happened. There were striking reactions of tension and emotional strain. One observer related:

> I observed a mature and initially poised businessman enter the laboratory smiling and confident. Within 20 minutes he was reduced to a twitching, stuttering wreck, who was rapidly approaching a point of nervous collapse. He constantly pulled on his earlobe, and twisted his hands. At one point he pushed his fist into his forehead and muttered: "Oh God, let's stop it." And yet he continued to respond to every word of the experimenter, and obeyed to the end.

Any understanding of the phenomenon of obedience must rest on an analysis of the particular conditions in which it occurs. The following features of the experiment go some distance in explaining the high amount of obedience observed in the situation.

1. The experiment is sponsored by and takes place on the grounds of an institution of unimpeachable reputation, Yale University. It may be reasonably presumed that the personnel are competent and reputable. The importance of this background authority is now being studied by conducting a series of experiments outside of New Haven, and without any visible ties to the university.
2. The experiment is, on the face of it, designed to attain a worthy purpose—advancement of knowledge about learning and memory. Obedience occurs not as an end in itself, but as an instrumental element in a situation that the subject construes as significant, and meaningful. He may not be able to see its full significance, but he may properly assume that the experimenter does.
3. The subject perceives that the victim has voluntarily submitted to the authority system of the experimenter. He is not (at first) an unwilling captive

impressed for involuntary service. He has taken the trouble to come to the laboratory presumably to aid the experimental research. That he later becomes an involuntary subject does not alter the fact that, initially, he consented to participate without qualification. Thus he has in some degree incurred an obligation toward the experimenter.

4. The subject, too, has entered the experiment voluntarily, and perceives himself under obligation to aid the experimenter. He has made a commitment, and to disrupt the experiment is a repudiation of this initial promise of aid.
5. Certain features of the procedure strengthen the subject's sense of obligation to the experimenter. For one, he has been paid for coming to the laboratory. In part this is canceled out by the experimenter's statement that:

   Of course, as in all experiments, the money is yours simply for coming to the laboratory. From this point on, no matter what happens, the money is yours.[2]

6. From the subject's standpoint, the fact that he is the teacher and the other man the learner is purely a chance consequence (it is determined by drawing lots) and he, the subject, ran the same risk as the other man in being assigned the role of learner. Since the assignment of positions in the experiment was achieved by fair means, the learner is deprived of any basis of complaint on this count. (A similar situation obtains in Army units, in which—in the absence of volunteers—a particularly dangerous mission may be assigned by drawing lots, and the unlucky soldier is expected to bear his misfortune with sportsmanship.)
7. There is, at best, ambiguity with regard to the prerogatives of a psychologist and the corresponding rights of his subject. There is a vagueness of expectation concerning what a psychologist may require of his subject, and when he is overstepping acceptable limits. Moreover, the experiment occurs in a closed setting, and thus provides no opportunity for the subject to remove these ambiguities by discussion with others. There are few standards that seem directly applicable to the situation, which is a novel one for most subjects.
8. The subjects are assured that the shocks administered to the subject are "painful but not dangerous." Thus they assume that the discomfort caused the victim is momentary, while the scientific gains resulting from the experiment are enduring.
9. Through Shock Level 20 the victim continues to provide answers on the signal box. The subject may construe this as a sign that the victim is still willing to "play the game." It is only after Shock Level 20 that the victim repudiates the rules completely, refusing to answer further.

These features help to explain the high amount of obedience obtained in this experiment. Many of the arguments raised need not remain matters of speculation, but can be reduced to testable propositions to be confirmed or disproved by further experiments.[3]

The following features of the experiment concern the nature of the conflict which the subject faces.

10. The subject is placed in a position in which he must respond to the competing demands of two persons: the experimenter and the victim. The conflict must be resolved by meeting the demands of one or the other; satisfaction of the victim and the experimenter are mutually exclusive. Moreover, the resolution must take the form of a highly visible action, that of continuing to shock the victim or breaking off the experiment. Thus the subject is forced into a public conflict that does not permit any completely satisfactory solution.
11. While the demands of the experimenter carry the weight of scientific authority, the demands of the victim spring from his personal experience of pain and suffering. The two claims need not be regarded as equally pressing and legitimate. The experimenter seeks an abstract scientific datum; the victim cries out for relief from physical suffering caused by the subject's actions.
12. The experiment gives the subject little time for reflection. The conflict comes on rapidly. It is only minutes after the subject has been seated before the shock generator that the victim begins his protests. Moreover, the subject perceives that he has gone through but two-thirds of the shock levels at the time the subject's first protests are heard. Thus he understands that the conflict will have a persistent aspect to it, and may well become more intense as increasingly more powerful shocks are required. The rapidity with which the conflict descends on the subject, and his realization that it is predictably recurrent may well be sources of tension to him.

13. At a more general level, the conflict stems from the opposition of two deeply ingrained behavior dispositions: first, the disposition not to harm other people, and second, the tendency to obey those whom we perceived to be legitimate authorities.

REFERENCES

Adorno, T., Frenkel-Brunswik, Else, Levinson, D. J., & Sanford, R. N. *The authoritarian personality.* New York: Harper, 1950.

Arendt, H. What was authority? In C. J. Friedrich (Ed.), *Authority.* Cambridge: Harvard Univer. Press, 1958. Pp. 81–112.Binet, A. *La suggestibilité.* Paris: Schleicher, 1900.

Buss, A. H. *The psychology of aggression.* New York: Wiley, 1961.

Cartwright, S. (Ed.) *Studies in social power.* Ann Arbor; University of Michigan Institute for Social Research, 1959.

Charcot, J. M. *Oeuvres complètes.* Paris: Bureaux du Progrès Médical, 1881.

Frank, J. D. Experimental studies of personal pressure and resistance. *J. Gen. Psychol.*, 1944, 30, 23–64.

Friedrich, C. J. (Ed.). *Authority.* Cambridge; Harvard Univer. Press, 1958.

Milgram, S. Dynamics of obedience, Washington: National Science Foundation, 25 January 1961. (Mimeo)

Milgram, S. Some conditions of obedience and disobedience to authority. *Hum. Relat.*, 1964, in press.

Rokeach, M. Authority, authoritarianism, and conformity. In I. A. Berg & B. M. Bass (Eds.), *Conformity and deviation.* New York; Harper, 1961. Pp. 230–257.

Snow, C. P. Either-or, *Progressive,* 1961 (Feb.), 24.

Weber, M. The theory of social and economic organization. Oxford: Oxford Univer. Press, 1947.

NOTES

1. A related technique, making use of a shock generator, was reported by Buss (1961) for the study of aggression in the laboratory. Despite the considerable similarity of technical detail in the experimental procedures, both investigators proceeded in ignorance of the other's work. Milgram provided plans and photographs of his shock generator, experimental procedure, and first results in a report to the National Science Foundation in January 1961. This report received only limited circulation. Buss reported his procedure 6 months later, but to a wider audience. Subsequently, technical information and reports were exchanged. The present article was first received in the Editor's office on December 27, 1961; it was resubmitted with deletions on July 27, 1962.
2. Forty-three subjects, undergraduates at Yale University, were run in the experiment without payment. The results are very similar to those obtained with paid subjects.
3. A series of recently completed experiments employing the obedience paradigm is reported in Milgram (1964).

(Received July 27, 1962)

READING 8

One of the most fascinating things about group dynamics is that the group as a whole often is very different from the sum of its parts. In other words, how successful a group, or what policy it decides to implement, or how competitive it acts, can be quite different from what one would predict based on averaging the talents, attitudes, or dispositions of all the group members. This intriguing discrepancy is illustrated throughout Chapter 8 (Group Processes). One such discrepancy is demonstrated in this creative study by Latané, Williams, and Harkins (1979). Anyone who has worked on a group project or been part of a team is likely to recognize what these authors call social loafing—when the individuals working together in a group don't produce as much or work as hard as they would if they were working individually. Note how the authors introduce their research by bringing together some seemingly contradictory findings from past research, and how they build their hypotheses in an attempt to understand and account for these contradictions. As you read this research, think about your own experiences with groups or teams and whether these experiences seem consistent with these results. How could you help prevent social loafing in your next group task?

Many Hands Make Light the Work: The Causes and Consequences of Social Loafing

Bibb Latané, Kipling Williams, and Stephen Harkins
Ohio State University

Two experiments found that when asked to perform the physically exerting tasks of clapping and shouting, people exhibit a sizable decrease in individual effort when performing in groups as compared to when they perform alone. This decrease, which we call social loafing, is in addition to losses due to faulty coordination of group efforts. Social loafing is discussed in terms of its experimental generality and theoretical importance. The widespread occurrence, the negative consequences for society, and some conditions that can minimize social loafing are also explored.

There is an old saying that "many hands make light the work." This saying is interesting for two reasons. First, it captures one of the promises of social life—that with social organization people can fulfill their individual goals more easily through collective action. When many hands are available, people often do not have to work as hard as when only a few are present. The saying is interesting in a second, less hopeful way—it seems that when many hands are available, people actually work less hard than they ought to.

Over 50 years ago a German psychologist named Ringelmann did a study that he never managed to get published. In rare proof that unpublished work does not necessarily perish, the results of that study, reported only in summary form in German by Moede (1927), have been cited by Dashiell (1935), Davis (1969), Köhler (1927), and Zajonc (1966) and extensively analyzed by Steiner (1966, 1972) and Ingham, Levinger, Graves, and Peckham (1974). Apparently Ringelmann simply asked German workers to pull as hard as they could on a rope, alone or with one, two, or seven other people, and then he used a strain gauge to measure how hard they pulled in kilograms of pressure.

This research was supported by National Science Foundation Grant GS40194.

The authors would like to thank Lewis Hinkle for technical assistance and Edward Diener, John Harvey, Norbert Kerr, Robert Kidd, George Levinger, Thomas Ostrom, Richard Petty, and Ladd Wheeler for their valuable comments.

S. Harkins is now an assistant professor of psychology at Northeastern University.

Requests for reprints should be sent to Bibb Latané, Behavioral Sciences Laboratory, Ohio State University, 404B West 17th Avenue, Columbus, Ohio 43210.

SOURCE: Latane, B., Williams, K., & Harkins, S. 1979. "Many Hands Make Light the Work: The Causes and Consequences of Social Loafing." *JOURNAL OF PERSONALITY AND SOCIAL PSYCHOLOGY, 37*, 822–832.

Rope pulling is, in Steiner's (1972) useful classification of tasks, maximizing, unitary, and additive. In a maximizing task, success depends on how much or how rapidly something is accomplished and presumably on how much effort is expended, as opposed to an optimizing task, in which precision, accuracy, or correctness are paramount. A unitary task cannot be divided into separate subtasks—all members work together doing the same thing and no division of labor is possible. In an additive task, group success depends on the *sum* of the individual efforts, rather than on the performance of any subset of members. From these characteristics, we should expect three people pulling together on a rope with perfect efficiency to be able to exert three times as much force as one person can, and eight people to exert eight times as much force.

Ringelmann's results, however, were strikingly different. When pulling one at a time, individuals averaged a very respectable 63 kg of pressure. Groups of three people were able to exert a force of 160 kg, only two and a half times the average individual performance, and groups of eight pulled at 248 kg, less than four times the solo rate. Thus the collective group performance, while increasing somewhat with group size, was substantially less than the sum of the individual efforts, with dyads pulling at 93% of the sum of their individual efforts, trios at 85%, and groups of eight at only 49%. In a way somewhat different from how the old saw would have it, many hands apparently made light the work.

The Ringelmann effect is interesting because it seems to violate both common stereotype and social psychological theory. Common stereotype tells us that the sense of team participation leads to increased effort, that group morale and cohesiveness spur individual enthusiasm, that by pulling together groups can achieve any goal, that in unity there is strength. Social psychological theory holds that, at least for simple, well-learned tasks involving dominant responses, the presence of other people, whether as co-workers or spectators, should facilitate performance. It is thus important to find out whether Ringelmann's effect is replicable and whether it can be obtained with other tasks.

The Ringelmann effect is also interesting because it provides a different arena for testing a new theory of social impact (Latané, 1973). Social impact theory holds that when a person stands as a target of social forces coming from other persons, the amount of social pressure on the target person should increase as a multiplicative function of the strength, immediacy, and number of these other persons. However, if a person is a member of a group that is the target of social forces from outside the group, the impact of these forces on any given member should diminish in inverse proportion to the strength, immediacy, and number of group members. Impact is divided up among the group members, in much the same way that responsibility for helping seems to be divided among witnesses to an emergency (Latané & Darley, 1970). Latané further suggests that just as psychophysical reactions to external stimuli can be described in terms of a power law (Stevens, 1957), so also should reactions to social stimuli, but with an exponent having an absolute value less than 1, so that the nth person should have less effect than the $(n - 1)$th. Ringelmann's asking his workers to pull on a rope can be considered social pressure. The more people who are the target of this pressure, the less pressure should be felt by any one person. Since people are likely to work hard in proportion to the pressure they feel to do so, we should expect increased group size to result in reduced efforts on the part of individual group members. These reduced efforts can be called "social loafing"—a decrease in individual effort due to the social presence of other persons. With respect to the Ringelmann phenomenon, social impact theory suggests that at least some of the effect should be due to reduced efforts on the part of group participants, and that this reduced effort should follow the form of an inverse power function having an exponent with an absolute value less than one.

The Ringelmann effect is interesting for a third reason: If it represents a general phenomenon and is not restricted to pulling on a rope, it poses the important practical question of when and why collective efforts are less efficient than individual ones. Since many components of our standard of life are produced through one form or another of collective action, research identifying the causes and conditions of inefficient group output and suggesting strategies to overcome these inefficiencies is clearly desirable.

For these three, and other reasons, we decided to initiate a program of research into the collective performance of individuals in groups.

EXPERIMENT 1

Clap Your Hands and Shout Out Loud

One of the disadvantages of Ringelmann's rope pulling task is that the equipment and procedures are relatively cumbersome and inefficient. Therefore, we decided to keep our ears open for other tasks that would allow us to replicate the Ringelmann finding conceptually and would provide the basis for extended empirical and theoretical analysis. We chose cheering and clapping, two activities that people commonly do together in social settings and that are maximizing, unitary, and additive. As with rope pulling, output can be measured in simple physical units that make up a ratio scale.

Method

On eight separate occasions, groups of six undergraduate males were recruited from introductory psychology classes at Ohio State University; they were seated in a semicircle, 1 m apart, in a large soundproofed laboratory and told, "We are interested in judgments of how much noise people make in social settings, namely cheering and applause, and how loud they seem to those who hear them. Thus, we want each of you to do two things: (1) Make noises, and (2) judge noises." They were told that on each trial "the experimenter will tell you the trial number, who is to perform and whether you are to cheer (Rah!) or clap. When you are to begin, the experimenter will count backwards from three and raise his hand. Continue until he lowers it. We would like you to clap or cheer for 5 seconds as loud as you can." On each trial, both the performers and the observers were also asked to make magnitude estimates of how much noise had been produced (Stevens, 1966). Since these data are not relevant to our concerns, we will not mention them further.

After some practice at both producing and judging noise, there were 36 trials of yelling and 36 trials of clapping. Within each modality, each person performed twice alone, four times in pairs, four times in groups of four, and six times in groups of six. These frequencies were chosen as a compromise between equating the number of occasions on which we measured people making noise alone or in groups (which would have required more noisemaking in fours and sixes) and equating the number of individual performances contributing to our measurements in the various group sizes (which would have required more noisemaking by individuals and pairs). We also arranged the sequence of performances to space and counterbalance the order of conditions over each block of 36 trials, while making sure that no one had to perform more than twice in a row.

Performances were measured with a General Radio sound-level meter, Model 1565A, using the C scale and the slow time constant, which was placed exactly 4 m away from each performer. The C scale was used so that sounds varying only in frequency or pitch would be recorded as equally loud. Sound-level meters are read in decibel (dB) units, which are intended to approximate the human reaction to sound. For our purposes, however, the appropriate measure is the effort used in generating noise, not how loud it sounds. Therefore, our results are presented in terms of dynes/cm^2, the physical unit of work involved in producing sound pressure.

Because people shouted and clapped in full view and earshot of each other, each person's performance could affect and be affected by the others. For this reason, the group, rather than the individual, was the unit of analysis, and each score was based on the average output per person. Results were analyzed in a $4 \times 2 \times 2$ analysis of variance, with Group Size (1, 2, 4, 6), Response Mode (clapping vs. shouting), and Replications (1, 2) as factors.

Results

Participants seemed to adapt to the task with good humor if not great enthusiasm. Nobody refused to clap or shout, even though a number seemed somewhat embarrassed or shy about making these noises in public. Despite this, they did manage to produce a good deal of noise. Individuals averaged 84 dB (C) clapping and 87 dB cheering, while groups of six clapped at 91 dB and shouted at 95 dB (an increment of 6 dB represents a doubling of sound pressure).

As might be expected, the more people clapping or cheering together, the more intense the noise and the more the sound pressure produced. However, it did not grow in proportion to the number of people: The average sound pressure generated *per person* decreased with increasing group size, $F(3, 21) = 41.5$, $p < .001$. People averaged about 3.7 dynes/cm^2 alone, 2.6 in pairs, 1.8 in foursomes, and about 1.5 in groups of six (Figure 1). Put another way, two-person groups performed at only 71% of the sum of their individual capacity, four-person groups at 51%, and six-person groups at 40%. As in pulling ropes, it appears that when it comes to clapping and shouting out loud, many hands do, in fact, make light the work.

People also produced about 60% more sound power when they shouted than when they clapped, $F(1, 7) = 8.79$, $p < .01$, presumably reflecting physical capacity rather than any psychological process. There

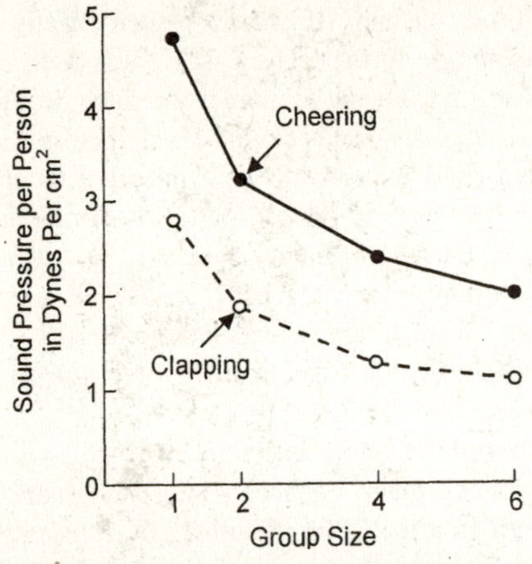

Figure 1. Intensity of noise as a function of group size and response mode, Experiment 1.

was no effect due to blocks of trials, indicating that the subjects needed little or no practice and that their performance was not deleteriously affected by fatigue. In addition, there were no interactions among the variables.

Discussion

The results provide a strong replication of Ringelmann's original findings, using a completely different task and in a different historical epoch and culture. At least when people are making noise as part of a task imposed by someone else, voices raised together do not seem to be raised as much as voices raised alone, and the sound of 12 hands clapping is not even three times as intense as the sound of 2.

Zajonc's (1965) elegant theory of social facilitation suggests that people are aroused by the mere presence of others and are thus likely to work harder (though not necessarily to achieve more) when together. Although social facilitation theory might seem to predict enhanced group performance on a simple task like clapping or shouting, in the present case it would not predict any effect due to group size, since the number of people present was always eight, six participants and two experimenters. Evaluation apprehension theory (Cottrell, 1972) would also not predict any effect as long as it is assumed that co-actors and audience members are equally effective in arousing performance anxiety. Therefore, these theories are not inconsistent with our position that an unrelated social process is involved. The results of Experiment 1 also can be taken as support for Latané's (1973) theory of social impact: The impact that the experimenters have on an individual seems to decrease as the number of coperformers increases, leading to an apparent drop in individual performance, a phenomenon we call social loafing.

However, there is an alternative explanation to these results. It may be, not that people exert less effort in groups, but that the group product suffers as a result of group inefficiency. In his invaluable theoretical analysis of group productivity, Steiner (1972) suggests that the discrepancy between a group's potential productivity (in this case *n* times the average individual output) and its actual productivity may be attributed to faulty social process. In the case of Ringelmann's rope pull, Steiner identifies one source of process loss as inadequate social coordination. As group size increases, the number of "coordination links," and thus the possibility of faulty coordination (pulling in different directions at different times), also increases. Steiner shows that for Ringelmann's original data the decrement in obtained productivity is exactly proportional to the number of coordination links.

Ingham et al. (1974) designed an ingenious experiment to determine whether the process losses found in rope pulling were mainly due to problems of coordinating individual efforts and the physics of the task, or whether they resulted from reductions in personal exertion (what we have called social loafing). First, they conducted a careful replication of Ringelmann's original rope-pulling study and found similar results—dyads pulled at 91% of the sum of their individual capacities, trios at 82%, and groups of six at only 78%.

In a second experiment, Ingham et al. cleverly arranged things so that only the individual's perception of group size was varied. Individuals were blindfolded and led to believe that others were pulling with them, but in fact, they always pulled alone. Under these conditions, of course, there is no possibility of loss due to faulty synchronization. Still there was a substantial drop in output with increases in perceived group size: Individuals pulled at 90% of their alone rate when they believed one other person was also pulling, and at only 85% with two to six others believed pulling. It appears that virtually all of the performance decrement in rope pulling observed by Ingham et al. can be accounted for in terms of reduced effort or social loafing.

With respect to clapping and especially shouting, however, there are several possible sources of coordination loss that might have operated in addition to social loafing: (a) Sound cancellation will occur to the extent that sound pressure waves interfere with each other, (b) directional coordination losses will occur to the extent that voices are projected toward different locations, and (c) temporal coordination losses will occur to the extent that moment-to-moment individual variations in intensity are not in synchrony. Our second experiment was designed to assess the relative effects of coordination loss and social loafing in explaining the failure of group cheering to be as intense as the sum of individual noise outputs.

EXPERIMENT 2

Coordination Loss or Reduced Effort?

For Experiment 2 we arranged things so that people could not hear each other shout; participants were asked to wear headphones, and during each trial a constant 90-dB recording of six people shouting was played over the earphones, ostensibly to reduce auditory feedback and to signal each trial. As a consequence, individuals could be led to believe they were shouting in groups while actually shouting alone. Ingham et al. (1974) accomplished this through the use of "pseudosubjects," confederates who pretended to be pulling with the participants but who in fact did not pull any weight at all. That is an expensive procedure—each of the 36 participants tested by Ingham et al. required the services of 5 pseudosubjects as well as the experimenter. We were able to devise a procedure whereby, on any given trial, one person could be led to believe that he was performing in a group, while the rest thought he was performing alone. Thus, we were able to test six real participants at one time.

Additionally, although we find the interpretation offered by Ingham et al. plausible and convincing, the results of their second experiment are susceptible to an alternative explanation. When participants were not pulling the rope, they stood and watched the pseudosubjects pull. This would lead people accurately to believe that while they were pulling the rope, idle participants would be watching (Levinger, Note 1). Thus, as the number of performers decreased, the size of the audience increased. According to Cottrell's evaluation apprehension hypothesis (1972), the presence of an evaluative audience should enhance performance for a simple, well-learned task such as rope pulling, and, although there is little supportive evidence, it seems reasonable that the larger the audience, the greater the enhancement (Martens & Landers, 1969; Seta, Paulus, & Schkade, 1976). Thus, it is not clear whether there was a reduced effort put forth by group members because they believed other people were pulling with them, or an increase in the effort exerted by individuals because they believed other people were watching them. In Experiment 2, therefore, we arranged to hold the size of the audience constant, even while varying the number of people working together.

Method

Six groups of six male undergraduate volunteers heard the following instructions:

> In our experiment today we are interested in the effects of sensory feedback on the production of sound in social groups. We will ask you to produce sounds in groups of one, two, or six, and we will record the sound output on the sound-level meter that you can see up here in front. Although this is not a competition and you will not learn your scores until the end of the experiment, we would like you to make your sounds as loud as possible. Since we are interested in sensory feedback, we will ask you to wear blindfolds and earphones and, as you will see, will arrange it so that you will not be able to hear yourself as you shout.
>
> We realize it may seem strange to you to shout as loud as you can, especially since other people are around. Remember that the room is soundproofed and that people outside the room will not be able to hear you. In addition, because you will be wearing blindfolds and headsets, the other participants will not be able to hear you or to see you. Please, therefore, feel free to let loose and really shout. As I said, we are interested in how loud you can shout, and there is no reason not to do your best. Here's your chance to really give it a try. Do you have any questions?

Once participants had donned their headsets and blindfolds, they went through a series of 13 trials, in which each person shouted four times in a group of six, once in a group of two, and once by himself. Before each trial they heard the identification letters of those people who were to shout.

Interspersed with these trials were 12 trials, two for each participant, in which the individual's headset was switched to a separate track on the stereophonic instruction tape. On these trials, everybody else was told that only the focal person should shout, but that individual was led to believe either that one other person would shout with him or that all six would shout.

Thus, each person shouted by himself, in actual groups of two and six, and in pseudogroups of two and six, with trials arranged so that each person would have approximately equal rest periods between the trials on which he performed. Each trial was preceded by the specification of who was to perform. The yells were coordinated by a tape-recorded voice counting backwards from three, followed by a constant 90-dB 5-sec recording of the sound of six people shouting. This background noise made it impossible for performers to determine whether or how loudly other people were shouting, or, for that matter, to hear themselves shout. Each trial was terminated by the sound of a bell. This sequence of 25 trials was repeated three times, for a total of 75 trials, in the course of which each subject shouted 24 times.

As in Experiment 1, the data were transformed into dynes/cm^2 and subjected to analyses of variance, with the group as the unit of analysis and each score based on the average output per person. Two separate 3×3 analyses of variance with group size (1,2,6) and trial block (1–3) were run, one on the output of trials in which groups actually shouted together, and one on the pseudogroup trials in which only one person actually shouted.

Results

Overall, participants shouted with considerably more intensity in Experiment 2 than in Experiment 1, averaging 9.22 dynes/cm2 when shouting alone, as compared to 4.73 dynes/cm2, $t(12) = 4.05$, $p < .01$. There are several plausible reasons for this difference. The new rationale involving the effects of reduced sensory feedback may have interested or challenged individuals to perform well. The constant 90-dB background noise may have led people to shout with more intensity, just as someone listening to music through headphones will often speak inappropriately loudly (the Lombard reflex). The performers may have felt less embarrassed because the room was soundproof and the others were unable to see or hear them. Finally, through eliminating the possibility of hearing each other, individuals could no longer be influenced by the output of the others, thereby lifting the pressure of social conformity.

As in Experiment 1, as the number of actual performers increase, the total sound output also increased, but at a slower rate than would be expected from the sum of the individual outputs. Actual groups of two shouted at only 66% of capacity, and groups of six at 36%, $F(2, 10) = 226$, $p < .001$. The comparable figures for Experiment 1 are 71% and 40%. These similarities between experiments suggest that our procedural changes, even though they made people unable to hear or see each other, did not eliminate their feeling of being in a group or reduce the amount of incoordination or social loafing.

The line connecting the solid circles in Figure 2 shows the decreased output per person when actually performing in groups. The dashed line along the top represents potential productivity—the output to be expected if there were no losses due to faulty coordination or to social loafing. The striped area at the bottom represents the obtained output per person in actual groups. Output is obviously lower than potential productivity, and this decrease can be considered as representing the sum of the losses due to incoordination and to reduced individual effort.

In addition to shouting in actual groups, individuals also performed in pseudogroups in which they believed that others shouted with them but in which they actually shouted alone, thus preventing coordination loss from affecting output. As shown in Figure 2, people shouted with less intensity in pseudo-groups than when alone, $F(2, 10) = 37.0$, $p < .0001$. Thus, group size made a significant difference even in pseudogroups in which coordination loss is not a factor and only social loafing can operate.

When performers believed one other person was yelling, they shouted 82% as intensely as when alone, and when they believed five others to be yelling, they shouted 74% as intensely. The stippled area defined at the top of Figure 2 by the data from the pseudo-groups represents the amount of loss due to social loafing. By subtraction, we can infer that the white area of Figure 2 represents the amount of loss due to faulty coordination. Since the latter comprises about the same area as the former, we can conclude that, for shouting, half the performance loss decrement is due to incoordination and half is due to social loafing.

Discussion

Despite the methodological differences between Experiments 1 and 2, both experiments showed that there is a reduction in sound pressure produced per person when people make noise in groups compared to when alone. People in Experiment 1 applauded and cheered in full view of each other, with all the excitement, embarrassment, and conformity that goes along with such a situation. In Experiment 2, no one could see or hear any other person. Only the experimenters could see the peo-

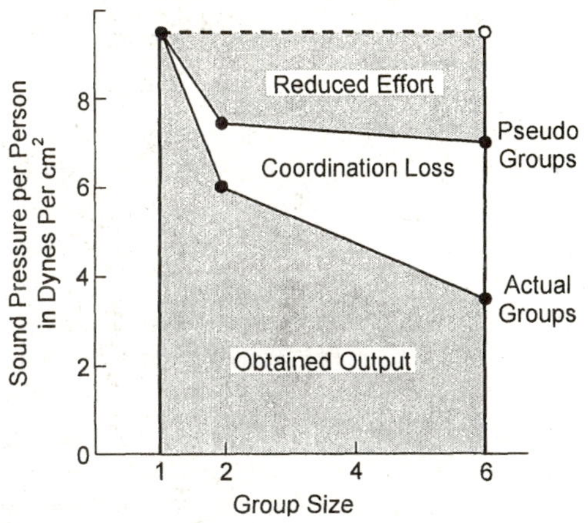

Figure 2. Intensity of sound produced per person when cheering in actual or perceived groups of 1, 2, and 6, as a result of reduced effort and faulty coordination of group efforts, Experiment 2.

ple perform. And finally, the rationale changed drastically, from the experimenters' interest in "judgments of how much noise people make in social settings" to their interest in "the effects of sensory feedback on the production of sound in social groups." Yet, despite differences in the task characteristics and supposed purpose, the two studies produced similar results. This points to the robust nature of both the phenomenon and the paradigm.

GENERAL DISCUSSION

Noise Production as Group Performance

Although we do not usually think about it that way, making noise can be hard work, in both the physical and the psychological sense. In the present case, the participants were asked to produce sound pressure waves, either by rapidly vibrating their laryngeal membranes or by vigorously striking their hands together. Although superficially similar in consequence, this task should not be confused with more normal outbreaks of shouting and clapping that occur as spontaneous outbursts of exuberant expressiveness. Our participants shouted and clapped because we asked them to, not because they wanted to.

This effortful and fatiguing task resulted in sound pressure waves, which, although invisible, can be easily and accurately measured in physical units that are proportional to the amount of work performed. The making of noise is a useful task for the study of group processes from the standpoint both of production and of measurement—people are practiced and skilled at making noise and can do so without the help of expensive or cumbersome apparatus, and acoustics and audio engineering are sufficiently advanced to permit sophisticated data collection. We seem to have found a paradigm wherein people get involved enough to try hard and become somewhat enthusiastic, yet the task is still effortful enough so that they loaf when given the opportunity.

The Causes of Social Loafing

The present research shows that groups can inhibit the productivity of individuals so that people reduce their exertions when it comes to shouting and clapping with others. Why does this occur? We suggest three lines of explanation, the first having to do with attribution and equity, the second with submaximal goal setting, and the third with the lessening of the contingency between individual inputs and outcomes.

1. Attribution and equity It may be that participants engaged in a faulty attribution process, leading to an attempt to maintain an equitable division of labor. There are at least three aspects of the physics and psychophysics of producing sound that could have led people to believe that the other persons in their group were not working as hard or effectively as themselves. First, individuals judged their own outputs to be louder than those of the others, simply because they were closer to the sound source. Second, even if everyone worked to capacity, sound cancellation would cause group outputs to seem much less than the sum of their individual performances. Finally, the perception of the amount of sound produced in a group should be much less than the actual amount—growing only as the .67 power of the actual amount of sound, according to Stevens's psychophysical power law (1975).

These factors may have led individuals to believe that the other participants were less motivated or less skillful than themselves—in short, were shirkers or incompetents. Thus, differences in the perception of sound production that were essentially the result of physical and psychophysical processes may have been mistakenly attributed to a lack of either skill or motivation on the part of the others, leading individuals to produce less sound in groups because there is no reason to work hard in aid of shirkers or those who are less competent.

This process cannot explain the results of Experiment 2, since the capacity to judge the loudness of one's own output, much less that of others, was severely impaired by the 90-dB background masking noise used to signal the trials. However, rather than "discovering" social loafing while participating in the experiment, the participants may have arrived with the preexisting notion that people often do not pull their own weight in groups. Thus, despite being unable to hear or see one another, lack of trust and the propensity to attribute laziness or ineptitude to others could have led people to work less hard themselves.

2. Submaximal goal setting It may be that despite our instructions, participants redefined the task and adopted a goal, not of making as much noise as possible, but merely of making enough noise or of matching some more or less well-defined standard. Individuals would clearly expect it to be easier to achieve this goal when others are helping, and might work less hard as a consequence. This, of course, would change the nature of noise production from what Steiner (1972) would term a *maximizing* task to an *optimizing* task. A maximizing task makes success a function of how much or how rapidly something is accomplished. For an optimizing task, however, success is a function of how closely the individual or group approximates a predetermined "best" or correct outcome. If participants in our experiments perceived sound production as an optimizing rather than a maximizing task, they might feel the optimal level of sound output could be reached more easily in groups than alone, thereby allowing them to exert less effort.

The participants in Experiment 2 could hear neither themselves nor others and would not be able to determine whether their output was obnoxious or to develop a group standard for an optimal level. Furthermore, in both experiments, the experimenters reiterated their request to yell "as loud as you can, every time," over and over again. Before the first trial they would ask the group how loud they were supposed to yell. In unison, the group would reply, "As loud as we can!" We think it unlikely that participants perceived the task to be anything other than maximizing.

3. Lessened contingency between input and outcome It may be that participants felt that the contingency between their input and the outcome was lessened when performing in groups. Individuals could "hide in the crowd" (Davis, 1969) and avoid the negative consequences of slacking off, or they may have felt "lost in the crowd" and unable to obtain their fair share of the positive consequences for working hard. Since individual scores are unidentifiable when groups perform together, people can receive neither precise credit nor appropriate blame for their performance. Only when performing alone can individual outputs be exactly evaluated and rewarded.

Let us assume that group members expect approval or other reward proportional to the total output of a group of n performers, but that since individual efforts are indistinguishable, the reward is psychologically divided equally among the participants, each getting $1/n$ units of reward. Under these assumptions, the average group, if it performed up to capacity and suffered no process loss, could expect to divide up n times the reward of the average individual, resulting in each member's getting $n \times 1/ n$, or n/n, units of reward, the same amount as an individual.

Although the total amount of reward may be the same, the contingency on individual output is not. Any given individual under these assumptions will get back only one nth of his own contribution to the group; the rest will be shared by the others. Even though he may also receive unearned one nth of each other person's contribution, he will be tempted, to the extent that his own performance is costly or effortful, to become a "free rider" (Olson, 1965). Thus, under these assumptions, if his own performance cannot be individually monitored, an individual's incentive to perform should be proportional to $1/n$.

Seligman (1975) has shown that animals and people become lethargic and depressed when confronted with tasks in which they have little or no control over the outcomes. Likewise, in our experiments, people may have felt a loss of control over their fair share of the rewards when they performed in groups, leading them also to become, if not lethargic and depressed, at least less enthusiastic about making lots of noise.

Since people were asked to shout both alone and in groups, they may have felt it smart to save their strength in groups and to shout as lustily as possible when scores were individually identifiable, marshalling their energy for the occasions when they could earn rewards. This line of reasoning suggests that if inputs were made identifiable and rewards contingent on them, even when in groups, it would be impossible for performers to get a free ride and they would have an incentive to work equally hard in groups of different sizes.

Social Loafing and Social Impact Theory

Each of these three lines of explanation may be described in terms of Latané's (1973) theory of social impact. If a person is the target of social forces, increasing the number of other persons also in the target group should diminish the pressures on each individual because the impact is divided among the group members. In a group performance situation in which pressures to work come from outside the group and individual outputs are not identifiable, this division of impact should lead each individual to work less hard. Thus, whether the subject is dividing up the amount of work he thinks should be performed or whether he is dividing up the amount of reward he expects to earn with his work, he should work less hard in groups.

The theory of social impact further stipulates the form that the decrease in output should follow. Just as perceptual judgments of physical stimuli follow power functions (Stevens, 1957), so also should judgments of social stimuli, and the exponent of the psychosocial power function should have an exponent of less than one, resulting in a marginally decreasing impact of additional people. Thus, social impact theory suggests that the amount of effort expended on group tasks should decrease as an inverse power function of the number of people in the group. This implication cannot be tested in Experiment 1 or with the actual groups of Experiment 2, inasmuch as coordination loss is confounded with social loafing. However, a power function with an exponent of –.14 accounted for 93% of the variance for the pseudogroups of Experiment 2. It appears that social impact theory provides a good account of both the existence and the magnitude of social loafing.

The Transsituational and Transcultural Generality of Social Loafing

The present research demonstrates that performance losses in groups occur with tasks other than rope pulling and with people other than prewar German workers. There are, in addition, other instances of experimental research that demonstrate similar cases of social loafing. For example, Marriott (1949) and Campbell (1952) have shown that factory workers produce less per person in larger groups than in smaller ones. Latané and Darley (1970) have found that the likelihood that a bystander will intervene in a situation in which someone requires assistance is substantially reduced by the addition of other bystanders who share in the responsibility for help. Wicker (1969) has found that the proportion of members taking part in church activities is lower in large than in small churches, presumably because the responsibility for taking part is more diffuse. Similarly, Petty, Harkins, Williams, and Latané (1977) found that people perceived themselves as exerting less cognitive effort on evaluating poems and editorials when they were among groups of other unidentifiable evaluators than when they alone were responsible for the task.

These experimental findings have demonstrated that a clear potential exists in human nature for social loafing. We suspect that the effects of social loafing have far-reaching and profound consequences both in our culture and in other cultures. For example, on collective farms (kolkhoz) in Russia, the peasants "move all over huge areas, working one field and one task one day, another field the next, having no sense of responsibility and no direct dependence on the results of their labor" (Smith, 1976, p. 281). Each peasant family is also allowed a private plot of up to an acre in size that may be worked after the responsibility to the collective is discharged. The produce of these plots, for which the peasants are individually responsible, may be used as they see fit. Although these plots occupy less than 1% of the nation's agricultural lands (about 26 million acres), they produce 27% of the total value of Soviet farm output (about $32.5 billion worth) (Yemelyanov, 1975, cited in Smith, 1976, p. 266). It is not, however, that the private sector is so highly efficient; rather, it is that the efficiency of the public sector is so low (Wädekin, 1973, p. 67).

However, before we become overly pessimistic about the potential of collective effort, we should consider the Israeli kibbutz, an example that suggests that the effects of social loafing can be circumvented. Despite the fact that kibbutzim are often located in remote and undeveloped areas on the periphery of Israel to protect the borders and develop these regions, these communes have been very successful. For example, in dairying, 1963 yields per cow on the kibbutz were 27% higher than for the rest of Israel's herds, and in 1960 yields were 75% higher than in England. In 1959, kibbutz chickens were producing 22% of the eggs with only 16% of the chickens (Leon, 1969). The kibbutz and the kolkhoz represent the range of possibilities for collective effort, and comparisons of these two types of collective enterprise may suggest conditions under which per person output would be greater in groups than individually.

Social Loafing as a Social Disease

Although some people still think science should be value free, we must confess that we think social loafing can be regarded as a kind of social disease. It is a "disease" in that it has negative consequences for individuals, social institutions, and societies. Social loafing results in a reduction in human efficiency, which leads to lowered profits and lowered benefits for all. It is "social" in that it results from the presence or actions of other people.

The "cure," however, is not to do away with groups, because despite their inefficiency, groups make possible the achievement of many goals that individuals alone could not possibly accomplish. Collective action is a vital aspect of our lives: From time immemorial it has made possible the construction of monuments, but today it is necessary to the provision of even our food and shelter. We think the cure will come from finding ways of channeling social forces so that the group can serve as a means of intensifying individual responsibility rather than diffusing it.

REFERENCE NOTE

1. Levinger, G. Personal communication, June 1976.

REFERENCES

Campbell, M. Group incentive payment schemes: The effects of lack of understanding and group size. *Occupational Psychology*, 1952, *26*, 15–21.

Cottrell, N. Social facilitation. In C. McClintock (Ed.), *Experimental social psychology*. New York: Holt, Rinehart & Winston, 1972.

Dashiell, J. F. Experimental studies of the influence of social situations on the behavior of individual human adults. In C. Murchison (Ed.), *A handbook of social psychology*. Worcester, Mass.: Clark University Press, 1935.

Davis, J. H. *Group performance*. Reading, Mass.: Addison-Wesley, 1969.

Ingham, A. G., Levinger, G., Graves, J., & Peckham, V. The Ringelmann effect: Studies of group size and group performance. *Journal of Experimental Social Psychology*, 1974, *10*, 371–384.

Köhler, O. Ueber den Gruppenwirkungsgrad der menschlichen Körperarbeit und die Bedingung optimaler Kollektivkroftreaktion. *Industrielle Psychotechnik*, 1927, *4*, 209–226.

Latané, B. *A theory of social impact*. St. Louis, Mo.: Psychonomic Society, 1973.

Latané, B., & Darley, J. M. *The unresponsive by-stander: Why doesn't he help?* New York: Appleton-Century-Crofts, 1970.

Leon, D. *The kibbutz: A new way of life*. London: Pergamon Press, 1969.

Marriott, R. Size of working group and output. *Occupational Psychology*, 1949, *23*, 47–57.

Martens, R., & Landers, D. M. Coaction effects on a muscular endurance task. *Research Quarterly*, 1969, *40*, 733–737.

Moede, W. Die Richtlinien der Leistungs-Psychologie. *Industrielle Psychotechnik*, 1927, *4*, 193–207.

Olson, M. *The logic of collective action: Public goods and the theory of groups*. Cambridge, Mass.: Harvard University Press, 1965.

Petty, R., Harkins, S., Williams, K., & Latané, B. The effects of group size on cognitive effort and evaluation. *Personality and Social Psychology Bulletin*, 1977, *3*, 579–582.

Seligman, M. *Helplessness*. San Francisco: Freeman, 1975.

Seta, J. J., Paulus, P. B., & Schkade, J. K. Effects of group size and proximity under cooperative and competitive conditions. *Journal of Personality and Social Psychology*, 1976, *34*, 47–53.

Smith, H. *The Russians*. New York: Ballantine Books, 1976.

Steiner, I. D. Models for inferring relationships between group size and potential group productivity. *Behavioral Science*, 1966, *11*, 273–283.

Steiner, I. D. *Group process and productivity*. New York: Academic Press, 1972.

Stevens, S. S. On the psychological law. *Psychological Review*, 1957, *64*, 153–181.

Stevens, S. S. A metric for the social consensus. *Science*, 1966, *151*, 530–541.

Stevens, S. S. *Psychophysics: Introduction to its perceptual, neural and social prospects*. New York: Wiley, 1975.

Wädekin, K. *The private sector in Soviet agriculture*. Los Angeles: University of California Press, 1973.

Wicker, A. N. Size of church membership and members support of church behavior settings. *Journal of Personality and Social Psychology*, 1969, *13*, 278–288.

Zajonc, R. B. Social facilitation. *Science*, 1965, *149*, 269–274.

Zajonc, R. B. Social psychology: *An experimental approach*. Belmont, Calif.: Brooks/Cole, 1966.

Received June 23, 1978

PART III
Social Relations

READING 9

At some point in their lives, most people enjoy an intimate romantic relationship, many get married, and some get divorced. How do intimate relationships progress over time? Is there a typical developmental pattern? Clearly, all marriages are different and cannot be squeezed into single mold. But recent studies show that some general patterns do emerge when large numbers of marital partners are periodically surveyed about their satisfaction. Recently, Kurdek (1999) reported on a longitudinal study of married couples in which he measured each partner's level of satisfaction every year for ten years. How did he measure satisfaction and what did he find? Is marriage an extended honeymoon? Do married couples in general become more satisfied over time, or less satisfied, or is there an uneven pattern of change? In the following article, Kurdek sought to answer these questions while, at the same time, noting that everyone is different and that no two marriages are alike.

The Nature and Predictors of the Trajectory of Change in Marital Quality for Husbands and Wives Over the First 10 Years of Marriage

Lawrence A. Kurdek
Wright State University

Four parameters of the trajectory of change in marital quality (initial status as well as linear, quadratic, and cubic patterns of change) were estimated for husbands and wives over the first 10 years of marriage (n = 522 couples at Year 1 and 93 couples at Year 10). Both husbands and wives started their trajectories of change at fairly high levels of marital quality and showed a cubic pattern of change such that marital quality declined fairly rapidly in the early years of marriage, stabilized, and then declined again. Whereas individual-differences variables predicted the initial status of the trajectory, husbands and wives living with only their biological children showed a steeper decline in marital quality than husbands and wives living without children or stepchildren.

I thank the couples who participated in this study and Steve Raudenbush for answering questions about hierarchical linear modeling.

Correspondence concerning this article should be addressed to Lawrence A. Kurdek, Department of Psychology, Wright State University, Dayton, Ohio 45435-0001. Electronic mail may be sent to larry.kurdek@wright.edu.

Marriage is usually described in developmental literature as a normative personal life event that occurs in early adulthood (e.g., Gould, 1978; Levinson, Darrow, Klein, Levinson, & McKee, 1978; G. E. Vaillant, 1977) and influences the nature of subsequent developmental tasks (e.g., Havighurst, 1972). The present study focuses on the complementary view that marriage itself can be viewed from a developmental perspective. For example, Kovacs (1983) regarded marriage not as a single life event but as a set of stages in which spouses attempt to achieve a balance between dependence and autonomy as they negotiate issues of control, power, and authority.

Despite evidence that approximately 90% of both men and women in the United States are married by the age of 45 (United States Bureau of the Census, 1997), that marital happiness is centrally important for adults' overall well-being (Glenn & Weaver, 1981), that there is substantial variability in the happiness of those who are in durable marriages (Heaton & Albrecht, 1991), and that nearly half of all marriages end in divorce (National Center for Health Statistics, 1991), there is currently a lack of descriptive information regarding both how marital quality changes and the variables that affect the pattern of this change.

SOURCE: Kurdek, L.A. 1999. "The Nature and Predictors of the Trajectory of Change in Marital Quality for Husbands and Wives over the First 10 Years of Marriage. *DEVELOPMENTAL PSYCHOLOGY, 35*, No. 5, 1283–1296.

Karney and Bradbury (1995) noted that one reason for the lack of this information is that few researchers have recruited both spouses from newly wed couples and repeatedly assessed their appraisals of marital quality over time with the same measure. These authors further noted that in the few studies that met these criteria, researchers usually studied change in marital quality by assessing differences in the means of each spouse's marital quality score over time. For example, MacDermid, Huston, and McHale (1990) found that husbands and wives reported equivalent declines in mean quality of satisfaction and love over three assessments spanning the first 2.5 years of marriage.

Karney and Bradbury (1997) argued that more precise information about the nature of change in marital quality can be obtained by focusing not on average levels of marital quality over time but rather on the *trajectory of change* in marital quality over time. Derived from growth curve analyses of longitudinal data collected over more than two time points, this trajectory includes information regarding the level of marital quality at the start of the marriage (e.g., high) and—depending on how many assessments are available—the number of bends or changes in the curve over time (see Cohen & Cohen, 1983, p. 233).

If data are available from at least four assessments, then one can determine whether the growth function that best describes the pattern of change in marital quality is linear, quadratic, or cubic. For a linear function, the rate of change is the same from assessment to assessment, and there are no bends in the growth curve. For a quadratic function, there is one phase of accelerated change resulting in one bend in the growth curve (e.g., marital quality may decline over the early years of marriage and then level off). Finally, for a cubic function, there are two phases of accelerated change resulting in two bends in the growth curve (e.g., marital quality may decline over the early years of marriage, level off, and then decline again).

In what appears to be the only report of findings from growth curve analyses of longitudinal data from newly wed couples, Karney and Bradbury (1997) obtained global assessments of marital quality from 54 pairs of first-married spouses up to eight times over the first 4 years of marriage. They found that a linear rather than a quadratic growth function fit the pattern of change in marital quality for both husbands and wives, that husbands and wives showed equivalent rates of linear decline in marital quality, and that husbands' rate of linear decline and wives' rate of linear decline were positively related. The finding that change in marital quality was not accelerated (i.e., that the quadratic growth function was not significant) is noteworthy because it is at odds with accounts that feelings of closeness and passion decline at a fairly rapid pace in the early stages of the relationship (Kovacs, 1983; Sternberg, 1986).

The first purpose of this study was to build on Karney and Bradbury's (1997) evidence regarding the normative pattern of change in marital quality for newlywed couples in two ways. First, newly wed spouses in remarriages after divorce as well as newly wed spouses in first marriages were assessed. The inclusion of remarried spouses is important because reports have shown that only 54% of all current marriages involve both spouses in first marriages (Clarke, 1995b). Second, spouses were assessed over the first 10 years of marriage rather than over only the first 4 years of marriage. The longer time span provided an opportunity to explore whether the growth curve of marital quality for spouses in fairly durable marriages had multiple bends (i.e., conformed to a cubic growth function).

In the current study, marital quality was assessed with Spanier's (1976) Dyadic Adjustment Scale, one of the most widely used measures in the literature on marital quality. Although this measure includes subscores regarding the level of agreement between partners on important issues, amount of shared activity, degree of expressed affection, and level of satisfaction with the relationship, these four subscores tend to be so highly intercorrelated that they conform to a single second-order factor (Sabourin, Lussier, Laplante, & Wright, 1991). Consequently, only the total score was used.

For each spouse, two questions regarding the growth curve for marital quality were of interest: (a) At what level of marital quality does the growth curve start, and (b) what is the growth function—linear (equal rates of change), quadratic (one bend or phase of accelerated change), or cubic (two bends or phases of accelerated change)—that best describes the pattern of change? On the basis of Karney and Bradbury's (1997) findings as well as the commonly held view that marriages begin at peak levels of positivity, the trajectory of change in marital quality for each spouse was expected to start at a high level of marital quality. Despite Karney and Bradbury's failure to obtain evidence of accelerated change, there was reason to expect one or even two phases of accelerated change. Consonant with a "honeymoon-is-over" effect (Kovacs, 1983; Sternberg, 1986), the decline in marital quality might be especially steep over the early years of the marriage and then stabilize. Further, consonant with a "7-year-itch" effect (Kovacs, 1983) as well as evidence that the median duration of marriage for divorcing couples is about 7 years (Clarke, 1995a), one might also expect that a second phase of accelerated change follows the period of stabilization.

In addition to determining which growth function best describes the pattern of change in marital quality, a growth curve analysis of longitudinal data on marital quality also provides a way to assess whether a variable that is a risk factor for marital distress exerts its deleterious effect on marital quality by being linked to low levels of marital quality at the start of the marriage or to a pattern of deterioration in marital quality over time. In their study of newly wed couples, Karney and Bradbury (1997) found that two risk factors assessed at the beginning of the marriage—psychological distress (neuroticism) and problematic conflict resolution styles—were related differently to the parameters of the growth trajectory. High levels of psychological distress predicted that spouses would begin the trajectory at low levels of marital quality, whereas frequent negative conflict resolution styles predicted declines in marital quality.

The second purpose of this study was to build on Karney and Bradbury's (1997) evidence regarding the factors that explained variability in each spouse's trajectory of change in marital quality. Of particular interest was whether three sets of variables predicted any of the four parameters of the trajectory of interest here—initial status as well as a linear, quadratic, or cubic pattern of change. The first set of predictor variables included information about each spouse's divorce history. This information was of interest because the probability of marital distress is high for spouses who have experienced multiple divorces (Clarke, 1995a; Wilson & Clarke, 1992). Consequently, spouses were categorized as having experienced no divorce (the reference group), one divorce, or multiple divorces. If people who remarry after multiple divorces are at risk for marital distress because they are quick to identify marital problems and have low thresholds for dealing with marital distress (Brody, Neubaum, & Forehand, 1988), then, compared with people who have not been divorced, they (as well as their spouses) may be especially likely to show early accelerated declines in marital quality rather than merely low levels of marital quality at the start of the marriage.

The second set of predictor variables included information regarding either the presence of residential stepchildren at the start of the marriage or the presence of any children born during the course of the marriage. The presence of residential stepchildren was relevant because spouses in stepfamilies have been thought to have unique sources of stress related to ill-defined social and legal roles for stepparents, the prevalence of myths holding the stepfamily to unachievable standards, and difficulties related to interacting with complex family systems that include former spouses and their kin (Ganong & Coleman, 1994).

The presence of biological children born during the course of the marriage was of interest because there is conflicting evidence regarding how marital quality changes over the course of the family life cycle. Data from retrospective reports (e.g., Burr, 1970) support the view that marital quality follows a U-shaped pattern such that marital quality is lowest when children are present, whereas data from prospective reports show that parents and nonparents do not differ in how marital quality changes over time (Karney & Bradbury, 1997; MacDermid et al., 1990; C. O. Vaillant & Vaillant, 1993).

In the present study, couples were divided into three child-related groups: couples in which husbands and wives never lived with either children or stepchildren over the course of the study (the reference group); couples in which husbands lived with only the children of their wives from a previous marriage (i.e., residential stepfather families); and couples in which husbands and wives lived with only their own biological offspring at some point during the study. Other child-status groups (e.g., couples with residential stepmothers and couples in which spouses lived with stepchildren and their own biological children) were too few in number to be included.

It seemed plausible that husbands with stepchildren might report lower initial levels of marital quality than those without children or stepchildren because the cost of having stepchildren is likely to be known at the beginning of the marriage (Ganong & Coleman, 1994). Alternatively, if interactions with stepchildren become increasingly negative as the stepchildren grow older and negotiate issues regarding personal autonomy (Hetherington & Clingempeel, 1992), then husbands who live with stepchildren may be especially likely to show declines in marital quality over time. Because previous findings regarding how a couple's own biological children affect marital quality are inconsistent, no hypotheses on this issue were advanced.

The final set of predictor variables included individual-differences variables known to be linked, either concurrently or prospectively, to marital quality. Studies of concurrent linkages have shown that partners with low evaluations of their spouses' dependability (Rempel, Holmes, & Zanna, 1985), strong dysfunctional beliefs about relationships (e.g., disagreements are destructive;

Eidelson & Epstein, 1982), low expressiveness (or "femininity"; Kurdek & Schmitt, 1986a), or high levels of psychological distress (Karney, Bradbury, Fincham, & Sullivan, 1994) tend to report low marital quality. Longitudinal studies indicate that wives with high levels of instrumentality (or "masculinity") tend to report decreases in marital satisfaction (Bradbury, Campbell, & Fincham, 1995).

Of interest here was whether values for these five individual-differences variables assessed at the beginning of the marriage showed intraspouse as well as cross-spouse relations to the four elements of each spouse's own trajectory of change in marital quality. That is, were husbands' own individual-differences variables as well as those of their wives linked to where each one began the trajectory as well as to each one's rate of linear, curvilinear, and cubic change? Although researchers have rarely examined intraspouse and cross-spouse effects, two studies are relevant here.

In the first study, Karney and Bradbury (1997) found that high levels of psychological distress (neuroticism) at the start of the marriage for both husbands and wives were linked to husbands' beginning the trajectory at low levels of marital quality. However, no such links were obtained for wives, and psychological distress was not related to the rate of linear change for either spouse. In the second study, Bradbury et al. (1995) found that wives' marital satisfaction tended to decline to the extent that they were high in instrumentality and that their husbands were low in both instrumentality and expressiveness. Because there was no compelling reason for these linkages to have occurred for only one spouse and because of the scarcity of information regarding what personality variables at the start of the marriage predict change in marital quality, only a general hypothesis was advanced. This was that husbands' and wives' problematic levels of the individual-differences variables assessed at the start of the marriage (i.e., low dependability of spouse, strong dysfunctional beliefs, high instrumentality, low expressiveness, and high psychological distress) would be linked to the low initial status of each one's own trajectory of change in marital quality.

METHOD

Participants

Participants were recruited from the lists of marriage licenses published in the *Dayton Daily News* from May 1986 through January 1988. Generally, licenses appeared 1 month after the marriage. Each couple was sent a letter that described the focus of the study as the identification of factors contributing to marital happiness. Although the initial letter indicated that the study would involve the completion of five annual mail surveys, there was sufficient interest in the study to extend it another 5 years. If both spouses were interested in participating in the study, they returned information regarding names and address in a postage-paid envelope. Of the 7,899 couples who received the letter, 1,407 indicated an interest in the study. This response rate of 18% is similar to those obtained from other studies that recruited participants from public records (e.g., 18% by Davila, Bradbury, Cohan, & Tochluk, 1997; and 17% by Spanier, 1976).

Completed surveys were returned by 538 couples at Year 1. This return rate of 38% is similar to the rate of 33% obtained by Kurdek and Schmitt (1986b) in a study that involved a survey of similar length but that required the anonymous participation of both partners. Because of their small numbers, couples in which a spouse was remarried after the death of a previous spouse and couples in which a spouse died in the course of the study were not included, leaving the base sample at Year 1 at 522 couples.

For these couples, the mean age at Year 1 was 29.09 years (SD = 7.54) for husbands and 27.05 years (SD = 6.72) for wives, and the mean length of cohabitation was 0.74 years (SD = 1.06). Nearly all of the husbands (95%) and wives (95%) were White. The modal level of education for each spouse was the completion of a baccalaureate degree (32% of husbands and 33% of wives), and most husbands (92%) and wives (79%) were employed. There were two modal levels of personal annual income for husbands: 15% earned between $15,000 and $19,999, and another 15% earned between $25,000 and $29,999. Twenty-three percent of the wives earned less than $5,000. The numbers of husbands with 0, 1, and multiple divorces were 339, 132, and 51, respectively, whereas the corresponding numbers for wives were 334, 131, and 57. The numbers of couples with no children, only biological children born after the marriage, and only residential stepchildren in stepfather families were 215, 140, and 77, respectively. Ninety couples did not belong to any of these child-status categories because they were members of fairly small subgroups (e.g., couples who experienced a premarital pregnancy or couples who had both biological children and stepchildren).

Procedure

At each annual assessment (Year 1 through Year 10), couples were mailed two identical surveys. The Year 1 survey included measures of background information, divorce history, child-related status, individual-differences variables, and marital quality. Follow-up surveys included measures of child-related status and marital quality. Spouses were directed to complete their surveys privately and not to discuss their answers until the surveys had been completed and returned in separate postage-paid envelopes. However, no checks were made to ensure that these directions were followed.

For the follow-up surveys, if completed surveys were not returned by both spouses within a 1-month period after they were mailed, a letter prompting a response was sent. In this letter, spouses also were given an opportunity to indicate whether they had separated or divorced (not distinguished) or to withdraw from the study. Three prompt letters were sent. If no response was received after the third letter, participants were notified that they would not be contacted further (i.e., they were dropped from the study), but they were asked to provide information on couple status (i.e., still living together or separated or divorced). The number of couples at each assessment is presented for each of the four outcome status categories (completed all assessments, separated, withdrew, and dropped) in Table 1. Bias in the sample of couples who completed all 10 assessments is addressed later.

TABLE 1
Number of Couples in Each Follow-Up Status Category by Year of Assessment

Year	Completed all Assessments	Separated	Withdrew	Dropped
1	522	–	–	–
2	392	–	–	–
3	307	21	16	48
4	262	13	6	26
5	230	7	6	19
6	197	6	15	12
7	150	7	29	11
8	130	3	9	8
9	113	1	11	5
10	93	1	7	12

Note. Dashes indicate that values were not computed.

Measure of Background Information at Year 1

Spouses provided information regarding age, gender, race, education (represented by eight intervals ranging from completion of less than seventh grade to the award of a doctorate), annual personal income (represented by 12 intervals ranging from $5,000 or less to $50,000 or more), and the number of months they had lived with their husbands or wives.

Measure of Divorce History at Year 1

Spouses provided information about their divorce history by selecting one of four options: (a) "This is my first marriage," (b) "I have been divorced, and this is my first remarriage," (c) "I have been divorced twice, and this is my second remarriage," or (d) "I have been divorced more than twice, and this is my third or more remarriage." Because only a few of the respondents selected option (d), they were combined with the respondents who selected option (c) to form a single multiple-divorce group.

Measure of Child-Related Status at Each Assessment

Spouses were asked to list the first name, the age, and the gender of each child living with them as well as their relationship to each child (e.g., mother or stepfather). From this information, three child-status groups were formed. These included couples in which husbands and wives never lived with either children or stepchildren, couples in which husbands lived with only the children of their wives from a previous marriage, and couples in which husbands and wives lived with only their biological children. Of the 140 couples who lived with only their biological children, the numbers making the transition to parenthood during the course of the first through the ninth assessment were 32, 31, 26, 23, 6, 11, 4, 5, and 2, respectively. The mean number and the mean age of children and stepchildren are presented in Table 2 by year of assessment. It is noteworthy that, on the average, biological children (53% of whom were female) were preschoolers and stepchildren (51% of whom were female) were adolescents.

Measures of Individual-Differences Variables at Year 1

Dependability of spouse Respondents used a 7-point scale ranging from 1 (*strongly disagree*) to 7 (*strongly* *agree*) to indicate how strongly they agreed with six items from the Dependability subscale of Rempel et al.'s (1985) Trust Scale (e.g., "I have found that my partner is a thoroughly dependable person, especially when it comes to things that are important"). High scores reflected high levels of spousal dependability. Cronbach's alpha for the summed composite score was .70 for husbands and .76 for wives. Means were 36.81 (SD = 5.07) for husbands and 36.28 (SD = 5.84) for wives. Additional psychometric properties of this score are described by Rempel et al.

Dysfunctional beliefs about relationships Respondents used a 6-point scale ranging from 0 (*very false*) to 5 (*very true*) to indicate how strongly they endorsed 32 beliefs from Eidelson and Epstein's (1982) Relationship Beliefs Inventory that included "disagreement is destructive" (e.g., "I take it as a personal insult when my partner disagrees with an important idea of mine"), "mindreading is expected" (e.g., "I get very upset if my partner does not recognize how I am feeling and I have to tell him/her"), "partners cannot change" (e.g., "My partner does not seem capable of behaving other than he/she does now"), and "sexual perfection is expected" (e.g., "I get upset if I think I have not completely satisfied my partner sexually"). High scores indicated strong dysfunctional beliefs. Cronbach's alpha for the summed composite score was .83 for husbands and .82 for wives. Means were 51.81 (*SD* = 13.51) for husbands and 50.59 (*SD* = 13.73) for wives. Additional psychometric properties of this score are presented by Bradbury and Fincham (1993).**Instrumentality and expressiveness** Respondents used a 7-point scale ranging from 1 (*never or almost never true*) to 7 (*always or almost always true*) to describe themselves in terms of instrumentality (11 items; e.g., "assertive, strong personality, dominant") and expressiveness (12 items; e.g., "affectionate, compassionate, eager to soothe hurt feelings"). Items were based on Kurdek's (1987) factor analysis of items from Bem's (1974) Sex Role Inventory (BSRI). High scores indicated high levels of instrumentality and expressiveness. Cronbach's alphas for the summed composite instrumentality and expressiveness scores were .86 and .88, respectively, for husbands and .86 and .87, respectively, for wives. For instrumentality, means were 55.77 (*SD* = 9.46) for husbands and 50.82 (*SD* = 9.98) for wives. For expressiveness, means were 67.46 (*SD* = 8.40) for husbands and 71.67 (*SD* = 7.28) for wives. Relevant information on the psychometric properties of scores derived from the BSRI is provided by Kurdek (1987) as well as by Brems and Johnson (1990).

Psychological distress Respondents used a 5-point scale ranging from 0 (*not at all*) to 4 (*extremely*) to indicate how much discomfort 90 problems from Derogatis's (1983) Symptom Checklist–90–Revised caused them during the past 7 days. Symptoms covered the areas of somatization, obsessions and compulsions, interpersonal sensitivity, depression, anxiety, hostility, phobic anxiety, paranoid ideation, and psychoticism. High scores indicated severe symptoms. Cronbach's alpha for the summed composite score was .97 for husbands and .97 for wives. Means were 41.28 (*SD* = 36.84) for husbands and 45.97 (*SD* = 38.29) for wives. Additional psychometric properties of this score are presented by Derogatis (1983) as well as by Schwarzwald, Weisenberg, and Solomon (1991). For descriptive purposes, correlations between all of the individual-differences scores for husbands and wives are presented in Table 3. Because correlations within spouses and between spouses were not high, each score was retained.

Measure of Marital Quality

At each assessment, marital quality was assessed by the total score from Spanier's (1976) 32-item Dyadic Adjustment Scale, for which high scores reflect high marital quality. Over the 10 assessments, Cronbach's alpha for the summed composite score (maximum value = 151) ranged from .90 to .96 for husbands and from .91 to .95 for wives. Additional psychometric properties of this score are reported by Kurdek (1992).

RESULTS

Bias in the Longitudinal Sample

Although the growth curve analyses used in this study included data from all 522 couples (see later), bias in the sample of couples who completed all 10 assessments was evaluated with a one-way (couple status) multivariate analysis of variance in which the 93 couples with all 10 assessments were compared with the 429 couples with fewer than 10 assessments on three sets of variables from Year 1. The first set included the following 11 demographic variables: husband's age, education, employment

TABLE 2
Mean Number of Children and Stepchildren, Mean Age (in Years) of Children and Stepchildren, and Sample Size (n) by Year of Assessment

	Children			Stepchildren		
Year	Number	Age	*n*	Number	Age	*n*
1	–	–	–	1.56	8.84	72
2	1.16	1.03	32	1.55	10.60	40
3	1.10	1.05	52	1.57	13.20	23
4	1.20	1.30	69	1.67	14.33	15
5	1.31	1.23	86	1.73	15.29	11
6	1.51	1.88	81	1.60	15.75	10
7	1.60	2.07	67	1.60	18.13	10
8	1.80	2.42	59	1.71	18.00	7
9	1.81	2.93	57	1.25	17.63	4
10	1.96	3.84	52	1.50	20.75	2

Note. Dashes indicate that values were not computed.

TABLE 3
Pearson Correlations Between Husband (H) and Wife (W) Year 1 Scores

Score	1	2	3	4	5	6	7	8	9	10
1. H dependability	–									
2. H beliefs	–.33**	–								
3. H instrumentality	.05	–.04	–							
4. H expressiveness	.24**	–.24**	.23**	–						
5. H distress	–.28**	.35**	–.02	–.14**	–					
6. W dependability	.21**	–.19*	–.04	.07	–.19**	–				
7. W beliefs	–.20**	.28**	–.01	–.12**	.12**	–.39**	–			
8. W instrumentality	.00	–.02	.13**	.19**	–.03	.02	–.10*	–		
9. W expressiveness	.11*	–.04	.13**	.10*	.03	.12	–.11*	.11*	–	
10. W distress	–.22**	.16**	.03	–.01	.20**	–.31**	.40**	–.06	–.03	–

Note. $N = 522$; * $p < .05$; ** $p < .01$.

TABLE 4
An Example of the Level 1 Data Setup for One Couple With Scores From the Dyadic Adjustment Scale (DAS) at Each Year of Assessment

		Husband				Wife			
Code	DAS	Intercept	Linear	Quadratic	Cubic	Intercept	Linear	Quadratic	Cubic
001	110	1	–9	6	–42	0	0	0	0
001	108	1	–7	2	14	0	0	0	0
001	109	1	–5	–1	35	0	0	0	0
001	118	1	–3	–3	31	0	0	0	0
001	117	1	–1	–4	12	0	0	0	0
001	116	1	1	–4	–12	0	0	0	0
001	130	1	3	–3	–31	0	0	0	0
001	118	1	5	–1	–35	0	0	0	0
001	124	1	7	2	–14	0	0	0	0
001	119	1	9	6	42	0	0	0	0
001	111	0	0	0	0	1	–9	6	–42
001	106	0	0	0	0	1	–7	2	14
001	101	0	0	0	0	1	–5	–1	35
001	109	0	0	0	0	1	–3	–3	31
001	104	0	0	0	0	1	–1	–4	12
001	112	0	0	0	0	1	1	–4	–12
001	106	0	0	0	0	1	3	–3	–31
001	113	0	0	0	0	1	5	–1	–35
001	116	0	0	0	0	1	7	2	–14
001	107	0	0	0	0	1	9	6	42

Note. The first 10 DAS scores are from the husband at Year 1 through Year 10, respectively, whereas the second 10 scores are from the wife.

status (0 = *unemployed*, 1 = *employed*), income, and number of divorces; wife's age, education, employment status (0 = *unemployed*, 1 = *employed*), income, and number of divorces; and years of cohabitation. The second set included the following 10 individual-differences variables: husband and wife versions of dependability of spouse, relationship beliefs, instrumentality, expressiveness, and psychological distress. Finally, the third set included husband and wife versions of the marital quality score.

The multivariate effect was significant for the set of demographic variables, $F(11, 510) = 5.91, p < .001$. Univariate analyses indicated that relative to husbands who did not complete all assessments, husbands who did had higher levels of education and higher personal annual incomes, $Fs(1, 520) = 39.05$ and 7.34, respectively, $ps < .01$. In addition, relative to wives who did not complete all assessments, wives who did had higher levels of education, $F(1, 520) = 43.14, p < .01$.

The multivariate effect was also significant for the set of individual-differences variables, $F(10, 511) = 3.77, p < .01$. Univariate analyses indicated that relative to husbands who did not complete all assessments, husbands who did had lower scores regarding dysfunctional beliefs and instrumentality, $Fs(1, 520) = 4.20$ and 5.41, respectively, $ps < .05$, and that relative to wives who did not complete all assessments, wives who did had higher scores for dependability and lower scores for dysfunctional beliefs, expressiveness, and psychological distress, $Fs(1, 500) = 6.39$, 15.82, 6.36, and 5.68, respectively, $ps < .05$. Finally, the multivariate effect for the two marital quality scores was not significant, indicating that the two groups of couples were equivalent on spouses' reports of relationship quality at the beginning of the marriage. Nonetheless, because of the other differences found, the current sample cannot be regarded as representative.

Statistical Issues

Determining where husbands and wives began their trajectory of change in marital quality and assessing whether the pattern of change in marital quality for each spouse was best captured by a linear, quadratic, or cubic growth function posed two problems regarding statistical analyses. First, because Pearson correlations between husbands' and wives' marital quality scores ranged from .56 to .64 over the 10 assessments, separate analyses could not be conducted for each spouse without biased tests of statistical significance (Kenny, 1996). Instead, one analysis needed to be done in which the four effects for one spouse (i.e., initial status as well as linear, quadratic, and cubic patterns of change) were estimated and tested for statistical significance with controls for the four effects of the other spouse. Second, because over the course of the study, couples separated, withdrew from the study, or were dropped from the study, sample size decreased from Year 1 to Year 10. To prevent the loss of information for couples without complete data, I needed to conduct analyses so that information from all couples could be used.

Both statistical problems were solved by conducting two-level hierarchical linear modeling analyses with version 4.04 of Bryk, Raudenbush, and Congdon's (1996) Hierarchical Linear Modeling (HLM) program. Raudenbush, Brennan, and Barnett's (1995) guidelines for analyzing data from marital dyads were followed (see Willett, Singer, & Martin, 1998, for a general discussion of growth modeling). In all two-level analyses, the model at Level 1 captured aspects of within-couple variability in marital quality, whereas the model at Level 2 captured facets of between-couples variability in each aspect of within-couple variability. Specifically, the model at Level 1 treated the couple as the unit of analysis and used a set of coded vectors (see Pedhazur, 1982, chap. 14) to define the four parameters of the trajectory of growth in marital quality for each spouse within each couple. An example of the Level 1 record of one couple with marital quality scores from the Dyadic Adjustment Scale at all 10 assessments is presented in Table 4.

As shown in this table, for each spouse, intercepts (i.e., estimates of initial status) were identified by dummy variables, and linear, quadratic, and cubic components of each spouse's growth curve were identified by sets of orthogonal polynomial contrasts that provided unique weights for the marital quality score at each of the 10 assessments (see Cohen & Cohen, 1983, p. 243). For example, the weights for the linear component were –9, –7, –5, –3, –1, 1, 3, 5, 7, and 9 for scores from Year 1 through Year 10, respectively. For couples with incomplete data, as many of the 10 assessment weights were assigned as there were assessments available.

In equation form (see Equation 1 below, where H = husband and W = wife), it can be seen that the Level 1 model simultaneously defined a cubic growth model for each spouse (four parameters for husbands and four parameters for wives), thereby controlling for the problem of partner interdependence:

Marital quality = H (intercept + linear component

+ quadratic component + cubic component)

+ W (intercept + linear component

+ quadratic component + cubic component). (1)

Because the HLM program (Bryk et al., 1996) first uses ordinary least-squares methods to estimate the eight parameters on an individual couple-by-couple basis, the problem of having couples with differing numbers of assessments in the same analysis was handled such that each couple had its own growth curve. These initial least-squares values were used to obtain more precise estimates of Level 1 effects using empirical Bayes methods such that Level 1 estimates were optimally derived so as to borrow strength from the information provided by the full sample (see Bryk et al., 1996, pp. 4–5).[1] Thus, the estimates reported here were based on data from the entire sample of 522 couples, resulting in a total of 4,792 assessments of marital quality for each spouse.

Estimating the growth curve for each spouse required that each of the eight parameters of the Level 1 model in Equation 1 become an outcome variable to be explained by variables in the Level 2 model, plus a random couple effect. Length of cohabitation was included in the Level 2 model as a control variable. Thus, the growth curve model that included the intercept (or initial status) and the linear, quadratic, and cubic components of change comprised Equation 1 at Level 1 and the following eight equations at Level 2:

H intercept = grand mean + length of cohabitation

+ random couple effect. (2)

H linear component = grand mean + length of cohabitation

+ random couple effect. (3)

H quadratic component = grand mean

+ length of cohabitation + random couple effect. (4)

H cubic component = grand mean + length of cohabitation

+ random couple effect. (5)

W intercept = grand mean + length of cohabitation

+ random couple effect. (6)

W linear component = grand mean + length of cohabitation

+ random couple effect. (7)

W quadratic component = grand mean

+ length of cohabitation + random couple effect. (8)

W cubic component = grand mean + length of cohabitation

+ random couple effect. (9)

Estimates of the Level 2 coefficients (fixed effects) as well as both the variance associated with each fixed effect and the covariation among the fixed effects (random effects) were accomplished through full maximum-likelihood methods which, in the present case, allowed the fit of nested models to be compared.

The Nature of the Trajectory of Change in Marital Quality

Four nested models were estimated to determine where spouses started the trajectory of change in marital quality and whether the growth curve for each spouse was best characterized as linear, quadratic, or cubic in nature. The first model (intercept) estimated only husband and wife intercepts. The second model (linear) estimated spousal intercepts and linear components of the growth curve. The third model (quadratic) estimated spousal intercepts and linear and quadratic components of the growth curve. Finally, the fourth model (cubic) estimated spousal intercepts and linear, quadratic, and cubic components of the growth curve. Thus, "higher order" models were tested with controls for "lower order" effects. Findings regarding the fixed effects (estimates of the parameters of the "best" growth curve) are presented before those relevant to the random effects (the amount of variability within each parameter and the correlations between those parameters).

Fixed effects The fit of a hierarchical linear model is assessed within the HLM program (Bryk et al., 1996) by a deviance statistic. Low values of this statistic reflect good fit. In the present study, the improved fit of increasingly more complex growth models was assessed by testing whether the decrease in the deviance statistic associated with going from the more simple to the more complex model was statistically significant. (The sample size for these tests changes because the relevant statistic is based on the number of cases with complete data.) These tests indicated that the linear model provided a better fit to the data than did the intercept model, $\chi^2(11, N = 392) = 1{,}357.81, p < .01$; that the quadratic model provided a better fit to the data than did the linear model, $\chi^2(15, N = 307) = 203.33, p < .01$; and that the cubic model provided a better fit to the data than did the quadratic model, $\chi^2(19, N = 197) = 118.83, p < .01$. Thus, of the four models, the cubic growth model provided the best fit to the pattern of change in marital quality.

The unstandardized coefficients for each of the four parameters of each spouse's cubic growth model are presented for husbands and wives in the top panel (Model 1) of Table 5. In the HLM program, these coefficients are tested for statistical significance with a *t* ratio. Following Karney and Bradbury (1997), I converted *t* ratios to effect-size *rs* to facilitate the interpretation of the coefficients.[2] Small, medium, and large effects were designated by *rs* of .10, .30, and .50, respectively (per Cohen, 1988). As shown in Table 5, the level of marital quality at the beginning of the trajectory was fairly high for both spouses. (Because the total Dyadic Adjustment Scale score was always greater than 0, both initial status effects had to be significant, so the relevant effect sizes are not presented.) As also shown in Table 5, the significant cubic effect for each spouse was medium in size.

For descriptive purposes, a graphical estimate of the nature of the growth curve for each spouse was derived by plotting the observed means of the marital quality scores obtained at each of the 10 assessments for the 93 couples who provided data for all years. The resulting graph is only an estimate, however, because—as noted earlier—the actual parameter estimates were based on information provided by the full sample of 522 couples. As shown in Figure 1, a cubic growth function best represented the pattern of change for each spouse because there were two bends in the growth curve. For each spouse, marital quality declined fairly rapidly over the first 4 years of marriage (the first phase of accelerated change), stabilized, and then declined again at about the 8th year of marriage (the second phase of accelerated change).[3]

Random effects The random effects associated with the cubic growth model addressed two issues. First, was there sufficient variability within each parameter of the cubic growth model to warrant retaining each

TABLE 5
Fixed Effects Estimates for Two Models of the Trajectory of Change in Marital Quality

	Husband			Wife		
Parameter	**Coefficient**	*t*	*r*	**Coefficient**	*t*	*r*
Model 1: Controlling for length of cohabitation						
Initial status	111.48	124.85**	–	111.04	117.56**	–
Growth curve						
Linear component	−0.69	−8.61**	−.52	−0.89	−9.98**	−.58
Quadratic component	0.37	4.79**	.32	0.28	3.67**	.25
Cubic component	−0.03	−4.75**	−.32	−0.03	−4.60**	−.31
Model 2: Controlling for length of cohabitation and follow-up status						
Initial status	115.45	79.32**	–	116.86	77.35**	–
Growth curve						
Linear component	−0.44	−4.47**	−.30	−0.54	−5.06**	−.34
Quadratic component	0.27	2.64**	.18	0.18	1.78	.13
Cubic component	−0.03	−3.24**	−.23	−0.03	−2.50**	−.18

Note. Dashes indicate that no value was calculated because the estimate for initial status had to be different from 0.
** $p < .01$.

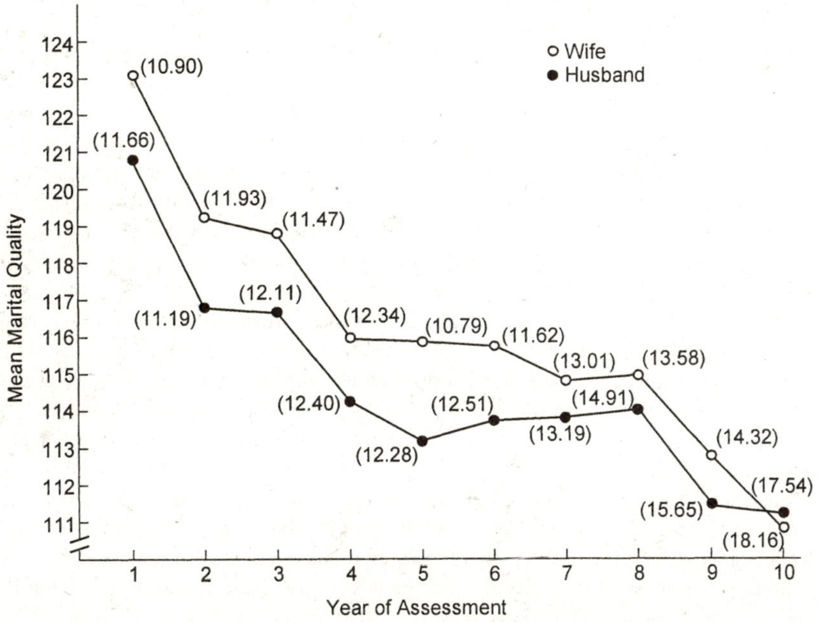

Figure 1. Mean marital quality scores (and standard deviations) by spouse and year of assessment for couples completing all 10 assessments ($n = 93$).

TABLE 6
Standard Deviations for Random Effects and Correlations Between Random Effects

Random effect	1	2	3	4	5	6	7	8
1. Husband initial	13.93							
2. Wife initial	.79	14.60						
3. Husband linear	.64	.51	0.81					
4. Wife linear	.56	.59	.88	0.97				
5. Husband quadratic	−.10	−.06	−.20	−.24	0.68			
6. Wife quadratic	.00	−.13	.00	−.02	.82	0.70		
7. Husband cubic	−.05	.10	−.16	−.27	−.06	−.24	0.05	
8. Wife cubic	.35	.42	.19	.02	−.44	−.57	.79	0.06

Note. Standard deviations are presented in the diagonal, and correlations are presented below the diagonal.

parameter in later analyses that were designed to account for such variability? The standard deviations for each of the eight random effects from the cubic model are presented in the diagonal of Table 6. The HLM program provides a chi-square test regarding the heterogeneity of the variance of each random effect. Because each of the eight resulting chi-square values was significant—$\chi^2(195, N = 197)$ ranged from 224.38 (for wife's cubic change) to 4,295.80 (for wife's initial status), *ps* < .01—the eight-parameter model was used in later analyses designed to explain the variability within each parameter.

The second issue was the extent to which husbands' trajectory of change in marital quality was related to that of their wives. Correlations among all of the random effects are presented below the diagonal of the data matrix in Table 6, from which cross-spouse correlations can be obtained. As shown in this table, because the husband-wife correlations were highly positive for initial status, linear change, quadratic change, and cubic change, spouses' trajectories of change in marital quality were very similar to one another. A multivariate test within the HLM program was run to determine whether the four parameters for husbands differed from the corresponding four parameters for wives. This test was significant, $\chi^2(4, N = 197) = 9.99$, $p < .05$. Subsequent univariate comparisons indicated that husbands and wives differed on only one of the four parameters: Relative to husbands, wives showed a steeper rate of linear change, $\chi^2(1, N = 197) = 8.68$, $p < .01$.

The Nature of the Trajectory of Change in Marital Quality With Controls for Longitudinal Outcomes

One possible concern with the cubic growth model just described is that it included data from couples with different outcome statuses over the course of the study. In particular, one might argue that the pattern of deterioration in marital quality just reported was due to the fact that spouses who separated or divorced were included with spouses who remained together. Consequently, a second cubic model was estimated in which Equations 2 through 9 (at Level 2) included three dummy variables that represented variability in outcome status (as well as controls for length of cohabitation). Because the couples with complete longitudinal data were used as the reference group, the dummy variables carried information about the extent to which couples who separated or divorced, withdrew from the study, or were dropped from the study differed from couples with complete longitudinal data.

The unstandardized weights associated with the three dummy variables are presented for each of the four parameters of the growth trajectory for each spouse in the top panel of Table 7. It can be seen that couples in which spouses separated or divorced differed from couples with complete longitudinal data in that the former group included husbands and wives with lower initial status and wives with steeper linear decreases: effect-size *rs* = –.30 (medium), –.46 (medium), and .29 (small), respectively. Couples who withdrew from the study differed from couples with complete longitudinal data in that the former group included wives with lower initial status: effect-size *r* = -.17 (small). Finally, couples who were dropped from the study differed from couples with complete longitudinal data in that the former group included husbands and wives with lower initial status and husbands and wives with steeper linear change: effect-size *rs* = –.18 (small), –.25 (small), –.14 (small), and –.18 (small), respectively.

With regard to the estimates of the parameters of the growth trajectory with controls for outcome status (as well as length of cohabitation), the degree to which increasingly more complex growth models improved the fit of the model to the data again was assessed. As in the previous analysis, the linear model provided a better fit to the data than did the intercept model, $\chi^2(17, N = 392) = 1{,}451.28$, $p < .01$; the quadratic model provided a better fit to the data than did the linear model, $\chi^2(21, N = 307) = 187.15$, $p < .01$; and the cubic model provided a better fit to the data than did the quadratic model, $\chi^2(25, N = 197) = 114.91$, $p < .01$. Thus, even with additional controls for outcome status, the cubic growth model still provided the best fit to the pattern of change in marital quality. However, as shown in the bottom portion of Table 5, the strength of the cubic effect was reduced from medium to small for both husbands and wives. Because the effects associated with outcome status were significant, following Karney and Bradbury (1997), I used the dummy variables representing these effects, along with length of cohabitation, as control variables in all subsequent analyses.

Explaining Variability in Each Parameter of the Trajectory of Change

Attention is now directed to whether spouses' divorce history, the presence of residential children or stepchildren, and spouses' individual-differences variables predicted any of the parameters that defined the cubic pattern of change in marital quality.

Divorce history For husbands and wives, the link between both their own divorce history and that of their spouse and each of the four parameters relevant to their own trajectory of change in marital quality was examined with a two-level model. The Level 1 model included husbands' own initial status, linear change, quadratic change, and cubic change as well as the four parallel terms for wives. At Level 2, each of these terms was explained by two sets of variables. These included the set of four control variables (length of cohabitation and the three dummy variables capturing information about outcome status) and a set of four dummy variables that carried information regarding the husband's own divorce history and that of the wife (no divorce, one divorce, or multiple divorces). Within this second set, two of the dummy variables represented variability in one spouse's own divorce history (with no divorce as the reference group), and the other two dummy variables represented variability in the divorce history of the other spouse (again, with no divorce as the reference group). Thus, eight equations with eight terms were specified at Level 2, four for each spouse.

The resulting unstandardized coefficients are presented in the second panel of Table 7. Although 2 of the 32 coefficients associated with comparisons between

TABLE 7
Unstandardized Coefficients Associated With Predictors of Each Parameter of the Trajectory of Change in Marital Quality

Predictor	Initial status		Linear change		Quadratic change		Cubic change	
	Husband	Wife	Husband	Wife	Husband	Wife	Husband	Wife
Outcome status (with controls for length of cohabitation)								
Separated vs. complete	−14.82**	−25.93**	−0.68	−2.60**	0.80	−0.51	0.03	−0.02
Withdrew vs. complete	−2.64	−5.32*	−0.27	−0.45	−0.06	−0.05	−0.01	0.00
Dropped vs. complete	−5.06**	−7.66**	−0.43*	−0.62**	0.18	−0.10	0.00	−0.02
Divorce history (with controls for length of cohabitation and outcome status)								
1 vs. none								
Husband	3.73	5.55**	0.10	0.18	0.12	0.26	0.01	0.00
Wife	−2.52	−1.88	−0.35*	−0.16	0.10	0.19	0.00	−0.01
Multiple vs. none								
Husband	0.82	1.89	−0.02	0.08	0.10	0.18	−0.05	0.00
Wife	−1.49	−0.52	−0.42	−0.46	−0.37	−0.46	−0.02	−0.02
Child status (with controls for length of cohabitation and outcome status)								
Biological vs. none	−4.87**	−3.46*	−0.48**	−0.35*	−0.24	−0.27	0.00	0.00
Step vs. none	−0.49	−2.10	−0.24	−0.36	−0.12	−0.19	0.00	−0.02
Other vs. none	−2.53	−1.03	−0.38	−0.21	−0.32	−0.20	−0.03	−0.02
Individual-differences variables (with controls for length of cohabitation and outcome status)								
Dependability								
Husband	0.95**	0.69**	−0.44	0.01	0.02	0.00	0.00	0.00
Wife	0.71**	1.17**	0.00	0.02	0.01	0.01	0.00	0.00
Dysfunctional beliefs								
Husband	−0.25**	−0.18**	−0.01	−0.01	0.00	0.00	0.00	0.00
Wife	−0.12**	−0.23**	0.00	0.00	0.00	0.00	0.00	0.00
Sex role self-concept								
Instrumentality								
Husband	0.05	−0.01	0.00	0.01	0.00	0.00	0.00	0.00
Wife	−0.03	−0.08	0.00	0.00	0.00	0.00	0.00	0.00
Expressiveness								
Husband	0.38**	0.26**	−0.02*	−0.01	−0.01	0.00	0.00	0.00
Wife	0.32**	0.43**	0.00	0.00	0.00	0.01	0.00	0.00
Psychological distress								
Husband	−0.12**	−0.08**	−0.01**	−0.01*	0.00	0.00	0.00	0.00
Wife	−0.05**	−0.07**	0.00	0.00	0.00	0.00	0.00	0.00

* $p < .05$. ** $p < .01$.

spouses with a history of one divorce and those with a history of no divorce were significant, they might best be regarded as chance findings. Of more substantive interest is the finding that none of the coefficients associated with comparisons between spouses with a history of multiple divorce and those with a history of no divorces was significant. Analyses not reported here indicated that Husband Divorce History × Wife Divorce History interactions also were not significant and that main effects for divorce history were still nonsignificant even when outcome status was not controlled.

The resulting unstandardized coefficients are presented in the second panel of Table 7. Although 2 of the 32 coefficients associated with comparisons between spouses with a history of one divorce and those with a history of no divorce were significant, they might best be regarded as chance findings. Of more substantive interest is the finding that none of the coefficients associated with comparisons between spouses with a history of multiple divorce and those with a history of no divorces was significant. Analyses not reported here indicated that Husband Divorce History × Wife Divorce History interactions also were not significant and that main effects for divorce history were still nonsignificant even when outcome status was not controlled.

Presence of residential children or stepchildren The link between whether the couple lived with children or stepchildren and each of the four parameters of the growth trajectory at Level 1 for each spouse was examined by including seven terms in each of the eight equations at Level 2. These included the set of four control variables (length of cohabitation and three dummy variables representing outcome status) and three dummy variables in which couples with no children were contrasted with each of three other groups: couples living with only their own biological children at some point in the study, couples in which the husband lived with only his stepchildren, and an "other" category that included the remaining couples. As can be seen from the unstandardized coefficients presented in the third panel of Table 7, relative to couples who did not live with any children, those who lived with only their biological children included husbands and wives with lower initial status for marital quality as well as stronger linear declines in marital quality: effect-size *rs* = −.19 (small), −.13 (small), −.21 (small), and −.14 (small), respectively.

In order to explore this linear effect in more detail, I tested a two-level model using data from only the 140 couples living with their biological children. The Level 1 model included four terms such that marital quality was defined in terms of the husband intercept, the husband linear component, the wife intercept, and the wife linear component. In turn, at Level 2, these four terms became outcome scores, each to be explained by five terms that captured much of the heterogeneity within this subsample of couples: years of cohabitation (as a control variable), year during which the transition to parenthood was made (ranging from 1 to 9), total number of children at last assessment (ranging from 1 to 4), total number of male children (ranging from 0 to 3), and mean age of all children (ranging from 1 to 8 years).

As can be seen from the unstandardized coefficients presented in Table 8, with controls for the other predictors at Level 2, year of transition and total number of children independently explained variability in each of the four parameters. Specifically, fathers and mothers who made the transition to parenthood relatively early started their respective trajectories of change at fairly low levels of marital quality, *rs* = .30 (medium) and .40 (medium), respectively, and they experienced relatively steep declines in marital quality, *rs* = .25 (small) and .35 (medium), respectively. In addition, fathers and mothers who had a relatively large number of children started their respective trajectories of change at fairly low levels of marital quality, *rs* = .18 (small) and .17 (small), respectively, and they experienced relatively steep declines in marital quality, *rs* = .24 (small) and .20 (small), respectively. In analyses not reported here, effects associated with the interaction between the timing of the transition to parenthood and total number of children, total number of male children, and mean age of all children were also examined. None of these effects was significant.

TABLE 8
Unstandardized Coefficients Associated with Predictors of Each Parameter of the Trajectory of Change in Marital Quality for Couples Living with Only Their Biological Children

	Initial status		Linear change	
Predictor	Husband	Wife	Husband	Wife
Year of transition to parenthood	2.33**	3.00**	0.16**	0.25**
No. of total children	4.10*	3.54*	0.44**	0.36*
No. of total male children	−2.48	−1.15	−0.16	−0.01
Mean age of all children	0.39	1.26	0.01	0.09

Note. Years of cohabitation was used as a control variable.
* $p < .05$. ** $p < .01$.

Individual-differences variables Because with two exceptions—instrumentality and expressiveness—the individual-differences variables did not form a coherent conceptual package, separate analyses were conducted for each variable. Instrumentality and expressiveness were considered together because they represented two dimensions of sex role self-concept. Thus, for dependability, dysfunctional beliefs, and psychological distress, each of the four parameters of a spouse's own trajectory of change in marital quality at Level 1 was explained for each spouse by the set of four control variables (length of cohabitation and three dummy variables carrying information about outcome status) and the self-version and spouse version of the individual-differences variable of interest, resulting in eight equations (four for each spouse) with six terms at Level 2. For the analyses involving sex role self-concept, self-versions of instrumentality and expressiveness and spouse versions of instrumentality and expressiveness were considered together, for a total of eight equations with seven terms at Level 2.

The resulting unstandardized coefficients are presented in the last panel of Table 7 and reveal one striking pattern: Independent intraspouse and cross-spouse effects were obtained for dependability of spouse, dysfunctional beliefs, expressivity, and psychological distress, but almost exclusively for the initial status of the trajectory of change. Specifically, husbands who began their trajectory of change at fairly low levels of marital quality at the start of their marriages regarded their wives as low in dependability (effect-size r = .42, medium), endorsed many dysfunctional beliefs about relationships (r = –.31, medium), saw themselves as low in expressiveness (r = .29, small), and reported high psychological distress (r = .38, medium). In addition, they also had wives who, at the start of the marriage, regarded them as low in dependability (effect-size r = .37, medium), endorsed many dysfunctional beliefs about relationships (r = –.16, small), saw themselves as low in expressiveness (r = .23, small), and reported high psychological distress (r = –.20, small).

In parallel fashion, wives who started their trajectory at fairly low levels of marital quality at the beginning of the marriage regarded their husbands as low in dependability (effect-size r = .54, large), endorsed many dysfunctional beliefs about relationships (r = –.29, small), saw themselves as low in expressiveness (r = .30, medium), and reported high psychological distress (r = .25, small). In addition, they also had husbands who, at the beginning of the marriage, regarded them as low in dependability (effect-size r = .32, medium), endorsed many dysfunctional beliefs about relationships (r = –.21, small), saw themselves as low in expressiveness (r = .20, small), and reported high psychological distress (r = .24, small).

DISCUSSION

The Nature of the Trajectory of Change in Marital Quality

The focus of this study was not on marriage as a static life event but on marital quality as a developmental phenomenon. Accordingly, the first purpose of this study was to describe the nature of change in marital quality over the first 10 years of marriage. Growth curve analyses were conducted on reports of marital quality from a sample of both spouses that is among the largest ever recruited and among the longest ever continuously assessed in this area of study. In order to explore rather complex patterns of change, a cubic growth curve was fitted for each spouse. This curve consisted of the level of marital quality with which the curve began and whether the pattern of change was characterized as changing at the same rate from assessment to assessment (linear), as having one phase of accelerated change (quadratic), or as having two phases of accelerated change (cubic).

Similar to the findings of Karney and Bradbury (1997), who used growth curve analyses to characterize the nature of change in marital quality for 54 first-married couples over the first 4 years of marriage, the growth curves of husbands and wives in the current study over the first 10 years of marriage were positively related to each other. In an extension of Karney and Bradbury's findings, husbands and wives in the present study (with controls for the length of time they had been living together) showed a similar pattern of cubic change such that marital quality declined fairly rapidly over the first 4 years of marriage (the first phase of accelerated change), stabilized, and then declined again at about the 8th year of marriage (the second phase of accelerated change). Although reduced in strength, the cubic growth effect remained significant for each spouse even when additional controls for the outcome status of couples over the course of this investigation (e.g., separated or divorced, withdrew from the study, were dropped from the study, or provided all 10 assessments) were introduced. Further, with these controls, the parameters of husbands' trajectories were equivalent to those of their wives.

As a normative account of how marital quality changes over time, the present findings have implications for how adult development is conceptualized. In his classic description of the developmental tasks of adulthood, Havighurst (1972) characterized early adulthood as a time of selecting a mate and adjusting to marriage and portrayed middle adulthood as a time of revitalizing marriage. The findings regarding change in marital quality over time suggest that early adulthood—a developmental period when most people still marry for the first time (United States Bureau of the Census, 1997)—might also be described as a time when one needs to be prepared for two sets of normative declines in marital quality. The first decline occurs over the early years of marriage, consistent with the common notion of a "honeymoon is over" effect (Kovacs, 1983; Sternberg, 1986). The second decline occurs at about the 8th year of marriage, consistent with the common notion of a 7-year-itch effect (Kovacs, 1983). Given evidence that evaluations of outcomes depend on the standards of evaluations used (see review by Higgins, Strauman, & Klein, 1986), the severity of some instances of marital distress might be mitigated by spouses' expecting and being prepared for "normal" periods of decline in marital quality.

One issue that merits further investigation is whether any specific dimensions of marital quality are most likely to decline over time. Addressing this issue is problematic for at least two reasons. First, there is as yet no well-articulated and empirically defended multidimensional model of marital quality (Fincham, 1998). Second, current measures that assess multiple dimensions of marital quality, such as Spanier's (1976) Dyadic Adjustment Scale, which was used in the present study, have the unfortunate psychometric property of highly intercorrelated subscores with attendant statistical problems of multicollinearity. Perhaps Sternberg's (1986) argument that love can be conceptualized in terms of intimacy, passion, and commitment is one starting point for further investigation into the structure of marital quality. It is possible, for example, that different components of marital quality change in different ways. For example, passion, because of its initial high extremes, may decline most quickly, whereas commitment, especially when viewed as barriers to leaving the marriage, may actually increase over time (Adams & Jones, 1997).

Accounting for Variability in the Trajectory of Change in Marital Quality

The second purpose of this study was to determine whether variability in any of the four parameters of the growth trajectory was accounted for by three sets of factors: spouses' divorce history, whether couples had children or stepchildren over the course of the study, and spouses' individual-differences variables assessed at the start of the marriage. The findings regarding divorce history were remarkable in that intrapartner and cross-partner effects were largely nonsignificant even when no controls were made for outcome status. This unexpected pattern of findings might be due to the fact that the group of multiply divorced spouses collapsed spouses that were divorced twice with those divorced more than twice.

In their discussion of "serial marriers," Brody et al. (1988) speculated that persons who have been divorced more than twice are at risk for psychological problems because of dysfunctional personality characteristics, unrealistic expectations of marriage, poorly developed negotiation and compromise skills, and cumulative negative stresses associated with living in a society in which serial marriers are regarded negatively. Unfortunately, the risk status of serial marriers could not be evaluated in this study because their number was too small to warrant including them as a distinct group.

The effects regarding having children or stepchildren are noteworthy because they indicate that relative to husbands and wives with no children or stepchildren, those who lived with only their biological children during the course of the study not only started their trajectories at lower levels of marital quality but also showed steeper linear declines in marital quality over time. Both of these effects are somewhat difficult to interpret because no information was available regarding the reasons why couples did not have children. For example, couples could want children eventually but postpone having them, deliberately choose not to have children, or not be able to have children for medical reasons (Houseknecht, 1987).

It is possible that spouses who eventually lived with only their biological children started their trajectories at lower levels of marital quality than those who never lived with any children or stepchildren because they were less motivated to maintain positive illusions about their relationships (Murray, Holmes, & Griffin, 1996). The perception that one's marital relationship is less than perfect may, in time, fuel one's desire to experience a parental relationship, perhaps as one way to compensate for emotional deficiencies within the marital relationship (Belsky, Youngblade, Rovine, & Volling, 1991). Alternatively, spouses who are highly invested in having children may regard their marriages as missing some critical element until children actually arrive.

The finding that relative to husbands and wives with no children or stepchildren, those who lived with only their biological children showed steeper linear declines in marital quality over time may be explained by the fact that in the present sample, most biological children were infants or preschoolers. It is possible that the presence of very young children acts as a barrier to ending even a marriage that is deteriorating (Cherlin, 1977). Consistent with the findings from this study that the decline in marital quality was especially likely for spouses who made the transition to parenthood fairly early in their marital careers and had many children, it is also plausible that the decline in marital quality is linked to an increase in the stressors of parenting that occur as young children develop (e.g., Belsky, Woodworth, & Crnic, 1996) and that leave parents with little time and energy to nurture their marital relationship. It would be of interest to determine whether marital quality stabilizes or even increases as children become more autonomous.

In light of discussions of the special stressors associated with living with stepchildren (see summary by Ganong & Coleman, 1994), the finding that the trajectory of change in marital quality for couples with no children or stepchildren was the same as that for spouses in stepfather families is consistent with Martin and Bumpass's (1989) finding that wives' bringing children into a remarriage does not affect the odds of marital success. It is possible that one of the factors that protected the marital quality of spouses in stepfather families was that the stepchildren in these families tended to be adolescents. Although raising adolescents in stepfather families has its own set of issues regarding discipline and control (Hetherington & Clingempeel, 1992), the relative autonomy of adolescents need not interfere with, and may even facilitate, the development of positive marital quality between mothers and stepfathers.

Finally, the effects associated with the individual-differences variables are of note in that they involved both intrapartner and cross-partner links for both husbands and wives only to the initial status of the trajectory of change in marital quality. Consistent with the findings of earlier studies assessing concurrent linkages between individual-differences variables and marital quality, spouses who started their trajectories at relatively low levels of marital quality also reported at the beginning of their marriages low dependability of spouse (Rempel et al., 1985), strong dysfunctional beliefs regarding relationships (Eidelson & Epstein, 1982), low expressiveness (Kurdek & Schmitt, 1986a), and high psychological distress (Karney et al., 1994). The present findings extend these earlier reports by also showing that these individual-differences variables have independent, parallel cross-spouse effects for both husbands and wives.

The findings that having children or stepchildren was linked to linear change in marital quality whereas individual-differences variables assessed at the start of the marriage were linked to the initial status of the trajectory of marital quality are reminiscent of Karney and Bradbury's (1997) findings that spousal interactional patterns (such as one might expect to occur in family systems with children) forecast linear declines in marital quality whereas spouses' individual-differences variables measured at the beginning of the marriage were linked only to the initial status of the trajectory. To the extent that identifying characteristics of persons predisposed to marital distress is deemed important (e.g., Holman, Larson, & Harmer, 1994), the inability of individual-differences variables to predict change in marital quality is sobering. However, given that this change may need to be understood in terms of dynamic tensions between spouses' developing needs and desires rather than in terms of their fairly stable intrapersonal predispositions (Montgomery, 1993), the inability of the individual-differences variables to predict change in marital quality is, in hindsight, not too surprising.

Limitations and Conclusions

The findings from this study need to be viewed with its limitations in mind, four of which are noted here. First, no claim can be made that the couples studied were representative of all newly wed couples because couples at the beginning of the study were disproportionately White and college educated. Second, although the growth curve analyses used all of the available data and controlled for outcome status, the rate of attrition was fairly high, and couples who provided data at all 10 assessments were biased with regard to demographic and individual-differences variables. Third, all of the data collected in this study were self-reported, with attending biases of self-presentation. Fourth, although the notion that marital quality changes in terms of two phases of accelerated change is a plausible interpretation of the cubic growth model, no analyses were conducted that tested precisely when the discontinuities in change occurred (Willett, 1997).

Despite these limitations, this study included a fairly large sample of newlyweds with diverse divorce histories who were studied annually for a longer period of time than in most other comparable studies. Overall, the findings (a) validate Karney and Bradbury's (1997) exhortation that marital researchers attend to the trajectory of change in marital quality; (b) suggest that a pattern of two phases of decline in marital quality is normative: and (c) document that whereas individual-differences variables at the start of the marriage are linked in an intraspouse and cross-spouse manner to the initial status of the trajectory of change in marital quality, only variables that tap some aspect of spousal interactions (such as whether they have children) are linked to the level of change in marital quality.

REFERENCES

Adams, J. M., & Jones, W. H. (1997). The conceptualization of marital commitment: An integrative analysis. *Journal of Personality and Social Psychology, 72*, 1177–1196.

Belsky, J., Woodworth, S., & Crnic, K. (1996). Trouble in the second year: Three questions about family interaction. *Child Development, 67*, 556–578.

Belsky, J., Youngblade, L., Rovine, M., & Volling, B. (1991). Patterns of marital change and parent-child interaction. *Journal of Marriage and the Family, 53*, 487–498.

Bem, S. L. (1974). The measurement of psychological androgyny. *Journal of Consulting and Clinical Psychology, 46*, 1053–1070.

Bradbury, T. N., Campbell, S. M., & Fincham, F. D. (1995). Longitudinal and behavioral analysis of masculinity and femininity in marriage. *Journal of Personality and Social Psychology, 68*, 328–341.

Bradbury, T. N., & Fincham, F. D. (1993). Assessing dysfunctional cognition in marriage: A reconsideration of the Relationship Belief Inventory. *Psychological Assessment, 5*, 92–101.

Brems, C., & Johnson, M. E. (1990). Reexamination of the Bem Sex-Role Inventory: The Interpersonal BSRI. *Journal of Personality Assessment, 55*, 484–498.

Brody, G. H., Neubaum, E., & Forehand, R. (1988). Serial marriage: A heuristic analysis of an emerging family form. *Psychological Bulletin, 103*, 211–222.

Bryk, A. S., & Raudenbush, S. W. (1992). *Hierarchical linear models: Applications and data analysis methods.* Newbury Park, CA: Sage.

Bryk, A. S., Raudenbush, S. W., & Congdon, R. T. (1996). *Hierarchical linear and nonlinear modeling with the HLM/2L and HLM/3L programs.* Chicago: Scientific Software International.

Burr, W. R. (1970). Satisfaction with various aspects of marriage over the life cycle: A random middle class sample. *Journal of Marriage and the Family, 32*, 29–37.

Cherlin, A. (1977). The effect of children on marital dissolution. *Demography, 14*, 265–272.

Clarke, S. C. (1995a). Advance report of final divorce statistics, 1989 and 1990. *Monthly Vital Statistics Report* (Vol. 43, No. 9, Supplement). Hyattsville, MD: National Center for Health Statistics.

Clarke, S. C. (1995b). Advance report of final marriage statistics, 1989 and 1990. *Monthly Vital Statistics Report* (Vol. 43, No. 12, Supplement). Hyattsville, MD: National Center for Health Statistics.

Cohen, J. (1988). *Statistical power analysis for the behavioral sciences.* Hillsdale, NJ: Erlbaum.

Cohen, J., & Cohen, P. (1983). *Applied multiple regression/correlation analysis for the behavioral sciences.* Hillsdale, NJ: Erlbaum.

Davila, J., Bradbury, T. N., Cohan, C. L., & Tochluk, S. (1997). Marital functioning and depressive symptoms: Evidence for the stress generation model. *Journal of Personality and Social Psychology, 73*, 849–861.

Derogatis, L. (1983). *SCL-90-R: Administration, scoring, and procedures manual.* Towson, MD: Clinical Psychometric Research.

Eidelson, R. J., & Epstein, N. (1982). Cognition and relationship maladjustment: Development of a measure of relationship beliefs. *Journal of Consulting and Clinical Psychology, 50*, 715–720.

Fincham, F. D. (1998). Child development and marital relations. *Child Development, 69*, 543–574.

Ganong, L. H., & Coleman, M. (1994). *Remarried family relationships.* Thousand Oaks, CA: Sage.

Glenn, N. D., & Weaver, C. N. (1981). The contribution of marital happiness to global happiness. *Journal of Marriage and the Family, 43*, 161–168.

Gould, R. L. (1978). *Transformations: Growth and change in adult life.* New York: Simon & Schuster.

Havighurst, R. J. (1972). *Developmental tasks and education.* New York: McKay.

Heaton, T. B., & Albrecht, S. L. (1991). Stable unhappy marriages. *Journal of Marriage and the Family, 53*, 747–758.

Hetherington, E. M., & Clingempeel, W. G. (1992). Coping with marital transitions. *Monographs of the Society for Research in Child Development. 57* (2–3, Serial No. 227).

Higgins, E. T., Strauman, T., & Klein, R. (1986). Standards and the process of self-evaluation: Multiple affects from multiple stages. In R. M. Sorrentino & E. T. Higgins (Eds.), *Handbook of motivation and cognition* (pp. 23–63). New York: Guilford Press.

Holman, T. B., Larson, J. H., & Harmer, S. L. (1994). The development and predictive validity of a new premarital assessment instrument. *Family Relations, 43*, 46–52.

Houseknecht, S. K. (1987). Voluntary childlessness. In M. B. Sussman & S. K. Steinmetz (Eds.), *Handbook of marriage and the family* (pp. 369–396). New York: Plenum.

Karney, B. R., & Bradbury, T. N. (1995). The longitudinal course of marital quality and stability: A review of theory, method, and research. *Psychological Bulletin, 118*, 3–34.

Karney, B. R., & Bradbury, T. N. (1997). Neuroticism, marital interaction, and the trajectory of marital satisfaction. *Journal of Personality and Social Psychology, 72*, 1075–1092.

Karney, B. R., Bradbury, T. N., Fincham, F. D., & Sullivan, K. T. (1994). The role of negative affectivity in the association between attributions and marital satisfaction. *Journal of Personality and Social Psychology, 66*, 413–424.

Kenny, D. A. (1996). Modes of nonindependence in dyadic research. *Journal of Social and Personal Relationships, 13*, 279–294.

Kovacs, L. (1983). A conceptualization of marital development. *Family Therapy, 3*, 183–210.

Kurdek, L. A. (1987). Sex role self scheme and psychological adjustment in coupled homosexual and heterosexual men and women. *Sex Roles, 17*, 549–562.

Kurdek, L. A. (1992). Dimensionality of the Dyadic Adjustment Scale: Evidence from heterosexual and homosexual couples. *Journal of Family Psychology, 6*, 22–35.

Kurdek, L. A., & Schmitt, J. P. (1986a). Interaction of sex role self-concept with relationship quality and relationship beliefs in married, heterosexual cohabiting, gay, and lesbian couples. *Journal of Personality and Social Psychology, 51*, 365–370.

Kurdek, L. A., & Schmitt, J. P. (1986b). Relationship quality of partners in heterosexual married, heterosexual cohabiting, gay, and lesbian relationships. *Journal of Personality and Social Psychology, 51*, 711–720.

Levinson, D. J., Darrow, C. N., Klein, E. B., Levinson, M. H., & McKee, B. (1978). *The seasons of a man's life.* New York: Knopf.

MacDermid, S. M., Huston, T. L., & McHale, S. M. (1990). Changes in marriage associated with the transition to parenthood: Individual differences as a function of sex-role attitudes and changes in division of household labor. *Journal of Marriage and the Family, 52*, 475–486.

Martin, T. C., & Bumpass, L. (1989). Trends in marital disruption. *Demography, 26*, 37–52.

Montgomery, B. M. (1993). Relationship maintenance versus relationship change: A dialectical dilemma. *Journal of Social and Personal Relationships, 10*, 205–223.

Murray, S. L., Holmes, J. G., & Griffin, D. W. (1996). The self-fulfilling nature of positive illusions in romantic relationships: Love is not blind, but prescient. *Journal of Personality and Social Psychology, 71*, 1155–1180.

National Center for Health Statistics. (1991). Advance report of final marriage statistics, 1988. *Monthly Vital Statistics Report* (Vol. 39, No. 12, Supplement 2). Hyattsville, MD: U.S. Public Health Service.

Pedhazur, E. J. (1982). *Multiple regression in behavioral research.* New York: Holt, Rinehart & Winston.

Raudenbush, S. W., Brennan, R. T., & Barnett, R. C. (1995). A multivariate hierarchical model for studying psychological change within married couples. *Journal of Family Psychology, 9*, 161–174.

Rempel, J. K., Holmes, J. G., & Zanna, M. P. (1985). Trust in close relationships. *Journal of Personality and Social Psychology, 49*, 95–112.

Rosenthal, R., & Rosnow, R. L. (1984). *Essentials of behavioral research: Methods and data analysis.* New York: McGraw-Hill.

Sabourin, S., Lussier, Y., Laplante, B., & Wright, J. (1991). Unidimensional and multidimensional models of dydadic adjustment: A hierarchical integration. *Psychological Assessment, 2*, 219–230.

Schwarzwald, J., Weisenberg, M., & Solomon, Z. (1991). Factor invariance of SCL-90-R: The case of combat stress reaction. *Psychological Assessment. 3*, 385–390.

Spanier, G. B. (1976). Measuring dyadic adjustment. *Journal of Marriage and the Family, 38*, 15–28.

Sternberg, R. J. (1986). A triangular theory of love. *Psychological Review, 93*, 119–135.

U.S. Bureau of the Census. (1997). *Statistical abstract of the United States: 1997.* Washington, DC: U.S. Government Printing Office.

Vaillant, C. O., & Vaillant, G. E. (1993). Is the U-curve of marital satisfaction an illusion? A 40-year study of marriage. *Journal of Marriage and the Family, 55*, 230–239.

Vaillant, G. E. (1977). *Adaptation to life.* Boston: Little, Brown.

Willett, J. B. (1997). Measuring change: What individual growth modeling buys you. In E. Amsel & K. A. Renninger (Eds.), *Change and development: Issues of theory, method, and application* (pp. 213–243). Mahwah, NJ: Erlbaum.

Willett, J. B., Singer, J. D., & Martin, N. C. (1998). The design and analysis of longitudinal studies of development and psychopathology in context: Statistical models and methodological recommendations. *Development and Psychopathology, 10*, 395–426.

Wilson, B. F., & Clarke, S. C. (1992). Remarriages: A demographic profile. *Journal of Family Issues, 13*, 123–141.

Received July 13, 1998
Revision received March 8, 1999
Accepted March 9, 1999

NOTES

1. The HLM program also provided information regarding whether the ordinary least-squares estimates of change were reliable. The reliability of each parameter is defined as the ratio of the variance of the true means to the variance of the estimates and depends on the number of observations per spouse, the magnitude of the variance associated with the true means, and the magnitude of the variance associated with measurement error. Generally, the reliability of the least-squares estimate of the mean increases with the number of observations per spouse, the amount of variance among spouses in their true means, and the number of items in the scale. In the current study, the reliabilities vary from couple to couple because the number of observations varies with the number of completed assessments. The HLM program calculated the average of these reliabilities with data from the 197 couples that had sufficient data for computation. The reliability values for intercept (initial status), linear change, quadratic change, and cubic change were .71, .50, .33, and .20 for husbands, respectively, and .72, .53, .34, and .26 for wives, respectively. Bryk and Raudenbush (1992, p. 202) recommended that average reliabilities should exceed .05 in order to avoid computational difficulties with the iterative computing routines. The current reliabilities exceeded this cutoff value and ensured that it was possible to use each spouse-specific change parameter to discriminate between couples.
2. According to Rosenthal and Rosnow (1984, p. 217), $r = \sqrt{[t^2/(t^2 + df)]}$. In HLM analyses, df = the number of Level 2 units (e.g., couples) – the number of Level 2 predictors – 1. By convention, r (which is always positive in sign) was assigned a positive or negative sign that matched the corresponding t ratio.
3. The two-level baseline model was also estimated with data from only the 93 couples with complete data. Estimates were similar to those obtained for the total sample. For husbands, respective unstandardized estimates for initial status the linear component, the quadratic component, and the cubic component were 114.65, –0.40, 0.19, and –0.03, with corresponding t ratios of 96.02, –4.83, 2.80, and –3.43, $ps < .01$. For wives, respective unstandardized estimates for initial status, the linear component, the quadratic component, and the cubic component were 116.23, –0.54, 0.12, and –0.03, with corresponding t ratios of 103.39, –6.73, 1.99, and –3.72, $ps < .05$. There was significant variability within each of the eight parameters, $\chi^2(92, N = 93)$ ranging from 115.17 (wife's cubic component) to 3,782.60 (husband's initial status), $ps < .05$.

READING 10

If you were in an emergency and needed help, would you rather there be one witness to your situation or several? Although common sense would suggest the latter, Latané and Darley's classic research on bystander intervention suggests that the answer may not be so obvious. Their research was inspired by the tragic death of a woman in New York City whose murder most likely could have been prevented had any of 38 witnesses to her attack intervened on her behalf. How could these bystanders have been so callous as to not even call the police until it was too late? Latané and Darley speculated that the presence of multiple bystanders may inhibit any one bystander from taking action. In this article they articulate some of the reasons why this may be, and report an ingeniously designed experiment that illustrates how the presence of multiple bystanders can even inhibit individuals from taking action in a potential emergency even when their *own* lives might be in danger! Consider how this experiment fits within the context of the discussion of bystander intervention in Chapter 10 (Helping), as well as how social comparison (Chapter **) and social influence (Chapter 9) processes are implicated in this research.

Group Inhibition of Bystander Intervention In Emergencies[1]

Bibb Latané[2]
Columbia University

John M. Darley[3]
New York University

Male undergraduates found themselves in a smoke-filling room either alone, with 2 nonreacting others, or in groups of 3. As predicted, Ss were less likely to report the smoke when in the presence of passive others (10%) or in groups of 3 (38% of groups) than when alone (75%). This result seemed to have been mediated by the way Ss interpreted the ambiguous situation; seeing other people remain passive led Ss to decide the smoke was not dangerous.

Emergencies, fortunately, are uncommon events. Although the average person may read about them in newspapers or watch fictionalized versions on television, he probably will encounter fewer than half a dozen in his lifetime. Unfortunately, when he does encounter one, he will have had little direct personal experience in dealing with it. And he must deal with it under conditions of urgency, uncertainty, stress, and fear. About all the individual has to guide him is the secondhand wisdom of the late movie, which is often as useful as "Be brave" or as applicable as "Quick, get lots of hot water and towels!"

Under the circumstances, it may seem surprising that anybody ever intervenes in an emergency in which he is not directly involved. Yet there is a strongly held cultural norm that individuals should act to relieve the distress of others. As the Old Parson puts it, "In this life of froth and bubble, two things stand like stone—kindness in another's trouble, courage in your own." Given the conflict between the norm to act and an individual's fears and uncertainties about getting involved, what factors will determine whether a bystander to an emergency will intervene?

We have found (Darley & Latané, 1968) that the mere perception that other people are also witnessing the event will markedly decrease the likelihood that an individual will intervene in an emergency. Individuals heard a person undergoing a severe epileptic-like fit in another room. In one experimental condition, the subject thought that he was the only person who heard the emergency; in another condition, he thought four other persons were also aware of the seizure. Subjects alone with the victim were much more likely to intervene on his behalf, and, on the average, reacted in less than one-third the time required by subjects who thought there were other bystanders present.

"Diffusion of responsibility" seems the most likely explanation for this result. If an individual is alone when he notices an emergency, he is solely responsible for coping with it. If he believes others are also present, he may feel that his own responsibility for taking action is lessened, making him less likely to help.

To demonstrate that responsibility diffusion rather than any of a variety of social influence processes caused this result, the experiment was designed so that the onlookers to the seizure were isolated one from another and could not discuss how to deal with the emergency effectively. They knew the others could not see what they did, nor could they see whether somebody else had already started to help. Although this state of affairs is characteristic of many actual emergencies (such as the Kitty Genovese murder in which 38 people witnessed a killing from their individual apartments without acting), in many other emergencies several bystanders are in contact with and can influence each other. In these situations, processes other than responsibility diffusion will also operate.

Given the opportunity to interact, a group can talk over the situation and divide up the helping action in an efficient way. Also, since responding to emergencies is a socially prescribed norm, individuals might be expected to adhere to it more when in the presence of other people. These reasons suggest that interacting groups should be better at coping with emergencies than single individuals. We suspect, however, that the opposite is true. Even when allowed to communicate, groups may still be worse than individuals.

Most emergencies are, or at least begin as, ambiguous events. A quarrel in the street may erupt into violence, but it may be simply a family argument. A man staggering about may be suffering a coronary or an onset of diabetes; he may be simply drunk. Smoke pouring from a building may signal a fire; on the other hand, it may be simply steam or air-conditioning vapor. Before a bystander is likely to take action in such ambiguous situations, he must first define the event as an emergency and decide that intervention is the proper course of action.

In the course of making these decisions, it is likely that an individual bystander will be considerably influenced by the decisions he perceives other bystanders to be taking. If everyone else in a group of onlookers seems to regard an event as nonserious and the proper course of action as nonintervention, this consensus may strongly affect the perceptions of any single individual and inhibit his potential intervention.

The definitions that other people hold may be discovered by discussing the situation with them, but they may also be inferred from their facial expressions or their behavior. A whistling man with his hands in his pockets obviously does not believe he is in the midst of a crisis. A bystander who does not respond to smoke obviously does not attribute it to fire. An individual, seeing the inaction of others, will judge the situation as less serious than he would if he were alone.

In the present experiment, this line of thought will be tested by presenting an emergency situation to individuals either alone or in the presence of two passive others, confederates of the experimenter who have been instructed to notice the emergency but remain indifferent to it. It is our expectation that this passive behavior will signal the individual that the other bystanders do not consider the situation to be dangerous. We predict that an individual faced with the passive reactions of other people will be influenced by them, and will thus be less likely to take action than if he were alone.

This, however, is a prediction about individuals; it says nothing about the original question of the behavior of freely interacting groups. Most groups do not have preinstructed confederates among their members, and the kind of social influence process described above would, by itself, only lead to a convergence of attitudes within a group. Even if each member of the group is entirely guided by the reactions of others, then the group should still respond with a likelihood equal to the average of the individuals.

An additional factor is involved, however. Each member of a group may watch the others, but he is also aware that the others are watching him. They are an audience to his own reactions. Among American males it is considered desirable to appear poised and collected in times of stress. Being exposed to public view may constrain an individual's actions as he attempts to avoid possible ridicule and embarrassment.

The constraints involved with being in public might in themselves tend to inhibit action by individuals in a group, but in conjunction with the social influence process described above, they may be expected to have even more powerful effects. If each member of a group is, at the same time, trying to appear calm and also looking around at the other members to gauge their reactions, all members may be led (or misled) by each other to define the situation as less critical than they would if alone. Until someone acts, each person only sees other nonresponding bystanders, and, as with the passive confederates, is likely to be influenced not to act himself.

This leads to a second prediction. Compared to the performance of individuals, if we expose groups of naive subjects to an emergency, the constraints on behavior in public coupled with the social influence process will lessen the likelihood that the members of the group will act to cope with the emergency.

It has often been recognized (Brown, 1954, 1965) that a crowd can cause contagion of panic, leading each person in the crowd to overreact to an emergency to the detriment of everyone's welfare. What is implied here is that a crowd can also force inaction on its members. It can suggest, implicitly but strongly, by its passive behavior, that an event is not to be reacted to as an emergency, and it can make any individual uncomfortably aware of what a fool he will look for behaving as if it is.

METHOD

The subject, seated in a small waiting room, faced an ambiguous but potentially dangerous situation as a stream of smoke began to puff into the room through a wall vent. His response to this situation was observed through a one-way glass. The length of time the subject remained in the room before leaving to report the smoke was the main dependent variable of the study.

Recruitment of subjects

Male Columbia students living in campus residences were invited to an interview to discuss "some of the problems involved in life at an urban university." The subject sample included graduate and professional students as well as undergraduates. Individuals were contacted by telephone and most willingly volunteered and actually showed up for the interview. At this point, they were directed either by signs or by the secretary to a "waiting room" where a sign asked them to fill out a preliminary questionnaire.

Experimental manipulation

Some subjects filled out the questionnaire and were exposed to the potentially critical situation while alone. Others were part of three-person groups consisting of one subject and two confederates acting the part of naive subjects. The confederates attempted to avoid conversation as much as possible. Once the smoke had been introduced, they stared at it briefly, made no comment, but simply shrugged their shoulders, returned to the questionnaires and continued to fill them out, occasionally waving away the smoke to do so. If addressed, they attempted to be as uncommunicative as possible and to show apparent indifference to the smoke. "I dunno," they said, and no subject persisted in talking.

In a final condition, three naive subjects were tested together. In general, these subjects did not know each other, although in two groups, subjects reported a nodding acquaintanceship with another subject. Since subjects arrived at slightly different times and since they each had individual questionnaires to work on, they did not introduce themselves to each other, or attempt anything but the most rudimentary conversation.

Critical situation

As soon as the subjects had completed two pages of their questionnaires, the experimenter began to introduce the smoke through a small vent in the wall. The "smoke" was finely divided titanium dioxide produced in a stoppered bottle and delivered under slight air pressure through the vent.[4] It formed a moderately fine-textured but clearly visible stream of whitish smoke. For the entire experimental period, the smoke continued to jet into the room in irregular puffs. By the end of the experimental period, vision was obscured by the amount of smoke present.

All behavior and conversation was observed and coded from behind a one-way window (largely disguised on the subject's side by a large sign giving preliminary instructions). If the subject left the experimental room and reported the smoke, he was told that the situation "would be taken care of." If the subject had not reported the presence of smoke by 6 minutes from the time he first noticed it, the experiment was terminated.

RESULTS

Alone condition

The typical subject, when tested alone, behaved very reasonably. Usually, shortly after the smoke appeared, he would glance up from his questionnaire, notice the smoke, show a slight but distinct startle reaction, and then undergo a brief period of indecision, perhaps returning briefly to his questionnaire before again staring at the smoke. Soon, most subjects would get up from their chairs, walk over to the vent, and investigate it closely, sniffing the smoke, waving their hands in it, feeling its temperature, etc. The usual alone subject would hesitate again, but finally walk out of the room, look around outside, and, finding somebody there, calmly report the presence of the smoke. No subject showed any sign of panic; most simply said, "There's something strange going on in there, there seems to be some sort of smoke coming through the wall . . . ."

The median subject in the alone condition had reported the smoke within 2 minutes of first noticing it. Three-quarters of the 24 people who were run in this condition reported the smoke before the experimental period was terminated.

Two passive confederates condition

The behavior of subjects run with two passive confederates was dramatically different; of 10 people run in this condition, only 1 reported the smoke. The other 9 stayed in the waiting room as it filled up with smoke, doggedly working on their questionnaire and waving the fumes away from their faces. They coughed, rubbed their eyes, and opened the window—but they did not report the smoke. The difference between the response rate of 75% in the alone condition and 10% in the two passive confederates condition is highly significant ($p < .002$ by Fisher's exact test, two-tailed).

Three naive bystanders

Because there are three subjects present and available to report the smoke in the three naive bystander condition as compared to only one subject at a time in the alone condition, a simple comparison between the two conditions is not appropriate. On the one hand, we cannot compare speeds in the alone condition with the average speed of the three subjects in a group, since, once one subject in a group had reported the smoke, the pressures on the other two disappeared. They legitimately could (and did) feel that the emergency had been handled, and any action on their part would be redundant and potentially confusing. Therefore the speed of the *first* subject in a group to report the smoke was used as the dependent variable. However, since there were three times as many people available to respond in this condition as in the alone condition, we would expect an increased likelihood that at least one person would report the smoke even if the subjects had no influence whatsoever on each other. Therefore we mathematically created "groups" of three scores from the alone condition to serve as a base line.[5]

In contrast to the complexity of this procedure, the results were quite simple. Subjects in the three naive bystander condition were markedly inhibited from reporting the smoke. Since 75% of the alone subjects reported the smoke, we would expect over 98% of the three-person groups to contain at least one reporter. In fact, in only 38% of the eight groups in this condition did even 1 subject report ($p < .01$). Of the 24 people run in these eight groups, only 1 person reported the smoke within the first 4 minutes before the room got noticeably unpleasant. Only 3 people reported the smoke within the entire experimental period.

Cumulative distribution of report times

Figure 1 presents the cumulative frequency distributions of report times for all three conditions. The figure shows the proportion of subjects in each condition who had reported the smoke by any point in the time following the introduction of the smoke. For example, 55% of the subjects in the alone condition had reported the smoke within 2 minutes, but the smoke had been reported in only 12% of the three-person groups by that time. After 4 minutes, 75% of the subjects in the alone condition had reported the smoke; no additional subjects in the group condition had done so. The curve in Figure 1 labeled "Hypothetical Three-Person Groups" is based upon the mathematical combination of scores obtained from subjects in the alone condition. It is the expected report times for groups in the three-person condition if the members of the groups had no influence upon each other.

It can be seen in Figure 1 that for every point in time following the introduction of the smoke, a considerably higher proportion of subjects in the alone condition had reported the smoke than had subjects in either the two passive confederates condition or in the three naive subjects condition. The curve for the latter condition, although considerably below the alone curve, is even more substantially inhibited with respect to its proper comparison, the curve of hypothetical three-person sets. Social inhibition of response was so great that the time elapsing before the smoke was reported was greater when there were more people available to report it (alone versus group $p < .05$ by Mann-Whitney U test).

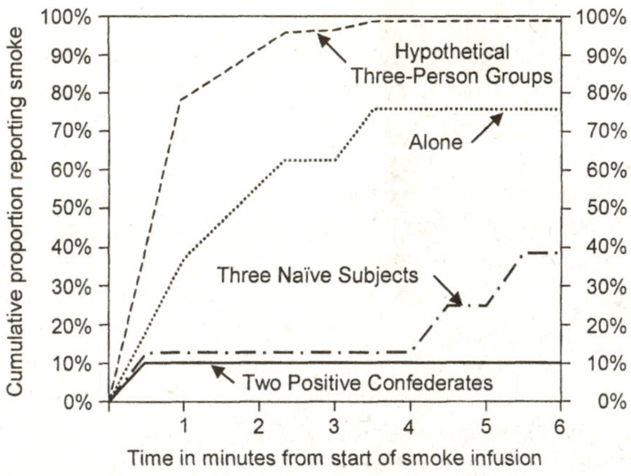

Figure 1. Cumulative proportion of subjects reporting the smoke over time.

Superficially, it appears that there is a somewhat higher likelihood of response from groups of three naive subjects than from subjects in the passive confederates condition. Again this comparison is not justified; there are three people free to act in one condition instead of just one. If we mathematically combine scores for subjects in the two passive confederates condition in a similar manner to that described above for the alone condition, we would obtain an expected likelihood of response of .27 as the hypothetical base line. This is not significantly different from the .37 obtained in the actual three-subject groups.

Noticing the smoke

In observing the subject's reaction to the introduction of smoke, careful note was taken of the exact moment when he first saw the smoke (all report latencies were computed from this time). This was a relatively easy observation to make, for the subjects invariably showed a distinct, if slight, startle reaction. Unexpectedly, the presence of other persons delayed, slightly but very significantly, noticing the smoke. Sixty-three percent of subjects in the alone condition and only 26% of subjects in the combined together conditions noticed the smoke within the first 5 seconds after its introduction ($p < .01$ by chi-square). The median latency of noticing the smoke was under 5 seconds in the alone condition; the median time at which the first (or only) subject in each of the combined together conditions noticed the smoke was 20 seconds (this difference does not account for group-induced inhibition of reporting since the report latencies were computed from the time the smoke was first noticed).

This interesting finding can probably be explained in terms of the constraints which people feel in public places (Goffman, 1963). Unlike solitary subjects, who often glanced idly about the room while filling out their questionnaires, subjects in groups usually kept their eyes closely on their work, probably to avoid appearing rudely inquisitive.

Postexperimental interview

After 6 minutes, whether or not the subjects had reported the smoke, the interviewer stuck his head in the waiting room and asked the subject to come with him to the interview. After seating the subject in his office, the interviewer made some general apologies about keeping the subject waiting for so long, hoped the subject hadn't become too bored and asked if he "had experienced any difficulty while filling out the questionnaire." By this point most subjects mentioned the smoke. The interviewer expressed mild surprise and asked the subject to tell him what had happened. Thus each subject gave an account of what had gone through his mind during the smoke infusion.

Subjects who had reported the smoke were relatively consistent in later describing their reactions to it. They thought the smoke looked somewhat "strange," they were not sure exactly what it was or whether it was dangerous, but they felt it was unusual enough to justify some examination. "I wasn't sure whether it was a fire but it looked like something was wrong." "I thought it might be steam, but it seemed like a good idea to check it out."

Subjects who had not reported the smoke also were unsure about exactly what it was, but they uniformly said that they had rejected the idea that it was a fire. Instead, they hit upon an astonishing variety of alternative explanations, all sharing the common characteristic of interpreting the smoke as a nondangerous event. Many thought the smoke was either steam or air-conditioning vapors, several thought it was smog, purposely introduced to simulate an urban environment, and two (from different groups) actually suggested that the smoke was a "truth gas" filtered into the room to induce them to answer the questionnaire accurately. (Surprisingly, they were not disturbed by this conviction.) Predictably, some decided that "it must be some sort of experiment" and stoically endured the discomfort of the room rather than overreact.

Despite the obvious and powerful report-inhibiting effect of other bystanders, subjects almost invariably claimed that they had paid little or no attention to the reactions of the other people in the room. Although the presence of other people actually had a strong and pervasive effect on the subjects' reactions, they were either unaware of this or unwilling to admit it.

DISCUSSION

Before an individual can decide to intervene in an emergency, he must, implicitly or explicitly, take several preliminary steps. If he is to intervene, he must first *notice* the event, he must then *interpret* it as an emergency, and he must decide that it is his personal *responsibility* to act. At each of these preliminary steps, the bystander to an emergency can remove himself from the decision process and thus fail to help. He can fail to notice the event, he can fail to interpret it as an emergency, or he can fail to assume the responsibility to take action.

In the present experiment we are primarily interested in the second step of this decision process, interpreting an ambiguous event. When faced with such an event, we suggest, the individual bystander is likely to look at the reactions of people around him and be powerfully influenced by them. It was predicted that the sight of other, nonresponsive bystanders would lead the individual to interpret the emergency as not serious, and consequently lead him not to act. Further, it was predicted that the dynamics of the interaction process would lead each of a group of naive onlookers to be misled by the apparent inaction of the others into adopting a nonemergency interpretation of the event and a passive role.

The results of this study clearly support our predictions. Individuals exposed to a room filling with smoke in the presence of passive others themselves remained passive, and groups of three naive subjects were less likely to report the smoke than solitary bystanders. Our predictions were confirmed—but this does not necessarily mean that our explanation for these results is the correct one. As a matter of fact, several alternatives are available.

Two of these alternative explanations stem from the fact that the smoke represented a possible danger to the subject himself as well as to others in the building. Subjects' behavior might have reflected their fear of fire, with subjects in groups feeling less threatened by the fire than single subjects and thus being less concerned to act. It has been demonstrated in studies with humans (Schachter, 1959) and with rats (Latané, 1968; Latané & Glass, 1968) that togetherness reduces fear, even in situations where it does not reduce danger. In addition, subjects may have felt that the presence of others increased their ability to cope with fire. For both of these reasons, subjects in groups may have been less afraid of fire and thus less likely to report the smoke than solitary subjects.

A similar explanation might emphasize not fearfulness, but the desire to hide fear. To the extent that bravery or stoicism in the face of danger or discomfort is a socially desirable trait (as it appears to be for American male undergraduates), one might expect individuals to attempt to appear more brave or more stoic when others are watching than when they are alone. It is possible that subjects in the group condition saw themselves as engaged in a game of "Chicken," and thus did not react.

Although both of these explanations are plausible, we do not think that they provide an accurate account of subjects' thinking. In the postexperimental interviews, subjects claimed, *not* that they were unworried by the fire or that they were unwilling to endure the danger; but rather that they decided that there was no fire at all and the smoke was caused by something else. They failed to act because they thought there was no reason to act. Their "apathetic" behavior was reasonable—given their interpretation of the circumstances.

The fact that smoke signals potential danger to the subject himself weakens another alternative explanation, "diffusion of responsibility." Regardless of social influence processes, an individual may feel less personal responsibility for helping if he shares the responsibility with others (Darley & Latané, 1968). But this diffusion explanation does not fit the present situation. It is hard to see how an individual's responsibility for saving himself is diffused by the presence of other people. The diffusion explanation does not account for the pattern of interpretations reported by the subjects or for their variety of nonemergency explanations.

On the other hand, the social influence processes which we believe account for the results of our present study obviously do not explain our previous experiment in which subjects could not see or be seen by each other. Taken together, these two studies suggest that the presence of bystanders may affect an individual in several ways; including both "social influence" and "diffusion of responsibility."

Both studies, however, find, for two quite different kinds of emergencies and under two quite different conditions of social contact, that individuals are less likely to engage in socially responsible action if they think other bystanders are present. This presents us with the paradoxical conclusion that a victim may be more likely to get help, or an emergency may be more likely to be reported, the fewer people there are available to take action. It also may help us begin to understand a number of frightening incidents where crowds have listened to but not answered a call for help. Newspapers have tagged these incidents with the label "apathy." We have become indifferent, they say, callous to the fate of suffering others. The results of our studies lead to a different conclusion. The failure to intervene may be better understood by knowing the relationship among bystanders rather than that between a bystander and the victim.

REFERENCES

Brown, R. W. Mass phenomena. In G. Lindzey (Ed.), *Handbook of social psychology.* Vol. 2. Cambridge: Addison-Wesley, 1954.

Brown, R. *Social psychology.* New York: Free Press of Glencoe, 1965.

Darley, J. M., & Latané, B. Bystander intervention in emergencies: Diffusion of responsibility. *Journal of Personality and Social Psychology*, 1968, 8, 377–383.

Goffman, E. *Behavior in public places.* New York: Free Press of Glencoe, 1963.

Latané, B. Gregariousness and fear in laboratory rats. *Journal of Experimental Social Psychology*, 1968, in press.

Latané, B., & Glass, D. C. Social and nonsocial attraction in rats. *Journal of Personality and Social Psychology*, 1968, 9, 142–146.

Schachter, S. *The psychology of affiliation.* Stanford: Stanford University Press, 1959.

(Received December 11, 1967)

NOTES

1. We thank Lee Ross and Keith Gerritz for their thoughtful efforts. This research was supported by National Science Foundation Grants GS 1238 and GS 1239. The experiment was conducted at Columbia University.
2. Now at the Ohio State University.
3. Now at Princeton University.
4. Smoke was produced by passing moisturized air, under pressure, through a container of titanium tetrachloride, which, in reaction with the water vapor, creates a suspension of tantium dioxide in air.
5. The formula for calculating the expected proportion of groups in which at least one person will have acted by a given time is $1 - (1 - p)^n$ where p is the proportion of single individuals who act by that time and n is the number of persons in the group.

READING 11

Understanding the causes of human aggression is an important mission for social psychology in this increasingly violent world. As is discussed in Chapter 11 of your textbook, the frustration-aggression hypothesis generated a great deal of attention when it was introduced in 1939, and the research it inspired caused it to be revised and modified in a variety of ways. Inspired by this research but also recognizing its limitations, Leonard Berkowitz offered an important contribution to our understanding of the situational determinants of aggression by emphasizing the roles of anger and thought on aggression. Berkowitz argued that when people are angry, they are in a state of readiness to aggress. Frustration is but one cause of anger. Whether or not an angered person will behave aggressively depends, in part, on whether aggression-enhancing cues are present in the situation. Berkowitz proposed that the presence of such a cue in a situation can automatically increase the likelihood of aggression. The aggression-enhancing cue examined in the study reported in this reading was the presence of weapons. Berkowitz and LePage addressed the question of "whether weapons can serve as aggression-eliciting stimuli, causing an angered individual to display stronger violence than he would have shown in the absence of such weapons." Note that Berkowitz and LePage did not investigate whether the presence of weapons would prompt people to *use* the weapons to aggress; rather, they examined the more subtle point of whether the presence of weapons would increase the underlying likelihood of responding aggressively that is, even if the weapons are not used in the actual aggression. As you read this article, consider the implications of this research for understanding aggression in general, but also for the ongoing debates about gun control and the prevalence of violence depicted in the media.

Weapons as Aggression-Eliciting Stimuli

Leonard Berkowitz and Anthony LePage
University of Wisconsin

An experiment was conducted to test the hypothesis that stimuli commonly associated with aggression can elicit aggressive responses from people ready to act aggressively. One hundred male university students received either 1 or 7 shocks, supposedly from a peer, and were then given an opportunity to shock this person. In some cases a rifle and revolver were on the table near the shock key. These weapons were said to belong, or not to belong, to the available target person. In other instances there was nothing on the table near the shock key, while for a control group 2 badminton racquets were on the table near the key. The greatest number of shocks was given by the strongly aroused Ss (who had received 7 shocks) when they were in the presence of the weapons. The guns had evidently elicited strong aggressive responses from the aroused men.

Human behavior is often goal directed, guided by strategies and influenced by ego defenses and strivings for cognitive consistency. There clearly are situations, however, in which these purposive considerations are relatively unimportant regulators of action. Habitual behavior patterns become dominant on these occasions, and the person responds relatively automatically to the stimuli impinging upon him. Any really complete psychological system must deal with these stimulus-elicited, impulsive reactions as well as with more complex behavior patterns. More than this, we should also be able to specify the conditions under which the various behavior determinants increase or decrease in importance.

The senior author has long contended that many aggressive actions are controlled by the stimulus properties of the available targets rather than by anticipations of ends that might be served (Berkowitz, 1962, 1964, 1965). Perhaps because strong emotion results in an increased utilization of only the central cues in the immediate situation (Easterbrook, 1959; Walters & Parke, 1964), anger arousal can lead to impulsive aggressive

SOURCE: Leonard Berkowitz and Anthony LePage. 1967. "Weapons as Aggression-Eliciting Stimuli," *JOURNAL OF PERSONALITY AND SOCIAL PSYCHOLOGY*, Vol. 7, No. 2, 202–207.

responses which, for a short time at least, may be relatively free of cognitively mediated inhibitions against aggression or, for that matter, purposes and strategic considerations.[1] This impulsive action is not necessarily pushed out by the anger, however. Berkowitz has suggested that appropriate cues must be present in the situation if aggressive responses are actually to occur. While there is still considerable uncertainty as to just what characteristics define aggressive cue properties, the association of a stimulus with aggression evidently can enhance the aggressive cue value of this stimulus. But whatever its exact genesis, the cue (which may be either in the external environment or represented internally) presumably elicits the aggressive response. Anger (or any other conjectured aggressive "drive") increases the person's reactivity to the cue, possibly energizes the response, and may lower the likelihood of competing reactions, but is not necessary for the production of aggressive behavior.[2]

A variety of observations can be cited in support of this reasoning (cf. Berkowitz, 1965). Thus, the senior author has proposed that some of the effects of observed violence can readily be understood in terms of stimulus-elicited aggression. According to several Wisconsin experiments, observed aggression is particularly likely to produce strong attacks against anger instigators who are associated with the victim of the witnessed violence (Berkowitz & Geen, 1966, 1967; Geen & Berkowitz, 1966). The frustrater's association with the observed victim presumably enhances his cue value for aggression, causing him to evoke stronger attacks from the person who is ready to act aggressively.

More direct evidence for the present formulation can be found in a study conducted by Loew (1965). His subjects, in being required to learn a concept, either aggressive or nature words, spoke either 20 aggressive or 20 neutral words aloud. Following this "learning task," each subject was to give a peer in an adjacent room an electric shock whenever this person made a mistake in his learning problem. Allowed to vary the intensity of the shocks they administered over a 10-point continuum, the subjects who had uttered the aggressive words gave shocks of significantly greater intensity than did the subjects who had spoken the neutral words. The aggressive words had evidently evoked implicit aggressive responses from the subjects, even though they had not been angered beforehand, which then led to the stronger attacks upon the target person in the next room when he supposedly made errors.

Cultural learning shared by many members of a society can also associate external objects with aggression and thus affect the objects' aggressive cue value. weapons are a prime example. For many men (and probably women as well) in our society, these objects are closely associated with aggression. Assuming that the weapons do not produce inhibitions that are stronger than the evoked aggressive reactions (as would be the case, e.g., if the weapons were labeled as morally "bad"), the presence of the aggressive objects should generally lead to more intense attacks upon an available target than would occur in the presence of a neutral object.

The present experiment was designed to test this latter hypothesis. At one level, of course, the findings contribute to the current debate as to the desirability of restricting sales of firearms. Many arguments have been raised for such a restriction. Thus, according to recent statistics, Texas communities having virtually no prohibitions against firearms have a much higher homicide rate than other American cities possessing stringent firearm regulations, and J. Edgar Hoover has maintained in *Time* magazine that the availability of firearms is an important factor in murders (Anonymous, 1966). The experiment reported here seeks to determine how this influence may come about. The availability of weapons obviously makes it easier for a person who wants to commit murder to do so. But, in addition, we ask whether weapons can serve as aggression-eliciting stimuli, causing an angered individual to display stronger violence than he would have shown in the absence of such weapons. Social significance aside, and at a more general theoretical level, this research also attempts to demonstrate that situational stimuli can exert "automatic" control over socially relevant human actions.

METHOD

Subjects

The subjects were 100 male undergraduates enrolled in the introductory psychology course at the University of Wisconsin who volunteered for the experiment (without knowing its nature) in order to earn points counting toward their final grade. Thirty-nine other subjects had also been run, but were discarded because they suspected the experimenter's confederate (21), reported receiving fewer electric shocks than was actually given them (7), had not attended to information given them about the procedure (9), or were run while there was equipment malfunctioning (2).

Procedure

General design Seven experimental conditions were established, six organized in a 2 × 3 factorial design, with the seventh group serving essentially as a control. Of the men in the factorial design, half were made to be angry with the confederate, while the other subjects received a friendlier treatment from him. All of the subjects were then given an opportunity to administer electric shocks to the confederate, but for two-thirds of the men there were weapons lying on the table near the shock apparatus. Half of these people were informed the weapons belonged to the confederate in order to test the hypothesis that aggressive stimuli which also were associated with the anger instigator would evoke the strongest aggressive reaction from the subjects. The other people seeing the weapons were told the weapons had been left there by a previous experimenter. There was nothing on the table except the shock key when the last third of the subjects in both the angered and nonangered conditions gave the shocks. Finally, the seventh group consisted of angered men who gave shocks with two badminton racquets and shuttlecocks lying near the shock key. This condition sought to determine whether the presence of *any* object near the shock apparatus would reduce inhibitions against aggression, even if the object were not connected with aggressive behavior.

Experimental manipulations When each subject arrived in the laboratory, he was informed that two men were required for the experiment and that they would have to wait for the second subject to appear. After a 5-minute wait, the experimenter, acting annoyed, indicated that they had to begin because of his other commitments. He said he would have to look around outside to see if he could find another person who might serve as a substitute for the missing subject. In a few minutes the experimenter returned with the confederate. Depending upon the condition, this person was introduced as either a psychology student who had been about to sign up for another experiment or as a student who had been running another study.

The subject and confederate were told the experiment was a study of physiological reactions to stress. The stress would be created by mild electric shocks, and the subjects could withdraw, the experimenter said, if they objected to these shocks. (No subjects left.) Each person would have to solve a problem knowing that his performance would be evaluated by his partner. The "evaluations" would be in the form of electric shocks, with one shock signifying a very good rating and 10 shocks meaning the performance was judged as very bad. The men were then told what their problems were, the subject's task was to list ideas a publicity agent might employ in order to better a popular singer's record sales and public image. The other person (the confederate) had to think of things a used-car dealer might do in order to increase sales. The two were given 5 minutes to write their answers, and the papers were then collected by the experimenter who supposedly would exchange them.

Following this, the two were placed in separate rooms, supposedly so that they would not influence each other's galvanic skin response (GSR) reactions. The shock electrodes were placed on the subject's right forearm, and GSR electrodes were attached to fingers on his left hand, with wires trailing from the electrodes to the next room. The subject was told he would be the first to receive electric shocks as the evaluation of his problem solution. The experimenter left the subject's room saying he was going to turn on the GSR apparatus, went to the room containing the shock machine and the waiting confederate, and only then looked at the schedule indicating whether the subject was to be angered or not. He informed the confederate how many shocks the subject was to receive, and 30 seconds later the subject was given seven shocks (angered condition) or one shock (nonangered group). The experimenter then went back to the subject, while the confederate quickly arranged the table holding the shock key in the manner appropriate for the subject's condition. Upon entering the subject's room, the experimenter asked him how many shocks he had received and provided the subject with a brief questionnaire on which he was to rate his mood. As soon as this was completed, the subject was taken to the room holding the shock machine. Here the experimenter told the subject it was his turn to evaluate his partner's work. For one group in both the angered and nonangered conditions the shock key was alone on the table (no-object groups). For two other groups in each of these angered and nonangered conditions, however, a 12-gauge shotgun and a .38-caliber revolver were lying on the table near the key (aggressive-weapon conditions). One group in both the angered and nonangered conditions was informed the weapons belonged to the subject's partner. The subjects given this treatment had been told earlier that their partner was a student who had been conducting an experiment.[3] They now were reminded of this, and the experimenter said the weapons were being used in some way by this person in his research (associated-weapons condition); the guns were to be disregarded. The other men were told simply the weapons "belong to someone else" who "must have been doing an experiment in here" (unassociated-weapons group), and they too were asked to disregard the guns. For the last treatment, one group of angered men found two badminton racquets and shuttlecocks lying on the table near the shock key, and these people were also told the equipment belonged to someone else (badminton-racquets group).

Immediately after this information was provided, the experimenter showed the subject what was supposedly his partner's answer to his assigned problem. The subject was reminded that he was to give the partner shocks as his evaluation and was informed that this was the last time shocks would be administered in the study. A second copy of the mood questionnaire was then completed by the subject after he had delivered the shocks. Following this, the subject was asked a number of oral questions about the experiment, including what, if any, suspicions he had. (No doubts were voiced about the presence of the weapons.) At the conclusion of this interview the experiment was explained, and the subject was asked not to talk about the study.

Dependent Variables

As in nearly all the experiments conducted in the senior author's program, the number of shocks given by the subjects serves as the primary aggression measure. However, we also report here findings obtained with the total duration of each subject's shocks, recorded in thousandths of a minute. Attention is also given to each subject's rating of his mood, first immediately after receiving the partner's evaluation, and again immediately after administering shocks to the partner. These ratings were made on a series of 10 13-point bipolar scales with an adjective at each end, such as "calm-tense" and "angry-not angry."

RESULTS

Effectiveness of Arousal Treatment

Analyses of variance of the responses to each of the mood scales following the receipt of the partner's evaluation indicate the prior-shock treatment succeeded in creating differences in anger arousal. The subjects getting seven shocks rated themselves as being significantly angrier than the subjects receiving only one shock ($F = 20.65, p < .01$). There were no reliable differences among the groups within any one arousal level. Interestingly enough, the only other mood scale to yield a significant effect was the scale "sad-happy." The aroused-seven-shocks men reported a significantly stronger felt sadness than the men getting one shock ($F = 4.63, p > .05$).

Aggression Toward Partner

A preliminary analysis of variance of the shock data for the six groups in the 3 × 2 factorial design yielded the findings shown in Table 1. As is indicated by the significant interaction, the presence of the weapons significantly affected the number of shocks given by the subject when the subject had received seven shocks. A Duncan multiple-range test was then made of the differences among the seven conditions means, using the error variance from a seven-group one-way analysis of variance in the error term. The mean number of shocks administered in each experimental condition and the Duncan test results are given in Table 2. The hypothesis guiding the present study receives good support. The strongly provoked men delivered more frequent electrical attacks upon their tormentor in the presence of a weapon than when nonaggressive objects (the badminton racquet and shuttlecocks) were present or when only the shock key was on the table. The angered subjects gave the greatest number of shocks in the presence of the weapons associated with the anger instigator, as predicted, but this group was not reliably different from the angered-unassociated-weapons conditions. Both of these groups expressing aggression in the presence of weapons were significantly more aggressive than the angered-neutral-object condition, but only the associated-weapons condition differed significantly from the angered-no-object group.

Some support for the present reasoning is also provided by the shock-duration data summarized in Table 3. (We might note here, before beginning, that the results with duration scores—and this has been a consistent finding in the present research program—are less clear-cut than the findings with number of shocks given.) The results indicate that the presence of weapons resulted in a decreased number of attacks upon the partner, although not significantly so, when the subjects had received only one shock beforehand. The condition differences are in the opposite direction, however, for the men given the stronger provocation. Consequently, even though there

TABLE 1
Analysis of Variance Results for Number of Shocks Given by Subjects in Factorial Design

Source	*df*	*MS*	*F*
No. Shocks received (A)	1	182.04	104.62*
Weapons association (B)	2	1.90	1.09
A × B	2	8.73	5.02*
Error	84	1.74	

*$p < .01$

TABLE 2
Mean Number of Shocks Given in Each Condition

	Shocks received	
Condition	1	7
Associated weapons	2.60_a	6.07_d
Unassociated weapons	2.20_a	5.67_{cd}
No object	3.07_a	4.67_{bc}
Badminton racquets	–	4.60_b

Note: Cells having a common subscript are not significantly different at the .05 level by Duncan multiple-range test. There were 10 subjects in the seven-shocks-received-badminton-racquets group and 15 subjects in each of the other conditions.

TABLE 3
Mean Total Duration of Shocks Given in Each Condition

	Shocks received	
Condition	1	7
Associated weapons	17.93_c	46.93_a
Unassociated weapons	17.33_c	39.47_{ab}
No object	24.47_{bc}	34.80_{ab}
Badminton racquets	–	34.90_{ab}

Note: The duration scores are in thousandths of a minute. Cells having a common subscript are not significantly different at the .05 level by Duncan multiple-range test. There were 10 subjects in the seven-shocks-received-badminton-racquet group and 15 subjects in each of the other conditions.

are no reliable differences among the groups in this angered condition, the angered men administering shocks in the presence of weapons gave significantly longer shocks than the nonangered men also giving shocks with guns lying on the table. The angered-neutral-object and angered-no-object groups, on the other hand, did not differ from the nonangered-no-object condition.

Mood Changes

Analyses of covariance were conducted on each of the mood scales, with the mood ratings made immediately after the subjects received their partners' evaluation held constant in order to determine if there were condition differences in mood changes following the giving of shocks to the partner. Duncan range tests of the adjusted condition means yielded negative results, suggesting that the attacks on the partner did not produce any systematic condition differences. In the case of the felt anger ratings, there were very high correlations between the ratings given before and after the shock administration, with the Pearson *rs* ranging from .89 in the angered-unassociated-weapons group to .99 in each of the three unangered conditions. The subjects could have felt constrained to repeat their initial responses.

DISCUSSION

Common sense, as well as a good deal of personality theorizing both influenced to some extent by an egocentric view of human behavior as being caused almost exclusively by motives within the individual, generally neglect the type of weapons effect demonstrated in the present study. If a person holding a gun fires it, we are told either that he wanted to do so (consciously or unconsciously) or that he pulled the trigger "accidentally." The findings summarized here suggest yet another possibility: The presence of the weapon might have elicited an intense aggressive reaction from the person with the gun, assuming his inhibitions against aggression were relatively weak at the moment. Indeed, it is altogether conceivable that many hostile acts which supposedly stem from unconscious motivation really arise because of the operation of aggressive cues. Not realizing how these situational stimuli might elicit aggressive behavior, and not detecting the presence of these cues, the observer tends to locate the source of the action in some conjectured underlying, perhaps repressed, motive. Similarly, if he is a Skinnerian rather than a dynamically oriented clinician, he might also neglect the operation of aggression-eliciting stimuli by invoking the concept of operant behavior, and thus sidestep the issue altogether. The sources of the hostile action, for him, too, rest within the individual, with the behavior only steered or permitted by discriminative stimuli.

Alternative explanations must be ruled out, however, before the present thesis can be regarded as confirmed. One obvious possibility is that the subjects in the weapons condition reacted to the demand characteristics of the situation as they saw them and exhibited the kind of behavior they thought was required of them. ("These guns on the table mean I'm supposed to be aggressive, so I'll give many shocks.") Several considerations appear to negate this explanation. First, there are the subjects' own verbal reports. None of the subjects voiced any suspicions of the weapons and, furthermore, when they were queried generally denied that the weapons had any effect on them. But even those subjects who did express any doubts about the experiment typically acted like the other subjects. Thus, the eight nonangered-weapons subjects who had been rejected gave only 2.50 shocks on the average, while the 18 angered-no-object or neutral-object men who had been discarded had a mean of 4.50 shocks. The 12 angered-weapon subjects who had been rejected, by contrast, delivered an average of 5.83 shocks to their partner. These latter people were evidently also influenced by the presence of weapons.

Setting all this aside, moreover, it is not altogether certain from the notion of demand characteristics that only the angered subjects would be inclined to act in conformity with the experimenter's supposed demands. The non-angered men in the weapons group did not display a heightened number of attacks on their partner. Would this have been predicted beforehand by researchers interested in demand characteristics? The last finding raises one final observation. Recent unpublished research by Allen and Bragg indicates that awareness of the experimenter's purpose does not necessarily result in an increased display of the behavior the experimenter supposedly desires. Dealing with one kind of socially disapproved action (conformity), Allen and Bragg demonstrated that high levels of experimentally induced awareness of the experimenter's interests generally produced a decreased level of the relevant behavior. Thus, if the subjects in our study had known the experimenter was interested in observing their *aggressive* behavior, they might well have given less, rather than more, shocks, since giving shocks is also socially disapproved. This type of phenomenon was also not observed in the weapons conditions.

Nevertheless, any one experiment cannot possibly definitely exclude all of the alternative explanations. Scientific hypotheses are only probability statements, and further research is needed to heighten the likelihood that the present reasoning is correct.

REFERENCES

Anonymous. A gun-toting nation. *Time*, August 12, 1966.

Berkowitz, L. *Aggression: A social psychological analysis.* New York: McGraw-Hill, 1962.

Berkowitz, L. Aggressive cues in aggressive behavior and hostility catharsis. *Psychological Review*, 1964, 71, 104–122.

Berkowitz, L. The concept of aggressive drive: Some additional considerations. In L. Berkowitz (Ed.), *Advances in experimental social psychology.* Vol. 2. New York: Academic Press, 1965. Pp. 301–329.

Berkowitz, L., & Geen, R. G. Film violence and the cue properties of available targets. *Journal of Personality and Social Psychology*, 1966, 3, 525–530.

Berkowitz, L., & Geen, R. G. Stimulus qualities of the target of aggression: A further study. *Journal of Personality and Social Psychology*, 1967, 5, 364–368.

Buss, A. *The psychology of aggression.* New York: Wiley, 1961.

Easterbrook, J. A. The effect of emotion on cue utilization and the organization of behavior. *Psychological Review*, 1959, 66, 183–201.

Geen, R. G., & Berkowitz, L. Name-mediated aggressive cue properties. *Journal of Personality*, 1966, 34, 456–465.

Loew, C. A. Acquisition of a hostile attitude and its relationship to aggressive behavior. Unpublished doctoral dissertation, State University of Iowa, 1965.

Walters, R. H., & Parke, R. D. Social motivation, dependency, and susceptibility to social influence. In L. Berkowitz (Ed.), *Advances in experimental social psychology.* Vol. 1. New York: Academic Press, 1964. Pp. 231–276.

NOTES

1. Cognitive processes can play a part even in impulsive behavior, most notably by influencing the stimulus qualities (or meaning) of the objects in the situation. As only one illustration, in several experiments by the senior author (cf. Berkowitz, 1965) the name applied to the

available target person affected the magnitude of the attacks directed against this individual by angered subjects.

2. Buss (1961) has advanced a somewhat similar conception of the functioning of anger.
3. This information evidently was the major source of suspicion; some of the subjects doubted that a student running an experiment would be used as a subject in another study, even if he were only an undergraduate. This information was provided only in the associated-weapons conditions, in order to connect the guns with the partner, and, consequently, this ground for suspicion was not present in the unassociated-weapons groups.

(Received October 5, 1966)

Reading 12

Five studies merged the priming methodology with the bystander apathy literature and demonstrate how merely priming a social context at Time 1 leads to less helping behavior on a subsequent, completely unrelated task at Time 2. In Study 1, participants who imagined being with a group at Time 1 pledged significantly fewer dollars on a charity-giving measure at Time 2 than did those who imagined being alone with one other person. Studies 2–5 build converging evidence with hypothetical and real helping behavior measures and demonstrate that participants who imagine the presence of others show facilitation to words associated with *unaccountable* on a lexical decision task. Implications for social group research and the priming methodology are discussed.

Crowded Minds: The Implicit Bystander Effect

Stephen M. Garcia and Kim Weaver
Princeton University

Gordon B. Moskowitz
Lehigh University

John M. Darley
Princeton University

Stephen M. Garcia, Kim Weaver, and John M. Darley, Department of Psychology, Princeton University; Gordon B. Moskowitz, Department of Psychology, Lehigh University.

Stephen M. Garcia was supported by a National Science Foundation graduate fellowship and by a graduate fellowship from the Program on Negotiation at Harvard Law School. We thank Deborah Prentice, Susan Fiske, Mark Hallahan, and Max Bazerman for their insightful comments and suggestions.

Correspondence concerning this article should be addressed to Stephen M. Garcia, Department of Psychology, Princeton University, Princeton, New Jersey 08544-1010. E-mail: smgarcia@princeton.edu

The *bystander apathy effect* is generally regarded as a well-established empirical phenomenon in social psychology (e.g., Darley & Latane, 1968; Latane & Darley, 1968; Latane & Nida, 1981). A person who faces a situation of another person in distress but does so with the knowledge that others are also present and available to respond is slower and less likely to respond to the person in distress than is a person who knows that he or she is the only one who is aware of the distress. The research demonstrating this effect, entirely appropriately, has manipulated the perceived presence of others and consistently has found this effect. Traditional theoretical accounts, such as the diffusion of responsibility explanation, focus on explaining how other actors present in the immediate situation influence would-be helpers' responses. A question left open that the present research seeks to begin to answer is at what level of calculational ideation this effect exists. In plainer English, does it depend on the respondent's calculations, either conscious or not, that there are other persons present who might help, or, at the other extreme, is it possible that simply imagining others may induce a similar mental state of diffused responsibility, regardless of whether those others are available to respond? Drawing on this latter perspective, our suggestion is that merely priming the presence of others at Time 1 can affect helping behavior on a completely unrelated task at Time 2, even when the primed others cannot possibly contribute to the helping task. If this is so, then the bystander apathy effect is not one that always must depend on a calculational effort but rather one that can be brought about by the priming of the presence of groups and the resulting mental state that is induced. Thus, real or imagined persons need not be built into the facets of a helping behavior situation for bystander apathy to occur.

SOURCE: Garcia, S. M., Weaver, K., Moskowitz, G. B. & Darley, J. M. 2002. "Crowded Minds: The Implicit Bystander Effect." *JOURNAL OF PERSONALITY AND SOCIAL PSYCHOLOGY*, *83*, No. 4, 843–853.

BYSTANDER APATHY

The classic bystander intervention studies (e.g., Clark & Word, 1974; Darley, Teger, & Lewis, 1973; Latane, 1970; Latane & Darley, 1968, 1970) have consistently shown that the presence of others inhibits helping behavior. However, current theoretical accounts stipulate that the immediate or imagined presence of others exerts its influence on helping because these others are involved in the situation at hand. In fact, if individuals know that immediate or imagined others cannot possibly help, then bystander apathy will not occur; individuals will behave as if alone (Bickman, 1972; Korte, 1971).

Along these lines, investigators have put forth several theoretical accounts of the bystander intervention findings. *Diffusion of responsibility* accounts (Darley & Latane, 1968) reflect the notion that as the number of people present in a situation increases, each individual feels less compelled or responsible to help. In fact, with so many people present, an individual might just assume that a victim is receiving help or that help is already on the way. *Social influence* (Darley & Latane, 1968; Darley et al., 1973) and *pluralistic ignorance* (Prentice & Miller, 1996) explanations, on the other hand, reflect the notion that people look to others to evaluate an emergency situation. If the others present are just standing around and appear calm, then would-be helpers infer that perhaps the situation really is not an emergency. Smoke spewing from a vent may just indicate a foggy vent, not a burning fire. Cacioppo, Petty, and Losch (1986) more recently offered another account for bystander apathy, namely, *confusion of responsibility*. This explanation argues that would-be helpers refrain from helping a victim in the presence of others because they do not want to be perceived as the perpetrator of the victim's pain and suffering. That is, in some cases, it might appear to observers that someone helping a victim is actually the cause of the victim's harm.

Although these situational accounts are compelling (for a review, see Latane & Nida, 1981) and are all likely contributors to bystander apathy, our purpose in this paper is to offer a *nonsituational* account that could provide an alternative or additional explanation for the findings. However, we hasten to add that situational and nonsituational accounts of bystander apathy need not be mutually exclusive. As we review, research on priming suggests that merely activating knowledge structures can affect social perception and behavior (e.g., Bargh, Chen, & Burrows, 1996; Higgins, Rholes, & Jones, 1977). In light of these findings, we seek to examine whether merely activating the construct of group in the minds of participants could also result in the bystander apathy effect. In particular, we are interested in examining whether activating the construct of a group of people who could not possibly help leads to an implicit bystander effect on a subsequent helping behavior.

PRIMING AFFECTS SOCIAL PERCEPTION AND BEHAVIOR

Bargh et al. (1996) defined priming as "the incidental activation of knowledge structures, such as trait concepts and stereotypes" (p. 230). Research has shown that the cognitive accessibility of these types of knowledge structures can have real and important effects on social perception and behavior (e.g., Carver, Ganellen, Froming, & Chambers, 1983; Dijksterhuis, Spears, & Lepinasse, 2000; Dijksterhuis & van Knippenberg, 1998; Epley & Gilovich, 1999; Higgins et al., 1977; Kawakami, Young, & Dovidio, 2000; Macrae & Johnston, 1998; Neuberg, 1988). More specifically, research on priming effects on social behavior has demonstrated that subtle cues or primes in the environment can subsequently affect behavior. For instance, in a new but already classic study, Bargh et al. (1996) found that priming the elderly stereotype can affect people's subsequent behavior. In their study, participants were primed through a scrambled sentence task. In the elderly condition, the sentences included words related to the elderly stereotype (e.g., *old, wrinkle, Florida*), whereas in the neutral condition, the scrambled sentences included age-nonspecific words. Findings showed that participants who were primed with the elderly stereotype walked out of the laboratory significantly more slowly than did participants in the neutral condition.

Similarly, other research looking at priming and behavior has found that individuals primed with the concept of professors perform better on a general knowledge test than do control participants (Dijksterhuis & van Knippenberg, 1998). The mechanism underlying these priming effects is based on the premise that triggering a knowledge structure such as a stereotype activates the semantic knowledge associated with it. This semantic knowledge includes, among other things, certain types of behaviors. For instance, part of the stored representation of elderly persons is that they walk slowly. Hence, when the construct or stereotype of an elderly person is primed in an individual, the behavioral representation is activated, and the individual walks more slowly.

In addition to influencing behavior directly, priming can also affect social perception and, as a consequence, influence behavior indirectly. In these cases, priming affects people's internal cues, which then spill over into their perceptions of other people and the social world. For instance, Higgins et al. (1977) demonstrated that priming individuals with concepts related to hostility leads them to perceive an ambiguous target person (e.g., Donald) as more hostile compared with individuals who do not receive hostility primes. Other research on *self-schemata* (e.g., Markus, 1977) and *chronic accessibility* (e.g., Bargh & Thein, 1985) speaks to the idea that people can have chronic cognitive filters that affect social perception. Research on relational schemas (Baldwin, 1994, 1995; Baldwin, Fehr, Keedian, Seidel, & Thomson, 1993; Baldwin, Keelan, Fehr, Enns, & Koh-Rangarajoo, 1996) also demonstrates that primes can affect social perception. Although the mechanism of these primes on social perception is similar to that of social behavior, one critical difference is that these primed or activated social representations color one's perspective of the world and subsequently have indirect effects on one's behavior. Behavioral primes, on the other hand, are directly linked to actual behaviors.

To better understand how primes can affect behavior indirectly through influencing social perception, we can look at competitive primes used in a Prisoner's Dilemma Game (Neuberg, 1988). In this study, participants were primed with either competitive or neutral primes and then began rounds of a Prisoner's Dilemma Game with another phantom participant. Participants made their first move before learning the move of the phantom participant. Results showed that the competitive primes had no effect on the participant's first move, indicating that the primes did not directly influence participants' behavior. However, participants with predisposed competitive dispositions who received competitive primes exhibited more competitive behavior on subsequent trials than did those participants with competitive predispositions who received neutral primes. These findings suggest that the competitive primes did not directly lead to competitive behavior but rather affected the participants' behavior indirectly through their distorted social perception of the phantom partner. In other words, the competitive lenses of these participants led them to perceive the phantom partner as being competitive only after they learned the partner's move. Their own behavior was affected when they responded in kind to what they perceived was a competitive partner.

PRIMING A SOCIAL CONTEXT

Research has clearly demonstrated that priming knowledge structures such as trait concepts, stereotypes, and behavior-related words can have real and important effects on both social perception and behavior. But what of more macro situations? Is it possible to prime a social context? For instance, can simply imagining being in a group at Time 1 affect behavior at Time 2? To this end, the present study examines whether it is possible to prime a social context or a psychological situation.

In a clever study, Epley and Gilovich (1999) examined whether priming could influence how people react to a social context, namely an Asch-like conformity situation. In their study, participants first completed a computer priming task in which they viewed either conformity (e.g., *comply, conform, obey*) or nonconformity (e.g., *challenge, defy, deviate*) primes. After completing the computer exercise, participants were led into another room with confederates in a conformity situation and were asked to rate attitude questions that were projected on a screen. Findings showed that those who were primed with conformity-related words were more likely to conform than were those primed with nonconformity words. This study was an important step in examining the effects of priming on how people behave in a social context. The present research seeks to build on this study by examining whether a social context itself can be brought to mind and, in turn, influence behavior.

THE IMPLICIT BYSTANDER EFFECT

Bystander apathy research shows that people do not always help in emergency situations, and the likelihood of each persons' helping decreases as the physical presence of other people becomes increased. Diffusion of responsibility accounts (e.g., Darley & Latane, 1968; Latane & Darley, 1968) explain that being in a group leads one to feel as if one is less responsible for helping or taking action, and this feeling of diminished responsibility or accountability then leads to inaction. Logically, then, any manner in which this feeling of diminished responsibility can be introduced should lead to similar behavior—inaction. For instance, priming notions of unaccountability should lead the concept to become more cognitively accessible. Once such increased accessibility, or perceptual fluency, occurs, it is likely to structure the manner in which people respond to situations. When a helping situation arises, people may search internal cues to determine whether they should help. If unaccountability has just been primed, they may help less.

We propose that being in or simply thinking about a group is enough to activate this construct, because part of the concept of being in a group is the notion of being lost in a crowd, being deindividuated, and having a lowered sense of personal accountability. Thus, although physically being in a group might lead one to experience these feelings, simply priming the notion of being in a group should also trigger or activate these concepts. Just as triggering a stereotype activates all the semantic knowledge associated with it, triggering an abstract concept such as being in a group should activate whatever knowledge is associated with that construct. In stereotyping research, we know that thinking about the elderly leads to notions of walking slowly being triggered despite these notions not being directly primed (Bargh et al., 1996). Similarly, thinking about African Americans leads to notions of hostility being triggered, despite these notions not being directly primed. Therefore, priming the psychological situation of being in a group should trigger the concepts associated with that situation. If this includes the sense of diminished responsibility and loss of accountability, as research suggests (e.g., Darley & Latane, 1968; Latane & Darley, 1968), then these notions should be triggered just as when one is in the physical presence of a group. Hence, priming the psychological situation of being in a group should lead to a bystander apathy effect whereby people are less likely to help because their internal cues reflect the increased fluency of unaccountability and suggest to them that helping is not required. We propose that implicit activation of concepts related to unaccountability operates much the same as explicit activation through physical presence in the midst of many others.

OVERVIEW

In the first three studies, we seek to establish the parallel that the implicit activation of the group leads to the same effect as does physically manipulating the presence of others. Hence, our central hypothesis is that individuals who merely imagine being in a group will exhibit less helping behavior on a subsequent, completely unrelated task. In the later studies, we seek to establish the mechanism underlying this proposed effect. Much like past research has shown that specific traits and behaviors are triggered by the activation of a broader stereotype, we assume that the specific concept of unaccountability and diffused responsibility is triggered by the activation of the concept of being with a group. To test this mechanism, we directly assess whether thinking about a group leads to heightened accessibility of these concepts.

STUDY 1

Method

Dining out study. In Study 1, we attempt to identify a linear relationship with number of people imagined and helping behavior. Previous research provides evidence that diffusion of responsibility can affect charitable donations (e.g., Wiesenthal, Austrom, & Silverman, 1983), so we decided to operationalize helping behavior in Study 1 as hypothetical contributions to charity. Previous research has also found that people respond similarly to hypothetical scenarios as they do to real helping situations (e.g., J. Baron & Miller, 2000; Davis, Mitchell, Hall, Lothert, Snapp, & Meyer, 1999; Laner, Benin, & Ventrone, 2001). Our prediction is that the more people participants imagine at Time 1, the less helping behavior they will exhibit at Time 2. More specifically, we predict that people who imagine being with a group of 30 people will exhibit less helping behavior at Time 2 than will those who imagine being with a group of 10 people, who, in turn, should exhibit less helping behavior than will those in the 1-person and neutral control conditions.

Participants. A total of 129 undergraduates from Princeton University participated in a between-subjects (social context: group of 30/group of 10/1 person/neutral control) questionnaire study. This questionnaire was part of a larger questionnaire packet for a Questionnaire Day hosted by the psychology department, and the key pages were imbedded in the packet itself. Participants were paid $8 for completing the entire questionnaire packet.

Procedure. Participants completed a two-page questionnaire. On Page 1, the *group of 30 condition* read as follows: "Imagine you won a dinner for yourself and 30 of your friends at your favorite restaurant." The *group of 10 condition* was identical but referenced 10 friends. The *one person control condition* was similar but focused on only one friend: "Imagine you won a dinner for yourself and a friend at your favorite restaurant." Next, all participants answered the filler question: "What time of day would you most likely make your reservation?" The choice set included the following times: 5 PM, 6 PM, 7 PM, 8 PM, 9 PM, or 10 PM.[1] Because this study was conducted within a larger questionnaire, our *neutral control condition* was simply the helping behavior dependent measure.

On Page 2, all participants read the helping behavior dependent measure, entitled Annual Charity Contribution. It read as follows: "Imagine you have long since graduated from college. What percentage of your annual after-tax earnings would you be willing to donate to charity? (Please Check)." At this point, participants could check one of the following percentage ranges: *1% or less, 2%–3%, 4%–5%, 6%–10%, 11%–15% 16%–20%, 21%–25%,* or *over 25%.* On completion of the entire questionnaire packet, participants were paid for their time.

Results and Discussion

To test our a priori prediction that a linear pattern would emerge such that participants in the group of 30 condition would pledge less of their income to charity than would those in the group of 10 condition, who in turn would pledge less than those in the 1 person and neutral control conditions, we assigned the following contrast weights to the conditions: –19.5 (group of 30 condition), 0.5 (group of 10 condition), 9.5 (1 person control condition), and 9.5 (neutral control condition). A contrast analysis suggests that our data significantly fit this linear pattern, $F(1, 125) = 4.14$, $p < .05$, and the residual was not significant, $F(2, 125) = 0.63$, $p > .5$. That is, the pattern suggests that participants who imagined a group of 30 people pledged less to charity than did those who imagined a group of 10 people, who in turn pledged less than did those who imagined one person or those in the control condition. See Table 1 for the means.

These results are consistent with the literature on diffusion of responsibility in that helping behavior decreased as the numbers of others imagined increased. However, these results shed new light on the diffusion of responsibility literature and suggest that imagined others need not be immediately present or connected to a helping behavior situation for the diffusion effect to occur. Indeed, merely imagining being with others at Time 1 was sufficient to create this diffusion effect.

TABLE 1
Mean Charity Contributions by Condition

Condition	Charity level *M*	*SD*
Group of 30	3.6	1.3
Group of 10	3.9	1.5
One person and neutral controls	4.2	1.6

Note. Response options ranged from 1= *1% or less to charity* to 8 *over 25%.*

STUDY 2

Method

The movies study. Whereas participants in Study 1 imagined being with friends, we attempt to show in Study 2 that when participants are primed with a situation that includes a group of strangers or being in the presence of a crowd they will likewise demonstrate less helping behavior. We compare results from the group prime condition with results from two control conditions, one in which participants were primed with one other person, and one in which they were not primed. As for our prediction, we hypothesized that individuals who imagine being in a crowded situation with many other people would pledge significantly fewer dollars to a university's annual giving campaign, compared with those individuals in our control conditions, which should not differ significantly from each other.

Participants. A total of 38 Harvard University and Princeton University undergraduates participated in a between-subjects (social context:group/one person/ neutral control) questionnaire study. Data from Harvard University participants were collected as part of a larger questionnaire packet during Questionnaire Day, and the key pages were imbedded within the packet. Data from the Princeton University participants were collected at the campus student center; only students who were sitting alone were approached to ensure that participants would not talk or confer with each other while completing the short questionnaire.

Procedure. Participants read one of three possible scenarios, two of which were about being at a movie theater. We chose the setting of a movie theater because we wanted the imagined setting to be away from the college campus. These scenarios manipulated whether participants thought about being with a friend in a crowded movie theater (*group condition*) or whether they thought about being alone with a friend in a movie theater (*one person control condition*). The group condition read as follows: "Imagine that you and a friend are sitting in a crowded movie theater. There are people in front of you, behind you, and to your sides. Although there are some children, the audience is mostly adults, and you are just watching the movie previews." The one person control condition was identical except that participants read about being alone with a friend at a movie theater: "Imagine that you and a friend are sitting alone in a movie theater. You and your friend have the entire theater to yourself, and you are just watching the movie previews." After reading the scenarios, all participants answered a filler question on a 7-point scale: "What room temperature would you prefer for the theater?" (1 = *very cool;* 7 = *very warm*). For the Princeton sample, the *neutral control condition* was simply, "What room temperature do you prefer in general?" (1 = *very cool;* 7 = *very warm*). The neutral control condition for the Harvard sample was simply the dependent variable below, as this dependent measure was already part of a larger questionnaire packet.

On Page 2, participants completed the dependent variable. Helping behavior was operationalized through an annual giving questionnaire. All participants read the following:

> Annual Giving is the yearly appeal (Harvard/Princeton) makes to all alumni, parents and friends for unrestricted funds which can be used immediately to meet the University's most important needs and opportunities. Now imagine you have long since graduated from (Harvard/Princeton). Of the following, which level of contribution do you foresee as your participation? (Please Check).

At this point, participants checked off one of the following dollar ranges: *$0, $1–49, $50–99, $100–249, $250–499, $500–999, $1,000–2,499, $2,500–4,999, $5,000–9,999, and $10,000 and above.* These dollar ranges were treated as a continuous variable (1 = *$0*; 10 = *$10,000* and above) in our analyses.

After completing the questionnaire, participants were thanked for their time and debriefed.

Results and Discussion

To test our a priori prediction that individuals in the group condition would pledge significantly fewer dollars than would those in the one person and neutral control conditions, we compared the mean of the group condition (M = 4.57, SD = 2.28) with that of the one person and control conditions (M = 6.50, SD = 2.62) and found a significant difference in the predicted direction, $F(1, 35) = 5.20$, $p < .05$. A follow up a priori comparison also confirmed that the one person (M = 6.92, SD = 2.43) and neutral control conditions (M = 6.08, SD = 2.84) did not significantly differ from each other, $F(1, 35)$ 0.66, $p > .4$. The College × Social Context interaction was not significant ($p > .5$), which suggests that the Harvard and Princeton samples yielded similar data patterns.

These results suggest that participants primed with the presence of many other people exhibited less helping behavior than did those who imagined being with one other person or those who were not primed. The pattern of results in this study gives credence to the argument that diffusion of responsibility, not self-awareness, is the best explanation for the effect. That is, a possible explanation for a difference between the one person and group conditions could be that there is an increase in helping behavior in the one person condition, as opposed to a decrease in the group condition. This alternative explanation may be plausible if we inadvertently manipulated self-awareness (e.g., Duval & Wicklund, 1972) in the one person condition. However, because participants in the group condition pledged fewer dollars than did those in the one person and neutral control conditions, which did not significantly differ from each other, the implication is that diffusion of responsibility underlies this effect, as opposed to increased self-awareness.

Moreover, this study demonstrates how diffusion of responsibility can spill over into a helping task for which the imagined others are not likely contributors or would-be helpers. That is, imagining a crowded movie theater arguably evokes thinking about a bunch of strangers. So, when asked about contributing to a university's annual giving campaign, participants should not logically expect strangers in a movie theater to have any motivation or compunction to donate to a Harvard or Princeton annual giving campaign. However, visualizing these imagined strangers still affected donation pledge levels. Hence, it seems that priming the presence of others can create an implicit bystander effect that spills over into a subsequent helping task.

STUDY 3

Method

Dining out study-real helping. In the next study, we wanted to replicate the finding that merely imagining the presence of others at Time 1 affects helping behavior at Time 2. We also wanted to generalize this effect to real helping behavior. That is, whereas Studies 1 and 2 demonstrated the effect with hypothetical giving, it is important to demonstrate it with real helping behavior. Again, our central hypothesis is that those primed with the presence of others will offer less helping behavior. We again compared results from the group condition with results from two control conditions, one in which participants imagined one other person, and one in which they were not primed.

Participants. A total of 129 undergraduates from Harvard, Princeton, and Rutgers participated in a between-subjects (social context: group/one person/neutral control) questionnaire design. Participants were recruited at campus student centers. Again, only those who were sitting by themselves were approached to prevent communication among participants.

Procedure. The participants completed a two-page questionnaire, which included the dining out primes of Study 1. On Page 1, the *group condition* read as follows: "Imagine you won a dinner for yourself and 10 of your friends at your favorite restaurant." The *one person control condition* was identical but focused on one friend: "Imagine you won a dinner for yourself and a friend at your favorite restaurant." Next, all participants answered the filler question: "What time of day would you most likely make your reservation?" The choice set included the following times: 5 PM, 6 PM, 7 PM, 8 PM, 9 PM, or 10 PM. The *neutral control condition* participants only read the filler question, which was slightly modified to "What time of day would you make a dinner reservation?"

On Page 2, we operationalized real helping behavior as volunteering to help out with an experiment being conducted in another room. More specifically, all participants read the following on Page 2: "In addition to this survey, we are conducting a brief experiment in another room. How much time are you willing to spend on this other experiment?" At this point, participants checked off one of the following minute intervals: *0 minutes, 2 minutes, 5 minutes, 10 minutes, 15 minutes, 20 minutes, 25 minutes,* and *30 minutes.*

After the questionnaires were collected, participants who had volunteered their time were ready (and some eager) to participate in another experiment. However, at that point, we explained to them our hypothesis and that there was actually no other experiment.

Results and Discussion

As in the previous studies, we made the a priori prediction that the group condition would differ significantly from the one person and neutral control conditions and that the one person and neutral control conditions would not differ significantly from each other. A comparison of the mean of the group condition (M = 2.34, SD = 2.99) with the mean of the one person and control conditions (M = 4.36, SD = 6.15) showed a significant difference in the predicted direction, $F(1, 126) = 3.98$, $p < .05$ (see Figure 1). A follow-up comparison confirmed that the one person control condition (M = 4.93, SD = 7.07) and the neutral control condition (M = 3.80, SD = 5.09) were not significantly different from each other, $F(1, 126) = 0.99$, $p > .3$.

These results suggest that participants who imagined a group of 10 people at Time 1 offered less helping assistance at Time 2 than did control participants, who either imagined 1 other person or saw no prime. Again, this data pattern is consistent with a diffusion of responsibility interpretation, as opposed to a self-awareness one, as the 1 person and neutral control conditions are not significantly different from each other. Another interesting aspect of this study is, again, the disconnect between those imagined and those who can help. That is, even though the participants in the group condition imagined their friends, these imagined friends were not in the immediate vicinity to offer helping behavior assistance. Hence, these results suggest that others need not be physically present for diffusion of responsibility to be created. Although we have demonstrated this implicit bystander effect with both real and hypothetical forms of helping behavior, in the next set of studies, we explore in more detail the mechanism or psychological processes behind the effect.

Study 4

Method

As discussed earlier, although the concept of reduced helping per se is not likely to be a part of the stored mental representation of a group or crowd, it is possible that the conceptual construct of being with a group or in the presence of others is linked to specific notions of deindividuation, being lost in a crowd, and a lowered sense of personal accountability. Rather than priming these constructs directly in the first studies, we assumed that they were triggered by thinking about being in a group. Much like past research has shown that specific traits and behaviors are triggered by the activation of a broader stereotype, we assume that the specific concept of diffused responsibility is triggered by the activation of the concept of being with a group. To test this assump-

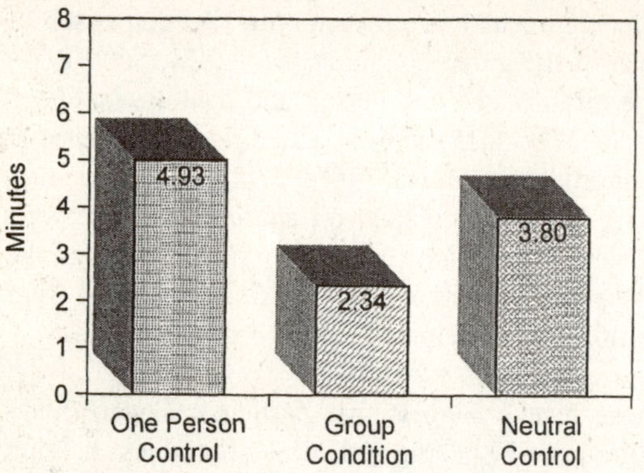

Figure 1. Study 3 helping behavior by condition.

tion, in Study 4 we directly assess whether thinking about a crowd leads to the heightened accessibility of concepts related to unaccountability. Hence, we seek evidence that concepts related to unaccountability and lack of responsibility are more accessible after participants imagine being with a group than after they imagine being with one other person.

Additionally, another interesting possibility is that thinking about being in a group or crowd triggers feelings of comfort and safety in numbers, and this might be what is disrupting helping behavior. Feeling a sense of comfort might lead one to interpret a helping situation as less in need of help. That is, when one feels comfortable and secure, one may look to an ambiguous helping situation, project one's own feelings, and see a situation that is more secure and comfortable than one might have otherwise surmised. If this explanation is correct, then participants in the group condition in Study 3 helped us out less with our study in the other room not because they felt less accountable but instead because they perceived us as being less in need than did those in the control conditions. Hence, to investigate this possibility, we also examined whether notions of safety and comfort become more accessible as a consequence of thinking about a group.

Participants. A total of 52 Lehigh University undergraduates participated in a between-subjects design (social context: group/one person/neutral control) study for course credit.

Procedure. Participants were escorted to individual experimental rooms equipped with computers. Participants then followed self-guided instructions through the software program MediaLab (Jarvis, 2002). MediaLab instructed participants that they would be completing a computer exercise in which letter strings would flash on the screen. The letter strings themselves would either be words or nonwords. Participants were told to press the keyboard key marked yes if the string of letters was a word or the key marked no if the string was a nonword. At this point, all participants performed a lexical decision practice exercise that included 30 trials—15 words (e. g., chair, table, door, knob) and 15 nonwords. All trials began with an orienting stimulus (+) that was presented in the center of the screen for 250 ms and was followed by a blank screen for 400 ms. The letter string (word or nonword) then appeared in the center of the screen for 50 ms. Once participants indicated word or nonword, another trial began.

After this trial session, the computer introduced participants to our manipulation. Participants in the group and one person control conditions read the movie scenario used in Study 2. Participants were randomly assigned to read one of the versions associated with the following conditions: group condition ("Imagine that you and a friend are sitting in a crowded movie theater ..") and one person control condition ("Imagine that you and a friend are sitting alone in a movie theater ..."). Participants in the neutral control condition read no version. After reading the scenario, participants answered the filler question on room temperature described in Study 2.

After this experimental manipulation, the computer instructed participants that they would do another lexical decision task. Forty-two letter strings were then presented in a random order. Again, each word or nonword was preceded by an orienting stimulus (+) that appeared for 250 ms and was followed by a blank screen for 400 ms. The word or nonword was then presented in the center of the computer screen for 50 ms.

Because most priming studies show facilitation effects, for our responsibility composite, we chose single words that were related to the concept of unaccountability. For our main unaccountability composite, we selected three synonyms of unaccountability-unaccountable, innocent, and exempt. 2 These words were matched to three neutral words representing the same degree of positivity to form a matched neutral composite (e. g., whimsical, impenetrable).

Six comfort-related words were also included: protected, safe, unthreatened, secure, comforted, and peaceful. These words were also matched to 6 neutral trait words (e. g. , diligent, intelligent). Finally, 5 neutral filler nouns (table, mountain, flower, program, and compass) and 19 nonwords were included. On completing the computer task, participants were thanked for their time and then debriefed about the purpose of the experiment.

Results

Data reduction. To analyze the reaction time data, we followed procedures outlined in Bargh and Chartrand (2000). Data points that were three standard deviations above or below the mean for each word were considered outliers and were dropped from subsequent analyses. This affected less than 3% of the data points. Because reaction time data are often skewed, we applied a log transformation to normalize the data to meet the assumptions of the statistical tests. Although the log transformed values were used in the analyses, we report the actual reaction time means in milliseconds.

Filler nouns. We analyzed participants' reaction times to the filler nouns first to ensure that participants in the group and control conditions did not show a difference in overall reaction time by condition. Results showed that there were no significant differences in response times to the filler nouns (group condition, $M = 516.00$, $SD = 129.00$; control conditions, $M = 526.00$, $SD = 99.00$), $F(1,49) = 0.42, p = .52$.

Unaccountable composite. Our a priori prediction was that individuals in the group condition would respond more quickly to the unaccountable composite words than would participants in the one person and neutral control conditions, whereas the two groups would show equal response times to the matched neutral words. To test this prediction, we conducted a planned contrast using standardized contrast scores (*L* score) computed for each participant. We multiplied the following contrast weights to our dependent measures: 1 (unaccountable words) and –1 (matched neutral words). This procedure resulted in L scores representing the sum of each participant's residual score after each score had been multiplied by the appropriate contrast weight (Rosenthal & Rosnow, 1985; Rosenthal, Rosnow, & Rubin, 2000). An analysis of these scores by type of prime yielded a significant difference in the predicted direction, $F(1, 50) = 5.27, p < .05$.[3] Participants in the group condition responded more quickly to the unaccountable composite words ($M = 517.00$ ms, $SD = 129.00$ ms) relative to those in the one person and neutral control conditions ($M = 587.00$ ms, $SD = 151.00$ ms). In contrast, those in the group ($M = 559.00$ ms, $SD = 158.00$ ms) and control ($M = 558.00$ ms,

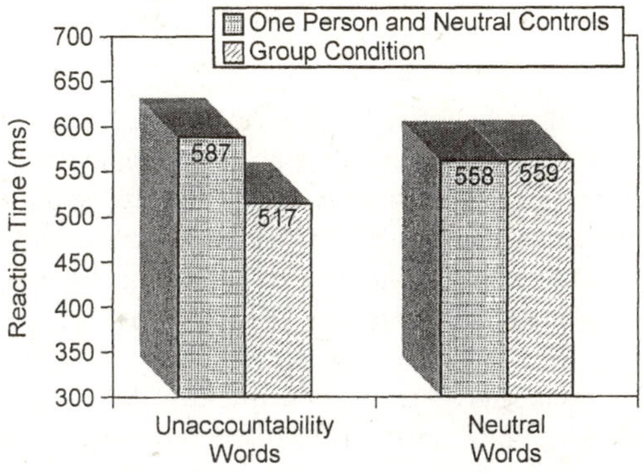

Figure 2. Study 4 reaction time (in ms) by condition and composite.

$SD = 140.00$ ms) conditions showed similar reaction times to the matched neutral words. See Figure 2 for means. A simple effects test on the unaccountable composite only, which does not take into account baseline reaction times to the matched neutral words, showed a marginally significant difference between the group condition and control conditions in the predicted direction, $F(1, 49) = 2.96$, $p = .09$. A simple effects test on the matched neutral composite showed no significant difference by condition, $F(1, 49) = 0.05$, $p = .81$, as expected.

We conducted a follow-up planned comparison on the *L* scores to ensure that the two control conditions did not differ from each other. This comparison indicated that the two control conditions (one person and neutral control) were not significantly different from each other, $F(1, 29) = 0.00, p = .97$.

Comfort composite. To test the possibility that thinking about a group has its effect on helping behavior because group or crowd primes thoughts about comfort, we performed a similar contrast using *L* scores. We multiplied the following contrast weights to our comfort dependent measures: 1 (comfort words) and –1 (matched neutral words). Results from this analysis did not reveal a significant difference by experimental condition, $F(1, 50) = 0.17, p = 68$.

Discussion

In light of these findings, it appears that merely imagining the presence of others or a crowded situation leads participants to respond more quickly to words related to the concept of unaccountability relative to matched neutral words. The fact that the crowded and control participants responded equally quickly to the matched neutral words indicates that this effect is specific to words related to unaccountability and is not due to participants in the group condition responding more quickly across the board. Hence, it seems that the increased accessibility of the concept *unaccountable* may be the mechanism by which priming the presence of others produces less helping on a subsequent, unrelated task. In addition, results from Study 4 are not consistent with the comfort hypothesis. Participants primed with a crowded situation did not respond significantly more quickly to words related to comfort than did those in the one person or neutral control conditions.

STUDY 5

Our purpose in Study 5 was twofold. First, we wanted to conceptually replicate the results of Study 4 to ensure the reliability of the reaction time findings. Second, we wanted to investigate whether the comfort hypothesis would be supported if we used a stronger group prime. For this reason, we not only had participants read the movie theater primes used in Study 4 but also asked them to list their thoughts about the theater for 3 min. The thought listing as a prime strength manipulation was modeled after one used by Dijksterhuis and van Knippenberg (1998), which showed that the longer individuals are exposed to primes, the stronger the effects are.

Method

Participants. A total of 74 Princeton University undergraduates participated in a between-subjects design (social context: group/one person/neutral control) study for course credit. Participants were run in individual experimental rooms.

Procedure. The entire procedure of Study 5 was the same as that used in Study 4, except for the prime manipulation. After the practice lexical decision session, the computer introduced participants to our manipulation. Participants in the group and one person control conditions read the movie scenario used in Studies 1 and 4 —*group condition* ("Imagine that you and a friend are sitting in a crowded movie theater. . . "), and *one person control condition* ("Imagine that you and a friend are sitting alone in a movie theater. . . "). They were then given a blank sheet of paper and were asked to list as many thoughts as came to mind for 3 min. Participants in the *neutral control condition* read no version and went directly to the reaction time task. The lexical decision task used the same words and the same specifications as did Study 4.

Results and Discussion

Data reduction. Before analyzing the reaction time data, we again followed procedures outlined in Bargh and Chartrand (2000) for dealing with reaction time data. Data points that were three standard deviations above or below the mean for each word were considered outliers and were replaced with missing values in subsequent analyses. This procedure again affected less than 3% of the data points. Because reaction time data are often skewed (for a discussion, see Bargh & Chartrand, 2000), we applied a log transformation to normalize the data to meet the assumptions of the statistical tests. Again, although we used logs in the analyses, we report the actual means in milliseconds.

Filler nouns. We analyzed participants' reaction times to the filler nouns first to ensure that participants in the group and control conditions did not show a difference in overall reaction time by condition. Results showed that those in the group condition (M = 436.00, SD = 73.00) and the control conditions (M = 446.00, SD = 94.00) responded equally to the filler nouns, $F(1, 71) = 0.23, p = .63$.

Unaccountable composite. Our a priori prediction was that individuals in the group condition would respond more quickly to the unaccountable composite words than would participants in the one person and neutral control conditions, whereas the two groups would respond equally quickly to the matched neutral words. To test this prediction, we again conducted a planned contrast using a standardized contrast score (L score) computed for each participant. We multiplied the following contrast weights to our dependent measures: 1 (unaccountable words) and –1 (matched neutral words). This resulted in L scores representing the sum of each participant's residual score after each score had been multiplied by the appropriate contrast weight. An analysis of these scores by experimental condition yielded a significant difference in the predicted direction, $F(1, 72) = 4.74, p < .05$. A simple effects test on the unaccountable composite words only showed that participants in the group condition responded more quickly to the unaccountable composite words (M = 429.00 ms, SD = 99.00 ms) than did those in the two control conditions (M = 476.00 ms, SD = 95.00 ms), $F(1, 71) = 5.20$, $p < .05$. In contrast, those in the group (M = 450.00 ms, SD = 101.00 ms) and control (M = 461.00 ms, SD = 94.00 ms) conditions showed similar reaction times to the matched neutral words, $F(1, 71) = 0.33$, $p = .57$. See Figure 3 for the means.

A follow-up comparison to ensure that the two control conditions did not differ in their L scores again showed that the two control conditions (one person and neutral control) were not significantly different, $F(1, 45)= 0.07$, $p = .80$.

Comfort composite. To examine the possibility that thinking about a group has its effect on helping behavior because group or crowd primes thoughts about comfort, we performed a similar contrast using L scores. We multiplied the following contrast weights to our comfort dependent measures: 1 (comfort words) and −1 (matched neutral words). Although the pattern of means was in the predicted direction, an analysis of these scores by experimental condition did not reveal a significant difference by condition, $F(1, 72) = 1.40$, $p = .24$. Despite the stronger prime, results from this analysis did not reveal a significant effect of social context on comfort L scores.

Exploring unaccountable and comfort. To further examine the relationship between unaccountable and comfort, we ran some additional regression analyses. Because Studies 4 and 5 were virtually identical (except for the duration of the prime), we collapsed the data from

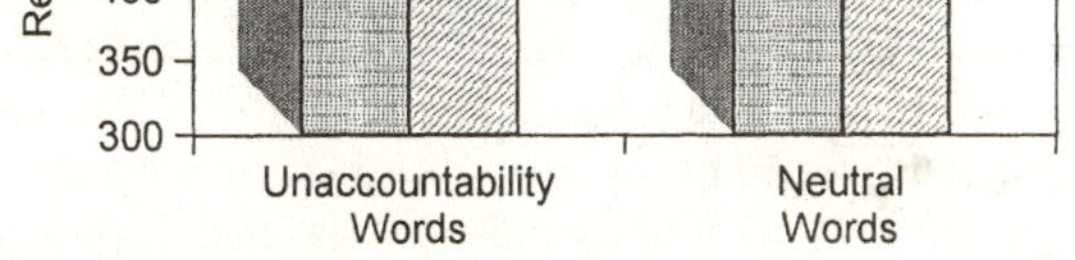

Figure 3. Study 5 reaction time (in ms) by condition and composite.

the two studies to increase the power for the analyses. Before collapsing the data, we first transformed the data from each of the two studies into standardized z scores and then concatenated these data sets.[4] Our goal for these analyses was twofold. First, we were interested in whether a boost in power would lend support to the comfort hypothesis and, if so, whether this relationship would hold when participants' reaction times to the unaccountable composite were held constant. Second, we wanted to investigate whether the relationship between social context (one person and neutral control/group) and unaccountable would hold if we controlled for participants' response times to the comfort composite.

To address these questions and thus further investigate the mechanism of the implicit bystander effect, we followed the procedures outlined in R. M. Baron and Kenny (1986) and Kenny, Kashy, and Bolger (1998). First, we were interested in whether the relationship between social context and the comfort composite would become significant with the boost in power brought about by collapsing the two studies. To test this, we dummy coded social context (1 = one person/control; 2 = group) and used it as the independent variable in the analyses. Regression analyses indeed showed that social context had a significant relationship with the comfort composite ($\beta = -.18$, $p < .05$). Then we tested whether the relationship between social context and the comfort composite would remain significant when we controlled for the unaccountable composite by treating it as a mediator. Social context had a significant relationship both with participants' reaction times to the comfort composite ($\beta = -.18$, $p < .05$) and with participants' reaction times to the unaccountable composite (the mediator in this case; $\beta = -.25$, $p < .01$). The unaccountable composite also had a significant relationship with the comfort composite while controlling for the effect of social context ($\beta = .73$, $p < .001$). However, when participants' reaction times to the unaccountable composite were controlled, the relationship between social context and comfort dropped dramatically ($\beta = .01$, $p = .94$).[5] A further analysis using the ratio of ab over the standard error of ab (see R. M. Baron & Kenny, 1986) revealed that including the unaccountable composite as a mediator produced a significant reduction in the relationship between condition and comfort (ratio = 2.76, $p < .01$).

The purpose of our second analysis was to test whether the relationship between social context and the unaccountable composite would remain significant when we controlled for the comfort composite by treating it as a mediator. Social context had a significant impact both on participants' reaction times to the unaccountable composite ($\beta = -.25$, $p < .01$) and on participants' reaction times to the comfort composite (the mediator in this case, $\beta = -.18$, $p < .05$). The comfort composite also had a significant relationship with participants' reaction times to the unaccountable composite when social context was controlled for ($\beta = .71$, $p < .001$). Results were not consistent with a mediational interpretation, however, because analyses showed that the relationship between social context and the unaccountable composite remained statistically significant, even when the comfort composite was controlled for ($\beta = -.13$, $p < .05$).[6]

These analyses suggest an intriguing dynamic between the concepts of unaccountable and comfort and suggest that the diffusion of responsibility explanation may provide a tighter account of the implicit bystander effect than does a comfort explanation. That is, a significant relationship exists between unaccountable thoughts and social context, even when one controls for words associated with comfort. However, comfort no longer has a significant relationship with social context when one controls for participants' reaction times to unaccountable words. Although these results do not categorically determine whether a diffusion of responsibility account is better than a comfort one, they do suggest that any relationship comfort has with social context may have something to do with responsibility. We speculate that some people may feel more comforted and secure as a consequence of feeling less responsible.

GENERAL DISCUSSION

The present studies help advance our current understanding of the bystander apathy literature by suggesting an alternative account in which imagined others need not be imbedded or implied in the helping situation at hand for the bystander apathy effect to be produced. That is, in our studies, individuals who just imagined the presence of others at Time 1 exhibited less helping behavior on a subsequent, completely unrelated task at Time 2, even when imagining others who could not possibly help out. For instance, imagining strangers in the movie theater should have no bearing on annual giving to a university alumni campaign, but from the current research it is clear that it does.

Although we feel this research provides evidence that, under some circumstances, a more social-cognitive account may be sufficient to explain bystander apathy, it by no means suggests that traditional accounts such as classic diffusion of responsibility (e.g., Darley & Latane, 1968) or confusion of responsibility (e.g., Cacioppo et al., 1986) are wrong. That is, our alternative account may interact with traditional ones in an additive or emergent way. Nevertheless, contrary to our current understanding of bystander apathy, the present research suggests that the presence of others need not be imbedded in or associated with the helping situation to exert diffusion of responsibility effects.

The present research also presents evidence that merely imagining a group can lead to lessened levels of responsibility. That is, from our reaction time studies, we have learned that participants who imagine the presence of others respond more quickly to words such as *unaccountable,* relative to participants in the control and one person conditions. Although diffusion of responsibility appears to characterize the mechanism behind the implicit bystander effect, future research must investigate more precisely how this mechanism works. The account that we put forth holds that a parallel of the explicit type of bystander apathy is what is being evidenced. That is, people who imagine group situations have notions of unaccountability triggered, and this leads them to see the situation as one that does not call for their personal help. However, there is the possibility that the mechanism through which the group primes exert an influence is less complicated than we surmised. Past research (e.g., Bargh et al., 1996; Dijksterhuis & van Knippenberg, 1998) has shown that primes can drive behavior unmediated through such construal processes. It remains wholly possible that bystander apathy could also be caused by behavioral manifestations of unaccountability, which are directly triggered by priming groups (or physically being in a group), and these behaviors interfere with or directly oppose helping behavior. The current studies do not distinguish between the construal hypothesis and the direct priming of behavioral manifestations, and, in fact, both processes are compatible with our data. What the data reveal is that the priming of group representations includes and simultaneously primes notions of lacking responsibility and accountability that appear to disrupt helping behavior. That is, even when one is not physically in a group, there is the possibility for an implicit bystander effect, in which diffusion of responsibility is triggered implicitly through primes and spreading activation.

Future Directions

From the present study, we know that priming the concept of group leads to the implicit bystander effect. However, an interesting avenue for future research is to examine whether priming the concept of being with a group below participants' level of conscious awareness still results in this effect. That is, one can envision words related to the concept of being with a group flashing on a computer screen to test whether the implicit bystander effect can be induced by unconscious priming. To the extent that activating the concept of a group or crowded situation makes accessible notions of unaccountability, it should not matter whether participants are aware of the group primes or whether they are primed below their conscious awareness. Nevertheless, this remains an empirical question.

Future research should also explore whether the type of group imagined plays a role in the implicit bystander effect. For instance, the interconnectedness of individuals in a group situation may influence responding. In classic bystander studies, the bystanders at hand often have no real social connection to each other except for being at the same place at the same time. That is, in these cases, the group is just a collection of independent individuals. Bystander apathy studies have also demonstrated this effect with bystanders with social connections to the others around them. In these cases, an individual may be a member of the group at hand. Along these lines, our studies provide evidence for the implicit bystander effect using both unconnected others and connected others. Namely, our dining out prime shows this effect with imagined acquaintances, whereas our movie theater prime shows the bystander effect when participants were simply imagining strangers. Although we grant that both types of primes lead to less helping behavior, it might be interesting to explore whether imagining one type of group becomes a stronger prime than another. Do people experience a greater sense of unaccountability when they are primed with being in an interconnected group than with being with random strangers?

Additionally, there is a possibility that some types of group primes may actually prime more helping behavior rather than less. For instance, leading people to think about groups of prosocial others, such as a group of lifeguards or doctors, may increase helping. Along these lines, manipulations that increase self-awareness (e.g., Duval & Wicklund, 1972) may also interact with group primes to increase helping behavior. For instance, if a person imagines that everyone in a crowded place is focused on him or her or if a person thinks of a crowded situation while standing in front of a mirror, helping will likely increase as people attempt to make their behavior consistent with their standards. Furthermore, level of identification with a particular group may affect how a group prime influences helping behavior. All of these questions are beyond the scope of this article and deserve future research.

CONCLUSION

Overall, this research suggests that priming the presence of others at Time 1 affects helping behavior on a completely unrelated task at Time 2. This research contributes to the priming methodology in that it primes a social context. Secondly, this research advances our understanding of bystander apathy and proposes an additional account for the bystander apathy effect. Future research must continue to explore the boundary conditions of the implicit bystander effect as well as the mechanisms that contribute to this process.

REFERENCES

Baldwin, M. W. (1994). Primed relational schemas as a source of self-evaluative reactions. *Journal of Social and Clinical Psychology, 13,* 380–403.

Baldwin, M. W. (1995). Relational schemas and cognition in close relationships. *Journal of Social and Personal Relationships, 12,* 547–552.

Baldwin, M. W., Fehr, B., Keedian, E., Seidel, M., & Thomson, D. W. (1993). An exploration of the relational schemata underlying attachment styles: Self-report and lexical decision approaches. *Personality and Social Psychology Bulletin, 19,* 746–754.

Baldwin, M. W., Keelan, J. P. R., Fehr, B., Enns, V., & Koh-Rangarajoo, E. (1996). Social-cognitive conceptualization of attachment working models: Availability and accessibility effects. *Journal of Personality and Social Psychology, 71,* 94–109.

Bargh, J. A., & Chartrand, T. L. (2000). The mind in the middle: A practical guide to priming and automaticity research. In H. T. Reis & C. M. Judd (Eds.), *Handbook of research methods in social and personality psychology.* Cambridge, England: Cambridge University Press.

Bargh, J. A., Chen, M., & Burrows, L. (1996). The automaticity of social behavior: Direct effects of trait concept and stereotype activation on action. *Journal of Personality and Social Psychology, 71,* 230–244.

Bargh, J. A., & Thein, R. D. (1985). Individual construct accessibility, person memory, and the recall-judgment link: The case of information overload. *Journal of Personality and Social Psychology, 49,* 1129–1146.

Baron, J., & Miller, J. G. (2000). Limiting the scope of moral obligations to help: A cross-cultural investigation. *Journal of Cross-Cultural Psychology, 31,* 703–725.

Baron, R. M., & Kenny, D. A. (1986). The moderator-mediator variable distinction in social psychological research: Conceptual, strategic and statistical considerations. *Journal of Personality and Social Psychology, 51,* 1173–1182.

Bickman, L. (1972). Social influence and diffusion of responsibility in an emergency. *Journal of Experimental Social Psychology, 8,* 438–445.

Cacioppo, J. T., Petty, R. E., & Losch, M. E. (1986). Attributions of responsibility for helping and doing harm: Evidence for confusion of responsibility. *Journal of Personality and Social Psychology, 50,* 100–105.

Carver, C. S., Ganellen, R. J., Froming, W. J., & Chambers, W. (1983). Modeling: An analysis in terms of category accessibility. *Journal of Experimental Social Psychology, 19,* 403–421.

Clark, R. D., & Word, L. E. (1974). Where is the apathetic bystander? Situational characteristics of the emergency. *Journal of Personality and Social Psychology, 29,* 279–287.

Darley, J. M., & Latane, B. (1968). Bystander intervention in emergencies: Diffusion of responsibility. *Journal of Personality and Social Psychology, 8,* 377–383.

Darley, J. M., Teger, A. L., & Lewis, L. D. (1973). Do groups always inhibit individuals' responses to potential emergencies? *Journal of Personality and Social Psychology, 26,* 395–399.

Davis, M. H., Mitchell, K. V., Hall, J. A., Lothert, J., Snapp, T., & Meyer, M. (1999). Empathy, expectations, and situational preferences: Personality influences on the decision to participate in volunteer helping behaviors. *Journal of Personality, 67,* 469–503.

Dijksterhuis, A., Spears, R., & Lepinasse, V. (2000). Reflecting and deflecting stereotypes: Assimilation and contrast in automatic behavior. *Journal of Experimental Social Psychology.*

Dijksterhuis, A., & van Knippenberg, A. (1998). The relation between perception and behavior, or how to win a game of trivial pursuit. *Journal of Personality and Social Psychology, 74,* 865–877.

Duval, T. S., & Wicklund, R. (1972). *The theory of objective self awareness.* New York: Academic Press.

Epley, N., & Gilovich, T. (1999). Just going along: Nonconscious priming and conformity to social pressure. *Journal of Experimental Social Psychology, 35,* 578–589.

Higgins, E. T., Rholes, W. S., & Jones, C. R. (1977). Category accessibility and impression formation. *Journal of Experimental Social Psychology, 13,* 141–154.

Jarvis, B. G. (2002). MediaLab Research Software (Version 2002) [Computer program]. New York: Empirisoft.

Kawakami, K., Young, H., & Dovidio, J. F. (2000). *Automatic stereotyping: Category, trait and behavior activations.* Manuscript submitted for publication.

Kenny, D. A., Kashy, D. A., & Bolger, N. (1998). Data analysis in social psychology. In D. Gilbert, S. Fiske, & G. Lindzey (Eds.), *The handbook of social psychology* (Vol. 1, pp. 233–265). Boston: McGraw-Hill.

Korte, C. (1971). Effects of individual responsibility and group communication on help-giving in an emergency. *Human Relations, 24,* 149–159.

Laner, M. R., Benin, M. H., & Ventrone, N. A. (2001). Bystander attitudes toward victims of violence: Who's worth helping? *Deviant Behavior, 22,* 23–24.

Latane, B. (1970). Field studies in altruistic compliance. *Representative Research in Social Psychology, 1,* 49–61.

Latane, B., & Darley, J, M. (1968). Group inhibition of bystander intervention. *Journal of Personality and Social Psychology, 10,* 215–221.

Latane, B., & Darley, J. M. (1970). *The unresponsive bystander: Why doesn't he help?* New York: Appleton-Century-Crofts.

Latane, B., & Nida, S. (1981). Ten years of research on group size and helping. *Psychological Bulletin, 89,* 308–324.

Macrae, C. N., & Johnston, L. (1998). Help, I need somebody: Automatic action and inaction. *Social Cognition, 16,* 400–417.

Markus, H. (1977). Self-schemata and processing information about the self. *Journal of Personality and Social Psychology, 35,* 63–78.

Neuberg, S. L. (1988). Behavioral implications of information presented outside of conscious awareness: The effect of subliminal presentation of trait information on behavior in the prisoner's dilemma game. *Social Cognition, 6,* 207–230.

Prentice, D. A., & Miller, D. T. (1996). Pluralistic ignorance and the perpetuation of social norms by unwitting actors. In M. P. Zanna (Ed.), *Advances in experimental social psychology* (Vol. 29, pp. 161–209). San Diego, CA: Academic Press.

Rosenthal, R., & Rosnow, R. (1985). Contrast analysis: Focused comparisons in the analysis of variance. New York: Cambridge University Press.

Rosenthal, R., Rosnow, R., & Rubin, D. (2000). *Contrasts and effect sizes in behavioral research: A correlational approach.* New York: Cambridge University Press.

Wiesenthal, D. L., Austrom, D., & Silverman, I. (1983). Diffusion of responsibility in charitable donations. *Basic and Applied Social Psychology, 4,* 17–27.

Received December 29, 2001
Revision received February 9, 2002
Accepted February 13, 2002

NOTES:

1. To rule out the possibility that making a dinner reservation entails more responsibility in our group prime than it does in our one person prime, we pretested these primes by asking 40 undergraduates to read the following in a between-subjects questionnaire: "Imagine you won a dinner for yourself and (1 or 10) of your friends at your favorite restaurant. You are calling to make the reservation for a time between 5 PM and 10 PM." We then asked them, "How important is your choice of reservation time?" (1 = *not important at all; 7 = extremely important*). Results showed that the importance ratings of those who read the one person prime ($M = 4.35$, $SD = 1.87$) and the group prime ($M = 4.15$, $SD = 1.09$) did not significantly differ from each other ($p > .68$), which suggests that the decision to make a dinner reservation time was no more important in the group condition than in the one person condition.
2. We considered including the term irresponsible; however, this term has a slightly different connotation than not responsible. More specifically, irresponsible seems to evoke thoughts of incompetence, whereas our intended usage of not responsible does not.
3. Note that we use the error term only for the groups involved in the between-subjects comparison (group/one person and neutral control) when the L scores involve a within-subject comparison.
4. Even before standardizing the scores, we initially concatenated the raw data from Studies 4 and 5 to verify that there were no significant interactions between social context (group/one person and neutral control) and school (Lehigh/Princeton) across our key dependent measures. All Fs were less than 1.00; unaccountable composite, $F(1, 122) = 0.05, p > .82$; comfort composite, $F(1, 122) = 0.05, p > .80$; unaccountable matched neutral, $F(1, 122) = 0.01, p > .90$; and comfort matched neutral, $F(1, 122) = 0.21, p > .64$.
5. Incidentally, these analyses yield similar results with the unstandardized data set combining Studies 4 and 5.
6. Again, these analyses yield similar results with the unstandardized data set combining Studies 4 and 5.

Reading 13

Five experiments examined effects of songs with violent lyrics on aggressive thoughts and hostile feelings. Experiments 1, 3, 4 and 5 demonstrated that college students who heard a violent song felt more hostile than those who heard a similar but nonviolent song. Experiments 2–5 demonstrated a similar increase in aggressive thoughts. These effects replicated across songs and song types (e.g., rock, humorous, nonhumorous). Experiments 3–5 also demonstrated that trait hostility was positively related to state hostility but did not moderate the song lyric effects. Discussion centers on the potential role of lyric content on aggression in short-term settings, relation to catharsis and other media violence domains, development of aggressive personality, differences between long-term and short-term effects, and possible mitigating factors.

Exposure to Violent Media: The Effects of Songs with Violent Lyrics on Aggressive Thoughts and Feelings

Craig A. Anderson and Nicholas L. Carnagey
Iowa State University

Janie Eubanks
Texas Department of Human Services

Craig A. Anderson and Nicholas L. Carnagey, Department of Psychology, Iowa State University; Janie Eubanks, Texas Department of Human Services, Austin, Texas.

Correspondence concerning this article should be addressed to Craig A. Anderson, Department of Psychology, W112 Lagomarcino Hall, Iowa State University, Ames, Iowa 50011-3180. E-mail: caa@iastate.edu

As evidenced by the creation of the Parents' Music Resource Center and the policy of labeling music products containing violent lyrics, many people are concerned with potential deleterious effects of listening to songs with violent lyrics. An accumulating body of scientific research spanning 4 decades supports the hypothesis that exposure to violent media is causally related to subsequent expression of aggression in both short- and long-term time frames (e.g., Anderson & Bushman, 2002a; Berkowitz, 1993; Bushman & Anderson, 2001). The vast majority of this research has focused on violent television and movies (Huesmann & Miller, 1994). Recently, a small but relatively consistent research literature has shown that short-term exposure to violent video games causes increases in aggression and aggression-related variables (Anderson & Bushman, 2001).

Nonetheless, there remains among the general population and many practitioners a very strong belief in the age-old *catharsis hypothesis*—the belief that experiencing and expressing aggressive emotions and thoughts will decrease subsequent aggressive thoughts, feelings, and emotions (Bushman, 2002; Bushman, Baumeister, & Stack, 1999). This ancient Greek idea, later popularized by Breuer and Freud (1893–1895/1955) and now usually labeled *venting*, states that aggressive impulses can be reduced by watching, reading, or singing about anger and aggression as well as by behaving in symbolically aggressive ways. Though the aggression catharsis hypothesis has been thoroughly explored and debunked in several entertainment media domains, there has been relatively little work on the effects of songs with violent lyrics on aggression-related variables such as aggressive thoughts and feelings.

SOURCE: Anderson, C. A. & Carnagery, N. L., & Eubanks, J. 2003. "Exposure to Violent Media: The Effects of Songs with Violent Lyrics on Aggressive Thoughts and Feelings." *JOURNAL OF PERSONALITY AND SOCIAL PSYCHOLOGY, 84*, 960–971.

MEDIA DIFFERENCES

There are numerous differences between watching violent television, playing violent video games, and listening to popular music. One is the lack of a video component to audio-only music. Another is that aggressive lyrical content of popular music is often discernible only to the most attentive of listeners, whereas video-based media (including music videos) make their violent content abundantly and graphically clear. Some rock music songs have such garbled lyrics that they have given rise to debates about what the lyrics are (e.g., "Louie, Louie"; "Inna-Godda-Da-Vida"; see Marsh, 1993). A third difference concerns attention. A large proportion of time spent listening to music involves paying attention to the music (not the lyrics) or to other tasks. Thus, effects of violent lyrics may generally be attenuated (relative to video-based media violence) simply because the lyrics are not processed by the listeners.

Nonetheless, there are valid reasons to worry about potentially harmful effects of violent music lyrics. Numerous studies have shown that aggressive words can prime aggressive thoughts, perceptions, and behavior (e.g., Anderson, Benjamin, & Bartholow, 1998; Bargh, Chen, & Barrows, 1996; Bargh & Pietromonaco, 1982). Indeed, such effects can occur even when the stimulus has not been consciously recognized (e.g., Bargh et al., 1996, Experiment 3). Furthermore, listeners are capable of recognizing themes of music (i.e., violence, sex, suicide, and Satanism) even when it is difficult to comprehend specific lyric content (Hansen & Hansen, 1991). Additionally, music stimuli are played repeatedly, both by radio stations as well as by listeners themselves.

Another difference between video-based entertainment and music concerns the amount of imagination needed or allowed to fill in details of the story being told. The lack of visual images in music both allows and requires listeners to imagine details. Concrete images probably play a major role in transfer of ideas from the video world to one's own real-world situations. When one's video antagonists are similar to one's real antagonists, violent solutions modeled in the video world are more likely to be attempted in the real world than when the video antagonists are dissimilar (Bandura, 1986; Berkowitz, 1993; Geen, 1990). The lack of concrete images in violent music may well allow listeners to imagine audio antagonists similar to real-world antagonists.

Thus, there are reasons to expect violent-lyric songs to be either more or less influential than violent video materials. The present article reports five experiments testing the hypothesis that brief exposure to songs with violent lyrics can increase two variables that are key mediators of situational influences on aggression: aggressive cognitions and aggressive affect. In the next section, we briefly review the existing research literature. Then we show why the general aggression model (GAM; Anderson & Bushman, 2001; Anderson & Huesmann, in press) suggests a focus on aggressive cognitions and affect.

PAST MUSIC RESEARCH

Experimental Studies of Music Videos

Several field and laboratory experiments have examined effects of aggressive music videos. Waite, Hillbrand, and Foster (1992) observed a significant decrease in aggressive behavior on a forensic inpatient ward after removal of Music Television (MTV). Peterson and Pfost (1989) found that exposing males to nonerotic violent music videos led to a significant increase in adversarial sexual beliefs and negative affect. Johnson, Jackson, and Gatto (1995) found that males who had been randomly assigned to view violent rap music videos became more accepting of the use of violence in dealing with interpersonal problems. Related research found that males and females exposed to violent rap music videos became more accepting of teen dating violence (Johnson, Adams, Ashburn, & Reed, 1995). College students exposed to rock music videos with antisocial themes produced a greater acceptance of antisocial behavior (Hansen & Hansen, 1990). Students were also more likely to accept stereotypic sex-role behavior after being exposed to music videos that displayed similar behavior (Hansen, 1989; Hansen & Hansen, 1988).

Music video studies are valuable in their own right, but they do not provide information about the effects of exposure to violent lyrics without video. Music videos are much more like other video media (TV, movies) in that they can tell a story with graphically violent images; the finding that they produce similar effects is not surprising.

Correlational Studies of Music Preference and Behavior

Correlational studies have suggested a connection between the kind of music youth listen to and various maladaptive behaviors and attitudes, though the direction of causality is not clear. Rubin, West, and Mitchell (2001) found that college students who preferred rap and heavy metal music reported more hostile attitudes than students who preferred other genres of music, such as alternative, adult contemporary, dance—soul, or country. Listeners to heavy metal music held more negative attitudes toward women. Rap music fans were more distrustful. Similarly, Took and Weiss (1994) found a correlation between preference for rap and heavy metal music and below-average academic performance, school behavior problems, drug use, arrests, and sexual activity. Still other studies have found correlations between music type preferences and a variety of maladaptive behaviors but have not specifically linked lyric preferences to those behaviors. (For a recent review, see Roberts, Christenson, & Gentile, in press.)

Experimental Studies of Music Without Video

Music Without Lyrics McFarland (1984) looked at the effects of exposure to tense, calm, or no-background music (without lyrics) on the emotional content of stories written for the Thematic Apperception Test. Participants who heard tense music wrote the most unpleasant stories. Like the music video studies, these results tell us little about lyric effects. However, they indicate that research on lyrics must control for effects of type of music.

Music With Lyrics Only a few studies have specifically examined the influence of violent songs on aggression-related variables. Interestingly, most have found no effects of lyrical content (e.g., Ballard & Coates, 1995; St. Lawrence & Joyner, 1991; Wanamaker & Reznikoff, 1989). For example, participants in Ballard and Coates's (1995) study heard one of six songs varying in genre (rap vs. heavy metal) and lyric (homicidal, suicidal, neutral). Lyric content had no impact on mood measures, including anger. In other studies showing no effect, the genre of the songs (heavy metal) made the lyrics nearly incomprehensible, a problem noted by the researchers themselves.

Barongan and Hall (1995) reported a study suggesting that antisocial lyrics can affect behavior, but the target behavior was not clearly aggressive; thus, its relevance to our work is unclear. Male college students listened to misogynous or neutral rap music, viewed three vignettes (neutral, sexual-violent, assaultive), and then chose one of the three vignettes to be shown to a female confederate. Those who had listened to the misogynous music were significantly more likely to choose the assaultive vignette.

Wester, Crown, Quatman, and Heesacker (1997) reported mixed results. Male undergraduates were exposed to either (a) sexually violent music and lyrics, (b) the same music without lyrics, (c) sexually violent lyrics without music, or (d) no music or lyrics. Results yielded no differences in negative attitudes toward women among the four groups. However, participants exposed to violent lyrics viewed their relationships with women as more adversarial.

Overall, the few published studies on the effects of exposure to songs with violent lyrics have produced mixed results, perhaps because of methodological problems involving confounds with arousal or lyrics that were indecipherable. We build on prior work by using a social-cognitive theoretical perspective that has emerged from aggression research in several different domains, including media violence.

Theoretical Perspective The theoretical basis for the present experiments comes from our earlier work on GAM (Anderson, 1997; Anderson, Anderson, & Deuser, 1996; Anderson & Bushman, 2002b; Anderson, Deuser, & DeNeve, 1995; Anderson & Dill, 2000; Anderson & Huesmann, in press). This model draws on empirical and theoretical contributions from several research groups, most notably the social-cognitive work of Bandura (1986), Berkowitz (1993), Crick and Dodge (1994), Geen (1990), Huesmann (1988), and Mischel (1973). Figure 1 presents the single-episode portion of this model. Effects of situational (e.g., violent media) and personality (e.g., trait hostility) input variables combine (sometimes interactively) to influence aggressive behavior by influencing the present internal state (cognition, affect, and arousal) and subsequent appraisal and decision processes. These main pathways are linked in Figure 1 by the bold lines with arrows. The dashed lines within the Present Internal State box indicate that these components affect each other. Because of potential arousal effects on other variables, it is important to control induced arousal when examining effects on cognition and affect. The focus of this article is lyric effects on current cognition and affect, so we do not discuss appraisal and action aspects of GAM.

According to GAM, long-term effects accrue via the development of highly accessible knowledge structures and emotional desensitization to violence by well-established social-cognitive learning and systematic desensitization processes. In brief, each media violence episode constitutes a learning trial in which one rehearses aggressive thoughts and primes aggression-related affects, creating and making chronically accessible hostile attitudes, beliefs, expectations, and scripts (Anderson & Bushman, 2002b; Anderson & Huesmann, in press.)

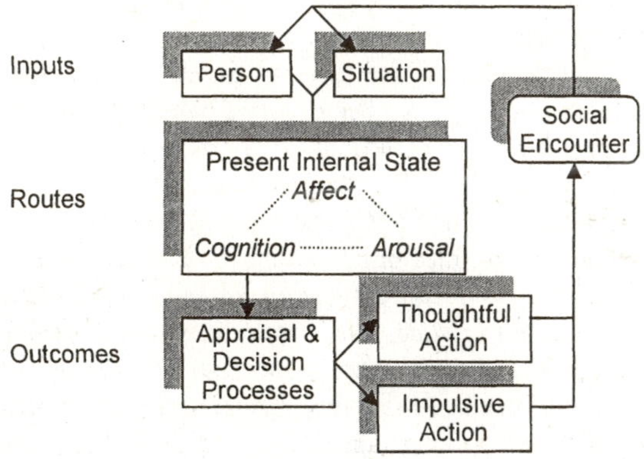

Figure 1. The general aggression model. Main pathways are linked by bold lines with arrows. Dashed lines within the Present Internal State box indicate that these components affect each other. From "Human Aggression," by C. A. Anderson & B. J. Bushman, 2002, *Annual Review of Psychology, 53,* p. 34. Copyright 2002 by Annual Reviews. Reprinted with permission.

OVERVIEW

The present studies investigated effects of violent songs on aggressive thought and affect, controlling for arousal effects by song selection and by measuring perceived arousal. We also investigated potential moderating effects of two variables: trait hostility and humorous content. Trait hostility was included for both theoretical and empirical reasons. GAM explicitly incorporates individual differences as factors important in each individual life episode and as something that develops from life experiences. Past research has demonstrated the importance of trait hostility in a variety of aggression contexts. For instance, the effects of exposure to violent movies sometimes (but not always) differ for people who score low versus high on measures of trait aggressiveness (Anderson, 1997; Bushman, 1995; Bushman & Geen, 1990). Similarly, aggressive personality has been linked to two aggression-related biases. Dill, Anderson, Anderson, and Deuser (1997) found that aggressive people are more likely to expect others to solve problems by use of aggressive behaviors (*hostile expectation bias*) and are more likely to see interpersonal interactions as aggressive encounters (*hostile perception bias*).

Humorous content was included both to test the generalizability of violent song effects and because past research suggests that humor might mitigate effects of aggression-stimulating variables (Baron, 1978; Berkowitz, 1970; Mueller & Donnerstein, 1977). Humorous (vs. nonhumorous) content may combine additively or interactively with violent (vs. nonviolent) content in their effects on subsequent aggressive thoughts and feelings. If they combine additively, then violent humorous songs should yield higher levels of aggressive affect and thought than nonviolent humorous songs but should be fairly comparable with no-song control conditions. If they combine interactively, then humorous songs should yield relatively low levels of aggressive thought and affect regardless of whether they are also violent or nonviolent.

Experiments 1 and 2 assessed effects of violent lyrics on state hostility and aggressive cognitions, respectively. Experiment 3 assessed effects of violent lyrics and trait hostility on state hostility and aggressive cognitions using a broader set of songs and a different measure of aggressive cognition. Experiments 4 and 5 examined the combined effects of violent humorous song lyrics on aggressive thought and affect and included trait hostility.

EXPERIMENT 1

Method

Participants Twenty-nine female and 30 male students from a large Midwestern university participated. About half were recruited by members of a senior psychology class as part of a class project. The rest were from the psychology participant pool in a later semester, and participated for extra credit. This experiment used a 2 (song) × 2 (sex) × 2 (participant pool) factorial design. The participant pool factor was included in the statistical analysis but had no reliable effects.

Songs We solicited suggestions from students from the same undergraduate population for pairs of contemporary rock songs that had the following characteristics. One song had to have clearly violent content, whereas the other had to have no (or minimal) violent content. Both had to be understandable, the same type (e.g., both hard rock or both soft rock), and about the same length. Finally, we wanted both songs to be by the same group. We used two songs, each about 5 min long, by the group Tool: "Jerk-Off " (violent; Tool, 1992, from the album *Opiate*) and "Four Degrees" (nonviolent; Tool, 1993, from the album *Undertow*).

Procedure After reading and signing a consent form, participants learned that the experiment involved how different songs affect performance on various tasks. They were to listen to a contemporary song, complete a couple of psychological tasks, and then answer a few questions about the song. Participants then listened to the assigned-song, completed the State Hostility Scale (SHS; Anderson et al., 1995), completed a longer unrelated task, and were debriefed.

The SHS contains 35 sentences describing current feelings (either hostile or friendly). For example, two hostile items read, "I feel like yelling at somebody" and "I feel furious." Respondents rate each sentence on a 5–point Likert-type scale (1 = *strongly disagree,* 3 = *neither agree nor disagree,* 5 = *strongly agree*). The friendly items are reverse scored. The scale typically produces internal reliability estimates in the .90–95 range, but three items ("I feel willful," "I feel tender," "I feel vexed") often show poor item-total correlations. "Willful" displayed a low item-total correlation in the present study, so we dropped it. Coefficient alpha was .96.

Results and Discussion

Sex was included in the analyses as a covariate rather than as another two-level factor.[1] The 2 (song: violent vs. nonviolent) × 2 (participant pool: volunteer vs. psychology) ANCOVA yielded two statistically reliable effects. As predicted, the violent song produced higher levels of state hostility than did the nonviolent song (*M*s = 2.60 and 2.19, respectively), $F(1, 54) = 5.97$, $MSE = 0.426$, $p < .02$. In addition, females reported higher levels of state hostility than males (*M*s = 2.62 and 2.17, respectively), $F(1, 54) = 6.71$, $MSE = 0.426$, $p < .02$.[2] This somewhat unusual finding is probably due to the fact that in our participant pool, females typically do not like hard rock music to the same extent as males.

These results indicate that the violent content of rock songs can increase feelings of hostility when compared with similar but nonviolent rock music. It is important to note that this violent lyrics effect occurred in the absence of any provocation. The low absolute level of the SHS means reflect this lack of provocation.

EXPERIMENT 2

Method

Experiment 2 was identical to Experiment 1 in all respects except that the dependent variable was a measure of aggressive cognition. Sixty-one undergraduates (30 females, 31 males) participated either as volunteers or as a part of their introductory psychology class.

The dependent variable was based on participants' ratings of a large number of word pairs from Bushman (1996). Bushman identified 10 words as clearly aggressive in meaning (*blood, butcher, choke, fight, gun, hatchet, hurt, kill, knife,* and *wound*) and 10 words as ambiguous in meaning, having both aggressive and nonaggressive meanings (*alley, animal, bottle, drugs, movie, night, police, red, rock,* and *stick*). Bushman showed that people who score high on trait hostility tended to perceive relatively greater similarity of meaning between pairs of aggressive and ambiguous words (from these two lists) than do people who score low on trait hostility.

We adapted Bushman's (1996) task in the following way. All possible pairs of these 20 words were presented to participants with instructions to rate each pair on how "similar, associated, or related" the paired words seemed to be. Ratings were made on 7-point scales anchored at 1 (*not at all similar, associated, or related*) and 7 (*extremely similar, associated, or related*). We calculated three average similarity scores for each participant: aggressive—aggressive word pairs (45), aggressive-ambiguous word pairs (100), and ambiguous-ambiguous word pairs (45). Our reasoning and predictions were quite simple. If listening to violent lyrics increases the accessibility of aggressive thoughts in semantic memory, then ambiguous words will tend to be interpreted in a relatively more aggressive way, leading to relatively higher similarity ratings of aggressive-ambiguous pairs. This same semantic priming process might also increase the perceived similarity of aggressive-aggressive pairs and of ambiguous-ambiguous pairs, but these increases should be small relative to the violent song effect on aggressive-ambiguous pairs. We used the other two word-pair types as within-subject controls. Thus, we predicted violent (vs. nonviolent) song participants to give larger similarity ratings of aggressive-ambiguous word pairs relative to their ratings of ambiguous-ambiguous and aggressive-aggressive word pairs.

Results and Discussion

We computed a contrast score reflecting the main prediction. We averaged each participant's aggressive-aggressive and ambiguous-ambiguous scores. From this control rating we then subtracted each person's aggressive-ambiguous score. On this contrast score, smaller scores indicate that the aggressive-ambiguous pairs were seen as relatively more similar (or less dissimilar) than the control-word pairs. We predicted that participants who heard the violent song would have significantly smaller contrast scores. An ANCOVA was conducted on this contrast.[3]

The 2 (song: violent vs. nonviolent) × 2 (subject pool: volunteer vs. introductory psychology) ANCOVA yielded only one reliable effect, the predicted main effect of music lyric content, $F(1, 56) = 4.24$, $MSE = 0.113$, $p < .05$. Table 1 presents the mean similarity ratings as a function of song and word-pair type.

As can be seen in Table 1, the violent song led to higher similarity ratings for aggressive-ambiguous word pairs than did the nonviolent song; the mean similarity score increased by almost half of a scale point (0.45) on a 7-point scale. The corresponding song effect on the control pairs (aggressive-aggressive and ambiguous-ambiguous) was much smaller; the mean similarity increase was just slightly more than a quarter of a scale point (0.27). As predicted, violent song participants had significantly smaller contrast scores. Figure 2 presents these results in a different way, clearly illustrating the violent-lyrics effect on aggressive cognition. In sum, hearing a violent rock song led participants to interpret the meaning of ambiguous words such as *rock* and *stick* in an aggressive way.

EXPERIMENT 3

Overview and Design

Broadening Aspects

Experiment 3 was designed to broaden our tests in three ways. First, on the basis of a pilot study, we used a larger set of 4 violent and 4 nonviolent songs. Twenty-six female and 24 male college students listened to 10 rock songs and rated how violent each was on a unidimensional scale anchored at 0 (*not at all*) and 10 (*extremely*). Two songs (with means of about 5.00), were dropped. The 4 selected nonviolent song means ranged from 2.19 to 4.11. The 4 selected violent song means ranged from 7.45 to 8.25. Each of the violent songs was rated as significantly more violent than each of the nonviolent songs, all *ps* < .0001. Participants in Experiment 3 listened to 1 of these 8 songs before completing the SHS and an aggressive thoughts accessibility measure.

Second, we examined potential moderating effects of trait hostility by including a modified version of the Caprara Irritability Scale (Anderson, 1997; Dill et al., 1997; Caprara et al., 1985). Third, we used a different procedure to measure accessibility of aggressive thoughts: Participants were timed as they read aggressive and nonaggressive words. An advantage of this reaction time task is that suspiciousness about the true purpose of the study is unlikely to influence responses (Anderson, 1997). The clear demand to read all words as quickly as possible effectively overrides any suspicion or hypothesis-related demands. One cannot intentionally speed up responses that are already given as quickly as possible. Attempts to selectively delay responses to one class of stimuli are easily detected by examining response time distributions.

Additional Controls Two other changes controlled for possible interpretational difficulties. We measured perceived arousal to check on our assumption that the violent and nonviolent songs did not differ in arousal properties. We also added a no-song control condition to assess

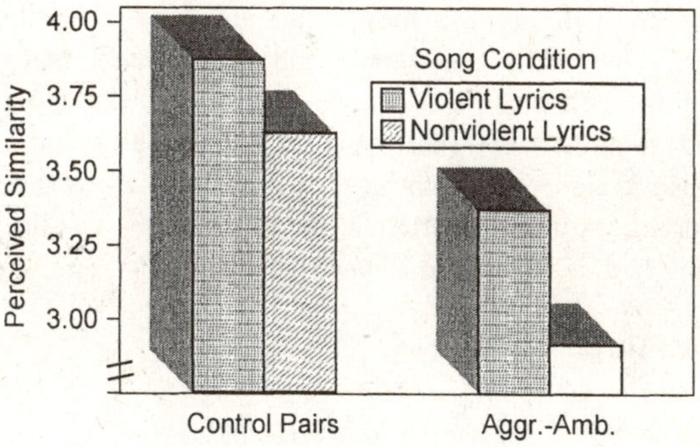

Figure 2. Perceived similarity differences between violent and nonviolent song conditions as a function of word-pair type. Aggr. = aggressive; Amb. = ambiguous.

TABLE 1
Effects of Violent Versus Nonviolent Song on Perceived Similarity of Aggressive-Aggressive (AgAg), Aggressive-Ambiguous (AgAm), and Ambiguous-Ambiguous (AmAm) Word Pairs

	Word-pair type				
Song	AgAg	AmAm	Control average: AgAg and AmAm	AgAm	Contrast: Control-Ag-Am
B	4.86	2.94	3.90	3.37	0.53
NV	4.60	2.66	3.63	2.92	0.71
V-NV diff.	0.26	0.28	0.27	0.45	0.28

Note: V = violent; NV = nonviolent; diff. = difference

whether the violent songs, the nonviolent songs, or both influenced state hostility and aggressive cognition. We expected this control condition to most closely resemble the nonviolent song condition.[4]

Finally, we counterbalanced the order in which the two dependent variables were assessed on the basis of other findings that measuring one aggression-related variable frequently changes the outcome of subsequently measured variables, a sort of *psychological uncertainty principle* (Lindsay & Anderson, 2000). Thus, the experiment used a 3 (song type) × 2 (order) × 2 (sex) factorial design with trait hostility as a continuous independent variable.

Method

Participants Eighty-three female and 79 male undergraduates at a large Midwestern university participated for class credit. Seven participants (4 females, 3 males) were dropped because they could not understand the lyrics. One additional female and 4 additional males were dropped because of procedural difficulties with the word pronunciation (WP) task. Three females and 2 males were dropped because of suspicion. There was no apparent sex or song pattern to these difficulties. The final sample had 75 female and 70 male participants.

Procedure

Preselection Because it was known that the sample size would be limited and that the power to detect a noncrossover interaction (between song condition and trait hostility) would be low, participants were preselected on trait hostility (cf. McClelland & Judd, 1993). Participants completed the Caprara Irritability Scale as part of a larger mass-testing questionnaire. Those who scored in the upper and lower quartiles were then called and signed up for participation. These pretest scores were used only to generate the list of names and phone numbers to be called and were discarded after the calling lists were generated. Thus, the experimenter was unaware of the participants' scores on this scale while calling and running experimental sessions.

General instructions After reading and signing consent forms, participants learned that they would be filling out several questionnaires, listening to a song, and doing some computer tasks. They were also told that "toward the end of the experiment you will fill out a questionnaire that will ask questions mainly about the song you listened to previously." This instruction was included to ensure that participants listened to the lyrics.

Trait hostility Next, participants completed an adaptation of the Caprara Irritability Scale (Caprara et al., 1985). The adaptation (Anderson, 1997; Dill et al., 1997) involved reverse scoring and using the 10 "friendly" filler items, along with the original 20 "irritable" items.

Songs After completing the trait hostility scale (THS), participants in the violent and nonviolent song conditions listened to one of eight songs. The four violent songs were "Shoot 'Em Up" by Cypress Hill (1991); "I Wouldn't Mind" by Suicidal Tendencies (1994); "Hit 'Em, Hard" by Run DMC (Simmons, McDaniels, Coward, Criss, & Gist, 1993); and "Jerk–Off" by Tool (1992). The four nonviolent songs were "Live at PJ's" by the Beastie Boys (1992); "Love vs. Loneliness" by Suicidal Tendencies (1994); "In the House" by Run DMC (Simmons, McDaniels, & Phillips, 1993); and "Finger Lickin' Good" by the Beastie Boys (1992). Participants then completed the dependent variables. Participants in the no-song condition went directly from the THS to the dependent variables.

State hostility The SHS was the same one described earlier. Preliminary analyses revealed that two items did not correlate well with the remaining 33 (*willful, tender*); they were dropped from subsequent analyses. Coefficient alpha was .96.

Word pronunciation This task involves reading words out loud as they appear on a computer screen, one per trial. A sound-activated voice key measures the latency between the word presentation and the point in time that participants name the word. The task was created in HyperCard 2.1 (Apple Computer, 1987–1999); the timer was triggered by a MacRecorder on a Macintosh computer. Ninety-six words were presented twice, a total of 192 trials. A different random order was used for each participant. The word list consisted of 24 aggressive words (e.g., *assault, choke*), 24 escape words (e.g., *abandon, desert*), 24 anxiety words (e.g., *insecure, foolish*), and 24 control words (e.g., *behold, listen*). The anxiety and escape words were also considered control words on the basis of previous studies (e.g., Anderson, 1997).

Other questionnaires After completing the second dependent variable, participants in the song conditions filled out two questionnaires designed to measure perceptions of how aroused or energized they were and their reactions to the song. Participants in the control condition, who had not yet heard any song, listened to a randomly selected nonviolent song before completing these two questionnaires.

The Perceived Arousal Scale (PAS: Anderson et al., 1995, 1996) contains 31 adjectives describing feelings of arousal (e.g., *energetic*) or lack of arousal (e.g., *listless*). Participants' ratings were based on how they felt "at the present moment" using 5-point Likert-type scales (1 = *very slightly or not at all,* 3 = *moderately*, 5 = *extremely*). The lack-of-arousal items are reverse scored. One item (*agitated*) displayed a low item-total correlation and was dropped. Coefficient alpha was .95.

On the Music Questionnaire participants rated how understandable and familiar the lyrics were using 11-point scales (0 = *not at all,* 5 = *moderately,* 10 = *perfectly*). They also indicated how much they thought about the purpose of the study as opposed to the tasks themselves (0 = *thought mostly about the purpose,* 3 = *thought equally about the purpose and the tasks,* 5 = *thought mostly about the tasks themselves*). The Music Questionnaire concluded with items designed to assess suspicion, focus of attention, and perceptions regarding effects of the song on later responses.

Results and Discussion

As in Experiments 1 and 2, sex was included as a covariate in all analyses. Task order was included as a factor because prior work has suggested that the priming effects tend to wear off fairly quickly, especially on state hostility. None of the task order effects were significant, but the state hostility results appeared somewhat different depending on task order, as is shown in a subsequent section.

Preliminary Analyses We first examined results from the PAS to see if the selected violent and nonviolent rock songs had similar arousal properties. The main effect of type of song did not approach significance, $F(1, 140) = 1.31$, $p > .25$. Thus, violent-lyric effects on other variables cannot be attributed to arousal differences. The only reliable effect on PAS was a negative relation to trait hostility, $F(1, 140) = 16.65$, $MSE = 0.512$, $p < .001$.

We next examined the Music Questionnaire ratings (understandability, familiarity, purpose, accuracy of suspicions, and estimated song influence on PAS, SHS, and WP). The two song conditions (violent vs. nonviolent) did not differ reliably on any of these variables ($ps > .20$).

Interestingly, there was one reliable sex effect and three reliable trait hostility effects on these Music Questionnaire items. Males ($M = 5.80$) rated the lyrics as more understandable than did females ($M = 4.90$), $F(1, 140) = 6.77$, $MSE = 4.900$, $p < .02$. Trait hostility was positively related to beliefs that the song influenced performance on PAS and on SHS, $Fs(1, 140) = 4.36$ and 4.34, $MSEs = 0.900$ and 0.987, $ps < .05$. Also, trait hostility was positively related to familiarity, $F(1, 140) = 4.78$, $p < .04$.

Trait hostility did not interact with the song manipulation in any of the analyses, so this interaction term was dropped from the statistical model. We then compared the control (no-song) and the nonviolent song conditions on WP and SHS. As expected, there were no reliable differences between these two conditions ($ps > .25$), so these conditions were combined into one larger nonviolent condition for all subsequent analyses.[5]

Main Analyses

State hostility Analyses ignoring task order yielded only a significant effect of trait hostility ($b = .21$), $F(1, 141) = 11.15$, $MSE = 0.411$, $p < .005$. Individuals who scored high on trait hostility tended to score high on state hostility. The violent song effect was in the predicted direction, with those who heard a violent song reporting higher levels of SHS ($Ms = 2.14$ and 1.98), but was not significant, $F(1, 141) = 2.02$, $p < .16$.

The lack of a reliable effect of song content on state hostility might appear to conflict with the results of Experiment 1. However, in Experiment 1 the SHS was administered immediately after the song. We therefore reanalyzed Experiment 3 SHS scores using only the 71 participants who completed the SHS first, even though the Task Order × Song Content interaction was not statistically reliable, $F(1, 139) = 2.20$, $p < .15$. Those who heard a violent song had significantly higher SHS scores ($M = 2.23$) than those who did not hear a violent song ($M = 1.92$), $F(1, 67) = 4.49$, $MSE = 0.378$, $p < .04$. Thus, it appears that the effect of listening to violent songs on state hostility is reliable, but it can be disrupted fairly easily by other intervening activities. SHS scores of participants who did the WP task first did not differ as a function of song condition, $F(1, 70) = 0$, *ns* ($Ms = 2.01$ and 2.06), in the violent song and nonviolent conditions.

Word pronunciation Preliminary analyses compared average reaction times to the three nonaggressive word types—anxiety, escape, and control words. As anticipated, there were no effects of sex, song, or trait hostility on these three word types (all *ps* > .10). Thus, they were averaged to form a nonaggressive word type. For the main analyses we subtracted average reaction time to aggressive words from the average reaction time to nonaggressive words. This WP measure is positive when aggressive words are more accessible than nonaggressive words; negative scores indicate the opposite.

As predicted, violent songs increased the relative accessibility of aggressive words. Those who listened to a violent song had larger WP scores (M = 11.1 ms) than those who had not listened to a violent song (M = 4.3 ms), $F(1, 141) = 3.91$, $MSE = 0.399$, $p = .05$. In addition, males produced higher WP scores than females (Ms = 13.6 and 1.7 ms, respectively), $F(1, 141) = 12.91$, $MSE = 0.399$, $p < .001$. Trait hostility was not systematically related to WP ($F < 1$).

Experiment 4

Overview and Design

Experiment 4 further tested the generality of the violent song effect on aggressive thoughts and feelings by using humorous songs and including trait hostility. A humorous violent song is likely to have two competing processes at work. The violent content may well prime aggressive thoughts and negative feelings. At the same time, the humorous content may produce positive feelings. If so, participants who hear the violent humorous song may well respond very much like no-song control participants, because these competing processes cancel each other out, especially for affective measures. A humorous nonviolent song does not have this competition problem. Only the positive aspects of the humorous content are at work. In other words, if humor and violent content combine additively, nonviolent humorous songs will yield levels of aggressive affect and thought that are significantly lower than levels obtained from violent humorous and no-song control conditions.

The experiment used a 3 (song) × 2 (order) × 2 (sex) factorial design, with trait hostility as a continuous variable. Participants were randomly assigned to hear either the violent humorous song, the nonviolent humorous song, or no song.[6] Half of the participants completed the SHS first, whereas the other half completed it after a cognitive task. A different measure of aggressive thought accessibility was used in this study, a word completion (WC) task. Finally, participants completed the PAS and the Music Questionnaire, as in Experiment 3.

Method

Participants Sixty-five female and 74 male students from a large Midwestern university successfully completed all portions of the experiment.

Dependent Variables The SHS, PAS, and Music Questionnaire were the same as in Experiment 3. Accessibility of aggressive thoughts was based on a WC task consisting of a list of 98 word fragments (Anderson, Flanagan, Carnagey, Benjamin, Eubanks, & Valentine, 2002). The respondent's task is to fill in the missing letters in order to form a word. Half of the fragments can be completed to form either aggressive or nonaggressive words (e.g., "h—t" can become *hit* or *hat*). Tasks similar to this have often been used as measures of implicit memory (e.g., Roediger, Weldon, Stadler, & Reigler, 1992). Accessibility of aggressive thoughts was the proportion of word completions that were aggressive.

Procedure After reading and signing a consent form, participants learned that the experiment was designed to see how songs affect thoughts and emotions. They then completed the measure of trait hostility. Next, participants either listened to one of the humorous songs (violent or nonviolent) or they continued directly to the dependent measures (no-song control). The songs were "A Boy Named Sue" (violent) by Johnny Cash (Silverstein, 1994) and "Hello Mudduh, Hello Fadduh!" (nonviolent) by Allan Sherman (1991). Next, participants completed the SHS and the WC task. Participants in the two song conditions then completed the Music Questionnaire. Those in the control condition listened to the nonviolent song and then completed the Music Questionnaire.

Results and Discussion

Preliminary Analyses Once again, sex and trait hostility were treated as covariates. One item was dropped from the PAS because of a low item-total correlation, leaving 30 items for the final scale. Coefficient alpha was .94. Final analyses on perceived arousal yielded only a main effect of sex, $F(1, 134) = 6.48$, $MSE = 0.452$, $p < .02$. Males scored higher than females on this measure (Ms = 3.35 and 3.05, respectively). The main effects of song, $F(2, 134) < 1.0$, and trait hostility, $F(1, 134) = 1.92$, $p > .15$, were both nonsignificant. Thus, any song or trait hostility effects on SHS or WC cannot be attributed to differences in arousal.

State Hostility One item was dropped from SHS because of low item-total correlations. Coefficient alpha was .94. The final analysis yielded significant main effects of trait hostility, (b = .27), $F(1, 134) = 34.24$, $MSE = 0.209$, $p < .0001$, and song, $F(2, 134) = 3.58$, $p < .05$. As predicted by an additive model of humor and violent content effects, the no-song control group (M = 1.97) and the humorous violent song group (M = 1.90), had essentially the same levels of SHS, $F(1, 134) = 0.55$. The violent (M = 1.90) and nonviolent (M = 1.72) song conditions were marginally different, $F(1, 134) = 3.52$, $p < .07$. Most important, as predicted by the additive model, the humorous nonviolent song group had significantly lower SHS scores than the average of humorous violent song and control groups, $F(1, 134) = 6.55$, $p < .02$.

Participants The Song × Task Order interaction was not significant ($F < 1$). Nonetheless, as before, we separately examined the SHS scores of the 70 participants who completed that scale first. The results were essentially the same as with the whole sample, except that the control mean was slightly smaller (instead of larger) than the humorous violent mean (Ms = 1.96 and 1.98, respectively). Once again there was a significant effect of trait hostility (b = .26), $F(1, 65) = 20.85$, $MSE = 0.205$, $p < .0001$. The violent (M = 1.98) and nonviolent (M = 1.75) song conditions were marginally different, $F(1, 65) = 3.44$, $p < .07$. The humorous nonviolent song condition produced a lower level of SHS than the average of the other two conditions, $F(1, 65) = 3.86$, $p < .06$.

Word Completions The final analysis yielded main effects of trait hostility and song condition. Trait hostility was positively related to WC (b = .011), $F(1, 134) = 4.21$, $MSE = 0.0029$, $p < .05$. The highest mean for proportions of aggressive WCs was in the humorous violent song condition (M = .229) and the lowest in the humorous nonviolent song condition (M = .200); the control group mean fell in between (M = .218), $F(2, 134) = 3.26$, $p < .05$. The humorous violent song yielded significantly higher WC scores than the humorous nonviolent song, $F(1, 134) = 6.46$, $p < .02$.

In summary, these results suggest that humorous and violent content essentially canceled each other out in terms of effects on state hostility but did not entirely do so for aggressive cognitions. Another way of summarizing these results is that the effects of violent lyrics on aggressive affect and cognition appear to apply to humorous songs as well as to more standard forms of popular music.

EXPERIMENT 5

Overview and Design

Experiment 5 further replicated Experiments 1–4. It tested the effects of violent lyrics and trait hostility on state hostility and aggressive cognition with both humorous and nonhumorous songs. The design was a 2 (violent or nonviolent music lyrics) × 2 (humorous or nonhumorous lyrics) factorial, with a no-song condition and trait hostility as a continuous independent variable. Different songs were used in Experiment 5 to further test generality.

Method

Eighty-two female and 69 male students at a large Midwestern university participated for partial course credit. One participant was dropped from all analyses because he failed to comply with experimental instructions. Aggressive cognition data from 1 male and 1 female were dropped because of procedural problems.

Procedure After reading and signing consent forms, participants learned that the experiment was investigating effects of music on mood. They were told that they would respond to a questionnaire (trait hostility), listen to a song, and then respond to two more questionnaires. To ensure that participants listened to the lyrics of the song, they were told that they would be asked questions about the song later in the experiment.

The trait hostility and SHS measures from Experiments 1–4 were used again. Coefficient alpha for trait hostility was .85. One SHS item, "I feel willful," had a low correlation with the other items and was dropped. Coefficient alpha was .96. The WC task from Experiment 4 assessed accessibility of aggressive thoughts.

The two humorous songs were "The Night Santa Went Crazy" (violent; Yankovic, 1996), and "Gump" (nonviolent; Yankovic, 1996) by Weird Al Yankovic. The two nonhumorous songs were "Country Death Song" (violent; Violent Femmes, 2000) and "I Held Her in My Arms" (nonviolent; Violent Femmes, 1986) by the Violent Femmes.

Participants in the no-song control condition went directly from the THS to the dependent variables. Half of the participants completed SHS first, whereas the other half first performed the WC task.

Results and Discussion

Analysis Strategy Sex and trait hostility were again treated as covariates. Preliminary analyses revealed no reliable effects of task order.

State Hostility For the total sample, there were significant main effects on SHS of music condition, F (4, 143) = 2.96, MSE = 0.361, $p < .03$, and trait hostility (b = .279), F (1, 143) = 15.45, $p < .0001$. The sex effect did not approach significance ($F < 1.0$). The two violent song conditions yielded significantly higher SHS scores than did the two nonviolent song conditions (*M*s = 2.95 and 2.72, respectively), $F(1, 143) = 4.88$, $p < .03$.

However, as in Experiment 3, the SHS effects were clearer for participants who completed that scale first. Figure 3 displays the means for the five conditions. For these 83 participants, contrasts examining the 2 (violent vs. nonviolent lyrics) × 2 (humorous vs. nonhumorous lyrics) conditions yielded a significant main effect of violent content, $F(1, 76) = 4.28$, $MSE = 0.387$, $p < .05$, and a marginally significant main effect of humorous content, $F(1, 76) = 2.97$, $p < .09$. Participants in the violent song conditions had higher SHS scores than those in the nonviolent song conditions (*M*s = 3.00 and 2.68, respectively). Those in the humorous song conditions had slightly lower state hostility scores than those in the nonhumorous conditions (*M*s = 2.71 and 2.98, respectively). The Humor × Violence interaction did not approach significance ($F < 1.0$).

As in Experiment 4, the least hostility was expressed by those who had just heard a song with nonviolent humorous lyrics ($M = 2.53$). Somewhat different from Experiment 4 was the finding that the no-song control mean ($M = 2.62$) was closer to the humorous nonviolent song than to the humorous violent song mean ($M = 2.89$).

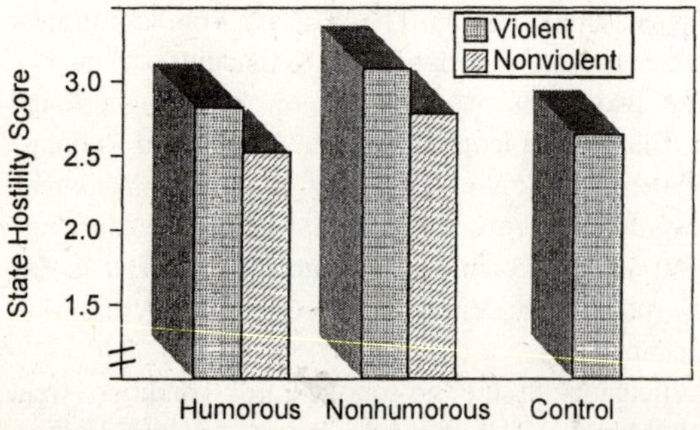

Figure 3. State hostility scores as a function of humorous and violent lyric content, Experiment 5.

The two conditions expected to yield the largest and smallest means—violent nonhumorous versus nonviolent humorous—did exactly that, and differed significantly (*M*s = 3.11 and 2.53, respectively), $F(1, 76) = 6.42$, $p < .02$. Trait hostility was also significantly related to SHS ($b = .288$), $F(1, 76) = 8.86$, $p < .01$. The sex effect was not significant, $F(1, 76) = 2.36$, $p > .12$.

Word Completions We computed the same proportion of aggressive WC scores as in Experiment 4. Males generated higher WC scores than females (*M*s = .291 and .220, respectively), $F(1, 141) = 15.00$, $MSE = 0.0117$, $p < .001$. Contrasts examining the 2 (violent vs. nonviolent lyrics) × 2 (humorous vs. nonhumorous lyrics) conditions yielded a significant main effect of violent content, $F(1, 141) = 6.16$, $p < .02$. Those who had listened to a violent song had higher WC scores than those who had heard a nonviolent song (*M*s = .279 and .228, respectively), mirroring the violent lyrics effect of Experiment 4. The no-song control condition yielded WC scores in between the violent and nonviolent conditions ($M = .268$), somewhat closer to the violent condition. This also mirrors the results of Experiment 4. Neither the humor main effect nor the Violence × Humor interaction approached significance (*F*s < 1.0).

Pooled Results To ensure an accurate summary of these five experiments, we pooled the violent (vs. nonviolent) song effects on aggressive affect and thought using meta-analytic techniques. We calculated the average $d+$ by dividing the difference between the relevant adjusted means by the pooled standard deviation.

Four experiments provided five independent tests of violent versus nonviolent lyrics on state hostility (one each from Experiments 1, 3, and 4; two from Experiment 5). As can be seen in the first three bars in Figure 4, violent lyrics increased state hostility overall ($d+ = .55$, $K = 5$, $N = 242$) as well as within nonhumorous ($d+ = .55$, $K = 3$, $N = 161$) and humorous ($d+ = .57$, $K = 2$, $N = 81$) conditions. The five independent effects on aggressive thoughts (one each from Experiments 2–4; two from Experiment 5) similarly yielded a significant effect overall ($d+ = .44$, $K = 5$, $N = 450$) as well as within nonhumorous ($d+ = .43$, $K = 3$, $N = 283$) and humorous ($d+ = .46$, $K = 2$, $N = 167$) conditions.

GENERAL DISCUSSION

Empirical Contributions

Two potentially problematic issues in music lyric research both revolve around the possibility that the comparison violent and nonviolent songs differ in ways that artifactually produce (or mask) differences in aggression-related dependent variables. In the present case, the two issues concern whether the obtained violent versus nonviolent song results were actually due to (a) systematic differences in the music itself rather than the lyrics or (b) differences in arousal properties. Across the five experiments, music characteristics of comparison songs were controlled in several different ways. In Experiments 1, 2, and 5, the violent and nonviolent songs were matched by the artists and were in much the same style. Furthermore, multiple violent and nonviolent songs were used in Experiments 3 and 5. Arousal was assessed and ruled out as a factor in Experiments 3 and 4. Across studies there were seven violent songs by seven artists and eight nonviolent songs by seven artists. The consistent results from these five experiments provide strong evidence that songs with violent lyrics increase aggression-related cognition and affect and that this effect is the result of the violence in the lyrics. It is not an artifact of confounded musical style, specific performing artist, or arousal.

The increase in aggressive thoughts was shown in three different ways. Violent songs led to more aggressive interpretations of ambiguously aggressive words (Experiment 2), increased the relative speed with which people read aggressive (vs. nonaggressive) words (Experiment 3), and increased the proportion of aggressive word completions (Experiments 4 and 5).

We used the same measure of aggressive feelings across studies because it and scales like it have been widely used and validated by numerous researchers. In Experiments 1, 3, 4, and 5, violent songs increased feelings of hostility, relative to appropriate nonviolent songs, in the absence of provocation or threat. These effects occurred across a variety of both humorous and nonhumorous songs and were not attributable to differences in arousal.

Furthermore, supplemental analyses revealed that the violent song effects did not interact with trait hostility in the three experiments that assessed this factor or with gender in any of the experiments. In sum, the consistency

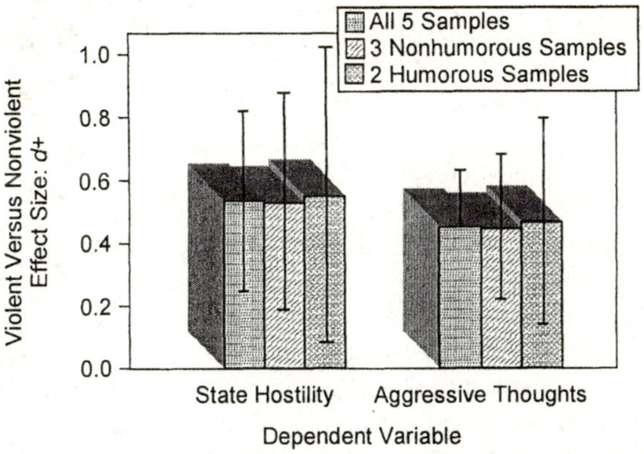

Figure 4. Pooled violent versus nonviolent lyric effect-sizes ($d+$) and 95% confidence intervals on state hostility and aggressive thoughts: All samples versus three nonhumorous samples versus two humorous samples. For state hostility, only the results from participants who completed the SHS first are included; *ns* = 242, 161, and 81. For aggressive thoughts, *ns* = 450, 283, and 167. Error bars represent 95% confidence intervals.

of results across songs, musical genre, artist, research method, trait hostility, and gender attests to the validity and generality of the obtained effects, as do the pooled results in Figure 4.

Implications for Violence

Our focus was on precursors to aggression, as outlined by GAM, rather than on aggressive behavior itself. The main reason for this focus was to allow in-depth testing and analysis of these critical precursors to aggression. These results support GAM-based predictions of how exposure to media violence influences present internal affective and cognitive states. Research on potential violent song effects on aggressive behavior becomes even more important now that we have clearly demonstrated that such songs increase aggressive thoughts and feelings.

GAM illustrates how exposure to media violence can produce both short- and long-term increases in aggressive behavior. In both contexts, violent lyrics most likely operate through both the affect and cognition routes, influencing appraisals of the situation and emotional state and (eventually) the behavioral decision.

Short-Term Effects: Priming Versus Venting

In the immediate situation, exposure to violent lyrics increases the accessibility of aggressive thoughts and affect. These results confirm GAM and the social-cognitive theories on which it is based in demonstrating priminglike effects and therefore add to the research literature contradicting popular notions of positive catharsis or venting effects on aggressive thoughts and feelings (Bushman, 2002; Bushman et al., 1999).

The violent-song-inspired increases in aggressive thoughts and feelings can influence perceptions of ongoing social interactions, coloring them with an aggressive tint. Such aggression-biased interpretations can, in turn, instigate a more aggressive response (verbal or physical) than would have been emitted in a nonbiased state, thus provoking an aggressive escalatory spiral of antisocial exchanges. In sum, listening to angry, violent music does not appear to provide the kind of cathartic release that the general public and some professional and pop psychologists believe.

Long-Term Effects

Direct effects Long-term effects operate in much the same manner, except that the proximate source of the high accessibility of aggressive cognitions and affects is the chronic state of the individual rather than a very recently heard violent song. Repeated exposure to violent lyrics may contribute to the development of an aggressive personality (Anderson & Bushman, 2002b; Anderson & Huesmann, in press), as is true for long-term TV violence effects (e.g., Eron, 1982; Huesmann, 1988; Huesmann & Guerra, 1997; Huesmann & Miller, 1994).

Indirect effects There may also be an indirect contribution, just as has been found in the TV literature. Specifically, short-term increases in aggression due to violent lyrics affect the person's social environment as well as the person. Close others (friends, family, peers, teachers) are influenced by these initially temporary increases in aggression and naturally respond to them in a negative way. Over time, these relationships deteriorate, and acquaintances begin to expect aggressive and conflictual interactions with the person and will therefore elicit further aggressive behaviors via well-established expectancy effects. In other words, repeated short-term media violence effects (lyrics, TV, movies, video games) can indirectly create a more hostile social environment, which further promotes the development of chronic hostility biases in the person's internal makeup—their perceptual and social scripts and schemata and related knowledge structures—in short, their personality.

Balance

Of course, there is reason to believe that this type of hostile thought and affect priming by violent songs may last only a fairly short time. Presumably, if the next song heard is nonviolent or if some other nonviolent event occurs, the short-term priming effects of violent lyrics will dissipate. This would seem especially likely if some positive event occurs. Furthermore, as noted earlier, lyrics are often secondary to the music itself, so much so that some violent songs have lyrics that are undecipherable.

At present, research on the effects of violent lyrics is in its infancy. There are now good theoretical and empirical reasons to expect effects of music lyrics on aggressive behavior to be similar to the well-studied effects of exposure to TV and movie violence and the more recent research efforts on violent video games. Additional research on music lyric effects is clearly needed, both short-term and longitudinal studies. GAM provides a useful framework for understanding the current studies and for guiding such future research.

REFERENCES

Anderson, C. A. (1997). Effects of violent movies and trait irritability on hostile feelings and aggressive thoughts. *Aggressive Behavior, 23,* 161–178.

Anderson, C. A., Anderson, K. B., & Deuser, W. E. (1996). Examining an affective aggression framework: Weapon and temperature effects on aggressive thoughts, affect, and attitudes. *Personality and Social Psychology Bulletin, 22,* 366–376.

Anderson, C. A., Benjamin, A. J., & Bartholow, B. D. (1998). Does the gun pull the trigger? Automatic priming effects of weapon pictures and weapon names. *Psychological Science, 9,* 308–314.

Anderson, C. A., & Bushman, B. J. (2001). Effects of violent video games on aggressive behavior, aggressive cognition, aggressive affect, physiological arousal, and prosocial behavior: A meta-analytic review of the scientific literature. *Psychological Science, 12,* 353–359.

Anderson, C. A., & Bushman, B. J. (2002a, March 29). The effects of media violence on society. *Science, 295,* 2377–2378.

Anderson, C. A., & Bushman, B. J. (2002b). Human aggression. *Annual Review of Psychology, 53,* 27–51.

Anderson, C. A., Deuser, W. E., & DeNeve, K. M. (1995). Hot temperatures, hostile affect, hostile cognition, and arousal: Tests of a general model of affective aggression. *Personality and Social Psychology Bulletin, 21,* 434–448.

Anderson, C. A., & Dill, K. E. (2000). Video games and aggressive thoughts, feelings, and behavior in the laboratory and in life. *Journal of Personality and Social Psychology, 78,* 772–790.

Anderson, C. A., Flanagan, M., Carnagey, N. L., Benjamin, A. J., Eubanks, J., & Valentine, J. C. (2002). *Specific effects of violent video game content on aggressive thoughts and behavior.* Manuscript submitted for publication.

Anderson, C. A., & Huesmann, L. R. (in press). Human aggression: A social-cognitive view. In M. A. Hogg & J. Cooper (Eds.), *Handbook of social psychology.*

Apple Computer. (1987–1999). *HyperCard 2.1.* Cupertino, CA: Author.

Ballard, M. E., & Coates, S. (1995). The immediate effects of homicidal, suicidal, and nonviolent heavy metal and rap songs on the moods of college students. *Youth and Society, 27,* 148–168.

Bandura, A. (1986). *Social foundations of thought and action: A social cognitive theory.* Englewood Cliffs, NJ: Prentice Hall.

Bargh, J. A., Chen, M., & Burrows, L. (1996). Automaticity of social behavior: Direct effects of trait construct and stereotype activation on action. *Journal of Personality and Social Psychology, 71,* 230–244.

Bargh, J. A., & Pietromonaco, P. (1982). Automatic information processing and social perception: The influence of trait information presented outside of conscious awareness on impression formation. *Journal of Personality and Social Psychology, 43,* 437–449.

Baron, R. A. (1978). Aggression-inhibiting influence of sexual humor. *Journal of Personality and Social Psychology, 36,* 189–197.

Barongan, C., & Hall, G. C. (1995). The influence of misogynous rap music on sexual aggression against women. *Psychology of Women Quarterly, 19,* 195–207.

Beastie, Boys. (1992). Finger lickin' good. On *In your head* [CD]. Nashville, TN: Capitol.

Beastie Boys. (1992). Live at PJ's. On *In your head* [CD]. Nashville, TN: Capitol.

Berkowitz, L. (1970). Aggressive humor as a stimulus to aggressive responses. *Journal of Personality and Social Psychology, 4,* 710–717.

Berkowitz, L. (1993). *Aggression: Its causes, consequences, and control.* New York: McGraw–Hill.

Breuer, J., & Freud, S. (1955). *Studies in hysteria* (Vol. 2, A. A. Brill, Trans.). London: Hogarth. (Original work published 1893–1895)

Bushman, B. J. (1995). Moderating role of trait aggressiveness in the effects of violent media on aggression. *Journal of Personality and Social Psychology, 69,* 950–960.

Bushman, B. J. (1996). Individual differences in the extent and development of aggressive cognitive-associative networks. *Personality and Social Psychology Bulletin, 22,* 811–819.

Bushman, B. J. (2002). Does venting anger feed or extinguish the flame? Catharsis, rumination, distraction, anger, and aggressive responding. *Personality and Social Psychology Bulletin, 28,* 724–731.

Bushman, B. J., & Anderson, C. A. (2001). Media violence and the American public: Scientific facts versus media misinformation. *American Psychologist, 56,* 477–489.

Bushman, B. J., Baumeister, R. F., & Stack, A. D. (1999). Catharsis, aggression, and persuasive influence: Self-fulfilling or self-defeating prophecies? *Journal of Personality and Social Psychology, 76,* 367–376.

Bushman, B. J., & Geen, R. G. (1990). Role of cognitive-emotional mediators and individual differences in the effects of media violence on aggression. *Journal of Personality and Social Psychology, 58,* 156–163.

Caprara, G. V., Cinanni, V., D'Imperio, G., Passerini, S., Renzi, P., & Travablia, G. (1985). Indicators of impulsive aggression: Present status of research on irritability and emotional susceptibility scales. *Personality and Individual Differences, 6,* 665–674.

Crick, N. R., & Dodge, K. A. (1994). A review and reformulation of social information processing mechanisms in children's adjustment. *Psychological Bulletin, 115,* 74–101.

Cypress Hill. (1991). Shoot'em up. On *Juice* (Original Soundtrack) [CD]. New York: MCA.

Dill, K. E., Anderson, C. A., Anderson, K. B., & Deuser, W. E. (1997). Effects of aggressive personality on social expectations and social perceptions. *Journal of Research in Personality, 31,* 272–292.

Eron, L. D. (1982): Parent-child interaction, television violence, and aggression of children. *American Psychologist, 37,* 197–211.

Geen, R. G. (1990). *Human aggression.* Pacific Grove, CA: Brooks/Cole.

Hansen, C. H. (1989). Priming sex-role stereotypic event schemas with rock music videos: Effects on impression favorability, trait inferences, and recall of subsequent male-female interaction. *Basic and Applied Social Psychology, 10,* 371–391.

Hansen, C. H., & Hansen, R. D. (1988). How rock music videos can change what is seen when boy meets girl: Priming stereotypic appraisal of social interactions. *Sex Roles, 19,* 287–316.

Hansen, C. H., & Hansen, R. D. (1990). Rock music videos and antisocial behavior. *Basic and Applied Social Psychology, 11,* 357–369.

Hansen, C. H., & Hansen, R. D. (1991). Schematic information processing of heavy metal lyrics. *Communication Research, 18,* 373–411.

Huesmann, L. R. (1988). An information-processing model for the development of aggression. *Aggressive Behavior, 14,* 13–24.

Huesmann, L. R., & Guerra, N. G. (1997). Children's normative beliefs about aggression and aggressive behavior. *Journal of Personality and Social Psychology, 72,* 408–419.

Huesmann, L. R., & Miller, L. S. (1994). Long-term effects of repeated exposure to media violence in childhood. In L. R. Huesmann (Ed.), *Aggressive behavior: Current perspectives* (pp. 153–186). New York: Plenum Press.

Johnson, J. D., Adams, M. S., Ashburn, L., & Reed, W. (1995). Differential gender effects on African American adolescents' acceptance of teen dating violence. *Sex Roles, 33,* 597–605.

Johnson, J. D., Jackson, L. A., & Gatto, L. (1995). Violent attitudes and deferred academic aspirations: Deleterious effects of exposure to rap music. *Basic and Applied Social Psychology, 16,* 27–41.

Lindsay, J. J., & Anderson, C. A. (2000). From antecedent conditions to violent actions: A general affective aggression model. *Personality and Social Psychology Bulletin, 26,* 533–547.

Marsh, D. (1993). *Louie Louie.* New York: Hyperion.

McClelland, G. H., & Judd, C. M. (1993). Statistical difficulties of detecting interactions and moderator effects. *Psychological Bulletin, 114,* 376–390.

McFarland, R. A. (1984). Effects of music upon emotional content of TAT stories. *Journal of Psychology, 116,* 227–234.

Mischel, W. (1973). Toward a cognitive social learning reconceptualization of personality. *Psychological Review, 80,* 252–283.

Mueller, C., & Donnerstein, E. (1977). The effects of humor-induced arousal upon aggressive behavior. *Journal of Research in Personality, 11,* 73–82.

Peterson, D. L., & Pfost, K. S. (1989). Influence of rock videos on attitudes of violence against women. *Psychological Reports, 64,* 319–322.

Roberts, D. F., Christenson, P. G., & Gentile, D. A. (in press). In D. Gentile (Ed.), *Media violence and children.* Westport, CT: Ablex Publishing.

Roediger, H. L., Weldon, M. S., Stadler, M. L., & Riegler, G. L. (1992). Direct comparison of two implicit memory tests: Word fragment and word stem completion. *Journal of Experimental Psychology: Learning, Memory, and Cognition, 18,* 1251–1269.

Rubin, A. M., West, D. V., & Mitchell, W. S. (2001). Differences in aggression, attitudes towards women, and distrust as reflected in popular music preferences. *Media Psychology, 3,* 25–42.

Sherman, A. (1991). Hello mudduh, hello fadduh! (A letter from camp). On *Dr. Demento 20th anniversary collection, disc one* [CD]. Santa Monica, CA: Rhino Records.

Simmons, J., McDaniels, D., Coward, R., Criss, A., & Gist, K. (1993). Hit 'em hard [Recorded by Run DMC]. On *down with the king* [CD]. New York: Profile Records.

Simmons, J., McDaniels, D., & Phillips, P. (1993). In the house [Recorded by Run DMC]. On *down with the king* [CD]. New York: Profile Records.

Silverstein, S. (1994). A boy named Sue [Recorded by Johnny Cash]. On *Johnny Cash super hits* [CD]. New York: Columbia Records.

St. Lawrence, J. S., & Joyner, D. J. (1991). The effects of sexually violent rock music on males' acceptance of violence against women. *Psychology of Women Quarterly, 15,* 49–63.

Suicidal Tendencies. (1994). I wouldn't mind. On *Suicidal for life.* [CD]. New York: Sony.

Suicidal Tendencies. (1994). Love vs. loneliness. On *Suicidal for life* [CD]. New York: Sony.

Took, K. J., & Weiss, D. S. (1994). The relationship between heavy metal and rap music and adolescent turmoil: Real or artifact? *Adolescence, 29,* 613–621.

Tool. (1992). Jerk-off. On *Opiate* [CD]. New York: BMG Music.

Tool. (1993). Four degrees. On *Undertow* [CD]. New York: Vo1cano Recordings/BMG.

Violent Femmes. (1990). I held her in my arms. On *The blind leading the naked* [CD]. New York: Warner Brothers.

Violent Femmes. (2000). Country death song. On *Hallowed ground* [CD]. Santa Monica, CA: Rhino Records.

Waite, B. M., Hillbrand, M., & Foster, H. G. (1992). Reduction of aggressive behavior after removal of Music Television. *Hospital and Community Psychiatry, 43,* 173–175.

Wanamaker, C. E., & Reznikoff, M. (1989). The effects of aggressive and nonaggressive rock songs on projective and structured tests. *The Journal of Psychology, 123,* 561–570.

Wester, S. R., Crown, C. L., Quatman, G. L., & Heesacker, M. (1997). The influence of sexually violent rap music on attitudes of men with little prior exposure. *Psychology of Women Quarterly, 21,* 497–508.

Yankovic, A. (1996). Gump. On *Bad hair day* [CD]. Santa Monica, CA: All American Music Group.

Yankovic, A. (1996). The night Santa went crazy. On *Bad hair day* [CD]. Santa Monica, CA: All American Music Group.

Received July 11, 2002
Revision received December 5, 2002
Accepted December 15, 2002

NOTES

1. Nonetheless, for all studies, preliminary analyses explored the possibility of sex interactions. There were none, thereby satisfying the homogeneity of slopes assumption of analysis of covariance (ANCOVA).
2. Unless otherwise indicated, reported means for all experiments are the appropriate least squares adjusted means, adjusted for other factors in the model such as sex and trait hostility. Significance levels are based on two-tailed tests.
3. The astute reader will realize that each effect in this between-subjects analysis of variance is identical to the interaction of that effect with the repeated-measures factor control versus aggressive-ambiguous.
4. Participants in the no-song control group actually heard a nonviolent song after they had completed all dependent variables except for the Music Questionnaire. This was done so that all groups would have the same cover story and the same debriefing.
5. For SHS, means for the control, nonviolent, and violent song conditions were 1.98, 1.98, and 2.14, respectively. For word pronunciation, corresponding means were 1.35, 5.93, and 11.08. Reported analyses simply treated all participants who heard a nonviolent song and those who completed the main dependent variables prior to hearing a song as if they were in one larger group. An alternative procedure for combining different conditions is to use equal contrast weights. Results were stronger with the contrast procedure for both dependent variables. Nonetheless, we report the simpler (and somewhat more conservative) procedure in the text.
6. Because it was known that sample size would be limited, participants were preselected on trait hostility using a 10-item version of Caprara's Irritability Scale. Students who scored in the upper and lower quartiles were called and signed up for participation. This was done to ensure that there would be an adequate number of participants scoring either high or low on trait hostility to allow for adequate analysis to be done on this independent variable.

PART IV

Applying Social Psychology

READING 14

Despite their persuasive impact on judges and juries, eyewitnesses to crimes are, in many ways, imperfect. As is discussed in Chapter 12 (Law), perceptions are limited by lighting, distance, and distraction; memories fade over time and as a result of interference; and the ability to retrieve a memory can be biased by suggestive questions, photographs, and lineups. In the following classic study, Loftus and Palmer (1974) began to develop what is now an important and well established theory: that eyewitness memories are constructed and then often reconstructed—not only on the basis of the observed event but from information obtained afterward, as from suggestive questions. As you read this article, ponder what it means about human memory and about the accuracy of eyewitness reports commonly used in criminal trials.

Reconstruction of Automobile Destruction: An Example of the Interaction Between Language and Memory

Elizabeth F. Loftus and John C. Palmer
University of Washington

Two experiments are reported in which subjects viewed films of automobile accidents and then answered questions about events occurring in the films. The question, "About how fast were the cars going when they smashed into each other?" elicited higher estimates of speed than questions which used the verbs collided, bumped, contacted, or hit in place of smashed. On a retest one week later, those subjects who received the verb smashed were more likely to say "yes" to the question, "Did you see any broken glass?", even though broken glass was not present in the film. These results are consistent with the view that the questions asked subsequent to an event can cause a reconstruction in one's memory of the event.

How accurately do we remember the details of a complex event, like a traffic accident, that has happened in our presence? More specifically, how well do we do when asked to estimate some numerical quantity such as how long the accident took, how fast the cars were traveling, or how much time elapsed between the sounding of a horn and the moment of collision?

It is well documented that most people are markedly inaccurate in reporting such numerical details as time, speed, and distance (Bird, 1927; Whipple, 1909). For example, most people have difficulty estimating the duration of an event, with some research indicating that the tendency is to overestimate the duration of events which are complex (Block, 1974; Marshall, 1969; Ornstein, 1969). The judgment of speed is especially difficult, and practically every automobile accident results in huge variations from one witness to another as to how fast a vehicle was actually traveling (Gardner, 1933). In one test administered to Air Force personnel who knew in advance that they would be questioned about the speed of a moving automobile, estimates ranged from 10 to 50 mph. The car they watched was actually going only 12 mph (Marshall, 1969, p. 23).

Given the inaccuracies in estimates of speed, it seems likely that there are variables which are potentially powerful in terms of influencing these estimates. The present research was conducted to investigate one such variable, namely, the phrasing of the question used to elicit the speed judgment. Some questions are clearly more suggestive than others. This fact of life has resulted in the legal concept of a leading question and in legal rules indicating when leading questions are allowed (*Supreme Court Reporter*, 1973). A leading question is simply one that, either by its form or content, suggests to the witness what answer is desired or leads him to the desired answer.

In the present study, subjects were shown films of traffic accidents and then they answered questions about the accident. The subjects were interrogated about the speed of the vehicles in one of several ways. For example, some subjects were asked, "About how fast were the cars going when they hit each other?" while others were

SOURCE: Loftus, E. F. & Palmer, J.C. 1974. "Reconstruction of Automobile Destruction: An Example of the Interaction Between Language and Memory" *JOURNAL OF VERBAL LEARNING AND VERBAL BEHAVIOR, 13*, 585–589,

asked, "About how fast were the cars going when they smashed into each other?" As Fillmore (1971) and Bransford and McCarrell (in press) have noted, *hit* and *smashed* may involve specification of differential rates of movement. Furthermore, the two verbs may also involve differential specification of the likely consequences of the events to which they are referring. The impact of the accident is apparently gentler for *hit* than for *smashed.*

EXPERIMENT I

Method

Forty-five students participated in groups of various sizes. Seven films were shown, each depicting a traffic accident. These films were segments from longer driver's education films borrowed from the Evergreen Safety Council and the Seattle Police Department. The length of the film segments ranged from 5 to 30 sec. Following each film, the subjects received a questionnaire asking them first to, "give an account of the accident you have just seen," and then to answer a series of specific questions about the accident. The critical question was the one that interrogated the subject about the speed of the vehicles involved in the collision. Nine subjects were asked, "About how fast were the cars going when they hit each other?" Equal numbers of the remaining subjects were interrogated with the verbs *smashed, collided, bumped*, and *contacted* in place of *hit*. The entire experiment lasted about an hour and a half. A different ordering of the films was presented to each group of subjects.

Results

Table 1 presents the mean speed estimates for the various verbs. Following the procedures outlined by Clark (1973), an analysis of variance was performed with verbs as a fixed effect, and subjects and films as random effects, yielding a significant quasi F ratio $F(5.55) = 4.65, p < .005$.

Some information about the accuracy of subjects' estimates can be obtained from our data. Four of the seven films were staged crashes; the original purpose of these films was to illustrate what can happen to human beings when cars collide at various speeds. One collision took place at 20 mph, one at 30, and two at 40. The means estimates of speed for these four films were: 37.7, 36.2, 39.7 and 36.1 mph, respectively. In agreement with previous work, people are not very good at judging how fast a vehicle was actually traveling.

TABLE 1
Speed Estimates for the Verbs Used in Experiment

Verb	Mean speed estimate
Smashed	40.8
Collided	39.3
Bumped	38.1
Hit	34.0
Contacted	31.8

Discussion

The results of this experiment indicate that the form of a question (in this case, changes of a single word) can markedly and systematically affect a witness's answer to that question. The actual speed of the vehicles controlled little variance in subject reporting, while the phrasing of the question controlled considerable variance.

Two interpretations of this finding are possible. First, it is possible that the differential speed estimates result merely from response-bias factors. A subject is uncertain whether to say 30 mph or 40 mph, for example and the verb *smashed* biases his response towards the higher estimate. A second interpretation is that the question form causes change in the subject's memory representation of the accident. The verb *smashed* may change a subject's memory such that he "sees" the accident as being more severe than it actually was. If this is the case, we might expect subjects to "remember" other details that did not actually occur, but are commensurate with an accident occurring at higher speeds. The second experiment was designed to provide additional insights into the origin of the differential speed estimates.

EXPERIMENT II

Method

One hundred and fifty students participated in this experiment, in groups of various sizes. A film depicting a multiple car accident was shown, followed by a questionnaire. The film lasted less than 1 min; the accident in the film lasted 4 sec. At the end of the film, the subjects received a questionnaire asking them first to describe the accident in their own words, and then to answer a series of questions about the accident. The critical question was the one that interrogated the subject about the speed of the vehicles. Fifty subjects were asked, "About how fast were the cars going when they smashed into each other?" Fifty subjects were asked, "About how fast were the cars going when they hit each other?" Fifty subjects were not interrogated about vehicular speed.

One week later, the subjects returned and without viewing the film again they answered a series of questions about the accident. The critical question here was, "Did you see any broken glass?" which the subjects answered by checking "yes" or "no." This question was embedded in a list totalling 10 questions, and appeared in a random position in the list. There was no broken glass in the accident but since broken glass is commensurate with accidents occurring at high speed, we expected that the subjects who had been asked the *smashed* question might more often say "yes" to this critical question.

Results

The mean estimate of speed for subjects interrogated with *smashed* was 10.46 mph; with *hit* the estimate was 8.00 mph. These means are significantly different, $t(98) = 2.00, p < .05$.

Table 2 presents the distribution of "yes" and "no" responses for the *smashed, hit,* and control subjects. An independence chi-square test on these responses was significant beyond the .025 level, $\chi^2(2) = 7.76$. The important result in Table 2 is that the probability of saying "yes," P(Y), to the question about broken glass is .32 when the verb *smashed* is used, and .14 with *hit*. Thus *smashed* leads both to more "yes" responses and to higher speed estimates. It appears to be the case that the effect of the verb is mediated at least in part by the speed estimate. The question now arises: Is *smashed* doing anything else besides increasing the estimate of speed? To answer this, the function relating P(Y) to speed estimate was calculated separately for *smashed* and *hit*. If the speed estimate is the only way in which effect of verb is mediated, then for a given speed estimate, P(Y) should be independent of verb. Table 3 shows that this is not the case. P(Y) is lower for *hit* than for *smashed*: the difference between the two verbs ranges from .03 for estimates of 1–5 mph to .18 for estimates of 6–10 mph. The average difference between the two curves is about .12. Whereas the unconditional difference of .18 between the *smashed* and *hit* conditions is attenuated, it is by no means eliminated when estimate of speed is controlled for. It thus appears that the verb smashed has other effects besides that of simply increasing the estimate of speed. One possibility will be discussed in the next section.

TABLE 2
Distribution of "Yes" and "No" Responses to the Question, "Did you See Any Broken Glass?"

	Verb Condition		
Response	Smashed	Hit	Control
Yes	16	7	6
No	34	43	44

DISCUSSION

To reiterate, we have first of all provided an additional demonstration of something that has been known for some time, namely, that the way a question is asked can enormously influence the answer that is given. In this instance, the question, "About how fast were the cars going when they smashed into each other?" led to higher estimates of speed than the same question asked with the verb *smashed* replaced by *hit*. Furthermore, this seemingly small change had consequences for how questions are answered a week after the original event occurred.

As a framework for discussing these results, we would like to propose that two kinds of information go into one's memory for some complex occurrence. The first is information gleaned during the perception of the original event; the second is external information supplied after the fact. Over time, information from these two sources may be integrated in such a way that we are unable to tell from which source some specific detail is recalled. All we have is one "memory."

Discussing the present experiments in these terms, we propose that the subject first forms some representation of the accident he has witnessed. The experimenter then, while asking, "About how fast were the cars going when they smashed into each other?" supplies a piece of external information, namely, that the cars did indeed smash into each other. When these two pieces of information are integrated, the subject has a memory of an accident that was more severe than in fact it was. Since broken glass is commensurate with a severe accident, the subject is more likely to think that broken glass was present.

There is some connection between the present work and earlier work on the influence of verbal labels on

TABLE 3
Probability of Saying "Yes" to, "Did You See Any Broken Glass?" Conditionalized of Speed Estimates

	Speed Estimate (mph)			
Verb Condition	**1–5**	**6–10**	**11–15**	**16–20**
Smashed	.09	.27	.41	.62
Hit	.06	.09	.25	.50

memory for visually presented form stimuli. A classic study in psychology showed that when subjects are asked to reproduce a visually presented form, their drawings tend to err in the direction of a more familiar object suggested by a verbal label initially associated with the to-be-remembered form (Carmichael, Hogan, & Walter, 1932). More recently, Daniel (1972) showed that recognition memory, as well as reproductive memory, was similarly affected by verbal labels, and he concluded that the verbal label causes a shift in the memory strength of forms which are better representatives of the label.

When the experimenter asks the subject, "About how fast were the cars going when they smashed into each other?", he is effectively labeling the accident a smash. Extrapolating the conclusions of Daniel to this situation, it is natural to conclude that the label, smash, causes a shift in the memory representation of the accident in the direction of being more similar to a representation suggested by the verbal label.

REFERENCES

Bird, C. The influence of the press upon the accuracy of report. *Journal of Abnormal and Social Psychology*, 1927, 22, 123–129.

Block, R. A. Memory and the experience of duration in retrospect. *Memory & Cognition*, 1974, 2, 153–160.

Bransford, J. D., & McCarrell, N. S. A sketch of a cognitive approach to comprehension. Some thoughts about understanding what it means to comprehend. In D. Palermo & W. Weiner (Eds.), *Cognition and the symbolic processes.* Washington, D.C.: V. H. Winston & Co., in press.

Carmichael, L., Hogan, H. P., & Walter, A. A. An experimental study of the effect of language on the reproduction of visually perceived form. *Journal of Experimental Psychology*, 1932, 15, 73–86.

Clark, H. H. The language-as-fixed-effect fallacy: A critique of language statistics in psychological research. *Journal of Verbal Learning and Verbal Behavior*, 1973, 12, 335–359.

Danill, T. C. Nature of the effect of verbal labels on recognition memory for form. *Journal of Experimental Psychology*, 1972, 96, 152–157.

Fillmore, C. J. Types of lexical information. In D. D. Steinberg and L. A. Jakobovits (Eds.), *Semantics: An interdisciplinary reader in philosophy, linguistics, and psychology.* Cambridge: Cambridge University Press, 1971.

Gardner, D. S. The perception and memory of witnesses. *Cornell Law Quarterly*, 1933, 8, 391–409.

Marshall, J. *Law and psychology in conflict.* New York: Anchor Books, 1969.

Ornstein, R. E. *On the experience of time.* Harmondsworth, Middlesex, England: Penguin, 1969.

Whipple, G. M. The observer as reporter: A survey of the psychology of testimony. *Psychological Bulletin*, 1909, 6, 153–170.

Supreme Court Reporter, 1973, 3: Rules of Evidence for United States Courts and Magistrates.

(Received April 17, 1974)

READING 15

Confession to a crime is a potent and incriminating form of evidence. When a defendant confesses to the police, even if he or she later claims that the confession was coerced, judges and juries vote for guilt and conviction. Yet every now and then, there are documented reports about innocent people who confess to crimes they did not commit as a mean of compliance, in response to pressures exerted during a police interrogation. In some cases, innocent suspects actually come to believe they may be guilty, indicating an even stronger form of influence, internalization. Is it really possible to convince people that they are guilty of an act they did not commit? Based on an analysis of actual cases, Kassin and Kiechel (1996) theorized that two factors increase the risk: (1) a suspect who lacks a clear memory of the event, and (2) the presentation of false evidence, a common police trick. As you will see, these researchers tested and supported this hypothesis in a laboratory experiment on false confessions. While reading this article, think about how it illustrates processes not only relevant to the psychology of law (Chapter 12), but also to social influence (Chapter 9) and persuasion (Chapter 7) research as well.

The Social Psychology of False Confessions: Compliance, Internalization, and Confabulation

Saul M. Kassin and Katherine L. Kiechel
Williams College

An experiment demonstrated that false incriminating evidence can lead people to accept guilt for a crime they did not commit. Subjects in a fast- or slow-paced reaction time task were accused of damaging a computer by pressing the wrong key. All were truly innocent and initially denied the charge. A confederate then said she saw the subject hit the key or did not see the subject hit the key. Compared with subjects in the slow-pace/no-witness group, those in the fast-pace/witness group were more likely to sign a confession, internalize guilt for the event, and confabulate details in memory consistent with that belief. Both legal and conceptual implications are discussed.

Address correspondence to Saul Kassin, Department of Psychology, Williams College, Williamstown, MA 01267.

In criminal law, confession evidence is a potent weapon for the prosecution and a recurring source of controversy. Whether a suspect's self-incriminating statement was voluntary or coerced and whether a suspect was of sound mind are just two of the issues that trial judges and juries consider on a routine basis. To guard citizens against violations of due process and to minimize the risk that the innocent would confess to crimes they did not commit, the courts have erected guidelines for the admissibility of confession evidence. Although there is no simple litmus test, confessions are typically excluded from trial if elicited by physical violence, a threat of harm or punishment, or a promise of immunity or leniency, or without the suspect being notified of his or her Miranda rights.

To understand the psychology of criminal confessions, three questions need to be addressed: First, how do police interrogators elicit self-incriminating statements (i.e., what means of social influence do they use)? Second, what effects do these methods have (i.e., do innocent suspects ever confess to crimes they did not commit)? Third, when a coerced confession is retracted and later presented at trial, do juries sufficiently discount the evidence in accordance with the law? General reviews of relevant case law and research are available elsewhere (Gudjonsson, 1992; Wrightsman & Kassin, 1993). The present research addresses the first two questions.

SOURCE: Kassin, S. I., & Kiechel, K.L. 1996. The Social Psychology of False Confessions: Compliance, Internalization, and Confabulation. *PSYCHOLOGICAL SCIENCE, 7*, 125–128. Reprinted by permission of Blackwell Science Ltd.

Informed by developments in case law, the police use various methods of interrogation—including the presentation of false evidence (e.g., fake polygraph, fingerprints, or other forensic test results; staged eyewitness identifications), appeals to God and religion, feigned friendship, and the use of prison informants. A number of manuals are available to advise detectives on how to extract confessions from reluctant crime suspects (Aubry & Caputo, 1965; O'Hara & O'Hara, 1981). The most popular manual is Inbau, Reid, and Buckley's (1986) *Criminal Interrogation and Confessions*, originally published in 1962, and now in its third edition.

After advising interrogators to set aside a bare, soundproof room absent of social support and distraction, Inbau et al. (1986) describe in detail a nine-step procedure consisting of various specific ploys. In general, two types of approaches can be distinguished. One is *minimization*, a technique in which the detective lulls the suspect into a false sense of security by providing face-saving excuses, citing mitigating circumstances, blaming the victim, and underplaying the charges. The second approach is one of *maximization*, in which the interrogator uses scare tactics by exaggerating or falsifying the characterization of evidence, the seriousness of the offense, and the magnitude of the charges. In a recent study (Kassin & McNall, 1991), subjects read interrogation transcripts in which these ploys were used and estimated the severity of the sentence likely to be received. The results indicated that minimization communicated an implicit offer of leniency, comparable to that estimated in an explicit-promise condition, whereas maximization implied a threat of harsh punishment, comparable to that found in an explicit-threat condition. Yet although American courts routinely exclude confessions elicited by explicit threats and promises, they admit those produced by contingencies that are pragmatically implied.

Although police often use coercive methods of interrogation, research suggests that juries are prone to convict defendants who confess in these situations. In the case of *Arizona v. Fulminante* (1991), the U.S. Supreme Court ruled that under certain conditions, an improperly admitted coerced confession may be considered upon appeal to have been nonprejudicial, or "harmless error." Yet mock-jury research shows that people find it hard to believe that anyone would confess to a crime that he or she did not commit (Kassin & Wrightsman, 1980, 1981; Sukel & Kassin, 1994). Still, it happens. One cannot estimate the prevalence of the problem, which has never been systematically examined, but there are numerous documented instances on record (Bedau & Radelet, 1987; Borchard, 1932; Rattner, 1988). Indeed, one can distinguish three types of false confession (Kassin & Wrightsman, 1985): *voluntary* (in which a subject confesses in the absence of external pressure), *coerced-compliant* (in which a suspect confesses only to escape an aversive interrogation, secure a promised benefit, or avoid a threatened harm), and *coerced-internalized* (in which a suspect actually comes to believe that he or she is guilty of the crime).

This last type of false confession seems most unlikely, but a number of recent cases have come to light in which the police had seized a suspect who was vulnerable (by virtue of his or her youth, intelligence, personality, stress, or mental state) and used false evidence to convince the beleaguered suspect that he or she was guilty. In one case that received a great deal of attention, for example, Paul Ingram was charged with rape and a host of satanic cult crimes that included the slaughter of newborn babies. During 6 months of interrogation, he was hypnotized, exposed to graphic crime details, informed by a police psychologist that sex offenders often repress their offenses, and urged by the minister of his church to confess. Eventually, Ingram "recalled" crime scenes to specification, pleaded guilty, and was sentenced to prison. There was no physical evidence of these crimes, however, and an expert who reviewed the case for the state concluded that Ingram had been brainwashed. To demonstrate, this expert accused Ingram of a bogus crime and found that although he initially denied the charge, he later confessed—and embellished the story (Ofshe, 1992: Wright, 1994).

Other similar cases have been reported (e.g., Pratkanis & Aronson, 1991), but, to date, there is no empirical proof of this phenomenon. Memory researchers have found that misleading postevent information can alter actual or reported memories of observed events (Loftus, Donders, Hoffman, & Schooler, 1989; Loftus, Miller, & Burns, 1978; McCloskey & Zaragoza, 1985)—an effect that is particularly potent in young children (Ceci & Bruck, 1993; Ceci, Ross, & Toglia, 1987) and adults under hypnosis (Dinges et al., 1992; Dywan & Bowers, 1983; Sheehan, Statham, & Jamieson, 1991). Indeed, recent studies suggest it is even possible to implant false recollections of traumas supposedly buried in the unconscious (Loftus, 1993). As related to confessions, the question is, can memory of one's own actions similarly be altered? Can people be induced to accept guilt for crimes they did not commit? Is it, contrary to popular belief, possible?

Because of obvious ethical constraints, this important issue has not been addressed previously. This article thus reports on a new laboratory paradigm used to test the following specific hypothesis: The presentation of false evidence can lead individuals who are vulnerable (i.e., in a heightened state of uncertainty) to confess to an act they did not commit and, more important, to internalize the confession and perhaps confabulate details in memory consistent with that new belief.

METHOD

Participating for extra credit in what was supposed to be a reaction time experiment, 79 undergraduates (40 male, 39 female) were randomly assigned to one of four groups produced by a 2 (high vs. low vulnerability) × 2 (presence vs. absence of a false incriminating witness) factorial design.

Two subjects per session (actually, 1 subject and a female confederate) engaged in a reaction time task on an IBM PS2/Model 50 computer. To bolster the credibility of the experimental cover story, they were asked to fill out a brief questionnaire concerning their typing experience and ability, spatial awareness, and speed of reflexes. The subject and confederate were then taken to another room, seated across a table from the experimenter, and instructed on the task. The confederate was to read aloud a list of letters, and the subject was to type these letters on the keyboard. After 3 min, the subject and confederate were to reverse roles. Before the session began, subjects were instructed on proper use of the computer—and were specifically warned not to press the "ALT" key positioned near the space bar because doing so would cause the program to crash and data to be lost. Lo and behold, after 60 s, the computer supposedly ceased to function, and a highly distressed experimenter accused the subject of having pressed the forbidden key. All subjects initially denied the charge, at which point the experimenter tinkered with the keyboard, confirmed that data had been lost, and asked, "Did you hit the 'ALT' key?"

Two forensically relevant factors were independently varied. First, we manipulated subjects' level of *vulnerability* (i.e., their subjective certainty concerning their own innocence) by varying the pace of the task. Using a mechanical metronome, the confederate read either at a slow and relaxed pace of 43 letters per minute or at a frenzied pace of 67 letters per minute (these settings were established through pretesting). Two-way analyses of variance revealed significant main effects on the number of letters typed correctly (Ms = 33.01 and 61.12, respectively; $F[1, 71] = 278.93$, $p < .001$) and the number of typing errors made (Ms = 1.12 and 10.90, respectively; $F[1, 71] = 38.81$, $p < .001$), thus confirming the effectiveness of this manipulation.

Second, we varied the use of *false incriminating evidence*, a common interrogation technique. After the subject initially denied the charge, the experimenter turned to the confederate and asked, "Did you see anything?" In the false-witness condition, the confederate "admitted" that she had seen the subject hit the "ALT" key that terminated the program. In the no-witness condition, the same confederate said she had not seen what happened.

As dependent measures, three forms of social influence were assessed: compliance, internalization, and confabulation. To elicit *compliance*, the experimenter handwrote a standardized confession ("I hit the 'ALT' key and caused the program to crash. Data were lost") and asked the subject to sign it—the consequence of which would be a phone call from the principal investigator. If the subject refused, the request was repeated a second time.

To assess *internalization*, we unobtrusively recorded the way subjects privately described what happened soon afterward. As the experimenter and subject left the laboratory, they were met in the reception area by a waiting subject (actually, a second confederate who was blind to the subject's condition and previous behavior) who had overheard the commotion. The experimenter explained that the session would have to be rescheduled, and then left the room to retrieve his appointment calendar. At that point, the second confederate turned privately to the subject and asked, "What happened?" The subject's reply was recorded verbatim and later coded for whether or not he or she had unambiguously internalized guilt for what happened (e.g., "I hit the wrong button and ruined the program"; "I hit a button I wasn't supposed to"). A conservative criterion was employed. Any reply that was prefaced by "he said" or "I may have" or "I think" was not taken as evidence of internalization. Two raters who were blind to the subject's condition independently coded these responses, and their agreement rate was 96%.

Finally, after the sessions seemed to be over, the experimenter reappeared, brought the subjects back into the lab, reread the list of letters they had typed, and asked if they could reconstruct how or when they hit the "ALT" key. This procedure was designed to probe for evidence of *confabulation*, to determine whether subjects would "recall" specific details to fit the allegation (e.g., "Yes, here, I hit it with the side of my hand right after you called out the 'A'"). The interrater agreement rate on the coding of these data was 100%.

At the end of each session, subjects were fully and carefully debriefed about the study—its purpose, the hypothesis, and the reason for the use of deception—by the experimenter and first confederate. Most subjects reacted with a combination of relief (that they had not ruined the experiment), amazement (that their perceptions of their own behavior had been so completely manipulated), and a sense of satisfaction (at having played a meaningful role in an important study). Subjects were also asked not to discuss the experience with other students until all the data were collected. Four subjects reported during debriefing that they were suspicious of the experimental manipulation. Their data were excluded from all analyses.

RESULTS AND DISCUSSION

Overall, 69% of the 75 subjects signed the confession, 28% exhibited internalization, and 9% confabulated details to support their false beliefs. More important, between-group comparisons provided strong support for the main hypothesis. As seen in Table 1, subjects in the slow-pace/no-witness control group were the least likely to exhibit an effect, whereas those in the fast-pace/witness group were the most likely to exhibit the effect on the measures of compliance ($\chi^2[3] = 23.84$, $p < .001$), internalization ($\chi^2[3] = 37.61$, $p < .001$), and confabulation ($\chi^2[3] = 18.0$, $p < .005$).

Specifically, although 34.78% of the subjects in the slow-pace/no-witness group signed the confession, indicating compliance, not a single subject in this group exhibited internalization or confabulation. In contrast, the two in dependent variables had a powerful combined effect. Out of 17 subjects in the fast-pace/witness cell, 100% signed a confession, 65% came to believe they were guilty (in reality, they were not), and 35% confabulated details to support their false belief (via chi-square tests, the differences in these rates between the slow-pace/no-witness control group and fast-pace/witness group were significant at *p*s < .001, .001, and .005, respectively).

TABLE 1
Percentage of subjects in each cell who exhibited the three forms of influence

Form of influence	No witness		Witness	
	Slow pace	Fast pace	Slow Pace	Fast pace
Compliance	35_a	65_b	89_{bc}	100_c
Internalization	0_a	12_{ab}	44_{bc}	65_c
Confabulation	0_a	0_a	6_a	35_b

Note. Percentages not sharing a common subscript differ at p < .05 via chi-square test of significance.

Additional pair-wise comparisons revealed that the presence of a witness alone was sufficient to significantly increase the rates of compliant and internalized confessions, even in the slow-pace condition ($\chi^2[1] = 12.18$, $p < .005$, and $\chi^2[1] = 16.39$, $p < .001$). There were no sex differences on any measures (i.e., male and female subjects exhibited comparable confession rates overall, and were similarly influenced by the independent variables).

The present study provides strong initial support for the provocative notion that the presentation of false incriminating evidence—an interrogation ploy that is common among the police and sanctioned by many courts—can induce people to internalize blame for outcomes they did not produce. These results provide an initial basis for challenging the evidentiary validity of confessions produced by this technique. These findings also demonstrate, possibly for the first time, that memory can be altered not only for observed events and remote past experiences, but also for one's own recent actions.

An obvious and important empirical question remains concerning the external validity of the present results: To what extent do they generalize to the interrogation behavior of actual crime suspects? For ethical reasons, we developed a laboratory paradigm in which subjects were accused merely of an unconscious act of negligence, not of an act involving explicit criminal intent (e.g., stealing equipment from the lab or cheating on an important test). In this paradigm, there was only a minor consequence for liability. At this point, it is unclear whether people could similarly be induced to internalize false guilt for acts of omission (i.e., neglecting to do something they were told to do) or for acts that emanate from conscious intent.

It is important, however, not to overstate this limitation. The fact that our procedure focused on an act of negligence and low consequence may well explain why the compliance rate was high, with roughly two thirds of all subjects agreeing to sign a confession statement. Effects of this sort on overt judgments and behavior have been observed in studies of conformity to group norms, compliance with direct requests, and obedience to the commands of authority. But the more important and startling result—that many subjects privately internalized guilt for an outcome they did not produce, and that some even constructed memories to fit that false belief—is not seriously compromised by the laboratory paradigm that was used. Conceptually, these findings extend known effects of misinformation on memory for observed events (Loftus et al., 1978; McCloskey & Zaragoza, 1985) and for traumas assumed to be buried in the unconscious (Loftus, 1993). Indeed, our effects were exhibited by college students who are intelligent (drawn from a population in which the mean score on the Scholastic Aptitude Test is over 1300), self-assured, and under minimal stress compared with crime suspects held in custody, often in isolation.

At this point, additional research is needed to examine other common interrogation techniques (e.g., minimization), individual differences in suspect vulnerability (e.g., manifest anxiety, need for approval, hypnotic susceptibility), and other risk factors for false confessions (e.g., blood alcohol level, sleep deprivation). In light of recent judicial acceptance of a broad range of self-incriminatory statements, increasing use of videotaped confessions at the trial level (Geller, 1993), and the U.S. Supreme Court's ruling that an improperly admitted coerced confession may qualify as a mere "harmless error" (*Arizona v. Fulminante*, 1991), further research is also needed to assess the lay jury's reaction to this type of evidence when presented in court.

Acknowledgments—This research was submitted as part of a senior honor's thesis by the second author and was funded by the Bronfman Science Center of Williams College.

REFERENCES

Arizona v. Fulminante, 59 U.S.L.W. 4235 (1991).

Aubry, A., & Caputo, R. (1965). *Criminal interrogation.* Springfield, IL: Charles C. Thomas.

Bedau, H., & Radelet, M. (1987). Miscarriages of justice in potentially capital cases, *Stanford Law Review, 40*, 21–179.

Borchard, E.M. (1932). *Convicting the innocent: Errors of criminal justice.* New Haven, CT: Yale University Press.

Ceci, S.J., & Bruck, M. (1993). Suggestibility of the child witness: A historical review and synthesis. *Psychological Bulletin, 113*, 403–439.

Ceci, S.J., Ross, D.F., & Toglia, M.P. (1987). Suggestibility of children's memory: Psycholegal implications. *Journal of Experimental Psychology: General, 116*, 38–49.

Dinges, D.F., Whitehouse, W.G., Orne, E.C., Powell, J.W., Orne, M.T., & Erdelyi, M.H. (1992). Evaluating hypnotic memory enhancement (hypermnesia and reminiscence) using multitrial forced recall. *Journal of Experimental Psychology: Learning, Memory, and Cognition, 18*, 1139–1147.

Dywan, J., & Bowers, K. (1983). The use of hypnosis to enhance recall. *Science, 222*, 184–185.

Geller, W.A. (1993). *Videotaping interrogations and confessions* (National Institute of Justice: Research in Brief). Washington, DC: U.S. Department of Justice.

Gudjonsson, G. (1992). *The psychology of interrogations, confessions, and testimony.* London: Wiley.

Inbau, F.E., Reid, J.E., & Buckley, J.P. (1986). *Criminal interrogation and confessions* (3rd ed.). Baltimore, MD: Williams & Wilkins.

Kassin, S.M., & McNall, K. (1991). Police interrogations and confessions: Communicating promises and threats by pragmatic implication. *Law and Human Behavior, 15*, 233–251.

Kassin, S.M., & Wrightsman, L.S. (1980). Prior confessions and mock juror verdicts. *Journal of Applied Social Psychology, 10*, 133–146.

Kassin, S.M., & Wrightsman, L.S. (1981). Coerced confessions, judicial instruction, and mock juror verdicts. *Journal, of Applied Social Psychology 11*, 489–506.

Kassin, S.M., & Wrightsman, L.S. (1985). Confession evidence. In S.M. Kassin & L.S. Wrightsman (Eds.), *The psychology of evidence and trial procedure* (pp. 67–94). Beverly Hills, CA: Sage.

Loftus, E.F. (1993). The reality of repressed memories. *American Psychologist, 48*, 518–537.

Loftus, E.F., Donders, K., Hoffman, H.G., & Schooler, J.W. (1989). Creating new memories that are quickly accessed and confidently held. *Memory and Cognition, 17*, 607–616.

Loftus, E.F., Miller, D.G., & Burns, H.J. (1978). Semantic integration of verbal information into visual memory. *Journal of Experimental Psychology: Human Learning and Memory, 4*, 19–31.

McCloskey, M., & Zaragoza, M. (1985). Misleading post-event information and memory for events: Arguments and evidence against memory impairment hypotheses. *Journal of Experimental Psychology, 114*, 3–18.

Ofshe, R. (1992). Inadvertent hypnosis during interrogation: False confession due to dissociative state; misidentified multiple personality and the satanic cult hypothesis. *International Journal of Clinical and Experimental Hypnosis, 40*, 125–156.

O'Hara, C.E., & O'Hara, G.L. (1981). *Fundamentals of criminal investigation.* Springfield, IL: Charles C. Thomas.

Pratkanis, A., & Aronson, E. (1991). *Age of propaganda: The everyday use and abuse of persuasion.* New York: W.H. Freeman.

Rattner, A. (1988). Convicted but innocent: Wrongful conviction and the criminal justice system. *Law and Human Behavior, 12*, 283–293.

Sheehan, P.W., Statham, D., & Jamieson, G.A. (1991). Pseudomemory effects and their relationship to level of susceptibility to hypnosis and state instruction. *Journal of Personality and Social Psychology, 60*, 130–137.

Sukel, H.L., & Kassin, S.M. (1994, March). *Coerced confessions and the jury: An experimental test of the "harmless error" rule*. Paper presented at the biennial meeting of the American Psychology-Law Society, Sante Fe, NM.

Wright, L. (1994). *Remembering Satan*. New York: Alfred A. Knopf.

Wrightsman, L.S., & Kassin, S.M. (1993). *Confessions in the courtroom*. Newbury Park, CA: Sage.

(Received 12/21/94; Accepted 2/22/95)

READING 16

Being rewarded for one's work helps to maintain motivation and commitment, but, as Chapters 3 (The Social Self), 7 (Attitudes), and 13 (Business) make clear, the effects of reward on motivation are complex. According to *equity theory*, for example, people want rewards to be equitable so that the ratio between inputs and outcomes should be the same for the self as it is for co-workers. Thus, if you feel overpaid or underpaid and cannot change the situation, you will experience distress and try to restore equity—perhaps by working more or less. Studying workers in a large insurance firm, Greenberg (1988) measured changes in productivity among those who were temporarily moved to offices that were larger, smaller, or equal to their rank within the company. Did office size affect performance, as predicted by equity theory, in an actual office setting? As you read this article, think about the implications of equity theory for motivation not only in the workplace but in close relationships and educational settings as well.

Equity and Workplace Status: A Field Experiment

Jerald Greenberg
Faculty of Management and Human Resources
The Ohio State University

In a field experiment, 198 employees in the underwriting department of a large insurance company were randomly reassigned on a temporary basis to the offices of either higher, lower, or equal-status coworkers while their own offices were being refurbished. The present study tested the hypothesis, derived from equity theory, that the status value of the temporary offices would create increases, decreases, or no change in organizational outcome levels. The resulting pattern of performance supported equity theory. Specifically, relative to those workers reassigned to equal-status offices, those reassigned to higher status offices raised their performance (a response to overpayment inequity) and those reassigned to lower status offices lowered their performance (a response to underpayment inequity). As hypothesized, the size of these performance changes was directly related to the magnitude of the status inconsistencies encountered. The value of these findings in extending equity theory to the realm of nonmonetary outcomes is discussed.

There can be little doubt about the existence of certain trappings of success in organizations—physical symbols (cf. Goodsell, 1977) reflecting the organizational status of job incumbents (Steele, 1973). Indeed, previous research has confirmed that certain indicators of status demarcation (cf. Konar & Sundstrom, 1985), such as large offices (Langdon, 1966), carpeting (Joiner, 1976), and proximity to windows (Halloran, 1978), are recognized as rewards symbolizing one's high standing in an organizational status hierarchy. Although these environmental rewards typically are associated with relatively high-status individuals, thereby reinforcing the social order of organizations (Edelman, 1978), there are some occasions in which the status of the job incumbent and the physical symbols associated with the status are not matched (Wineman, 1982). Such instances may be recognized as cases of status inconsistency (cf. Stryker & Macke, 1978) and, as such, reactions to them may be explained by equity theory (e.g., Adams, 1965; Walster, Walster, & Berscheid, 1978).

According to equity theory, workers who receive levels of reward (i.e., outcomes) higher or lower than coworkers who make equivalent contributions to their jobs (i.e., inputs) are considered overpaid and underpaid, respectively. Such inequitable states have been shown to result in dissatisfaction and to bring about increases and decreases, respectively, in job performance (for a review, see Greenberg, 1982). As such, the present investigation addresses whether the characteristics of an employee's workspace influence his or her perceptions of equitable treatment on the job. If the characteristics of one's work space are perceived as constituting part of one's work-related rewards, then it follows that receiving work-space-derived rewards greater or less than coworkers of equal status may create conditions of overpayment and underpayment inequity, respectively. The focal ques-

SOURCE: Greenberg, Jerald, "Equity and Workplace Status: A Field Experiment," *Journal of Applied Psychology,* 1988, Vol. 73, No. 4, 606–613.

tion of the present investigation is whether equity theory explains the reactions of persons encountering consistencies and inconsistencies between their job status and the rewards offered by their work space.

Although there is little direct evidence bearing on this question, managers have intuitively believed and long advocated the importance of basing office design decisions on employees' ranks in their organizations' status hierarchies as a mechanism for ensuring equitable treatment (Robichaud, 1958). According to equity theory, an employee's work space may be recognized as an element of equitable treatment insofar as it is perceived as a reward that reflects his or her organizational status. Indeed, previous research (e.g., Konar, Sundstrom, Brady, Mandel, & Rice, 1982) has shown that several elements of work space, such as the nature of the furnishings, amount of space, capacity for personalization, and the ability to control access by others, have been found to covary with workers' relative status rankings (for reviews, see Becker, 1981, 1982; Davis, 1984; Sundstrom, 1986).

Although previous researchers have not incorporated work-space elements into equity theory-based predictions directly, extrapolations from existing research suggest that reactions to work-space characteristics may be predictable from equity theory. For example, Burt and Sundstrom (1979) found in a field study that workers who were underpaid financially were less dissatisfied with their pay if they worked under conditions that were more environmentally desirable than those who did not receive additional work-space-related benefits. These results suggest that the desirable working conditions constituted an additional reward that offset the dissatisfaction created by inadequate monetary payment. Such a finding is consistent with the possibility that workers' reactions to their work spaces may be explained by equity theory. Inequities created by nonmonetary rewards have also been studied by Greenberg and Ornstein (1983), who found that experimental subjects who were overpaid by receiving an inappropriately high job title responded by increasing their job performance, as predicted by equity theory. Thus, much as an inappropriately high job title resulted in attempts to redress overpayment inequity by raising inputs, similar reactions may result from overpayments created by the introduction of work-space elements that are inappropriately lavish for one's organizational ranking.

On the basis of this logic, the present study tested hypotheses derived from equity theory in an organizational setting in which the refurbishing of offices necessitated the reassignment of employees to temporary offices. Specifically, I hypothesized that employees reassigned to offices of higher status workers (i.e., those who are overpaid in terms of office status) would be more productive than those reassigned to offices of other equal-status workers. Similarly, employees reassigned to offices of lower status worker (i.e., those who are underpaid in terms of office status) would be expected to be less productive than those reassigned to offices of other equal-status workers.

Following from equity theory's proposition that the magnitude of the inequity-resolution efforts will be proportional to the magnitude of the inequity (Adams, 1965; Walster et al., 1978), it was expected that improvements or decrements in performance would be greater the larger the over- or underpayments, respectively. Employees reassigned to offices of workers two levels above them would be expected to perform at a higher level than employees reassigned to offices of more modestly overpaid workers one level above them. Similarly, employees reassigned to offices of workers two levels below them would be expected to perform at a lower level than employees reassigned to offices of more modestly underpaid workers one level below them.

METHOD

Subjects

The 198 participants in the study (123 men and 75 women) were drawn from three groups of salaried employees in the life insurance underwriting department of a large insurance company. There were 91 underwriter trainees (*Mdn* age = 24 years; *Mdn* job tenure = 8 months), 60 associate underwriters (*Mdn* age = 28 years; *Mdn* job tenure = 1 year, 9 months), and 47 underwriters (*Mdn* age = 31 years; *Mdn* job tenure = 3 years, 2 months). All of these employees were charged with the responsibility for reviewing and either approving or disapproving applications for life insurance on the basis of the extent to which information uncovered in their investigations satisfied the company's criteria for risk. The primary difference in responsibility for the three groups was the monetary size of the policies they were permitted to approve.

Design

Because the offices of the underwriting department were being refurbished, an opportunity presented itself for studying the behavior of employees working temporarily (10 consecutive work days) in offices regularly assigned to higher, lower, or equally ranked coworkers in the underwriting department. With the cooperation of the participating organization, assignment to temporary office conditions was made at random.[1] The reassignment made it possible to create conditions of potential overpayment (assignment to a higher status office), underpayment (assignment to a lower status office), or equitable payment (assignment to an equal-status office), as well as the degree of inequitable payment (office assignment either one or two levels above or below the worker's status). To create control groups, some workers in each employee group remained in their own permanent offices during the study period. Table 1 summarizes the experimental design and reports the number of subjects assigned to each condition.

In addition to these between-subjects elements, the design of the present study also included time as a within-subjects element. Repeated measures of the dependent variables were taken at six intervals; the second week before reassignment to a temporary office, the first week before reassignment, the first week during the reassignment period, the second week during reassignment, the first week back in one's permanent office after reassignment, and the second week after reassignment.

TABLE 1
Summary of Study Design

Worker group/ temporary office	*n*	Payment condition
Trainee		
Other trainee	42	Equitably paid
Associate	18	One-step overpaid
Underwriter	12	Two-steps overpaid
Own	19	Control
Associate		
Trainee	18	One-step underpaid
Other associate	18	Equitably paid
Underwriter	12	One-step overpaid
Own	12	Control
Underwriter		
Trainee	12	Two-steps underpaid
Associate	12	One-step underpaid
Other underwriter	12	Equitably paid
Own	11	Control

Procedure

Office assignment procedure Before the study began, workers (except those in the control groups) were informed that they would have to work for 2 consecutive 5-day work weeks in other offices while their own offices were being refurbished.[2] So as to not disrupt performance, but allowing ample time for workers to gather their belongings, workers were informed of the impending temporary move 2 workdays in advance. Workers drew lots to determine their temporary office assignments and were not permitted to switch these assignments. This procedure helped safeguard against the possibility that reactions to office assignments could be the result of perceived managerial favoritism or hostility resulting from an undisclosed (and potentially capricious) basis for the office assignments. The procedure also controlled against any possible self-selection bias in office reassignments.

Office characteristics The offices used in the study were those regularly assigned to either underwriter trainees, associate underwriters, or underwriters. In the organization studied, as in others (e.g., Harris, 1977; Kleinschrod, 1987), the offices of workers of different status-rankings differed along several predetermined, standardized dimensions. Consensual knowledge of such differences helped reinforce the status differences between the offices used in the study.[3] The key physical characteristics of the offices used in the experiment are described in Table 2. Although these dimensions were known within the host organization to reflect status differential, it is instructive to note that they are not idiosyncratic. Indeed, these dimensions are among those found in the survey study by Konar et al. (1982) to be associated with status differences among employees in other organizations.

As shown in Table 2, the offices of associate underwriters were shared by fewer office mates, allowed more space per person, and had larger desks than the offices of underwriter trainees. Underwriters' offices were always completely private (used by only one person), allowed the most space per person, and had the largest desks. In addition, the underwriters' offices had doors, whereas the offices of underwriter trainees and associate underwriters did not. The use of these status markers (cf. Konar & C Sundstrom, 1985) is in keeping with previous studies showing that higher status is associated with the use of unshared, private offices (Sundstrom, Burt, & Kamp,

TABLE 2
Physical Characteristics of Offices

	Offices		
Physical characteristic	**Underwriter trainees (n = 15)**	**Associate underwriters (n = 30)**	**Underwriters (n = 47)**
No. of occupants per office	6[a]	2	1
Presence of door	No	No	Yes
Occupant space (m^2 per occupant)	21.34	29.87	44.81
Desk size (m^2)	1.14	1.32	1.53

Note. Because the host company standardized office characteristics as a function of employee status, there was very little or no variation in the values reported here.
[a] One of the 15 offices that was larger than the others housed seven underwriter trainees; the remaining 14 housed six.

1980), greater floorspace (Harris, 1977), larger desks (Wylie, 1958), and the option to limit access to oneself by the presence of doors (Geran, 1976).

Performance measure The principal dependent measure was job performance in reviewing applications for life insurance. It was the practice of the company studied to derive corrected performance scores for all underwriters. (Such measures typically were used, in part, as the basis for performance evaluations and pay raises.) Raw performance measures were computed weekly on the basis of the number of cases completed. These were then adjusted by supervisory personnel for decision quality, the complexity of the cases considered (both of which were based on predetermined criteria), and the number of hours spent reviewing application files, resulting in a corrected performance score. So as to provide a basis of comparison for interpreting these scores, the mean corrected performance scores of the workers studied in the 2 months prior to the present investigation was 49.2. Because this score was not significantly different than the two prereassignment scores observed in this investigation, $F < 1.00$, *ns*, there is no reason to believe that the study period was in any way atypical.

Questionnaire measures To help explain the performance measure, questionnaire data were collected as supplementary measures. These questionnaires were administered at three times: one week before reassignment, one week into the reassignment period, and one week after reassignment.

To measure job satisfaction, the 20-item general satisfaction scale of the Minnesota Satisfaction Questionnaire (MSQ; Weiss, Dawis, England, & Lofquist, 1967) was used. It requires participants to indicate whether they are *very satisfied, satisfied, neither satisfied nor dissatisfied, dissatisfied*, or *very dissatisfied* with respect to a broad range of job dimensions, such as "the feeling of accomplishment I get from the job" and "the freedom to use my own judgment." This scale was chosen because it has excellent psychometric properties (Price & Mueller, 1986) and because its use enhances comparability with other tests of equity theory using the same measure (e.g., Pritchard, Dunnette, & Jorgenson, 1972). For the present sample, coefficient alpha was .88.

An additional set of questions was designed to determine the extent to which workers recognized the outcome value of their office environments. As such, a measure of environmental satisfaction was derived by asking subjects, "How pleased or displeased are you with each of the following aspects of your current work environment?": privacy, desk space, floorspace, noise level, lighting, furnishings, and overall atmosphere. Scale values could range from *extremely displeased* (1) to *extremely pleased* (7), Coefficient alpha was computed to be .82.

Finally, a separate item asked, "How would you characterize the overall level of rewards you are now receiving from your job?" Scale values could range from *extremely low* (1) to *extremely high* (7).

Manipulation checks As the basis for explaining performance differences in terms of the inequities caused by status differences in office assignments, it was necessary to establish that workers correctly perceived the status differences of their temporary offices and, also, had unaided and unimpaired opportunities to perform in their temporary offices. Accordingly, checklist questions addressing these matters were administered at the end of the first week in the temporary offices (at the same time as the second administration of the questionnaire measures). Because these questions were not applicable to workers in the control group, the checklist was not administered to them.

Specifically, to determine whether subjects recognized the status differences between their regular offices and their temporary offices, they were requested to respond to a checklist item that asked, "Is your temporary office usually assigned to a coworker of: lower status than you, equal status to you, or higher status than you?" An additional checklist item asked subjects, "Relative to your regular office, do the facilities found in your temporary office: help you do your job better, enable you to do your job equally well, or cause you to do your job more poorly?"

RESULTS

Manipulation Checks

Subjects' responses to the questionnaire item asking them to identify the relative status attached to their temporary offices showed that they were, in fact, aware of the similarities or differences between their own offices and their temporary ones. Virtually all of the subjects assigned to the offices of equal-status others recognized those offices as being of equal status. All of the subjects assigned to offices of higher and lower status others (whether one or two steps higher or lower) recognized the hierarchical level of those offices. This evidence supports the claim that subjects were aware of the status similarities or differences they encountered during the course of the study and that the manipulations of status were successful.

Another manipulation check sought to ensure that subjects' performance differences could not be attributed to differential opportunities to perform their jobs while in the temporary offices. In response to a checklist item, virtually all 198 participants reported that the facilities in their temporary offices enabled them to perform their jobs as well as they did in their regularly assigned offices. These data discount the possibility that performance increases or decreases noted while in the temporary offices were the result of opportunities provided by or thwarted by office conditions.

Preliminary Analyses

Prior to testing hypotheses, analyses were conducted on the work performance data to determine whether combining the various cells that composed the identically defined payment conditions shown in Table 1 was justified. This was done by including the identically defined groups (as a between-subjects factor) and the observation time (as a repeated measure) in mixed-design analyses of variance (ANOVAS). Justification for combining the responses of the identically defined groups required finding no significant differences between groups, either as main effects or in interactions with the observation time.

As shown in Table 1, four distinct payment conditions were identified by more than one group of workers. Specifically, three groups of workers (those reassigned to equal-status offices) were identified as equitably paid, three groups of workers (those who remained in their own offices) were identified as control subjects, two groups of workers (those assigned to offices one status level higher) were identified as one-step overpaid, and two groups of workers (those assigned to offices one status level lower) were identified as one-step underpaid. Separate ANOVAS for the groups defining each of these four payment conditions revealed no significant main effects of group membership and no interaction of group membership with time, all values of $F < 1.00$, *ns*. Accordingly, distinct payment conditions were created by combining the data for the identically defined groups.

Performance Measure

To test hypotheses regarding the effects of payment equity on task performance, a 6 × (6) mixed-design ANOVA was used, in which the six payment conditions composed the between-subjects factor and the six observation periods composed the within-subjects factor. A significant interaction effect between these two factors was obtained, $F(25, 950) = 8.41, p < .001$; the corresponding means are displayed in Figure 1.

Simple effects tests were performed to compare the six payment groups at each of the time periods. These tests revealed no significant differences between groups during each of the two weeks before reassignment, in both cases, $F < 1.00$ *ns*, and also during the second week after reassignment, $F < 1.00$, *ns*. How ever, significant differences between groups were found as workers readjusted to their permanent offices

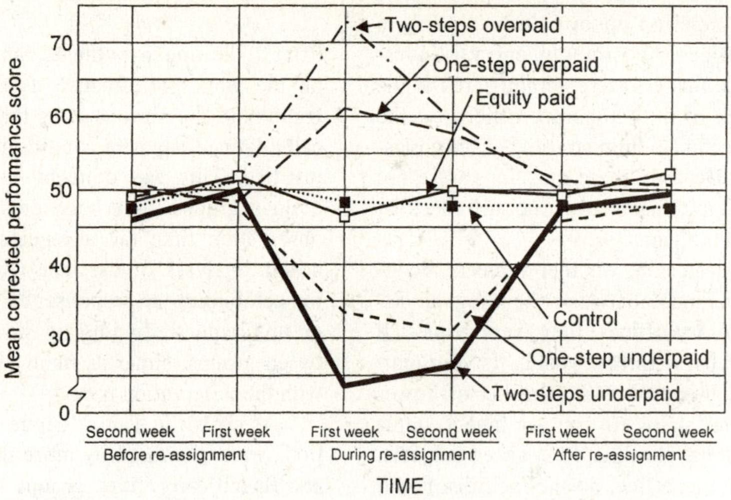

Figure 1. Mean job performance for each payment group over time.

during the first week after reassignment, $F(5, 192) = 2.85$, $p < .025$. Newman-Keuls tests (this and all subsequent Newman-Keuls tests are based on an alpha level of .05) revealed that significant differences existed between workers in the one-step overpaid group and the one-step underpaid group, whereas those in the remaining groups were not significantly different from each other.

Significant differences emerged in simple effects tests comparing payment groups during the first week of reassignment, $F(5, 192) = 13.99$, $p < .001$. Newman-Keuls tests revealed that the performance of the equitably paid group and the control group did not differ significantly. However, compared with this base level, the one-step overpaid group was significantly more productive and the one-step underpaid group was significantly less productive. Additional comparisons showed that those who were two-steps overpaid were significantly more productive than those who were one-step overpaid, and that those who were two-steps underpaid were significantly less productive than those who were one-step underpaid. Thus, for the first week during reassignment, all hypotheses were supported.

During the second week of reassignment, a significant simple effect of payment group was found as well, $F(5, 192) = 11, 60$, $p < .001$. As in the first week of reassignment, Newman-Keuls tests showed the equivalence of the control group and the equitably paid group. Also, as in the first week of reassignment, those who were one-step overpaid and underpaid performed significantly higher and lower than these base levels, respectively. The magnitude of inequity hypothesis was only partially supported during the second week of reassignment: Those who were two-steps underpaid were less productive than those who were one-step underpaid, but those who were two-steps overpaid did not perform at significantly higher levels than those who were one-step overpaid (although the difference between the means was in the predicted direction).

This finding is the result of a significant drop in performance from the first week during reassignment to the second week among those who were two-steps overpaid, $t(11) = 5.56$, p <.001 (this and subsequently reported t tests are two-tailed), indicating that the extreme initial reaction to gross overpayment was not sustained. By contrast, the failure to find significant differences between the first and second reassignment weeks for the one-step overpaid group, $t(29) = 1.98$, *ns*, the one-step underpaid group, $t(29) = .76$, *ns*, and the two-steps underpaid group, $t(11) = .88$, *ns*, suggests that the impact of these inequities was relatively stable over time.

Questionnaire Measures

Correlations between the questionnaire measures were uniformly low. Specifically, the MSQ scores were not significantly correlated with either the environmental satisfaction measures ($r = .04$) or the self-reports of overall reward ($r = .07$). Likewise, the environmental satisfaction measure and the self-reports of overall reward were not significantly correlated with each other (r = .03). The statistical independence of these measures justifies the use of separate univariate analyses.

As in the case of the performance measure, a set of preliminary analyses was performed for each questionnaire measure that showed nonsignificant differences between the various groups defining each payment condition, all values of $F < 1.00$, *ns*. Accordingly, the same six payment conditions that were used for the performance measure were created in analyses of the questionnaire measures. However, because there were three questionnaire-administration periods (as opposed to six performance-measurement periods), analyses of the questionnaire items were based on 6 × (3) mixed-design ANOVAS.

A significant Payment × Time interaction was found for responses to the MSQ, $F(10, 389) = 3.01$, $p < .005$. A simple effects test found this interaction to be the result of between-group differences during the reassignment period, $F(5, 192) = 2.59$, $p < .01$, and no significant differences either before or after the reassignment, in both cases $F < 1.00$, *ns*. Newman-Keuls comparisons of the means within the reassignment period revealed significantly lower levels of satisfaction reported by workers who were two-steps underpaid (M = 44.15) compared with any of the other cells (combined m = 75.50), none of which were significantly different from each other.

Analyses of the environmental satisfaction questionnaire also revealed a significant interaction effect, $F(10, 389) = 3.65$, $p < .001$. Simple effects tests found that both the prereassignment and the postreassignment levels of satisfaction were not significantly different from each other, in both cases, $F < 1.00$, *ns*, although significant differences emerged during the reassignment period, $F(5, 192) = 3.18$, $p < .01$. Newman-Keuls tests showed that compared with the equitably paid group and the control group (which were not significantly different from each other; combined M = 29.75), the two overpaid groups were significantly higher (although not significantly different from each other; combined M = 40.50) and the two underpaid groups were significantly lower (although not significantly different from each other; combined M = 18.10).

Self-reports of overall reward received also revealed a significant Payment × Time interaction, $F(10, 389) = 3.74$, $p < .001$. Although perceived reward levels were not significantly different at the prereassignment and postreassignment sessions, in both cases, $F < 1.00$, *ns*, significant differences emerged during the reassignment period, $F(5, 192) = 3.61$, $p < .005$. Newman-Keuls tests comparing these means revealed that those who were two-steps overpaid (M = 5.90) reported significantly higher reward levels than either those who were only one-step overpaid, equitably paid, or in the control group (the means for which were not significantly different from each other; combined M = 4.33). The means for these groups, however, were significantly higher than the means for those who were either one- or two-steps underpaid (which were not significantly different from each other; combined M = 2.75).

DISCUSSION

The results of the present study provide strong support for hypotheses concerning the status value of offices (Edelman, 1978; Konar &: Sundstrom, 1985) as outcomes amenable to analysis by equity theory (e.g., Adams, 1965). The performance increases demonstrated by overpaid workers and the decreases demonstrated by underpaid workers in the present study take their place among many other studies that successfully support equity theory predictions (see reviews by Greenberg, 1982, 1987). The unique contribution of the present work, however, is the finding that conditions of overpayment and underpayment were able to be created by manipulating nonmonetary outcomes—elements of the work environment associated with organizational status.

Implications

As such, these findings support Adams's (1965) claim that "job status and status symbols" (p. 278) constitute outcomes in the equity equation, a notion that is just beginning to receive empirical support (e.g., Greenberg &. Ornstein, 1983). This is in contrast to the well-established impact of monetary outcomes demonstrated in the equity theory literature (Greenberg, 1982, 1987). The specific vehicle of status examined in the present work, the physical environment of offices, although previously recognized by students of office design (e.g., Becker, 1981, 1982; Steele, 1973), heretofore has received scant attention as a possible determinant of workers' equity perceptions (e.g., Burt & Sundstrom, 1979). The present work extends the findings of research by Konar et al. (1982), which demonstrated that certain physical features of offices are related to organizational status by showing that these physical symbols of status demarcation operate as outcomes amenable to equity theory analysis. As such, the present findings provide a useful complement to the accumulated literature on office design (e.g., Davis, 1984; Konar et al., 1982; Sundstrom, 1986) by providing an explanatory mechanism that may account for employees' reactions to their work environments (e.g., Wineman, 1982).

The present investigation also supports equity theory's prediction that the reaction to an inequity will be proportional to the magnitude of the inequity experienced (Adams, 1965, p. 281). Specifically, underpaid workers were found to reduce their performance (i.e., lower their inputs) more when they were extremely underpaid (i.e., assigned offices of others two steps below them) than when they were more moderately underpaid (i.e., assigned offices of others one step below them). Likewise, workers who were more overpaid (i.e., assigned to offices of others two steps above them) raised their performance more than those who were more moderately overpaid (i.e., assigned to offices of others one step above them). This set of findings is particularly noteworthy in that it is one of only a few studies (e.g., Leventhal, Allen, & Kemelgor, 1969) that directly manipulate the magnitude of the inequity encountered. As such, it is notable in attempting to reverse a trend toward the "striking absence of attempts to quantify the magnitude of inputs and outcomes, and thus inequities in the research literature on equity" (Adams & Freedman, 1976, p. 52).

Of particular interest in the present research is observed tendency for overpayment inequity to bring about overall lower levels of performance increments than did underpayments bring about performance decrements. Such a finding is in keeping with Adams's (1965) supposition that the threshold for experiencing overpayment inequity is higher than that for underpayment inequity. Similarly, several studies (see review by Walster et al., 1978) have shown that reactions to underpayment are more pronounced than reactions to overpayment. The overall weaker effects of overpayment demonstrated in the present study appear to be the result of lower performance levels in the second week of overpayment than in the first week. Similar temporary effects of overpayment have been demonstrated in both laboratory (e.g., Greenberg & Ornstein, 1983) and field (e.g., Pritchard et al., 1972) settings. Such findings are in keeping with theoretical assertions that reactions to in equity may be moderated by the passage of time (Cosier & Dalton, 1983). Knowing that their overpayment was only going to be temporary, workers may have had little motivation to redress the inequity they experienced by sustaining high levels of performance (Greenberg, 1984). In contrast to the sustained effects of underpayment, more precise explanations for the diminished effects of overpayment over time are lacking and should be recognized as a topic in need of future research.

Further evidence for the less potent effects of overpayment relative to underpayment are provided by the job satisfaction data. Significantly lower levels of satisfaction were found only for the most extremely underpaid workers, but not for overpaid workers, thereby corroborating the weaker effects of overpayment demonstrated by Pritchard et al. (1972). In this regard, it is essential to note that the failure to find more pronounced differences on the job satisfaction measure does not weaken the equity-theory-based interpretation of the present findings. Although equity theory postulates that behavioral reactions to inequity are driven by attempts to alleviate feelings of dissatisfaction (Walster et al., 1978), it has been argued elsewhere (Greenberg, 1984) that such affective mediation has not been clearly demonstrated in previous research and may not be a necessary precondition for behavioral reactions to inequity.

Indeed, an equity theory analysis of the pattern of observed performance differences is supported by other questionnaire findings. Specifically, during the reassignment period, extremely overpaid workers reported receiving higher rewards and extremely underpaid workers reported receiving lower rewards than equitably paid workers. Apparently the office-assignment manipulation was successful in getting workers to perceive changes in their outcome levels. Specific evidence attesting to the fact that these overall rewards were the result of the work environment is provided by the findings of the environmental satisfaction questionnaire: During the reassignment period, overpaid workers reported greater satisfaction, and underpaid workers reported less satisfaction, compared with equitably paid workers (and compared with their reactions to their permanent offices). Such evidence not only shows that workers were aware of the differences in their work environments, but also that changes in environmental satisfaction levels (outcomes) may account for the observed performance differences (inputs).[4]

Limitations and Future Research Directions

Prompted by the diminished impact of overpayment overtime found in the present study, one cannot help but wonder how long the observed effects of status-based inequities would persist. Before managers can be advised to manipulate workplace elements as a tactic for improving subordinates' attitudes or job performance (cf. Goodsell, 1977; Ornstein, in press), future longitudinal investigations need to be conducted to determine the persistence of the presently observed effects (or any reactions to inequity; Cosier & Dalton, 1983). Previous research suggesting that workers suspecting such manipulative intent might actually lower their performance (Greenberg & Ornstein, 1983) would dictate against intentional manipulations of inequity for instrumental purposes (Greenberg, 1982; Greenberg & Cohen, 1982). Clearly, future research is needed to determine the long-term reactions to inequities.

Additional future research is needed to help determine the relative contributions of the specific environmental elements manipulated in the present study. Indeed, the complex set of manipulations that defined relative status in the present study makes it impossible to determine which specific features may have had the greatest impact on the results. For example, we cannot determine from the present study whether the results were due to subjects' knowledge of the status of the office's permanent resident or of the status value of any of the furnishings or design (cf. Davis, 1984; Sundstrom, 1986). Although the inherent confounding of these features was necessary to enhance the validity of this field experiment, it would appear useful to isolate these factors in future laboratory experiments to determine their individual contributions (as outcomes) to inequity effects.

CONCLUSION

Given the importance of the workplace environment as a determinant of workers' job attitudes (Oldham & Fried, 1987; Sundstrom et al., 1980), it should not be surprising to find that workers' assignment to offices was related to their perceived level of job rewards and to their actual job performance. In this regard, equity theory proved to be a useful mechanism for explaining workers' reactions to temporarily encountered environmental conditions. As such, this work broadens the potential horizons of research and theory on organizational justice (Greenberg, 1987), as well as that on workplace environments (Becker, 1981; Sundstrom, 1986). As the rapprochement between these lines of investigation develops, we may well begin to understand the potential of the work environment as a tool for use by practicing managers (cf. Goodsell, 1977; Ornstein, in press; Steele, 1973).

REFERENCES

Adams, J. S. (1965). Inequity in social exchange. In L. Berkowitz (Ed.), *Advances in experimental social psychology* (Vol. 2, pp. 267–299). New York: Academic Press.

Adams, J. S., & Freedman, S. (1976). Equity theory revisited: Comments and annotated bibliography. In L. Berkowitz & E. Walster (Eds.), *Advances in experimental social psychology* (Vol. 9, pp. 43–90). New York: Academic Press.

Becker, F. D. (1981). *Workspace*. New York: Praeger.

Becker, F. D. (1982). *The successful office.* Reading, MA: Addison-Wesley.

Burt, R. E., & Sundstrom, E. (1979, September). Workspace and job satisfaction: Extending equity theory to the physical environment. In H. M. Parsons (Chair), *Physical environments at work.* Symposium presented at the 87th Annual Convention of the American Psychological Association, New York.

Cosier, R. A., & Dalton, D. R. (1983). Equity theory and time: A reformulation. *Academy of Management Reviews*, 8, 311–319.

Davis, T. R. V. (1984). The influence of the physical environment in offices. *Academy of Management Review*, 9, 271–283.

Edelman, M. (1978). *Space and social order.* Madison, WI: University of Wisconsin, Institute for Research on Poverty.

Geran, M. (1976). Does it work? *Interior Design*, 47(2), 114–117.

Goodsell, C. T. (1977). Bureaucratic manipulation of physical symbols: An empirical study. *American Journal of Political Science*, 21, 79–91.

Greenberg, J. (1982). Approaching equity and avoiding inequity in groups and organizations. In J. Greenberg & R. L. Cohen (Eds.), *Equity and justice in social behavior* (pp. 389–435). New York: Academic Press.

Greenberg, J. (1984). On the apocryphal nature of inequity distress. In R. Folger (Ed.), *The sense of injustice: Social psychological perspectives* (pp. 167–186). New York: Plenum Press.

Greenberg, J. (1987). A taxonomy of organizational justice theories. *Academy of Management Review*, 12, 9–22.

Greenberg, J., & Cohen, R. L. (1982). Why justice? Normative and instrumental interpretations. In J. Greenberg & R.

L. Cohen (Eds.), *Equity and justice in social behavior* (pp. 437–469). New York: Academic Press.

Greenberg, J., & Ornstein, S. (1983). High status job title as compensation for underpayment: A test of equity theory. *Journal of Applied Psychology*, 68, 285–297.

Halloran, J. (1978). *Applied human relations: An organizational approach*. Englewood Cliffs, NJ: Prentice-Hall.

Harris, T. G. (1977, October 31). Psychology of the New York work space. *New York*, pp. 51–54.

Joiner, D. (1976). Social ritual and architectural space. In H. Proshansky, W. Ittleson, & L. Rivlin (Eds.), *Environmental psychology: People and their physical settings* (2nd ed., pp. 224–241). New York: Holt, Rinehart & Winston.

Kleinschrod, W. A. (1987, July). A balance of forces. *Administrative Management*, 48(7), 18–23.

Konar, E., & Sundstrom, E. (1985). Status demarcation in the office. In J. Wineman (Ed.), *Behavioral issues in office design* (pp. 48–66). New York: Van Nostrand.

Konar, E., Sundstrom, E., Brady, C., Mandel, D., & Rice, R. W. (1982). Status demarcation in the office. *Environment and Behavior*, 14, 561–580.

Langdon, F. J. (1966). *Modern offices: A user survey* (National Building Studies Research Paper No. 41, Ministry of Technology, Building Research Station). London: Her Majesty's Stationery Office.

Leventhal, G. S., Allen, J., & Kemelgor, B. (1969). Reducing inequity by reallocating rewards. *Psychonomic Science*, 14, 295–296.

Louis Harris & Associates, Inc. (1978). *The Steelcase national study of office environments: Do they work?* Grand Rapids, MI: Steelcase.

Oldham, G. R., & Fried, Y. (1987). Employee reactions to workspace characteristics. *Journal of Applied Psychology*, 72, 75–80.

Ornstein, S. (in press). Impression management through office design. In R. Giacolone & P. Rosenfeld (Eds.), *Impression management in organizations*. Hillsdale, NJ: Erlbaum.

Price, J. L., & Mueller, C. W. (1986). *Handbook of organizational measurement*. Marshfield, MA: Pitman.

Pritchard, R. D., Dunnette, M. D., & Jorgenson, D. O. (1972). Effects of perceptions of equity and inequity on worker performance and satisfaction. *Journal of Applied Psychology*, 56, 75–94.

Robichaud, B. (1958). *Selecting, planning, and managing office space*. New York: McGraw-Hill.

Steele, F. (1973). *Physical settings and organizational development*. Reading, MA: Addison-Wesley.

Stryker, S., & Macke, A. S. (1978). Status inconsistency and role conflict. In R. H. Turner, J. Coleman, & R. C. Fox (Eds.), *Annual review of sociology* (Vol. 4, pp. 57–90). Palo Alto, CA: Annual Reviews.

Sundstrom, E. (1986). *Work places*. New York: Cambridge University Press.

Sundstrom, E., Burt, R., & Kamp, D. (1980). Privacy at work: Architectural correlates of job satisfaction and job performance. *Academy of Management Journal*, 23, 101–117.

Walster, E., Walster, G. W., & Berscheid, E. (1978). *Equity: Theory and research*. Boston: Allyn & Bacon.

Weiss, D. J., Dawis, R. V., England, G. W., & Lofquist, L. H. (1967). *Manual for the Minnesota Satisfaction Questionnaire*. Minneapolis: University of Minnesota, Industrial Relations Center.

Wineman, J. D. (1982). Office design and evaluation: An overview. *Environment and Behavior*, 14, 271–298.

Wylie, H. L. (1958). *Office management handbook* (2nd ed.). New York: Ronald Press.

NOTES

1. The number of employees within each worker group assigned to each condition was predetermined by the number of available offices and the number of desks per office. To maintain the characteristics of the permanent offices while they were used as temporary offices, the number of temporary residents assigned to an office was kept equal to the number of its permanent residents. Further stimulating the permanent characteristics of the offices, while also avoiding possible confoundings due to having mixed-status office mates, all multiple-employee offices were shared by equal-status coworkers.
2. To keep constant the amount of time that all of the workers spent in their temporary offices, none were allowed to return to their permanent offices in advance of the 2-week period, even if the work was completed ahead of schedule. The physical separation of the various offices and the placement of construction barriers made it unlikely that workers could learn of any possible early completions. Because the 2 weeks allowed for completion of the offices was liberally budgeted, no delays in returning to permanent offices were necessitated.
3. A preexperimental questionnaire conducted among employees of the host organization indicated strong consensual agreement about the existence and nature of symbols of status demarcation in their organization. In responding to an open-ended question, 222 employees

surveyed identified the four dimensions listed in Table 2 most frequently (from 75% to 88%) as reflective of status differences in their organization. Such findings are in keeping with those reported in more broad-based survey research (Louis Harris & Associates, 1978).

4. Unfortunately, however, because these questionnaires were administered only once during the reassignment period, the responses cannot be used to gauge changes in affective reactions within this critical period.

Received September 15, 1987
Revision received December 18, 1987
Accepted February 17, 1988

READING 17

Until recently, the medical community did not know if psychological factors such as stress could "get into" the body's immune system. As the exciting research presented in Chapter 14 (Health) reflects, however, health researchers today working in the field of psychoneuroimmunology (*psycho* for mind, *neuro* for nervous system, and *immunology* for the immune system) find that stress produces a wide range of disabling effects on the body—including an increased risk of chronic back pain, upper respiratory infections, arthritis, and some forms of cancer. This range of effects suggests that stress may weaken the immune system—the first line of defense against illness. Does this mean that people who are under stress are more likely to get sick? To answer this question, Sheldon Cohen and others (1993) paid volunteers to spend nine days and nights in a medical experiment, where they reported on life stress and then received randomized exposure to a common cold virus. The question: Were those suffering high levels of stress more likely to catch the cold than those with lower levels of stress? As you read this innovative study, ask yourself: Would you have agreed to participate in it? What are the health implications of the results?

Negative Life Events, Perceived Stress, Negative Affect, and Susceptibility to the Common Cold

Sheldon Cohen, David A. J. Tyrrell, and Andrew P. Smith

After completing questionnaires assessing stressful life events, perceived stress, and negative affect, 394 healthy Ss were intentionally exposed to a common cold virus, quarantined, and monitored for the development of biologically verified clinical illness. Consistent with the hypothesis that psychological stress increases susceptibility to infectious agents, higher scores on each of the 3 stress scales were associated with greater risk of developing a cold. However, the relation between stressful life events and illness was mediated by a different biologic process than were relations between perceived stress and illness and negative affect and illness. That these scales have independent relations with illness and that these relations are mediated by different processes challenges the assumption that perceptions of stress and negative affect are necessary for stressful life events to influence disease risk.

Sheldon Cohen, Department of Psychology, Carnegie Mellon University; David A. J. Tyrrell, Medical Research Council's Common Cold Unit, Salisbury, England; Andrew P. Smith, Health Psychology Research Unit, University of Wales College of Cardiff, Cardiff, Wales.

This research was supported by grants from the National Institute of Allergies and Infectious Disease (A123072) and the Office of Naval Research (N00014-88-K-0063), by a Research Scientist Development Award to Sheldon Cohen from the National Institute of Mental Health (MH00721), and by the Medical Research Council's Common Cold Unit.

We are indebted to S. Bull, R. Dawes, J. Greenhouse, J. Middleton, H. Parry, M. Sargent, J. Schlarb, S. Trickett; the medical, nursing, and technical staff of the Common Cold Unit; and the volunteers for their contribution to the research.

Correspondence concerning this article should be addressed to Sheldon Cohen, Department of Psychology, Carnegie Mellon University, Pittsburgh, Pennsylvania 15213-3890.

It is commonly believed that life stressors increase susceptibility to infectious disease. When demands imposed by events exceed ability to cope, a psychological stress response is elicited (Lazarus & Folkman, 1984). This response is composed of negative cognitive and emotional states. In turn, these states are thought to alter immune function through autonomic nerves that connect the central nervous system to immune tissue (D. L. Felten, Felten, Carlson, Olschowka, & Livnat, 1985; S. Y. Felten & Olschowka, 1987), through the action of hormones whose release is associated with negative affectivity (Shavit, Lewis, Terman, Gale, & Liebeskind, 1984), or through stress-elicited changes in health practices such as smoking and alcohol consumption (Cohen & Williamson, 1991; Kiecolt-Glaser & Glaser, 1988).

Direct connections between stress and various functions of the immune system have been found in both field (e.g., Kiecolt-Glaser & Glaser, 1991) and laboratory settings (e.g., Manuck, Cohen, Rabin, Muldoon, & Bachen, 1991; Naliboff et al., 1991). However, it is unclear whether the immune changes related to stress in these studies are of the type or magnitude that would influence susceptibility to infection (Jemmott & Locke, 1984; Laudenslager, 1987). There is also research directly assessing the relation between stress and upper respiratory infections in community samples (see review in Cohen & Williamson, 1991). Several of these studies provide evidence that social stressors increase risk for verified upper respiratory disease (Graham, Douglas, & Ryan, 1986; Meyer & Haggerty, 1962). This work, however, did not control for the possible effects of stressful events on exposure to infectious agents (as opposed to their effects on host resistance) or provide evidence about other behavioral and biologic mechanisms through which stress might influence susceptibility to infection. Moreover, the literature on this topic is not entirely consistent with several studies failing to find a relation between stress and respiratory disease (Alexander & Summerskill, 1956; Cluff, Cantor, & Imboden, 1966).

Viral-challenge studies, in which volunteers who complete stress scales are intentionally exposed to a cold or influenza virus, have provided only weak support for a relation between stress and susceptibility to upper respiratory infections (Broadbent, Broadbent, Phillpotts, & Wallace, 1984; Totman, Kiff, Reed, & Craig, 1980; Greene, Betts, Ochitill, Iker, & Douglas, 1978; Locke & Heisel, 1977). This work, however, suffers from a wide range of methodological flaws (Cohen & Williamson, 1991). Individual studies suffer from insufficient sample sizes, concurrent administration of drugs, lack of information on overall rates of infection in response to the dose of virus administered, and lack of controls for important predictors of susceptibility such as preexisting antibodies to the infectious agent, gender, and age (see Jackson et al., 1960). They also fail to control for the possible role of stress-elicited changes in health practices such as smoking and alcohol consumption.

Part of the problem in establishing a relation between stress and new cases of disease is that there is little agreement within or across disciplines on how stress should be defined or measured. As addressed earlier, this article is concerned with *psychological stress*, that is, negative cognitive and emotional states elicited when persons perceive that their demands exceed their ability to cope (Lazarus & Folkman, 1984). However, even within this constrained area, there is considerable controversy as to how such a state should be assessed (e.g., Cohen, 1986; Dohrenwend & Shrout, 1985; Lazarus, DeLongis, Folkman, & Gruen, 1985). In an article published in a medical journal (Cohen, Tyrrell, & Smith, 1991), we reported that psychological stress, operationally defined as an index including negative life events, perceived stress, and negative affect, predicted susceptibility to colds among 394 initially healthy persons we intentionally exposed to upper respiratory viruses. We justified the use of the stress index on the basis of a factor analysis indicating that the three measures formed a single principal component, providing evidence that the scales measure a common underlying concept. By using a single index, we were able to substantially reduce the number of analyses and hence Type I error. The psychological stress index provided a robust and valid measure in that it showed a linear relation with risk for developing colds, and in that the relation between the stress index and susceptibility was unaffected by controls for a series of environmental, psychological, behavioral, and immunological factors. However, combining the three scales masked information that examination of the individual scales might tell us about the stress process. Although the scales are correlated with one another, each taps a somewhat different component of the psychological stress experience.

In this article, we present further data from our prospective study of persons intentionally exposed to upper respiratory viruses. Healthy persons were administered the three stress scales, three personality scales, and measures of health practices, and then they were experimentally exposed to one of five cold viruses or placebo. The association between stress and the development of biologically verified clinical disease was examined with use of a control for baseline (prechallenge) antibodies to the challenge virus, the identity of the challenge virus, allergic status, weight, the season, the number of subjects housed together, the infectious status of any subjects sharing housing, and various demographic factors. We examine the relation between each of the three separate stress scales and risk for clinical colds, evaluate potential pathways through which each might influence susceptibility, and discuss the differences in terms of the components of psychological stress that each of the scales assess.

METHOD

The subjects were 154 men and 266 women who volunteered to participate in trials at the Medical Research Council's Common Cold Unit (CCU) in Salisbury, England. All reported no chronic or acute illness or regular medication regimen on their applications and were judged in good health following clinical and laboratory examination on arrival at the unit. Pregnant women were excluded. Volunteers' ages ranged from 18 to 54 years, with a mean of 33.6 and standard deviation of 10.6. Twenty-two percent did not complete their secondary education, 51% completed secondary education but did not attend a university, and 27% attended a university for at least 1 year. Volunteers were reimbursed for their traveling expenses and received free meals and accommodations. The trial was approved by the Harrow District Ethical Committee and informed consent was obtained from each volunteer after the nature and possible consequences of the study were fully explained.

Procedure

During their first 2 days at the CCU, volunteers were given a thorough medical examination, completed a series of self-reported behavioral protocols including psychological stress, personality, and health practice questionnaires, and had blood drawn for immune and cotinine assessments. Subsequently, volunteers were exposed using nasal drops, to a low infectious dose of one of five respiratory viruses: rhinovirus types 2 (RV2; $n = 86$), 9 (RV9; $n = 122$), and 14 (RV14; $n = 92$), respiratory syncytial virus (RSV; $n = 40$), and coronavirus type 229E (CV; $n = 54$). An additional 26 volunteers received saline. One or two viruses were used in each individual trial, and volunteers were randomly assigned to virus and saline conditions. Viral doses were intended to simulate those that occur in person-to-person transmission, and they resulted in illness rates of between 20% and 60%. For 2 days before and 7 days after viral challenge, volunteers were quarantined in large apartments (alone or with 1 or 2 others). Starting 2 days before viral challenge and continuing through 6 days after the challenge, each volunteer was examined daily by a clinician using a standard respiratory sign-symptom protocol (Beare & Reed, 1977). Examples of items on the protocol include sneezing, watering of eyes, nasal stuffiness, nasal obstruction, postnasal discharge, sinus pain, sore throat, hoarseness, cough, and sputum. The protocol also included an objective count of the number of tissues used daily by a volunteer and body temperature (oral) assessed twice each day. Approximately 28 days after the viral challenge a second serum sample was collected by volunteers' own physicians and shipped back to the CCU. All investigators were blind to volunteers' psychological status and to whether they received virus or saline.

Psychological Stress

Three kinds of measures of psychological stress were used: (a) number of major stressful life events judged by the respondent as having a negative impact, (b) perception that current demands exceed capabilities to cope, and (c) current negative affect. The major stressful life events scale consisted of events that might happen in the life of the respondent (41 items) or close others (26 items). The events were a subset of those appearing in the List of Recent Experiences (Henderson, Byrne, & Duncan-Jones, 1981) and were chosen because of their potential for negative impact and the relatively high frequency of occurrence in population studies. Respondents were asked which of the items had occurred during the last 12 months. They were asked to rate each event they reported as having either a positive or negative impact on their lives. A few items such as death of a spouse or child were assumed to be consensually negative, and the respondent was not asked for an impact rating. The scale score was the number of negative events (either consensual or respondent rated) reported by the subject. Because the scores were highly skewed (57% reported two or fewer events, range was 0–14), with some irregularities in the smoothness of the distribution, we used two different approaches to life-event analyses. In the first, we retained the continuous scaling by using a $\log_{10}$ transformation of the raw data. In the second, we transformed life events into a dichotomized variable: two or fewer events versus more than two events. The 10-item Perceived Stress Scale (PSS-10; Cohen & Williamson, 1988) was used to assess the degree to which situations in life are perceived as stressful (reliability in this sample, $\alpha = .85$). Items in the PSS-10 were designed to tap how unpredictable, uncontrollable, and overloading respondents find their lives. Finally, the negative affect scale included 15 items from Zevon and Tellegen's (1982) list of negative emotions. The items included distressed, nervous, sad, angry, dissatisfied with self, calm (reverse scored), guilty, scared, angry at yourself, upset, irritated, depressed, hostile, shaky, and content (reverse scored). A 5-point (0–4) Likert-type response format was used to report affect intensity during the last week ($\alpha = .84$). Both the PSS-10 and negative affect scores were approximately normally distributed, and their raw (continuous) scores were used as predictors in the regression analyses. Stressful life events were correlated .35, $p < .001$, and .35, $p < .001$, with PSS-10 and negative affect, respectively. Negative affect was correlated .65, $p < .001$, with the PSS-10. Point biserial correlations between dichotomized stressful life events and PSS-10 and life events and negative affect were .32, $p < .001$, and .32, $p < .001$, respectively.

For comparison, we also present data based on analyses using the psychological stress index used in our earlier article (Cohen, Tyrrell, & Smith, 1991). All three stress scales formed a single principal component, with loadings of .66, .86, and .86, respectively, providing evidence that the scales measure a common underlying concept. Hence we formed an index combining the three measures as an indicator of psychological stress. Because life events were not normally distributed, an index based on normalized scores was not appropriate. Instead, the index was created by quartiling each scale and summing quartile ranks for each subject (1 for lowest quartile and 4 for highest), resulting in a stress index ranging from 3 to 12. The quartiles were 0, 1–2, 3–4, and 5–14 for the life-events scale; 0–10, 11–14, 15–18, and 19–33 for the PSS-10; and 0–7, 8–13, 14–20, and 21–49 for the negative affect scale. Index scores were approximately normally distributed.

Infections and Clinical Colds

Infectious diseases result from the growth and action of microorganisms or parasites in the body (see Cohen & Williamson, 1991). Infection is the multiplication of an invading microorganism. It is possible for a person to be infected (for the microorganism to replicate) without developing clinical symptoms. Clinical disease occurs when infection is followed by the development of symptomatology characteristic of the disease.

Biological verification of infection can be accomplished by establishing that an infectious agent is present or replicating in tissue, fluid, or both. We use two common procedures for detecting a replication of a specific virus. In the viral isolation procedure, nasal secretions are cultured (put in a medium that stimulates virus replication). If the virus is present in nasal secretions, it will grow in the medium and can be detected. Alternatively, we can indirectly assess the presence of a replicating virus by looking at changes in serum antibody levels to that virus. Antibodies are protein molecules that attach themselves to invading microorganisms and mark them for destruction or prevent them from infecting cells. An invading microorganism (i.e., infection) triggers the immune system to produce antibody. (*Antibody* is also called *immunoglobulin* [Ig]). Because each antibody recognizes only a single type of microorganism, the production of antibody to a specific infectious agent is evidence for the presence and activity of that agent.

Assays for viral isolation and viral-specific antibody levels Nasal wash samples for viral isolation were collected before inoculation and on Days 2–6 after viral inoculation. They were mixed with broth and stored in aliquots at –70°C. Rhinoviruses were detected in O-Hela cells, respiratory syncytial virus in Hep2 cells, and coronavirus in the C-16 strain of continuous human fibroblast cells. When a characteristic cytopathic effect was observed, the tissue culture fluids were passaged into further cultures and identity tests on the virus were performed. Rhinoviruses and coronaviruses were confirmed by neutralization tests with specific rabbit immune serum, and respiratory syncytial virus by immunofluorescent staining of culture cells.

Levels of neutralizing antibodies and of specific antiviral immunoglobulin A (IgA) and immunoglobulin G (IgG) were determined before and 28 days after the viral challenge. Neutralizing antibodies (for rhinoviruses only) were determined by neutralization tests with homologous virus (Al Nakib & Tyrrell, 1988). Results were recorded as the highest dilution showing neutralization, and a fourfold rise was regarded as significant. Suitable, neutralizing tests were not available for RSV and CV.

Viral specific IgA and IgG levels for rhinoviruses (Barclay & Al Nakib, 1987), CV (Callow, 1985), and RSV (Callow, 1985) were determined by enzyme-linked immunosorbent assays. This test detects antibody which correlates with neutralization titers, is associated with resistance to infection, and increases in response to infection (Al Nakib & Tyrrell, 1988).

Operational definitions of infection and clinical colds A volunteer was deemed infected if a virus was isolated after the challenge or if there was a significant rise in viral-specific serum antibody after the challenge, that is, a fourfold increase in neutralizing antibody (rhinoviruses only) or an IgG or IgA increase of two standard deviations greater than the mean of nonchallenged volunteers (all viruses). Eighty-two percent (325) of the volunteers receiving virus were infected. Nineteen percent (5) of the volunteers receiving saline were infected. We attributed infections among the saline group to volunteer transmission of virus to others housed in the same apartment. A control for person-to-person transmission is included in the data analysis.

At the end of the trial, the clinician judged the severity of each volunteer's cold on a scale ranging from *nil* (0) to *severe* (4). Ratings of *mild cold* (2) or greater were considered positive clinical diagnoses. Volunteers also judged the severity of their colds on the same scale. Clinician diagnosis was in agreement with self-diagnosis for 94% of the volunteers. Volunteers were defined as having developed *clinical colds* if they were both infected and diagnosed by the clinician as having a clinical cold. Of the 394 volunteers participating in the trials, 38% (148) developed clinical colds. None of the 26 saline controls developed colds.

Seven persons with positive clinical diagnoses but no indication of infection were excluded from the sample because we assumed the illness was caused by pretrial exposure to another virus. Analyses including them (by definition no clinical cold and no infection) resulted in identical conclusions.

Body Temperature and Mucus Weights

Because clinical diagnoses can be influenced by how subjects present their symptoms, we independently evaluated the associations between each stress measure and two clinical signs not subject to self-presentation bias: body temperature and mucus weights. Body temperature (degrees centigrade) was taken each morning and afternoon with an oral thermometer. An average daily temperature ([morning + afternoon]/2) was calculated for the day before and each day following the viral challenge. Mucus weights were determined by collecting tissues used by subjects in sealed plastic bags. The bags were weighed, and the weight of the tissues and the bags was subtracted. Daily mucus weights (in grams) were calculated for both before and after the viral challenge. The prechallenge measure was based on the mucus weight on the day before challenge. The postchallenge measures were based on the weights from Days 1 to 5 after the challenge. To obtain an approximately normally distributed variable, we used the $\log_{10}$ of both pre- and postchallenge mucus weights in the analyses.

Standard Control Variables

We used a series of control variables that might provide alternative explanations for a relation between stress and illness. These include prechallenge serostatus for the experimental virus, age, gender, education, allergic status, weight, season, number of others the volunteer was housed with, whether an apartment mate was infected, and challenge virus.

Prechallenge serostatus refers to whether a subject had antibody to the virus before experimental exposure, that is, was previously exposed to the virus. Serostatus was defined as positive when a volunteer had a neutralizing prechallenge antibody titer greater than 2 for rhinoviruses and a prechallenge antibody level greater than the sample median for CV and RSV. Forty-three percent of volunteers were seropositive before the challenge, including 55% for RV2, 48% for RV9, 20% for RV14, 50% for RSV, and 50% for CV.

Age and gender were based on self-report. Because age was not normally distributed it was scored categorically on the basis of a median split: 18–33 or 34–54. Scores on education were based on a 9-point self-report scale ranging from *no schooling* (0) to *doctoral degree* (8). Allergic status was based on physician interview questions regarding allergies to food, drugs, or other allergens. Persons reporting any allergy were defined as *allergic*. A ponderal index (weight/height^3) was used to control for volunteers' weight. We used the number of hours of daylight on the first day of the trial as a continuous measure of the season. Number of daylight hours was correlated .80 ($p < .001$) with the average temperature on the same day. A control for the possibility that person-to-person transmission rather than the virus inoculation might be responsible for infection or clinical colds was also included. Because person-to-person transmission would only be possible if an apartment mate was infected by the vital challenge, the control variable indicated whether any housing mate was infected. Finally, *challenge virus* is a categorical variable representing the experimental virus to which a volunteer was exposed.

Health Practice Measures

Health practices including smoking, drinking alcohol, exercise, quality of sleep, and dietary practices were assessed as possible pathways linking stress and susceptibility. Cotinine as assessed in serum by gas chromatography was used as a biochemical indicator of smoking rate because it provides an objective measure of nicotine intake that is not subject to self-report bias (Feyerabend & Russell, 1990; Jarvis, Tunstall-Pedoe, Feyerabend, Vesey, & Saloojee, 1987). We used the $\log_{10}$ of the average of the two (before and 28 days after challenge) cotinine measures as an indicator of smoking rate. (The correlation between the two measures was .95, $p < .001$, $N = 348$). The correlation between the $\log_{10}$ average cotinine and the $\log_{10}$ self-reported number of cigarettes smoked per day was .96 ($p < .001$, $N = 372$).

The remaining health practices were assessed by questionnaire before the viral challenge (see Cohen et al., 1991). Average number of alcoholic drinks per day was calculated using separate estimates of weekday and weekend drinking. A half pint, bottle, or can of beer, glass of wine, and shot of whisky contain approximately equal amounts of alcohol and were each treated as a single drink. We use the $\log_{10}$ of average number of drinks per day as an indicator of drinking. The exercise index included items on the frequency of walking, running, jogging, swimming, aerobics, and work around the house. The quality of sleep index included items on feeling rested, difficulty falling asleep, and awakening early; and the dietary habit index was made up of items designed to assess concern with a healthy diet and included frequencies of eating breakfast, fruits, and vegetables.

Personality Measures

Because psychological stress could reflect stable personality styles rather than responses to environmental stressors, self-esteem and personal control (two personality characteristics closely associated with stress) were assessed before the viral challenge. Self-esteem was measured by the self-regard and social confidence subscales of the Feelings of Inadequacy Scale (Fleming & Watts, 1980; $\alpha = .89$), and personal control by the personal efficacy and interpersonal control subscales of the Spheres of Control Scale (Paulhus, 1983; $\alpha = .76$). A third personality characteristic, introversion-extraversion was also assessed because of an existing literature suggesting that introverts were at higher risk for infection (Broadbent et al., 1984; Totman et al., 1980). It was assessed by the Eysenck Personality Inventory (Eysenck & Eysenck, 1964; $\alpha = .80$).

Statistical Analysis

As expected, none of the saline control subjects developed colds and hence the analyses include only persons receiving a virus. The primary analysis tests whether each of the psychological stress measures is associated with greater rates of clinical colds. Secondary analyses assess the importance of the two components of the definition of a clinical cold, infection and illness (clinical symptomatology), in accounting for an association of stress and clinical colds. Specifically, we determined whether the relation between stress and colds was attributable to increases in infection or to increases in diagnosed colds among infected persons.

Logistic regression was used to predict these dichotomous outcomes (Hosmer & Lemeshow, 1989). We used a regression procedure that provides estimated regression coefficients for each independent variable adjusted for all other variables in the equation. Probability values are based on the change in log-likelihood that would result if each variable were entered as the last variable in a stepwise regression. This is analogous to testing whether a variable accounts for a significant increment in explained variance in a linear regression model.

We report a sequential series of analyses. In the first analysis, only the psychological stress measure was entered as a predictor. In the second, we entered the standard control variables along with the stress measure and tested whether there was a significant change in log-likelihood when the stress index was added to the equation. Education, weight, season, and number of apartment mates were entered as continuous variables and the remainder of the standard controls as dummy (categorical) variables (Hosmer & Lemeshow, 1989).

Additional analyses tested possible roles of health practices and personality variables in the relation between stress and clinical colds. In all cases, we added these variables to a regression equation that included standard controls, and we report the adjusted coefficient and the probability value based on the change in log-likelihood when the stress measure is added to the equation. These analyses are extremely conservative, testing the significance of the stress measures after adding as many as 16 control variables.

Repeated measures analysis of covariance was used in supplementary analyses of continuous outcomes: postchallenge mucus weights and body temperature. In each case, prechallenge scores and standard control variables were used as covariates.

RESULTS

Stress and Susceptibility to Clinical Illness

Figure 1 presents separate rates of clinical colds for those above and below the median of each stress measure. Rates for the psychological stress index are also presented for comparison (Cohen et al., 1991). As apparent from the figure, highly stressed persons have higher rates of colds irrespective of the stress scale, although this difference is

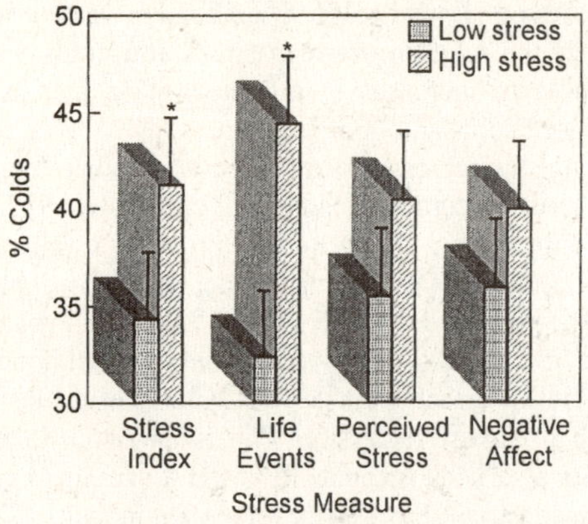

Figure 1. Observed associations between each of the stress measures and rates of clinical colds for the entire sample (N = 394). (Standard errors are indicated by vertical lines $^*p < .05$.)

statistically reliable only with the psychological stress index and stressful life events. Both the index and life events predicted colds when they were the only predictor in the equation ($b = .10, p < .02$ for the index; $b = .74, p < .04$ for continuous life events variable; and $b = .51, p < .02$ for dichotomous life events), as well as when the 10 control variables were entered into the equation ($b = .10, p < .04$ for the index; $b = .75, p = .06$ for continuous and $b = .46$, $p < .05$ for dichotomous life events).

To determine whether any of the effects reported above might be attributable to relations between stress and health practices, we ran an additional set of conservative analyses including smoking rate, drinking rate, diet, exercise, and sleep quality in the equations along with the 10 standard control variables. The addition of health practices did not significantly alter the results of any of the equations described earlier (b = .12, $p < .02$ for the index; $b = .73, p = .08$ for continuous and $b = .46, p = .06$ for dichotomous life events).

In the analyses presented so far, each of the stress measures was evaluated in separate equations. However, the data suggest the possibility that the effects of life events were independent of the effects of the other two measures. Because of the high correlation of perceived stress and negative affect, all three stress measures could not be entered into the same equation. Instead, we fit two models to the clinical cold data. In the first we entered life events, perceived stress, and their residualized interaction and in the second we entered life events, negative affect, and their residualized interaction. Life events was the only reliable predictor even approaching significance in any of the equations. For the equation with perceived stress, $b = .68$ and p = .08 when the continuous variable was used, and $b = .47$ and $p < .04$ when the dichotomous variable was used. For the equation with negative affect, $b = .74$ and p = .05 when the continuous variable was used, and $b = .50$ and $p < .03$ when the dichotomous variable was used. The reliable effect of life events in these models indicates that the component of stressful life events that predicts clinical illness is independent of what is measured by the two remaining scales. The lack of reliable interactions also suggests that the influence of life events is independent of the level of either perceived stress or negative affect.

In our previous article, we found that being housed with another person who became infected (and thus infectious) partly obscured the effects of stress on colds. This occurred because persons with infectious roommates may be reexposed to the virus after vital challenge. This was in contrast to persons without infectious roommates; who received a single dose-controlled exposure. Hence, we ran a set of additional regression equations predicting clinical colds including only the 91 subjects without infectious roommates (28 of these people had no roommates). Although these analyses resulted in a substantial loss of statistical power, they provided some information on how the separate scales fare when a major source of noise is eliminated from the analyses. Each equation included the standard control variables and the five health practices. As in the analyses including all subjects, clinical illness rates were higher for those with higher levels of stress as assessed by all of the measures (see Figure 2). These relations were statistically reliable in the cases of the stress index ($b = .32, p < .02$), perceived stress (b =. 14, $p < .02$), and negative affect ($b = .09, p < .03$), but marginally reliable at best in the case of life events (b = .58, *ns* for the continuous variable; $b = 1.12, p = .08$ for the dichotomous variable).

Stress and Infection

Recall that to be infected means that the challenge virus replicates within the body. This is detected directly in culture (viral isolation) or indirectly through establishing significant increases in viral-specific antibody. A person can be infected without developing clinical illness. The following analyses include all subjects and assess whether the reported relations between the various stress

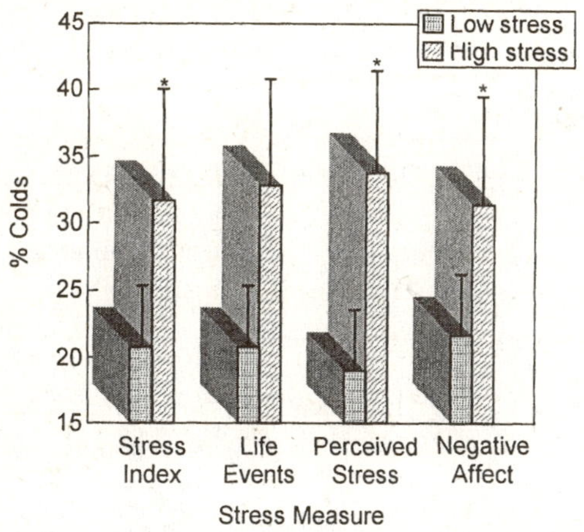

Figure 2. Observed associations between each of the stress measures and rates of clinical colds for the sample without infectious roommates ($n = 91$). (Standard errors are indicated by vertical lines $*p < .05$.)

measures and clinical colds are partly or wholly attributable to an association between these scales and increased infection.

Table 1 presents rates of infection for those below and above the median for each of the three stress measures as well as the stress index. As apparent from the table, while infection rates are higher for those above the median on all four measures, these differences are reliable for the stress index ($b = .15, p < .01$; $b = .17, p < .01$ with standard controls; $b = .18, p < .01$ with health practices), perceived stress ($b = .05, p < .03$; $b = .04, p = .05$ with standard controls; $b = .05, p = .06$ with health practices), and negative affect ($b = .04, p < .01$; $b = .05, p < .01$ with standard controls; $b = .06, p < .01$ with health practices), but not for either continuous or dichotomous life events.

Are the relations between perceived stress and infection and negative affect and infection independent of life events? When life events is entered into an equation with perceived stress and their residualized interaction, only the relation between perceived stress and infection approaches significance ($b = .04, p = .06$ for continuous variable; $b = .05, p < .05$ for the dichotomous variable). Similarly, when entered into a regression with negative affect and their residualized interaction, only negative affect is reliable ($b = .04, p < .02$ for the continuous variable; $b = .04, p < .02$ for the dichotomous variable). This suggests that the components of perceived stress and negative affect that predict clinical illness are mostly independent of what is measured by the life events scale.

Results from analyses of the 91-subject subsample were similar to those found in the entire sample. In a regression equation including standard controls and health practices, both perceived stress ($b = .16, p < .02$) and negative affect ($b = .13, p < .01$) were associated with infection. The stress index was marginally related ($b = .27, p = .07$). Life events (both continuous and dichotomous) were not.

Stress and Clinical Symptomatology Among Infected Persons

To be defined as clinically ill, persons must exhibit both infection and clinical symptoms. The following analyses were designed to assess whether the reported relations between the various stress measures and clinical colds were partly or wholly attributable to associations between stress and becoming sick (developing clinical symptoms) after infection. Because these analyses included only persons who were infected, the results are independent of earlier analyses predicting infection.

Table 1 presents rates of clinical colds among infected persons for those above and below the median on each stress measure as well as the stress index. As apparent from the table, only life events approached reliable prediction of colds among infected persons (for continuous variable, $b = .68, p = .08$; $b = .62, p = .16$ with standard controls; $b = .58, p = .21$ with standard controls and health practices; for dichotomous variable $b = .50, p < .03$; $b = .44, p = .08$ with standard controls; $b = .46, p = .08$ with standard controls and health practices).

Was the relation between life events and colds among infected persons independent of perceived stress and negative affect? Stressful life events still predicted clinical illness in both equations including perceived stress and their interaction ($b = .74, p = .08$ for continuous variable; $b = .51, p < .04$ for dichotomous variable) and equations including negative affect and their interaction ($b = .82, p = .06$ for continuous variable; $b = .56, p < .02$ dichotomous variable). This suggests that the component of stressful life events that predicts clinical illness among infected persons is independent of what is measured by the two remaining scales.

In the analyses presented so far, the diagnosis of illness was based on clinical judgment. Additional analyses investigated the associations of life events with two purely objective measures of disease manifes-

TABLE 1
Observed Percentage of Infection and Clinical Colds Among Infected Subjects by Scores on the Stress Index and by Scores on the Three Individual Measures of Stress for the Entire Sample and for the Subsample Without Infectious Roommates

	Entire sample		Sample without infectious roommates	
Score	% infected (n = 394)	% colds among infected subjects (n = 325)	% infected (*n* = 91)	% colds among infected subjects (*n* = 68)
Stress index				
Low	78.7	43.2	72.9	28.6
High	86.3**	47.7	76.7*	42.4
No. of stressful life events				
Low	80.9	40.1	73.6	28.2
High	84.6	52.5**	76.3	44.8
Perceived stress scale				
Low	78.4	44.2	69.4	26.5
High	86.7**	46.8	81.0*	44.1
Negative affect				
Low	76.9	45.8	67.4	32.3
High	88.2**	45.4	82.2**	37.8

* $p < .10$ in model without controls. ** $p < .05$ in model without controls.

tation: mucus weight and average body temperature. Only persons defined as infected were included. These analyses were repeated measure analyses of covariance. The covariate in the mucus weight analysis was the mucus weight on the day before viral challenge and in the temperature analysis, the temperature on the day before viral challenge. The repeated measure was the dependent variable at each of 5 days following challenge. Although life events were not associated with changes in mucus weights after challenge, those with high numbers of life events had greater increases in temperature after challenge than those with low numbers of events, $F(1, 319) = 6.37, p < .02$. Average daily postchallenge temperatures adjusted for prechallenge temperatures are depicted in Figure 3. There was no relation between stressful life events and prechallenge temperatures (36.41 °C for two or fewer events and 36.48 °C for more than two). An analysis adding the 10 standard control variables as covariates produced similar results, $F(1, 306) = 5.40, p < .03$. The interaction between life events and time (repeated measures) did not approach reliability in either analysis. In sum, the relation between life events and clinical diagnosis among infected persons was associated with a biological marker of disease and hence not attributable to stress-elicited biases in symptom presentation.

Analyses of the 91-subject subsample (actually only the 68 who were infected) did not indicate reliable effects of any of the measures on clinical illness for infected persons. This is probably attributable to the substantial loss of power. Although not statistically reliable, the rates of colds among infected people were higher for stressed persons no matter which of the stress scales was used (see Table 1).

Personality or Stress?

In a regression equation predicting colds and including only the three personality measures as predictors, there was a marginal ($b = -.01, p = .12$) relation between decreased self-esteem and increased colds. However, this association does not exist when the relation is adjusted for the 10 standard control variables ($p = .42$). There is no association between either personal control or introversion-extraversion and colds in either equation.

In our earlier article, we demonstrated that the association between the psychological stress index and clinical colds was independent of the three personality measures. Because there was some indication that self-esteem might play a role in susceptibility in the disaggregated analyses, we conducted analyses adding self-esteem to the regression equations including the stan-